Indiana Railroad
The Magic Interurban

George K. Bradley

Indiana Railroad
The Magic Interurban
by George K. Bradley

Bulletin 128 of the Central Electric Railfans' Association

Library of Congress Catalog Card Number 91-70886
International Standard Book Number 0-915348-28-4

Published by Central Electric Railfans' Association
Post Office Box 503, Chicago, Illinois 60690-0503
United States of America

Copyright © 1991 by Central Electric Railfans' Association
Portions on freight service © 1950, 1975 by CERA

All rights reserved. Unless permission is granted by the copyright owner, this material shall not be copied, reproduced, or coded for reproduction by any electrical, mechanical, or chemical process, or combination thereof, now known or later developed

Printed and bound in the United States of America

Indiana Railroad: The Magic Interurban was designed by William D. Markowski, Park Ridge, Illinois and assembled by Roy G. Benedict, Chicago, Illinois. Color separations and printing negatives were by Jim Walter Color Separations, Beloit, Wisconsin; typesetting by S Printing Company of Illinois and Apple Printing, Troy, Michigan. Printing and binding were contracted to Interurban Press, Glendale, California. Editorial assistance was provided by Roy G. Benedict. Photographs and illustrations in this volume are from a variety of sources and the ownership is identified wherever possible

CERA bulletins are technical and educational historical studies by members of the Central Electric Railfans' Association, working without salary, with a particular knowledge and interest in the subject. CERA is an Illinois not-for-profit corporation. This book is consistent with CERA's purpose of fostering the study of the history, equipment and operation of electric railways. If you can provide additional information, or believe that any statement herein is inaccurate or incomplete, please send CERA documentation supporting such amendment, citing your sources

CERA Directors 1988-1991

Norman Carlson	Donald L. MacCorquodale	William Reynolds
Phillip F. Cioffi	Bruce G. Moffat	David Sadowski
Walter R. Keevil	Stanford A. Nettis	William M. Shapotkin
Frederick D. Lonnes	Charlie W. Petzold	Jeffrey L. Wien

Contents

Maps
- Ownership and abandonment dates 4
- Track-circuit block signals 61
- Principal towns served 201

Index to places reached
- Cities, towns and other passenger traffic generators 203
- Siding locations (in employee timetables):
  - Muncie-Anderson-Indianapolis Division 60
  - Northern Division 116
  - Other rail routes 209

Acknowledgments 7

Prelude: An Eventful Trip 11
  The situation of central Indiana utilities in 1929

Chapter

1 A Solid Foundation 19
  Companies comprising Indiana Railroad System:
  - Terre Haute, Indianapolis & Eastern Traction Company .. 19
  - Union Traction Company of Indiana 19
  - Northern Indiana Power Company 20
  - Indiana Service Corporation 20
  - Indianapolis, Columbus & Southern Traction Company .. 21
  - Indianapolis as an interurban center 21
  - The Schoepf-McGowan syndicate 22
  - Samuel Insull 24
  - Middle West Utilities Company 26
  - Competition by automobiles and motor buses 27

2 Consolidating Indiana 29
  - Insull-Morgan plan: Indiana Electric Corporation 29
  - Midland United Company 31
  - Receivership of Union Traction 31
  - A different plan: a consolidated organization 32
  - Purchase of Union Traction by Midland United 34
  - Receivership of THI&E 34
  - Abandonment of portions of THI&E 35

3 Out of Nowhere—Indiana Railroad 37
  - Creation of Indiana Railroad 37
  - Purchase of THI&E by Midland United 39
  - Indianapolis Street Railway 40
  - Track and roadway 41
  - Electric power 42
  - Passenger and freight terminals 45
  - Freight car interchange with steam railroads 47
  - Operation of freight trains 48
  - Freight car interchange with other interurbans 49
  - Freight train schedules 50
  - Kentucky Avenue freight terminal, Indianapolis 53
  - Potential for coal movements across the System 54
  - Signal systems 56

4	**The Highspeeds**	67	**10** **Death Comes for the Railroad** 147	
	Rolling stock on the System in 1930	67	Approval of conversion of remaining lines 147	
	Design of the new "highspeed" cars	68	Attempts to sell the highspeeds 147	
	Highspeeds' delivery	70	Arrangements for rail service abandonment 149	
	Highspeeds in operation	72	Arrival of replacement buses 151	
	Safety of train operation	76	The last day of rail passenger service 151	
	Peak route mileage	77	Closing down the rail line 153	
			The remaining trains of Public Service Company ... 154	
5	**The Roller Coaster**	79	**11** **Aftermath** 157	
	Rolling stock on the System in 1931	79	Emergence of Indiana Railroad from receivership ... 157	
	Abandonments in 1931-1932	79	Sale of Indiana Railroad by Midland United 158	
	Reduction in frequency of passenger service	83	Public Service Company's lease problem 159	
	Feustel's death	83	Columbus collision 160	
	Fall of Insull empire	86	End of rail passenger service 160	
6	**Politics and Bowman Elder**	89	**12** **The Motor Bus Era** 163	
	Indianapolis Railways	91	Indiana Railroad bus operations 163	
	Reduced bus operations	91	Expand or sell: the only options 165	
	Lower fares	92	Indianapolis & Southeastern Trailways 168	
	Bowman Elder, receiver of Indiana Railroad	93	Southeastern Trailways, Inc. 168	
	Indiana Railroad System in 1933-1934	95		
	Formal leases for the Indiana Railroad System	97	**13** **City Service** 171	
	Coal train operations	99	Kokomo 171	
	Change of Louisville terminal	101	Logansport, Wabash and Peru 172	
7	**1935-1936—The Good Years**	103	Jeffersonville and Columbus 173	
	Purchase of ten Northern Indiana Railway cars	104	New Albany 174	
	Railway Post Office cars	105	Muncie 177	
	Car fires	107	Anderson 179	
	Conversion of older cars for one-man operation ..	108	Marion 182	
	Pick-up and delivery of freight	112	Richmond 188	
	Expansion: Richmond-Dayton line	113	Terre Haute 190	
	Was it the Inflexible Flyer?	115	**14** **Isolated Freight Operations** 195	
	A difficult day on the Northern Division		The Binkley Mine 195	
8	**1937—Strike!**	119	Southern Indiana Railway, Inc. 197	
	Terre Haute streetcar strike	120	Western Indiana Gravel Company 199	
	Ohio River flood	120	An abbreviated equipment roster 200	
	End of Northern Division passenger service	120	<u>Appendix</u>	
	Anderson strike	122	**A** **Public Timetables** 201	
	Abandonment of Dayton line	124	System timetable of September 27, 1931 201	
	Settlement of strike	125	List of public timetables (rail operations) 202	
	Winter's Punch	127	**B** **Employee Timetables** 208	
	Fighting the cold and snow of winter		**Bibliography** 223	
9	**Rolling Downhill (1938-1940)**	131		
	Railfan trips	131		
	Conversion of Peru rail line to buses	133		
	Charter passenger services	139		
	Abandonment of Louisville line	141		
	Conversion of Terre Haute rail line to buses	143		
	Expansion of intercity motor truck service	143		

The ornament appearing on this page and elsewhere in the book is the Indiana Railroad herald as painted on the side of the company's top-drawer rolling stock. For use in *Indiana Railroad: The Magic Interurban* it was drafted by Herb Harnish, Fort Wayne, Indiana.

Page 1 Highspeed 57, running as northbound train 8 on October 20, 1940, is about to enter the south end of the Muncie Traction Terminal trainshed. The car is going east on Howard Street, just crossing Mulberry Street where the tracks in the left foreground branch off to the freight house. *James P. Shuman photo*

Left The *Dixie Flyer* roars off the dusty streets of Edinburg, Indiana one summer day in the mid-1930's. It's "dropping" one of the block signals which protect much of the high-speed open track. At this rate it will be in the Louisville station on time two hours from now. *Ewing Dale photo*

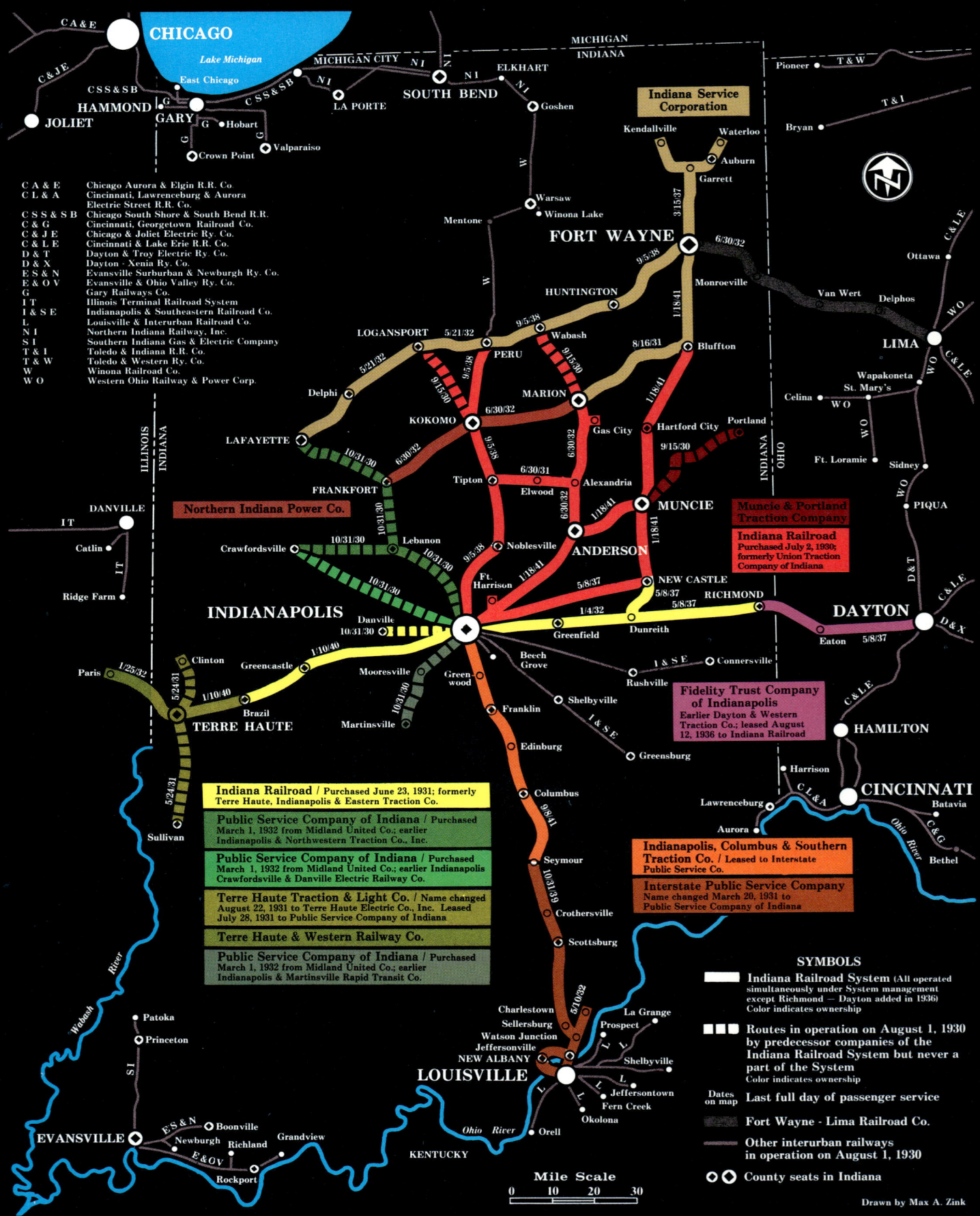

Above Highspeed 58 is being used for a CERA special on October 20, 1940. On the southbound trip from Fort Wayne to Muncie it pauses at the Eaton station. The big old frame station building is located on the outside of the curve. *James P. Shuman photo*

Below En route Indianapolis, Railway Post Office car 376 stops at the west end of Anderson street running. It is on another leg of the same trip. Belt siding, visible beyond the car, was named for the railroad which crossed at this location. *James P. Shuman photo*

Above In 1907, THI&E bought a number of larger, 61-foot cars from Cincinnati Car Company. The much rebuilt 29 is on East Washington Street in Indianapolis, working the line to Richmond, in 1930. *Wilbourne B. Cox photo, George Krambles collection*

Below Built in 1906, THI&E 68 was one of several dozen similar cars built by the Cincinnati Car Company for the Schoepf-McGowan syndicate's Indiana and Ohio properties. It was still in use in 1931 when Indiana Railroad was formed. *Bass Photo Company, Indiana Historical Society*

Acknowledgments

As Central Electric Railfans' Association enters its second half century, fond memories of the Indiana Railroad return to older CERA members who rode the lines, just as to the younger members who have heard so much about it. During CERA's early years, railfan trips over this huge interurban electric line spanned nearly the whole Hoosier State from Fort Wayne on the northeast to Jeffersonville on the south (and beyond to Louisville, Kentucky) and to Terre Haute on the west. As a great "draw" to bring railfans together, especially those from Indiana and the Chicago area, the Indiana Railroad System helped swell the ranks of the young CERA. Many a friendship that continues today originated on an orange interurban car lettered with the magic name: "INDIANA RAILROAD."

Fortunately many railroad enthusiasts photographed the line and collected information about it. The documentary record of this railway is unusually strong. This book depends on the people who generously loaned their photographs, printed materials and personal recollections.

In researching this book the author had the pleasure of working with not only many fans of the railroad, but also professionals who had a part over fifty years ago in shaping its operations or who guide successor companies. These include Russ Powell, one of two surviving motormen; George Krambles, an engineering trainee in 1936; Marty Kramer, president of Southeastern Trailways, Inc.; Bill Elder, president of Southern Indiana Railway and son of the Indiana Railroad's receiver; and Don Walker, assistant chief engineer for track and roadway.

Contributors to this book include:

Allen County-Fort Wayne Public Library
Anderson Public Library
The late Edwin P. Belknap
Roy G. Benedict
Allan Berner
Dr. Howard R. Blackburn
George K. Bradley
Philip E. Buchert
Frank E. Butts
Norman Carlson
The late Stanley O. Chausse
The late James F. Cook
Ewing Dale
Steve Davidson
Detroit Public Library
Neff Dykes
William L. Elder
The late Walter Fidler
Robert E. Geis
General Steel Industries, Inc.
Richard H. George
F. Gerald Handfield, Jr.
The late Herbert G. Harnish
John D. Horachek
The late John Hoschek
John F. Humiston
Indiana Historical Society Library
Indiana Museum of Transportation
Indiana State Archives
Indiana State Library
William C. Janssen
The late Vane A. Jones
George Krambles
Martin Kramer
Gordon E. Lloyd
Loyola University (Chicago): Michael Grace, S.J.
Malcolm D. "Mac" McCarter
Madison County (IN) court records
Marion County (IN) court records
Jerry Marlette
Robert V. Mehlenbeck
Jack M. Miller
The late George Moore
The late Ronald A. Morris
Motor Bus Society, Inc.
Muncie Indiana Transit System
Muncie Public Library
David W. Peat
Ralph A. Perkin
Tim Peterson
Russell Powell
Craig Pressler
The late Jerry D. Pruden
Public Service Company of Indiana
Walter Sampson
James P. Shuman
Willard Sinnett
George M. Smerk
Southeastern Trailways, Inc.
Southern Indiana Railway
Robert M. Stacy
William A. Steventon
The late Frank Summers
Eugene Van Dusen
Donald H. Walker
Robert Wills
George Yater
George Zies
Harry Zillmer
Maximilian A. Zink

Right Four key contributors appear in this 1979 photo taken on a Chicago Transit Authority trip hosted by George Krambles. They are, left to right, Edwin P. Belknap, James F. Cook, Jerry D. Pruden and George Krambles.
George Krambles collection

Above Line car 763 was many times rebuilt. It still shows some of its original form as a "Robertson" style car body from St. Louis Car Company. On October 19, 1940 the 763 came north from Muncie to tension some very slack trolley wire at Sprang siding near the county line separating Allen and Wells counties.
James P. Shuman photo

Left With the Indianapolis skyline in the distant background, one-man car 430 rolls toward Ben Davis on the Terre Haute line in the summer of 1939. Though only about six miles from the Traction Terminal, it had already left the state capital's metropolitan area.
Ronald P. Morris collection

Above It's summer 1939; one-man 427-series cars still serve the Terre Haute line. The 439 is in the yards while a sister car, southbound on Capitol Avenue in front of the Indiana State House, makes a morning departure. *Dr. Howard R. Blackburn photo*

Below A late afternoon view of RPO 375 westbound on Pearl Street in Fort Wayne. This May 19, 1940 photo was made on the north side of the Fort Wayne terminal. The 375 will be backed into Track 3 and face north for departure. *William E. Schreiber collection*

Above It's 3:40 PM and Union Traction's trains 517 and 514 meet at Hartford City. Southbound car 440 takes the siding alongside the station in this time-honored daily ritual. *Jerry D. Pruden collection*

Below Union Traction posed brand-new 427 and a second car from the same series for publicity. The artist's sketch was used for timetables and advertisements. *George K. Bradley collection*

Prelude

An Eventful Trip

The station door swung wide and two men stepped out. They walked to the rear of a waiting interurban car where a large metal sign, leaning against the coupler, listed the train stops. At the car steps, the two, no strangers to the conductor, were cordially greeted, "Good morning, Mr. Feustel, good morning, Mr. Insull." Soon after the two settled into their seats, the red Union Traction Company car moved out of the Fort Wayne station on its nearly four-hour journey to Indianapolis.

On that fall day the car sped southward through Yoder, Ossian and into the Bluffton station. There after the crew changed, the car left the tracks of the Indiana Service Corporation (ISC) and headed south over the lines of the Union Traction Company of Indiana. As Samuel Insull, Jr. recalled, nearly fifty years later, the car seemed to make a number of time-consuming stops. However, on a largely single-track rail system, a missed meet of an opposing train—by even a couple of minutes—could produce what might appear to be excessive delays to one who was more accustomed to a multi-track main line or suburban railroad.

The hindrances might have been seen as an omen. Certainly any delay would frustrate two of the most powerful public utility men in Indiana. Samuel Insull, Jr. was president and Robert Feustel was the executive vice-president of Midland United Company, the senior Indiana holding company of the Insull utility empire. Midland United controlled large electric and gas utility companies plus several hundred miles of interurban and city railway systems. Union Traction was not one of them ... and not because they hadn't tried! In more ways than one, Union Traction was a problem to Insull and Feustel on that day in 1929.

The two were traveling to Indianapolis, the state capital, for the opening hearings on the proposed merger of sixteen electric and transportation companies into a new organization, the Indiana Electric Corporation, a carefully planned conglomerate valued at $70,000,000. This merger would later be viewed as a link between the past and the future. It was an assemblage of utility and traction companies whose heritage began with the Schoepf-McGowan syndicate of the early 1900's. The last survivor of the syndicate had been Randal Morgan. He and the elder Samuel Insull had started a "rationalization" of the northern Indiana utilities as early as 1923. The product would be a new consolidation as large, if not larger, than the earlier syndicate's properties. During the next four years, Morgan had died (1926) and the merger petition had been presented to the Public Service Commission of Indiana in September 1928. Now, over a year later, the hearings were scheduled to begin in December 1929. The regulatory commission was friendly to the Insull interests but even this usually reliable panel could not be counted upon at this time. Feustel and Insull hoped for success but both had their doubts.

Earlier in 1929, the Insull interests approached the receiver of the Union Traction Company to discuss obtaining control of that system and particularly its power company subsidiary. The bonds of the bankrupt company were held under a deposit agreement by several committees representing the bondholder groups. The proposed Insull utility consolidation was well known and seemed to promise something for everyone with an interest in the old properties. This was a mistake! Some Union Traction bondholders, hoping to be included, wanted far more than their share might realize in any sale. Insull and Feustel, contemplating the problems confronting their consolidation plans, realized that the dissident Union Traction bondholders might make a stir. This could cause a disappointing delay and have an effect on the main merger. They would wage a good fight for the Indiana Electric Corporation's acquisition of the Terre Haute, Indianapolis and Eastern Traction Company (THI&E) but the prospects for this plan were diminishing. There were too many "ifs" and the chances of crossing all the hurdles were slim.

As the Union Traction car paused under the Muncie train shed and then headed toward Anderson, Insull and Feustel's conversations continued. If one plan wouldn't work, then another would be needed. That, according to Insull, was when the two came up with the

Above Railway Post Office car 376, with CERA's drumsign, on October 20, 1940, is in Taft siding west of Anderson on the eastbound leg of the fan trip. Highspeed 57, running as train 17 bound for Indianapolis, is flying by. The distant interlocking tower belongs to the paralleling Big Four Railroad. *James P. Shuman photo*

Below The same special car is Indianapolis-bound at Bucy substation. The parking-meter-like unit near the switch stand is a switch indicator connected to the signal system. A movable pan in the trolley wire, rodded to the switch, helped insure trolley poles would go where the cars did! *William E. Schreiber collection*

Above The Anderson shop lead tracks with car 58 on May 20, 1940 as the car nears the end of its brilliant career. In this last year of the Indiana Railroad's operation, some maintenance extras such as removing grass from the once-neat yard tracks have been stopped.
William E. Schreiber photo

Below Highspeeds at Fort Wayne: The 73 is a Pullman-built coach-baggage car; the 54, an ACF coach-parlor car. This is a mid-morning November 17, 1940 view. Track 1 and the east curves are out of service: the remaining route enters from the west via Main Street and departs on Pearl Street.
William E. Schreiber photo

Above In 1924 Interstate Public Service Company posed car 153 and parlor-buffet car 161, as the *Dixie Flyer*, along with a new White intercity motor coach. The narrow road, full of tight turns, was typical of the main Indianapolis-Louisville highway. *Motor Bus Society, Inc. Library*

germ of a new plan. From this moment Insull and Feustel probably began to lose interest in the Indiana Electric Corporation merger. It was probably a losing cause. Now a more expansive plan seemed appropriate.

What did they have? They controlled three major electric power utilities with interurban rail lines: Indiana Service Corporation, Interstate Public Service Company and Northern Indiana Power Company. Insull also controlled Northern Indiana Public Service Company, an electric and gas utility, Gary Railways and the Chicago South Shore & South Bend, an electric railroad.

Eventually the THI&E and the Union Traction Company, or pieces of them, would be accessible to their Midland United Company and then a huge area of Indiana could be electrically interconnected by Midland-owned companies.

Feustel was the senior officer in Indiana for the Insull utility companies. Indiana Service Corporation (ISC), his home company, was the best balanced utility in overall city and intercity rail operations. It probably had the best and most talented transportation operating staff which Feustel had either collected or inherited from the earlier leadership of Sam Greenland, who now headed the St. Louis Public Service Company.

The next logical step would be a coordination of the Indiana Insull rail operations. Feustel had already suggested bringing the top operating rail people to Indianapolis to place all city and interurban rail and bus operations of ISC, Interstate and Northern Indiana Power under one management with headquarters in the Traction Terminal Building. The economics and improved efficiency would be typical of Insull-managed properties. There would be no change in ownership or company identity and therefore no room for complaint from any stock or bondholders. Operations might be united under one name for further simplification. All the power companies and the rail properties could be operated to the best advan-

Above Before Indiana Railroad, twelve interurban lines of four separate companies connected the capital to much of Indiana. The Traction Terminal symbolized their cooperation. Waiting in mid-1928 are THI&E car 20 on the "Ben Hur" to Crawfordsville and 51 on the "Northwestern" to Lafayette, Interstate's 117 on a Columbus local, I&C 609 signed Greensburg and two Union traction cars: wooden 279 and a steel "400."
Richard H. George collection

tage of the entire group. The plan was seen as the way of the future and was soon announced to the public.

As the interurban car hurried along into Pendleton, past Fort Harrison, through Lawrence, along 38th Street to Orchard and then south onto the streets of Indianapolis, the two men's discussions probably changed to more immediate subjects but the coordination idea would come up again—and very soon. Eventually Midland would find the right combination.

In the center of the city the car turned off the street and rumbled to a halt under the huge train shed of the Traction Terminal where Feustel and Insull stepped to the pavement. The two were now on the center stage of the Indiana interurbans, a scene created through an earlier common ownership of several major electric rail lines.

Robert Feustel and Sam Insull, Jr., walked from the interurban car to the terminal building passing by rail cars of many colors: tuscan red, pullman green, sand yellow, orange and other hues. The two men would soon command and change this colorful array and alter the course of Indiana utilities—especially the interurbans. A whole new and unique rail system would arise on the Indiana plains in an atmosphere of apparent idyllic happiness. With it would come the fondly remembered, and perhaps most magic, interurban: the Indiana Railroad.

Above Steel interurban cars on the "new" *Wabash Valley Flyer* in 1926. Baggage-passenger 379 and parlor car 390, "Little Turtle," are westbound at Andrews siding.

Right A young man meets a lady alighting from the *Flyer's* parlor car at the Fort Wayne terminal. The conductor is Quell Etter. *Both: Bradley-Harnish collection*

Left Southbound highspeed 61 departs Muncie on a fall 1940 day. The rapidly setting sun leaves long shadows: the same might be said for the rail line. "Muncie Local" is displayed on a train bound for New Castle because that city's name is not on the highspeed's sign curtains.
Frank E. Butts photo

Chapter 1
A Solid Foundation

Left Long before Indiana Railroad: Indianapolis and Greenfield Rapid Transit Company's 45 passes under a steam railroad bridge. The newly-laid and unballasted track suggests this was a very early trip before the line was completed. *David W. Peat collection*

Indiana Railroad, a creation of 1930, was possible because of the extensive network of electric railways already in place. The building of the Indiana interurbans began thirty years before, and by 1912 all major construction was completed. Some of these intercity lines never reached projected terminal cities, having been cut short by the financial panics of 1903 and 1907. After 1907, new construction money was generally not available. Only a few lines were built in the following years. Several truncated and financially weak lines remained as branches of the main lines. Most of the Indiana interurban trackage was still in existence in 1929: about 1700 route miles out of the approximately 1800 miles that had been built.

The greater portion of the Indiana mileage was in central Indiana, radiating from Indianapolis, with the Wabash River valley being the northern edge. Most of the remaining trackage was in northwestern Indiana where three companies, the Chicago South Shore and South Bend Railroad, the Chicago, South Bend and Northern Indiana Railway and the Gary Railways controlled the main lines in five northern-tier counties. One line, the Winona Railroad, appropriately using the slogan "The Connecting Link," tied the two areas together. A separated and unrelated group of electric lines was centered on Evansville in the southwest corner of the state.

The central lines, including the Indianapolis-Louisville route, were the subject of Sam Insull, Jr. and Robert Feustel's talks. They were interested particularly in those that had an electric power business. Their extensive high-lines, rights-of-way and commercial and residential distribution systems offered an opportunity for a large interconnected electric power network. Acquisition of strategically located companies not already in the Insull group would greatly expand Insull's power territory. Each of these rail/power companies had a distinct history. To understand the electric railway and power situation leading to the Indiana Railroad requires stepping back to the halcyon days of building interurbans beginning with the earliest construction in the 1890's and ending with the virtual completion before 1910.

The Terre Haute, Indianapolis & Eastern Traction Company's beginnings dated to July 16, 1893 when the Brazil Rapid Transit Company ran a small city streetcar over three miles of track, built alongside the National Road (later U.S. 40), from Brazil to Harmony. It wasn't until 1900 that the Terre Haute Electric Company extended a line from Terre Haute to Brazil. A few years later that company built lines from Terre Haute north to Clinton and south to Sullivan. The Indianapolis & Greenfield Rapid Transit Company opened a line between the two cities in its title extending from Irvington, the end of the East Washington Street city car line in Indianapolis, on June 19, 1900. This line was extended eastward to Richmond with a major branch from Dunreith to New Castle and a minor branch from Cambridge City to Milton. An extension east of Richmond connected with the Dayton & Western's interurban line west from Dayton, Ohio. Dayton was a major junction point in the Ohio network of electric railways. Over a period of years trackage was built westward from Indianapolis to connect with the Terre Haute-Harmony tracks for a through route. A line was also built from Indianapolis to Danville (Indiana) where the original plan had been to continue west to connect with the line from Terre Haute. All of these companies were pulled together in 1907 to form the THI&E. The THI&E then leased the Indianapolis & Northwestern Traction Company, Inc. and its line from Indianapolis to Lafayette with a branch from Lebanon to Crawfordsville; the Indianapolis, Crawfordsville & Danville Electric Railway Company with its line from Indianapolis to Crawfordsville and hopes to reach Danville (Illinois); and the Indianapolis & Martinsville Rapid Transit Company with a line between the two named cities. The THI&E also constructed a line from Terre Haute to Paris, Illinois. In addition, the THI&E had city lines at Terre Haute and Richmond and held stock control of the Indianapolis streetcar system.

The THI&E, over a period of years, acquired and built extensive electric power generating and distribution facilities. These, and the interurban power distribution system, meant the company was the major electric power supplier in a wide area.

The Union Traction Company of Indiana was a direct outgrowth of the city streetcar systems at Anderson and Marion. The Marion Electric Street Railway Company built a suburban line south to Jonesboro and then east, across the Mississinewa River to Gas City. This six-mile route was opened on August 1, 1893 with small low-speed single-truck city streetcars. From Anderson, Charles L. Henry, an attorney, promoted and built an 11-mile electric line north to Alexandria with the first through run being made on January 1, 1898. Henry bought a group of 45-foot double-truck passenger motor cars and trailers that resembled contemporary steam railroad equipment. These were not the first large electric cars in the state as the line between South Bend and Mishawaka had been using six large cars since 1895. Henry's use of the larger cars and his popularizing of the word "interurban," which had been frequently used before, set the standard for later intercity electric railways. Henry promoted the interurban idea on any available forum and is often credited with the title, "Father of the Interurban."

The instant success of the Anderson-Alexandria line prompted rapid expansion of electric lines throughout the Indiana "Gas Belt" where industries were quickly moving to take advantage of cheap and plentiful fuel. The Marion company, soon to be part of the Union Traction Company, built south to Summitville and met

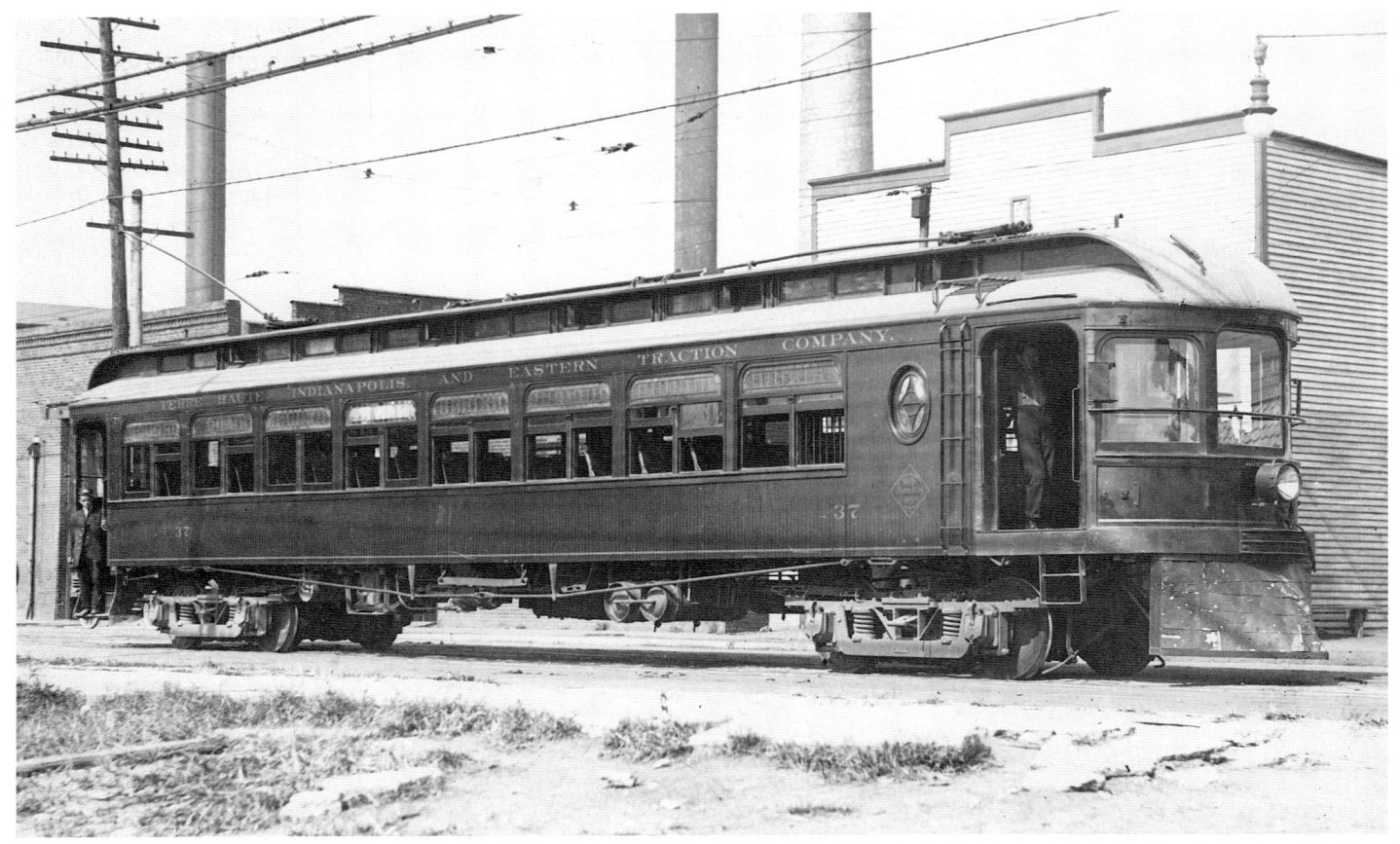

Above THI&E's 60-foot interurban car 37 eastbound on West Washington Street near the Indianapolis Street Railway Company's shop. These cars were design classics—THI&E's finest!
David W. Peat collection

an extension north from Alexandria. The 34-mile Anderson-Marion through route was opened in late 1898. At the same time a line was built west from Alexandria to Elwood which was extended to Tipton in 1902. The important Indianapolis-Anderson-Muncie route was completed in 1901. Another line was projected from Alexandria to Muncie. The route was completely graded, the bridge abutments completed and some steel bridge work was in place before the 1903-04 financial panic halted construction. It was never completed.

Union Traction built little after 1904 but acquired extensive trackage by leasing a new line from Indianapolis north to Kokomo where the line branched into lines to Peru and Logansport. A line from Marion to Wabash was acquired in the same year. During 1905, an interstate route was completed from Dayton, Ohio to Muncie. The Indiana portion, from Muncie to Union City, became the property of Union Traction. In 1903, a major line was built from Muncie to Bluffton, connecting with a Bluffton-Fort Wayne line. The Muncie-Bluffton line was leased by the Union Traction Company. In 1912, the Indianapolis, New Castle and Eastern Traction Company with a line from Indianapolis to Muncie, by way of New Castle, was leased. This line was always known as "The Honey Bee Route" based on its straight-line construction in a "bee-line" between Indianapolis and New Castle. The Honey Bee later leased the Muncie and Portland Traction Company and that route came into the Union Traction. The Union Traction had a 10-mile branch from Anderson to Middletown which was part of a projected Anderson-New Castle route. Union Traction, the largest of the Indiana interurbans, also had comprehensive city streetcar systems at Anderson, Marion and Muncie.

Union Traction generated its own power and originally had a number of small electric power plants. Following the completion of a large generating station at Anderson most of the others were closed. A system covering this large area had an extensive power distribution network. This offered some fine possibilities to sell power so a subsidiary, Traction Light and Power, was established to sell power to 50 small communities.

The Northern Indiana Power Company was centered at Kokomo. The Kokomo, Marion & Western built from Kokomo to Marion in two spurts starting in 1903 and completing in 1905. A subsidiary company built west from Kokomo to Frankfort in 1912. The two were merged into the Indiana Railways & Light Company with the company's electric power business becoming more important than the interurban lines and the Kokomo streetcars. In 1922, the Chicago-based combination of electric power companies, headed by Samuel Insull, acquired control of the company and it became the Northern Indiana Power Company. The name always created some confusion as Kokomo and the east-west territory is, at best, north-central Indiana and the words "northern Indiana" were already in use by a major consumers gas producing company and another interurban rail company.

Centered at Fort Wayne was the Indiana Service Corporation. This company, in the early 1900's, under the banner of the Fort Wayne & Wabash Valley Traction Company, built a long interurban line, following the Wabash River valley from Fort Wayne to Lafayette. It connected with the Union Traction Company at Wabash, Peru and Logansport. A Fort Wayne-Indianapolis through interurban route was undertaken jointly by the Wabash Valley and Union Traction. A similar situation existed through the Wabash Valley's Fort Wayne to Bluffton branch in connection with the Union Traction. In 1920, the Wabash Valley Lines were reorganized as the Indiana Service Corporation. Control of the ISC was acquired by the Insull interests in 1925. The interurban north from Fort Wayne to Kendallville and Waterloo became part of the ISC as did The Marion & Bluffton Traction Company with a line between those two cities. ISC had a major street railway system at Fort Wayne and lesser operations at Wabash, Peru and Logansport. (Earlier the Lafayette streetcars had been included.) From its earliest days, the ISC and its predecessors had been in the electric power business with many industrial, commercial and residential customers. After 1920, ISC had the operating control of the Fort Wayne to Lima, Ohio route. This line, which later became the Fort Wayne-Lima Railroad, was a major connecting link between the Indiana and Ohio interurban networks. The Lima line was a power customer of the ISC as it had no electric power generating station of its own. East from Fort Wayne to the Ohio line, where the ISC's electric service territory ended, there was only one small town so the right-of-way and overhead lines were of little interest to the ISC. (The ISC story is detailed in *Fort Wayne and Wabash Valley Trolleys* by George K. Bradley and published in 1983 by Central Electric Railfans' Association.)

The Indianapolis, Greenwood and Franklin Railroad built the first interurban line into Indianapolis. It began operating cars south to Greenwood in the first weeks of January 1900. Franklin was reached later. The Indianapolis, Columbus & Southern Traction Company (IC&S) succeeded the earlier company and, by 1907, had extended the rail line through Columbus to Seymour. The IC&S was a financially strong interurban, locally financed by members of three Columbus banking and investment families.

The Indianapolis & Cincinnati Traction Company (I&C) controlled two lines running southeasterly from Indianapolis to terminals at Connersville and Greensburg. The company was never very successful as a rail property but it did develop a modest tributary power business. In a 1928 reorganization the power and rail facilities were sold to two different groups. The successor Indianapolis & Southeastern Railroad Company modernized the rail service with brightly painted moderate-speed lightweight interurban cars and new motor buses. The buses offered a connecting service from Greensburg to Cincinnati.

Indianapolis became the focal point of the interurban industry in Indiana. Twelve long interurban routes radiated from the Indianapolis hub. (A thirteenth property, the six-mile Beech Grove Traction Company, was classified as an interurban company even though it used the tracks of the Indianapolis Street Railway for nearly half the total distance.) Of the twelve, Union Traction controlled three, THI&E had six, the IC&S had one and the I&C had two.

Below Muncie and Portland Traction Company's car 103 at Albany station. A shorter car for a shorter line but even so the finest vehicle on the town's streets.
Jerry D. Pruden collection

Above The Wabash Valley's 61-foot parlor-buffet car 502. The "Ivanhoe" and three sister cars provided a service comparable to that of competing steam railroads.
Herb Harnish collection

By 1903 the principal owners of the Indianapolis Street Railway Company became interested in the interurban companies that used their streetcar lines. The involvement was interesting and it was not necessarily planned.

Thomas Dolan, president, and Randal Morgan, first vice-president, of the United Gas Improvement Company, had a large investment in the Citizens' Street Railway Company, of Indianapolis, when that company became embroiled in some financial and political difficulties in 1899. They called in Hugh J. McGowan, their very successful gas company manager in Kansas City. McGowan set up a new unified company, Indianapolis Street Railway Company, and became its president. The Cincinnati Street Railway was controlled by investors associated with Dolan and Morgan. McGowan was also named president of the Cincinnati Traction Company, which leased the street railway, upon its formation on February 21, 1901. He gave up the Cincinnati position in October of the same year and was succeeded by William Kesley Schoepf who was also Chairman of the Executive Committee of the Cincinnati Traction Company. For the next ten years the combination of Schoepf-McGowan grew to be the dominant force in Midwest interurban circles.

The money that these two shrewd and competent managers required came from Philadelphia financiers. They included, besides Dolan and Morgan, George and Peter Widener, William and George Elkins, and J. Levering Jones. These men had financial resources far beyond those of many other electric traction promoters. They could ride out financial panics which wrecked some other promoters. It also put them in a position to pick up the pieces cheaply when some weaker investor combine stumbled.

Schoepf devoted most of his efforts to Ohio where he put together a number of companies into the Ohio Electric Railway. In 1907, it consisted of about 500 route miles of interurban railway. The Indiana operations were treated differently—not amalgamated into a single corporate organization—and grew into several large but separate companies.

McGowan acquired control of the Union Traction Company (UT) in 1902. The UT had about 120 miles of line in operation. It was building and expanding. About this same time, George McCulloch, a newspaper publisher and associate of Morgan's, was getting the public credit for a new Indianapolis-to-Kokomo route. One of the hallmarks of the Schoepf-McGowan syndicate's methods was the careful use of "front" men, like McCulloch, as promoters and builders to mask the source of capital. The syndicate owners knew that shrewd landholders would demand higher prices if they knew the real source of the capital. Several "grass roots" companies turned out to be Schoepf-McGowan promotions.

The Union Traction system grew to 415 route miles. Two other Schoepf-McGowan properties, put together in the first decade of the twentieth century, were the Fort Wayne & Wabash Valley Traction Company (approximately 140 route miles) and the Terre Haute, Indianapolis & Eastern Traction Company (a complex collection of owned and leased properties totaling 400 route miles). This gave the Schoepf-McGowan properties over 1,400 route miles of interconnected interurban lines, including three connecting lines between the Indiana and Ohio properties, plus the city street railway systems of Cincinnati, Indianapolis, Fort Wayne, Terre Haute and several other cities. It was a mighty traction empire!

The empire had its monuments to mark its achievement. Hugh McGowan conceived the idea of a large office building and train terminal to serve as a headquarters for the electric lines. The Indianapolis Traction Terminal, costing over a million dollars, was completed in August 1904 and opened to traffic on September 12, 1904. This greatest of all interurban stations had a huge trainshed covering nine tracks. The shed spanned 133 feet, was 185 feet long and easily accommodated 18 large interurban cars. The shed was an integral part of the nine-story Romanesque style office building designed by the Chicago firm of D. H. Burnham and Company. Its location on the northwest corner of Illinois and Market Streets was ideal as it was only a block from the State Capitol, a block from the monument circle (designed as the center of the city) and one and one-half blocks from the city's busiest commercial intersection. Eventually all of the Indianapolis interurbans except the Beech Grove Traction Company ran their trains through the terminal and most maintained offices in the building. The traffic was very heavy with over 100,000 arriving and departing trains annually during the peak years of the interurbans. These were easily handled because with nine tracks, the terminal had been planned to serve interurban lines that were never built or not completed as projected. The Indianapolis Traction Terminal remained the interurban heart and hub of the industry for nearly forty years and as a bus terminal for twenty more. It was Hugh McGowan's monument—later his memorial.

The great terminal had been built by the Indianapolis Traction & Terminal Company, which was formed in 1902 for that purpose and to acquire control of the Indianapolis Street Railway Company. (In 1919, the situation was reversed, in a corporate reorganization, with a new Indianapolis Street Railway Company assuming the operations and obtaining control of the Traction Terminal Corporation. The THI&E held stock control of these companies after 1907, and the bonds were, largely, held by the same interests as the other Schoepf-McGowan properties.)

Below Union Traction Company's 246 at Eaton during the high-water conditions following the 1913 floods, which created havoc for the Indiana interurban lines. The conductor's boots were an essential item. *Jerry D. Pruden collection*

Above Busy West Market Street in Indianapolis from the Soldiers and Sailors Monument with the handsome Indiana State Capitol as a backdrop. This view (circa 1910) shows four cars leaving the Traction Terminal. The first turns south on Capitol Avenue, the second follows closely, the third is a THI&E car swinging into Market Street and the fourth eases past the entrance gates. *George K. Bradley collection*

The Schoepf-McGowan syndicate combine began to come apart about 1910. On September 21, 1910, the Fort Wayne & Wabash Valley Traction Company suffered the Kingsland wreck, a catastrophe that took 41 lives. The company went through reorganization with some of the Philadelphia personalities still involved but without the usual Philadelphia capital input. Then, on December 19, 1911, Hugh McGowan, only 51 years old, died following a long illness. The final break came early in the morning of April 15, 1912 when George Widener and his son Harry went to the bottom with the *RMS Titanic*. After that only Randal Morgan remained as an active participant in Indiana utility affairs and in particular the THI&E.

While one combination was disintegrating, another was just starting. This one, Chicago-based, grew out of a plan to improve and expand electric power generation and distribution on a vast scale whose potential was recognized by only a limited number of visionaries. Samuel Insull was one of these rare men.

Sam Insull had learned shorthand as a very young man in his native England and became an expert stenographer. Through a stroke of luck he went to work for the London representatives of a man he admired, Thomas A. Edison. Insull learned everything he could about the technical side of the Edison business while pursuing his secretarial duties. He impressed several of the top Edison men in London, including Edward H. Johnson, who thought the young Insull might be useful to Edison.

Upon his return to the United States, Johnson arranged for Insull to come to New York and to bring some current business data with him. Insull arrived early on one evening in February 1881 and, by eight o'clock that same evening, found himself with Johnson in Edison's office. He gave the men a detailed briefing of the current worth of each of the Edison London properties so that they could be pledged to raise capital for the expanding light and power business. Edison, in his rather casual manner, almost automatically accepted the young man as his personal secretary and Insull was soon keeping track of whatever needed to be done for the Edison companies and Edison himself. Working in this atmosphere of new technology and exploration was fast-paced. To market Edison's lights, the team had to invent a generating and distribution system and then compete against the gas lighting interests. Initially, the financial backers of the companies favored the sale of small isolated power plants for each building or installation because these achieved a short-term gain while the large central power stations required a long-term large capital investment. Fortunately, the central station proponents prevailed. During this time Insull worked hard for Edison and, in turn, Edison rewarded him very well.

A rising new power demand came from the rapid conversion of street railways from animal to electric power boosting the need for central station power, equipment and motors. This business grew rapidly (there were only two street railways using electric power at the end of 1885—in South Bend, Indiana and Baltimore, Maryland) and among the Edison-controlled companies was the Sprague Electric Railway & Motor Company. For more manufacturing capacity, the Edison Machine Works was moved from New Jersey to Schenectady, New York, with Insull in charge of the new plant.

In 1890 all of the Edison companies were consolidated under the name of Edison-General Electric. Insull, as second vice-president, became the executive officer in charge of all light and power manufacturing. Under his central control only the new company name was used on all products. Among others, the Sprague name was taken off of street railway motors and installations and his former company absorbed. (The innovative Sprague was bitter about this.) Edison-General Electric's chief competitor was the younger, highly aggressive, and almost as large, Thomson-Houston Electric Company of Lynn, Massachusetts. Both companies were growing faster than their finances would allow, and the interested New York and Boston banking houses suggested the two companies merge. The consolidation became effective June 1, 1892 under the new banner of General Electric Company.

Charles A. Coffin of Thomson-Houston became the president of the new company. Most of the new officers were from Thomson-Houston with Sam Insull the exception. He was offered the number three position in the new company—similar to his previous situation, but with much larger responsibilities in manufacturing. By this time Insull believed that the real future was in the electric power generation and distribution business.

The directors of the Chicago Edison Company, already one of the larger local lighting companies, were looking for a new president. Insull took the job effective July 1, 1892. Before he left, his New York friends held a farewell banquet for him attended by some of the most important figures in the electric business including Thomas A. Edison, Edward H. Johnson, Charles A. Coffin, Eugene Griffin (first vice-president of General Electric), Thomas Commerford Martin (editor of *Electrical World*), John I. Beggs (North American Company and later Milwaukee Electric), Henry Villard (financier, head of North American Company and the former Edison-General Electric Company), H. Ward-Leonard (motor-generators and other innovations), S. Dana Greene (General Electric engineering and marketing), Carl Schurz (politician and educator) and others.

In Chicago, Insull did everything bigger and better. Though his plans were avant-garde, they soon became the standard of the industry. Very little was known about practical and economical use of central station power. Aggressive sales policies and innovations plus the philosophy that electric lights were not a luxury item saw the Chicago Edison Company expand. As this company grew so did Insull's credibility in the Chicago business community. He cemented this by his ability to go to England and personally sell $1,200,000 in bonds for his company's growth. He also locked out an electric utility competitor by gaining control of the erstwhile rival Commonwealth Electric Company, later merged into today's Commonwealth Edison Company. As Insull's success and reputation grew, he became involved in many electric power companies and grew wealthy in the process.

In 1901 Insull appeared as a named director of the Chicago & Indiana Air Line Railway Company, an interurban electric railway projected from South Bend, Indiana to Chicago. This company shifted to Cleveland financial hands and became the Chicago, Lake Shore & South Bend Railroad, commonly known as the South Shore Lines. Insull apparently dropped out of this Indiana project early but reappeared at the other end of the state.

Above Samuel Insull (circa 1920)
Loyola University of Chicago Archives

Samuel Insull was very close to his family and he shared his good fortune with them. His younger brother Martin came to the United States and was given the formal college education that Sam had missed. Martin worked as a trouble shooter for his brother and was innovative in his own right. In 1902 some of Insull's banker associates asked him to look into some properties they owned in and around New Albany, Indiana. Insull acquired the controlling interest in the distressed firms and sent Martin out to manage the properties.

Martin soon proved very able and began expanding the operation. He soon collected electric, gas, streetcar, and interurban companies with a value estimated at nearly five million dollars. These included the New Albany Street Railroad Company (a local street railway) and the Louisville & Northern Railway & Lighting Company (interurban lines in the New Albany area).

By 1912 it would have been ideal to sell the combined property at a handsome profit as Insull had done on previous occasions. But this time he did something different that would have a profound effect on the Indiana utilities and the utility industry in general. At the suggestion of a broker friend, Insull formed a holding company. If it worked, Insull and any associates involved stood to profit. If it didn't work, the loss would not be disastrous.

A holding company could issue its own securities for cash and obtain operating capital needed for whatever expansion might be planned. The holding company could make money in three ways: It could (1) charge fees for the construction of a physical plant, (2) charge for financing companies or (3) build operating companies into sound money makers. The first two procedures were frowned upon by Insull while the third appealed to him as an honest growth route. Capital growth and time were fundamental to the third plan. This method could build a company into a great success and expand the base of control of corporate officers and shareholders. Insull already had all the money he might desire, but the idea of control and the possibilities of the holding company must have attracted him.

Middle West Utilities Company was incorporated in May 1912 as a holding company with Samuel Insull as president and Martin Insull as vice-president. Its first move was a consolidation of the New Albany properties under the banner of the Interstate Public Service Company. From that point onward, Middle West continued to grow through the acquisition and expansion of existing smaller companies.

Interstate Public Service Company, too, could expand due to the strong financial backing of the holding company. The Indianapolis & Louisville Traction Company was purchased in March 1912. The Indianapolis, Columbus and Southern Traction Company was leased for 999 years on September 7, 1912 at an initial rental of $92,000 per annum (perhaps the smartest deal ever made by the owners of an interurban company). End-to-end connections of the separate companies meant Interstate now had interconnected power transmission lines, several power plants and the electric power business in a sizable and growing area in southern and central Indiana. In addition to a rail line from Indianapolis to Louisville and three city rail systems, Interstate became a modern, well-run and profitable public utility company under the leadership of Harry Reid, one of Martin Insull's top men.

Below The properties the public knew as "THI&E Lines" at the beginning of the Indiana Railroad era had a complicated past. The "Greenfield Line" built most of the route east from Indianapolis: as far as Dublin. THI&E purchased it in 1907. Four other divisions—northwest and southwest of the capital and around Terre Haute—continued under separate ownership, only leased to THI&E. *David W. Peat collection*

Above Ward B. Hiner's new Mack buses lined up for the dedication of the Red Ball bus terminal. The intercity motor coaches were, like the interurbans, providing cheaper rides than the steam railroads.

Photo by Bass Photo Company, Indiana Historical Society Library

The larger Indiana interurbans did reasonably well until after the first World War. But then rising costs cut into their profit margins. With the exception of some newer passenger equipment, there had been little done in the way of expansion or improvements. Most of the new equipment was city streetcars to pacify the more vocal urban population. The interurban industry's funding had left many lines perilously close to the brink of financial disaster and the delicate balance was about to be upset by, not only increased costs, but the rise of the internal combustion engine for automobiles and buses accompanied by an expanding network of paved highways.

By the mid-twenties, the interurban companies found themselves caught up in a common problem for traction companies. Intercity motor-bus operators sought passengers with the interurban rail lines a prime target. Indiana bus companies were no exception. By 1925, several bus firms were trying to get favorable legislation which would allow them to operate without regulation by the Public Service Commission. The commission continued to regulate in what the commission perceived as the public interest.

Some of the bus companies were a reflection of the owner and his personality directed the business more than a balance sheet. By the mid-twenties, overexpansion resulted in routes being established and withdrawn when they proved to be losers. Rate cutting to steal business, not only from the interurbans and steam railroads but other bus companies as well, was common. At one point, several Indiana companies had to revise their schedules because they published schedule times that supported the interurban company claims of buses exceeding the speed limits. The electric railways bought up a number of these bus companies and started some of their own to protect and, sometimes, expand their territory. Joint rail and bus service allowed some interurbans to finally reach the cities in their corporate titles.

The various interurbans reacted differently. Indiana Service Corporation through purchase and its own efforts offered a comprehensive service covering Fort Wayne and northeastern Indiana. Interstate Public Service Company, to protect its territory, put routes in and out of service with the speed of a yo-yo. Union Traction installed competing buses on its main line from Indianapolis to Muncie and Anderson to Marion and then added more routes as the need and/or opportunity arose. The THI&E was slow to react and enter the bus business and soon found Hiner's Red Ball Lines, Inc. paralleling several rail lines. Ward B. Hiner soon became one of the largest bus operators in Indiana. He bought a substantial number of buses (40 in the first quarter of 1925) and built a large Indianapolis Union Bus Terminal. The low fares could not support this ambitious effort and Red Ball went bankrupt in late 1925 with Fred I. Jones being named as receiver. Jones also headed Hoosier Stage Lines and some have hinted that he had direct links with the THI&E management. Early in 1926, Jones arranged a sale of his and the Red Ball routes to the THI&E's bus subsidiary, Indiana Motor Transit Company, and to Union Traction. The buses reverted to the manufacturers who, in turn, sold some of them to the new route owners. By the end of 1929 the Indiana interurban railroads controlled most competing bus routes and were firmly in the local and intercity bus business. There had been a cost in all of this maneuvering which was not offset by increased ridership. In almost every case the combined total of bus and rail passengers declined each year. The company's return on the bus investment balanced against the decline in rail passengers produced an overall negative effect. The bus purchases were, at best, a defensive action by an industry already in financial trouble.

Chapter 2
Consolidating Indiana

Left Interstate Public Service Company's *Dixie Flyer* departs from the Indianapolis Traction Terminal. The 151 leads parlor-buffet car 161, "Franklin," whose occupants are being served lunch on the train. They'll be in Louisville before dinnertime.
Motor Bus Society, Inc. Library

In 1923, Samuel Insull and Randal Morgan (the only remaining member of the Schoepf-McGowan syndicate still active in Midwest utility affairs) began the integration of their Indiana utilities complex. The business concept of this rationalization was to integrate the electric and gas utilities into sensible, geographically oriented operating units all in the control of a single holding company. Some of the predecessor companies would be absorbed to facilitate the administration of this complex. The interurban railroads and the street railways were, by this time, only a part of the electric power load. This was a dramatic change from the past yet it was a graphic indication of the success of the utilities. In many cases, the rail lines had provided the heaviest demand for power during the early days of the electric utilities. The street railways and interurbans were practical, and very visible, demonstrations of the use of electricity. The interurban rights-of-way served as routes for high-tension power lines and these railways played a role in the expansion of rural electrification. The linear patterns of the rail systems found some rail/power companies operating far afield from their home operations and, in some cases, in their competitors' service territory. It was this interconnecting maze of small companies that cried for rationalization if the electric utility industry was to continue to grow.

The electric railway demand for electricity remained fairly constant and progressively became a decreasing percentage of the total electric load as the utilities were very successful in adding new customers, especially industries, commercial establishments and homes. Some of the utilities distributed gas to the same group of customers. The environment created the need for a beneficial and rational approach. Insull and Morgan had the vision to see what rationalization could do for the future of the utility industry.

Insull and Morgan planned a series of corporate mergers and consolidations of the Indiana properties they presently owned followed by the acquisition of others. Insull would set up the program with Morgan's blessings. Morgan was interested in building a more stable concern that would produce solid profits and resolve some problems of isolated properties that had little prospect of growth. The plan would benefit Morgan and other investors financially and simplify operating problems. The Insull interests saw a chance for profit and improved managerial possibilities.

Morgan's United Gas Improvement Company held the dominant control in northern Indiana. United had acquired the Northern Indiana Gas & Electric Company (with a service territory—mostly gas—scattered across the state) in 1910 and this marked the entry of holding company ownership into Indiana public utilities. United, in 1916, acquired Indiana Lighting Company which controlled gas properties from Fort Wayne to Lafayette.

Meanwhile, Insull's own new holding company, The Public Service Investment Company, was incorporated on June 22, 1924. (The name was changed to Midland Utilities Company on August 19, 1924.) Midland Utilities gained control of the Calumet Gas & Electric Company, the Chicago South Shore & South Bend Railroad, Gary Railways, Indiana Service Corporation and some smaller properties. The Calumet Gas & Electric's name was changed to Northern Indiana Public Service Company (NIPSCO) on January 28, 1926. NIPSCO absorbed Northern Indiana Gas & Electric on June 3, 1926 and the new organization became one of Midland Utilities Company's holdings and a major northern Indiana electric and gas utility, a position it enjoys today (1991). This Morgan-Insull transaction moved very smoothly. The next one did not.

Morgan was the principal owner of the Terre Haute, Indianapolis & Eastern Traction Company, which had grown into a sizable electric utility with a sprawling interurban rail system. In 1925, Morgan and Insull contemplated consolidating the THI&E with some properties of the American Public Utilities Company (then controlled by United Gas Improvement) and merging these with several other Insull properties.

The plan surfaced when Morgan and Insull, using the investment banking house of Halsey, Stuart & Company as "readjustment managers," proposed bringing the electric light, power and traction business of central and northwest Indiana under one company. The Indianapolis Street Railway was controlled by the THI&E but both Insull and Robert I. Todd, president of both the THI&E and the Indianapolis Street Railway, stated it would not be included in the merger. (The company was completing plans to close its own generating station, upgrade its distribution system and, as a transportation company, become a customer.)

On January 30, 1926, according to the *Electric Railway Journal,* Insull was "reported to have said that the interests he represented were not going into the consolidation primarily from the traction viewpoint, but . . . closer traction relations were certain, with through interurban service at high speed possible from Chicago to Louisville." (Possible, yes, but not too likely because of the indirect route and considerable low-speed track.) The deal between Morgan and Insull was based on electric power and not rail lines. The plan was delayed and eventually changed following Morgan's unexpected death on March 20, 1926 at the age of 72.

The plan moved along through 1926, all of 1927 and into 1928 with little apparent progress. In July 1928, an announcement was made that the THI&E-controlled properties and the Central Indiana Power Company would be merged into the Indiana Electric Corporation (a separate company created in 1921 to build the Dresser power station located south of Terre Haute on the Wabash River). All of the THI&E rail lines would be

Above THI&E freight motor 150 and a trailer box car wait in a siding on the Crawfordsville line while a paralleling Peoria & Eastern Atlantic-type steam locomotive hustles by with a passenger train.
George K. Bradley collection

included with the exception of the three leased lines from Indianapolis to Lafayette, Martinsville and Crawfordsville. Those three—the Indianapolis & Martinsville Rapid Transit Company, the Indianapolis & Northwestern Traction Company, Inc. and the Indianapolis, Crawfordsville & Danville Electric Railway Company—would be assigned to a proposed new company to be known as the Indiana Central Rapid Transit Company. No formal action on this proposed company was taken at this time but it was indicated it would be comprised exclusively of the three lines leased by the THI&E.

By August 28, 1928 a final petition for a formal merger of sixteen electric power and transportation companies valued at $70,000,000 was filed with the Public Service Commission of Indiana. As before, the Indianapolis Street Railway was omitted. The surprise was the omission of the three leased THI&E lines in this initial filing. They were money losers as were several of the THI&E's own. The merger would have a better chance without the inclusion of the losing properties. But, by the time the final proposal was completed and submitted, the three lines were reinstated.

The plan was broad in scope and sizable in proportions and action was slow. The Public Service Commission's chairman stated there would be a careful and detailed study of the entire plan. An auditing firm would be hired to review all of the facts and financial data. The Insull forces also presented their supportive and appropriate exhibits to support their case. By October 1929, a year later, most of the preliminary work was complete. Shortly thereafter the Commission announced public hearings on the merger, described as a "combination in the public interest," would open on December 2, 1929. Opposition was anticipated from several sectors including the rate-paying customers.

The rationalization of Indiana utilities proceeded with the Indiana Electric Corporation making the better newspaper headlines. The holding companies' activities were well chronicled, although less colorful, and were usually relegated to the financial pages. That sector of the public that could see the physical results probably didn't care about the financial actions.

Midland Utilities Company's control of several key utilities was not readily obvious to the general public. What the public saw was the outstanding rehabilitation of the Chicago area interurbans and, especially in Indiana, the modernization of the Chicago South Shore & South Bend Railroad. Most knew that the South Shore, like the other two high-speed Chicago interurbans (the Chicago North Shore & Milwaukee Railroad Company and Chicago Aurora & Elgin Railroad Company) were Insull properties. Additionally, some of the public saw the Midland Utilities modernization of the Gary Railways and Indiana Service Corporation. To some there appeared to be no connection. However all were major Indiana companies controlled by the Midland Utilities company. The senior officers of all these companies were Samuel Insull, Samuel Insull, Jr. and Robert M. Feustel with the senior Insull placing the other two in charge of daily operations. Feustel, the president of the Indiana Service Corporation, was the chief adviser to Samuel Insull, Jr. There were also three other top officials to act as advisers to Sam Jr. on various Indiana utilities matters: Morse Dell Plaine and Samuel E.

Mulholland of NIPSCO and Charles W. Chase of Gary Railways. Midland Utilities was an important first step but it was limited in scope.

An umbrella company, the Midland Utilities Investment Company, was incorporated on December 26, 1928. This was part of the overall consolidation of Indiana utilities. On January 2, 1929, the new firm was given controlling interest in the Midland Utilities Company. Interstate Public Service Company was also transferred from Middle West Utilities to the new company. The controlled companies were only coordinated, not merged, and continued to run as individual units. The railroad and power portions of each utility would be unofficially separated. Charles Chase noted at the time that the Gary Railways (now controlled by Midland Utilities) would be little involved in the coordinated rail scheme but that by considering the state as a whole a more comprehensive program could be developed. (Chase's observation was safe as the Gary property was unique. Principally a streetcar operation, its lightweight lines handled little freight and had almost no potential for development.) The coordinated plan would not be executed until the end of 1929. Prior to that time, on August 29, 1929, the new organization changed its name to Midland United Company.

The largest Indiana interurban property was the Union Traction Company of Indiana. An independent, it would be valuable in any comprehensive statewide plan. Union Traction was a north-central Indiana interurban with over 400 route miles, partly owned and partly leased from non-operating subsidiaries. It had a subsidiary, Traction Light & Power Company furnishing electricity to fifty small communities and many rural customers along the interurban rail lines—but not to key cities such as Anderson, Muncie or Marion. This power subsidiary was a valuable asset and it made money. The company also had a sizable bus operation. Being big did not promise solvency. Union Traction's own interurban lines were not losing money as operating units, but most of the leased lines were either marginal or deficit operations. The prospects were not good as the 1928 net operating revenue had fallen to only 26% of 1923, the last year of solvency.

The company entered receivership on December 31, 1924 as the net operating revenue was not sufficient to meet the interest on the bonds of the underlying companies. Arthur W. Brady, who had been president of the company since 1904, was named receiver. He continued to operate but did not adopt or affirm the lease of the Muncie & Portland Traction Company because of certain financial guarantee requirements in that lease. The leased Muncie, Hartford & Fort Wayne Railway was the essential mainline link in the Indianapolis-Muncie-Fort Wayne route. The bonds of this underlying leased company were held by the Guardian Trust Company. In 1925 Guardian Trust unsuccessfully filed for foreclosure and sale of this company to protect their claims on the property.

Brady managed to hold the Union Traction together and actually upgraded his mainline service through the acquisition of 15 new passenger cars. He was faced with declining ridership, even with the new cars, from a total of 14,405,000 passengers in 1924 to 10,855,000 in 1928. Of this amount over one million were motor bus passengers on city and intercity routes.

Some resolution of Union Traction's problem was required. As it stood, the receiver had to pursue money matters through the courts. The court declared liens of the various mortgages on the company were superior to all other creditor claims and demands. This included all purchases and injury judgments. Liquidation would probably be the only way to close out the debts. The predicament was not unnoticed by the Insull interests.

Representatives of three groups of Union Traction bondholders met in Philadelphia in July 1929 and accepted a purchase proposal from Midland Utilities Investment Company (later Midland United Company). Notices were sent to the bondholders recommending acceptance of the proposal and suggesting their bonds be deposited with the committee. Unless the offer was withdrawn before September 3, the company would be sold.

This offer was made after Midland United officials had reviewed Union Traction's possibilities and discussed the situation with Arthur Brady. Although the offer was accepted by the active bondholder committee, a group of dissident bondholders (none of whom were interested enough to present any ideas or serve on the bondholders protective committee) started legal action to block the sale to Midland United.

The *Electric Railway Journal News*, on August 31, 1929, noted that Union Traction had been in receivership for almost five years and, "Hampered as he has been during that time, the receiver, Arthur W. Brady, has done a good job with little assistance from the bondholders. —Now some of the bondholders have discovered the property has real potentialities. . . . the question arises why the bondholders have not cleaned house, invested the money necessary to make the road a paying proposition and gained for themselves the profits they now fear will fall to others." The publication also commented it was solely interested in seeing the road restored and they supported the Insulls' proposition because they seemed to be the only ones willing to devote the time, work and money to the project.

The dissident bondholders obtained a temporary injunction and blocked the sale of the Union Traction to Midland United at least until the end of October 1929. At that time they hoped to obtain a permanent injunction by suggesting improprieties on the part of the committee and the receiver.

The motive of this action remains undisclosed. Possibly the motive was to hold out for more money.

The last few months of 1929 must have looked like the low point for the Insull Indiana consolidation effort. Actually, it slipped a bit further but the corner was about to be turned and success lay just ahead. Several Insull-sponsored actions would sink or be allowed to sink, and a new plan—that would work—would emerge. Sam Insull, Jr. and Robert Feustel were already putting the basics together.

First, public hearings on the Indiana Electric Corporation merger were started on December 2, 1929 preceded by opposition testimony from James Ogden, attorney general of Indiana. Ogden presented his legal opinion that Indiana commission law provided no authority for the merger of companies supplying dissimilar services or not operating in the same localities. Ogden also indicated that this question of whether similar services were rendered and whether sound public policy allows such consolidations would have to be determined by the commission. This placed an additional burden on the commission. The hearings were adjourned on December 10.

Articles of incorporation were finally filed, during the first week of December. They provided that the Indiana Central Rapid Transit Company, Inc. would "own, construct, purchase, lease" interurbans. It was announced that the company's purpose would be the acquisition of THI&E's 61-mile Indianapolis-Richmond line, the 11-mile Dunreith-New Castle branch and the Richmond city lines, all of which were to be excluded from the merger.

The merger plan hearings, after the Commission took the testimony, were adjourned for over three months, reopened on March 16, and concluded on March 21, 1930. The Insull interests' final summary had been given by Patrick J. Lucey, Chicago attorney for the company, who stated, "We are not amateurs in utility operation and finance. We come on behalf of the best and largest utility operating organization in the country to take over interurban lines that are now almost defunct and revitalize them with money and management."

That statement may have done more to help the opposition because the interurbans involved were nearly defunct and some people who had slept easy in the early years of the merger plan, when large capital was mentioned, were now uneasy six months after the stock market collapse of October 1929. By mid-April the Commission set down its determination that the Indiana Electric Company merger was based on an unsound financial set-up that would not serve the public interest. The merger was denied and the plan was abandoned!

The denial precipitated a disaster for the THI&E. In financial straits, although solvent, the company had borrowed more than $2,000,000 in short-term notes in anticipation of the merger's approval. Unable to meet the current obligations, following the merger denial, the company was placed in receivership in Marion County Superior Court on April 2, 1930 with Elmer Stout, president of the Fletcher-American National Bank of Indianapolis, named as receiver.

Coordinated operation of the Midland United-controlled properties had moved ahead since late in 1929. All the utility executive and general office departments would be consolidated into one group. Individual corporate identities would be retained. Operation of the central organization was located in the Indianapolis Traction Terminal Building. For example, E. Van Arsdale, who had succeeded Harry Reid as head of Interstate (Reid had become the executive in charge of Middle West's eastern subsidiaries) continued as the head of his company but with the emphasis on the electric power operations. The entire group was under Samuel Insull, Jr. and Robert Feustel.

A further step was announced in March 1930 when Henry Bucher was named general railway executive of the Midland United's rail properties (except the CSS&SB

Below Union Traction Company's publicity department posed motor car 402 and parlor car "Indiana" on Meridian Street north of Anderson shops. Two-car *Hoosierland* trains like this were run each day though not over this branch to Marion. *George K. Bradley collection*

and Gary Railways). Bucher, a long-time associate of Feustel, had been ISC's railway manager since 1924. He moved his operations to Indianapolis to add a rail link to the utility consolidation and to obtain the advantages of one general supervisor for rail operations. In reality, he had a scattered operation. Interstate Public Service Company's line went south from Indianapolis to Louisville, ISC's lines ran across the north-central part of the state plus a joint operation over two Union Traction lines, while Northern Indiana Power Company had a 50-mile line from Frankfort to Marion, where it had an end-to-end connection with ISC's Marion & Bluffton route, and intersected a north-south Union Traction line.

Not so visible was the new consolidated organization. Feustel and Bucher, over the next few months, drew on a wealth of good middle management people. Many of these people came from ISC's interurban engineering force in Fort Wayne. Officers and executives of other utilities in the Insull holdings, particularly Midland United and Midland Utilities, did multiple duty, serving several companies. The pooling of talents brought the services of many skilled and highly qualified people to the rail operations. The shared management meant that several interurbans could be operated under the direction of one supervisory organization. Coordination of services and schedules was expected to work for the benefit of shippers and passengers and to reduce operating expenses. It would work better if all of the rail lines were connected.

However, the primary business of Midland United and its subsidiaries was electric power generation and distribution, the manufacturing and distribution of gas and manufactured ice for commercial customers. Every move Midland made involved electric power or gas. The Indiana Electric Corporation merger had been conceived by Insull and Morgan to consolidate electric and gas properties. The move to acquire Union Traction was to gain Traction Light & Power and the electric power lines, most of which were on the railway right-of-way. These transmission lines interconnected otherwise separated portions of other Midland power companies. The rail lines could be viewed primarily as users of electric power. Rather large users in the economy of 1930, when some sizable industries still depended on steam to run their plants by mechanical transmission!

Meanwhile, Arthur Brady precipitated action on the Union Traction proceedings by asking for a court decree, in late May 1930, to settle accounts, determine liens and sell the property. At the end of February he had been authorized to, and did, abandon the Muncie-Union City and Anderson-Middletown lines. He had also petitioned for abandonment of the Marion-Wabash, Muncie-Portland and Kokomo-Logansport lines with hearings to be held on June 3 and June 5 respectively. On June 6 the court ordered the property to be sold at auction on July 2.

In June 1930, Midland United finalized the earlier agreement with the committees representing the bond-

Below On Friday, October 23, 1931 some of the 15,000 teachers in attendance at the Indiana State Teachers' Association convention await trains and buses in the concourse of the Indianapolis Traction Terminal.
George K. Bradley collection

Above Samuel Insull, Jr. (circa 1935)
Loyola University of Chicago Archives

holders of the Union Traction and its underlying companies. Apparently the dissidents were satisfied or silenced as approximately 60% of the outstanding bondholders approved the sale. Reportedly, Midland paid $2,829,000 for $14,201,000 (approximately 20¢ on the dollar) of outstanding first mortgage bonds.

On July 2, 1930, Midland United, through its secretary B. P. Shearon, purchased the Union Traction at the court-ordered sale for $3,923,933. This included over 400 miles of street railway and interurban lines plus Traction Light & Power, the subsidiary power company. The Kokomo-Logansport and Marion-Wabash lines, although included in the sale, were Union Traction operations pending abandonment and their operation remained in Brady's hands. The real estate of the already abandoned lines to Union City and Middletown plus some never used rights-of-way were also included. As part of the final court decree, the Muncie-Portland line, also pending abandonment, was returned to its owners—The Muncie & Portland Traction Company. There was no intention of continued operation by that company so trains continued to run under Brady's direction.

Only a few hours after the Union Traction purchase, Midland United announced that an agreement had been reached with bondholders controlling 70% of the THI&E for the purchase of the outstanding bonds. The offer was $750 for each $1000 bond with the total purchase price believed to be about 3.6 million dollars.

The THI&E bond purchase offer covered only a part of its large assets. The offer included those properties owned directly by the THI&E (Brazil-Indianapolis-Richmond line, Dunreith-New Castle line, Indianapolis-Danville line, Richmond city lines and the West Tenth Street, Indianapolis generating station). In addition control of the leased Terre Haute Traction & Light Company was acquired. Centered at Terre Haute, this latter company owned or controlled the interurban route east to Brazil, the route from Terre Haute to Paris, Illinois (the Illinois portion under the name of Terre Haute & Western Railway), the lines north to Clinton and south to Sullivan, the Terre Haute city lines and commercial electric generating stations at Terre Haute and Brazil. THI&E also controlled, but did not own, the leased lines from Indianapolis to Lafayette, Martinsville and Crawfordsville. The Terre Haute electric power facility was the only bright spot in this lackluster galaxy. Overall, the rail lines had lost money since 1924. That year only $64,000 appeared as rail profit on the income statement. The number of passengers had fallen by eight million from over 24 million in 1924 to just under 16 million in 1929. This poor showing and position was one of the reasons for the failure of the Indiana Electric Corporation merger plan. The credibility of the THI&E as a solvent profit maker declined each year. It was also easy to see that only the electric power portion was profitable.

Above Robert M. Feustel (circa 1928) *George K. Bradley collection*

Receiver Elmer Stout was placed in the position of having to untangle the THI&E and simplify the complex situation. Fortunately, he had the complete cooperation of the Insull interests and Feustel in particular. This was underscored by Feustel's statement at the time of the bond purchase, "We feel that these properties have a better chance of being made to pay a return than any of the others and if we acquire control we will enter on a program of financial reorganization and rehabilitation. As to the operation of the interurban lines which are operated by the THI&E, we are not interested."

The THI&E proper included the 19-mile Indianapolis-to-Danville (Indiana) line which came in the July 2 bond purchase. Stout petitioned to abandon this money loser on August 6. Final approval was received and the last car ran on October 31, 1930.

Midland then made an offer on August 20 to buy the bonds of the three THI&E-leased interurban lines on a salvage basis. The incentive to make any bid was the modest amount of electric light and power business along with the high tension distribution system attached to the three lines. A proposal was put forward to cover this salvage value plus some of the bondholder committee expenses. The terms for the $1000 first mortgage bonds—the only securities of value—were $195 for each bond of the Indianapolis & Martinsville Rapid Transit Company, $220 for each bond of the Indianapolis, Crawfordsville & Danville Electric Railway and $80 for each of the Indianapolis & Northwestern Traction Company bonds.

The three lines were placed in separate receiverships, with Stout as receiver, on September 2, 1930. Unable to finance continued operation of the three lines, Stout petitioned for abandonment of all three in mid-September. Simultaneously with the Danville line, on October 31, they disappeared into the Halloween night along with the ghosts and hobgoblins.

The termination of the Crawfordsville line ended the long-hoped-for linking of the Indiana-Ohio interurbans with the Illinois Traction system (ITS) which was (by the late twenties) partly owned by Insull interests. The Illinois line had, for a long time, interchanged freight with the steam roads and much of the line was built to standards for handling railroad cars built to Master Car Builders (MCB) standards. The Crawfordsville line was capable of operating MCB equipment from the Indianapolis city limits westward to Crawfordsville. An extension plus a hoped for interurban by-pass at Indianapolis might have produced a new source of freight revenues for the lines controlled by and the interests friendly to Insull. As late as 1928, Donald Walker, the assistant chief engineer of the THI&E, and Charles Handshy, of the ITS, did a "horse-back" survey of the proposed Crawfordsville-Danville (Illinois) route. A major bridge over the Wabash River and generally rough terrain made the forty-mile projected route too costly.

Motor buses replaced most of the abandoned lines. THI&E's subsidiary Indiana Motor Transit, Inc. was involved as was American Stages, Inc. (controlled by THI&E officials). Greyhound Lines' Pennsylvania-Indiana General Transit Company picked up the rights to serve added cities on their existing runs through Martinsville and Lafayette. Other operators were also interested in some of the shorter local services.

Stout was now rid of the worst losers and those most easily separated. The Indianapolis-Greenfield-Richmond line reportedly lost $142,311 during the nine months of 1930 that Stout operated the line. On February 26, 1931 he petitioned to abandon this 69-mile line, but no action was taken. The Terre Haute & Western line to Paris (Illinois) continued. The leased Illinois company, also insolvent, had a separate receiver.

The THI&E control of the financially troubled Indianapolis Street Railway Company sent that system into a separate receivership. On April 18, 1930, George C. Forrey, Jr., vice president of Fletcher-American National Bank, was named receiver. A separate plan, removing the Indianapolis property from the THI&E organization, would be proposed by Midland United.

Midland United, in 1930, continued some of the power company realignments. NIPSCO transferred its Lafayette, Frankfort, Lebanon and Crawfordsville districts to Public Service Company of Indiana in return for Public Service's Goshen, Warsaw and Monticello districts. The move confined the two companies to more compact service areas.

Below Interstate's 11 AM *Dixie Flyer* departs from Indianapolis Traction Terminal on its 117 mile, 3 hour 45 minute trip to Louisville. Seven trains made this run each day. The bus terminal next door issued Interstate's own, competing, motor coaches to Franklin, along the line, and to Louisville with the latter runs taking only 5 minutes longer than the trains. *Motor Bus Society, Inc. Library*

Chapter 3
Out of Nowhere— Indiana Railroad

Left Westbound car 438 (a two-man car) enters Morgan's siding in Brazil on September 15, 1935. *William C. Janssen photo*

Indiana Railroad appeared in a magical puff of the finest public relations smoke. That euphonious—almost perfect—title was easily remembered and was to the point. Feustel and Insull, plus all their talented help, could not have done better. In the briefest period, a time of necessity, they came up with a brilliant name that was meaningful to all potential customers, descriptive of the line's geographic boundaries and so unifying that all Hoosiers could point with pride. Indiana Railroad bespoke something bright and different in a dreary time when something positive was needed.

Midland United's plans had been dramatically changed in a brief period between the April 1930 abandonment of the Indiana Electric Corporation merger plan and the acquisition of the Union Traction on July 2, 1930. The Indiana Electric Corporation had been turned down by the Public Service Commission, and the Union Traction was in receivership. Both were failures. Disassociation from both, through a new identity, was the best route. Midland owned the Indiana Central Rapid Transit Company name but that was associated with several THI&E lines and the tarnished corporate merger plan. Over a dozen ISC interurban cars carried the all-too-similar, but meaningless, "Indiana Central Lines" slogan. Now, near the end of June 1930, a successor company to Union Traction was needed.

Bob Feustel and Sam Insull, Jr. carefully considered these ideas through the winter and spring of 1930. Suddenly the pieces fell together in rapid succession, in sensible form, and quick, decisive action was taken. Midland peeked into its corporate attic and pulled out a no longer used but viable Indiana corporate charter.

The cover page carried the name "Gary Connecting Railroad," incorporated in Indiana on July 20, 1920 to succeed to rail properties held by an earlier company with a similar name. The Gary Connecting Railroad properties were merged into the Gary Railways Company on August 15, 1925 and the corporate shell went into the file. Now, hastily pulled out, the shell was put to use by filing articles of reorganization with the Indiana Secretary of State on July 14, 1930. A corporate name change and charter provisions, with a wide scope of operations described, were approved as part of the reorganized company. Indiana Railroad was born!

At the court sale of the Union Traction, B. P. Shearon had purchased the Traction Light & Power Company separately and it became a subsidiary of Midland United. The company had purchased some of its electric power, for the 50 small towns and villages it served, from Union Traction generating plants. The relationship was continued for a period of time until new connections were made.

A few small communities along the interurban lines continued to receive electricity from Indiana Railroad. But the separation of Traction Light & Power was part of the arrangement to make Indiana Railroad strictly a rail utility while retaining only those generating units required for the operations. Union Traction's Anderson power station, that Indiana Railroad inherited, was an antique—close to an operating museum. (Sam Insull, Jr. later recalled that obsolescent installation: "I'll never forget going into the Anderson generating station. Those acres and acres of reciprocating engines.")

The splitting of the power and rail facilities placed Indiana Railroad on its own as a separate company operating its own rail lines. The division left no room for the rate-paying customers of the power companies to complain about the use of power revenues for rail expenses. In this manner, the basic problem of the Indiana Electric Corporation merger plan was eliminated. Unique to interurban railways, the company had no outstanding bonded debt, and only five shares of stock, of an authorized 50,000 shares were issued. All five were held by Midland United Company. Indiana Railroad would have a fresh start, as a new company, with Midland absorbing the substantial initial cost involved in the purchase of the former Union Traction rail property and advancing unsecured money to get the company going. The purchase cost might have been considered as a write-off for those values other than the power facilities. There was no formal agreement stating the amount, if any, that would be repaid. Midland's public plans for Indiana Railroad indicated no intention or expectation of repayment for the rail facilities. The company would survive on its rail operating earnings, if any, without having any revenues paid to the bondholders. This was a simple financial operating method that would demonstrate whether the Indiana Railroad could survive and continue to operate. Total control was in Midland United's hands. Their creation of the new company and putting it into operation was the first step toward the building of a "super interurban."

With the purchase of Union Traction, the Insull-controlled central and southern Indiana lines were connected into one interurban rail network which Midland hoped would be economically sound. The entire operation, Indiana Railroad plus the other rail lines, was classed as the "Indiana Railroad System." A single management coordinated the rail operations of all four companies (Indiana Railroad, Indiana Service Corporation, Northern Indiana Power Company, Interstate Public Service Company). However, all the accounting was handled for the respective companies, as before, to record profit and loss tallies for the various lines. Indiana Railroad collected passenger and freight revenues, returning a certain portion to each company based on ownership of the rail route used. No leases formalized the relations between the companies. It was a somewhat loose "gentlemen's agreement" but it succeeded.

On August 1, less than a month after the purchase, Indiana Railroad began operating the former Union Traction Company rail properties. Directors of the new company had already met on July 30 at the Insull offices in Chicago and elected officers of the company. They were: Samuel Insull, chairman; Samuel Insull, Jr., chairman of the executive committee; Robert M. Feustel, president; William A. Sauer, vice-president; Henry Bucher, vice-president and general manager; George F. Mitchel, treasurer; Bernard P. Shearon, secretary; and Edwin J. Booth, comptroller. A number of appointments were made to head various departments. Most of these appointments were extensions of the responsibilities of the Midland United rail management group. L. M. Brown, a director of the new company and former general manager of Interstate Public Service Company's rail lines, was named general superintendent of Indiana Railroad as well as the other Midland interurbans. Harry V. Norford became general superintendent of maintenance of way, a position that he held with ISC. J. Allen Greenland, superintendent of transportation for the ISC city lines, was placed in charge of the 11 city systems. The large Fort Wayne city lines remained under direct ISC control. Most of the Union Traction top officers and managers were replaced. Heber La Monte, superintendent of motive power, and E. E. Slick, claims adjuster, retained their Union Traction capacities in the new organization.

A new timetable was issued on August 1, 1930. With the exception of several minor revisions and corrections, it was identical in appearance to the last Union Traction timetable. It was printed in the same color and still carried the Union Traction herald on the cover. Listed in the timetable, and still operating, were the three one-time Union Traction lines that Arthur Brady as receiver had petitioned to abandon. On August 8, 1930 the Public Service Commission authorized the abandonment of the Muncie & Portland Traction Company's line and the former Union Traction Marion-Wabash and Kokomo-Logansport lines. All three abandonments were to be effective at the end of service on September 15, 1930. Indiana Railroad, by agreement, operated the lines for Brady. They had been separated in the sale and were Arthur Brady's responsibility but the only solution was to have the new company, which now owned all the rolling stock, operate the three lines for him. In the case of the Muncie & Portland, Brady was acting for Frank C. Ball, the Muncie & Portland's president. Freight and passenger service continued until the abandonment date.

The Indiana Railroad System's first joint timetable, of September 28, 1930, consolidated the routes and services of all four companies. Missing were the routes up for abandonment at the time of the purchase. They had quietly coasted into oblivion as part of Arthur Brady's wind-up of affairs which were largely completed by the end of the year. The three lines were dismantled over the next year by Indiana Railroad crews.

Motor coach service operated by Fred Burch of Hammond would replace the Kokomo-Logansport service as an extension of Burch's route to Logansport. Lake Shore Coach Lines petitioned to take over the service between Muncie and Portland. Several truck operators jumped in to offer service to cities that would no longer be reached by the interurban.

Long-distance motor coaches were operated by Indiana Railroad from Indianapolis to Marion via

Below Union Traction's elderly 273 relettered for Indiana Railroad. Muncie-New Castle schedule until the middle of 1932. Wooden 273 and 275 were refurbished and placed in regular service on the
George Krambles collection

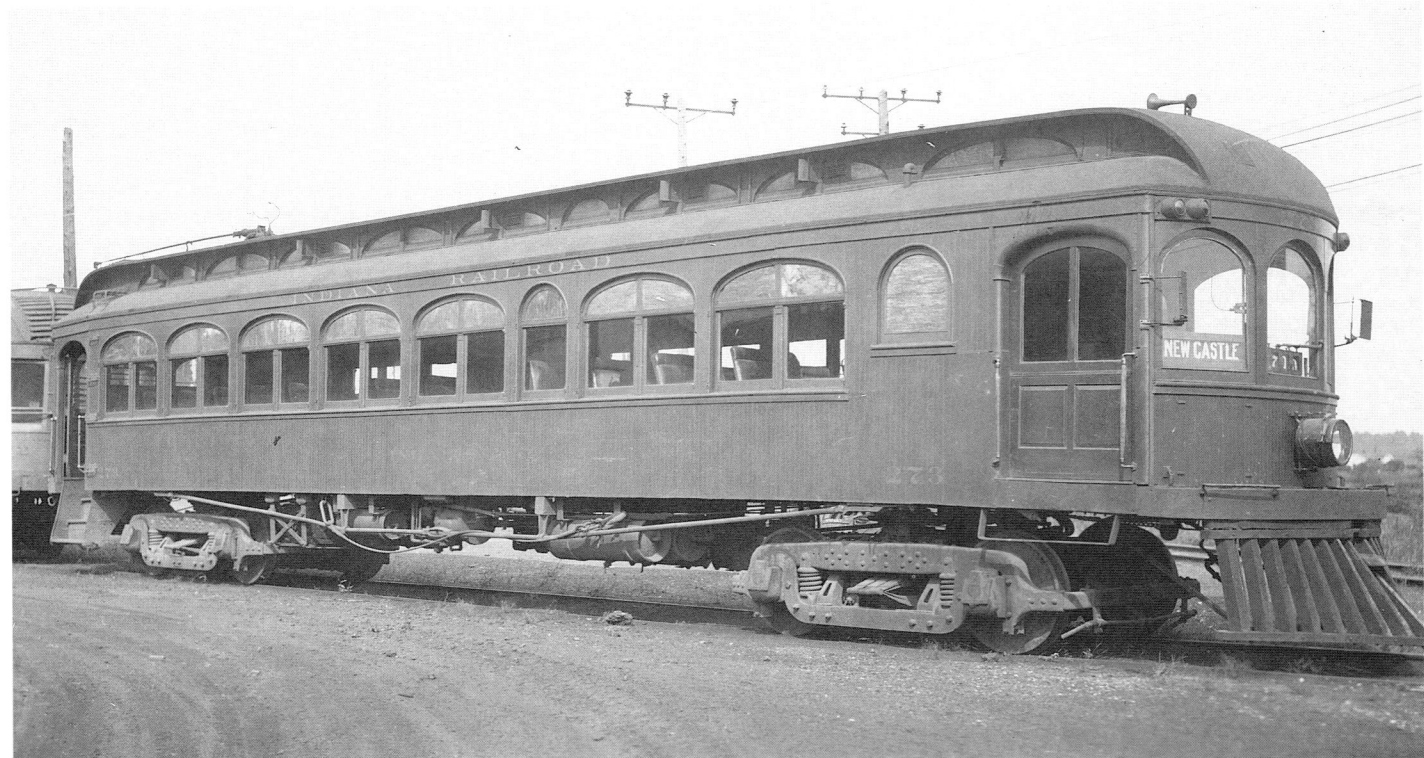

Above The line west of Brazil, built early, had a narrow right-of-way along the National Road and minimum grading. New pavement widened the highway (hence Millers siding is practically in the roadway) in this April 30, 1939 view. A company employee is at the semaphore-type switch stand ready to open the switch so the 435 can back out once the oncoming train has made the meet. *John F. Humiston photo*

Anderson. The Interstate had three motor coach runs, each way, between Indianapolis and Louisville. These local service buses on paralleling routes had travel times almost identical to rail cars. Frequent suburban Indianapolis-Greenwood-Franklin bus service was also maintained by Interstate.

The existing parlor-dining car trains from Indianapolis to Fort Wayne and Louisville as well as the Indianapolis-Louisville sleeping car service continued as in the past. There were few real surprises or changes in the new timetable except improved Indianapolis-Fort Wayne limited times on both routes by 15 to 25 minutes. Many people didn't even know the difference in management. To those that took a second look at the car exteriors, the red Union Traction cars showed the only change. The old name was painted out and the Indiana Railroad name substituted. Many of the assorted red, yellow and orange wooden and steel cars frequenting the Indianapolis Traction Terminal were now operating under the "system" management.

Indiana Railroad rolled into 1931 on a buoyant and positive note. This could be the company's best year. Some of the long-range plan began to fall into place with the reverse twist of having a variety of potential problems solved by the passage of time. Sam Insull, Jr., Robert Feustel, and Elmer Stout may have arranged the scenario that would resolve the consolidation problem. (A document exists, dated January 5, 1931, carrying the title "Division of the THI&E company property, owned and leased, 1/5/31" assigning segments to Midland United subsidiaries.)

By March of 1931, the THI&E transportation properties had shrunk to the Terre Haute-Indianapolis-Richmond main line with part of that under a petition for abandonment, the New Castle-Dunreith branch, three short lines radiating from Terre Haute, the Terre Haute and Richmond city operations and the intercity bus routes of the subsidiary Indiana Motor Transit Company. A March 9 legal action, that was most likely arranged by Stout and Midland United officials, brought the Fidelity-Philadelphia Trust Company (Philadelphia), speaking as trustees for a mortgage agreement, into the Marion County Superior Court in Indianapolis. That mortgage secured a sizable amount of outstanding bonds. If the trustee pushed for a prior lien claim on all the company's holdings, the receiver could be forced into an immediate sale of all the properties as he would have no cash to operate the company. A forced sale would work in the Insull interests' favor because they controlled the largest portion of the bonds. It would put them in the best position to bid for the remaining equity in the property—and probably when they wanted to bid.

Stout, continuing in his role as receiver, on April 8 petitioned for the abandonment of two of the deficit-ridden Terre Haute short lines. (The leased Terre Haute Traction & Light's Sullivan and Clinton lines totalled some 38 miles.) They were abandoned on May 24, 1931. In slightly over a year, Stout had pared approximately 230 route miles from the sprawling THI&E. About 175 miles still remained. Stout then filed a petition to sell the THI&E. Superior Court Judge Russell J. Ryan ordered the property sold at foreclosure on June 23.

Bernard P. Shearon bid $2,500,000 on behalf of the Midland United Company. His was the only bid offered (and the only one expected) in this public sale, but it had been determined in advance that the bid amount

Above The summer sun is beating down on Wabash Avenue in Terre Haute. Though the street is paved, westbound car 430, still in Union Traction red with the Indiana Railroad name added, is raising some dust. Bill Janssen is anticipating the long, hot, dry walk downtown in the car's wake. Two-man operation was still the practice in this 1934 view.
William C. Janssen photo

would be acceptable to the court—a relatively common procedure when settlement agreements beneficial to all parties have been resolved.

As per the plan of January 5, 1931, the THI&E system would be divided among three of Midland United Company's subsidiaries: Indiana Railroad, Public Service Company of Indiana and Indiana Industrial Land Company. Public Service Company of Indiana was the former Interstate whose name was changed on March 20, 1931 to more accurately reflect the geographical operating territory of the company. The stockholders, on April 15, had authorized the company to reorganize to allow for expanded operations.

The Public Service Commission, on July 25, approved Indiana Railroad's acquisition of the interurban lines from Indianapolis to Brazil and Indianapolis to Richmond (with a branch from Dunreith to New Castle), the city streetcar lines in Richmond, the abandoned Indianapolis-Danville line and Indiana Motor Transit Company (which was operating four intercity bus routes from Indianapolis to Terre Haute, Crawfordsville and Richmond and along the Rockville Road). The additions greatly increased the scope of the Indiana Railroad and the system. Also included in the sale was the THI&E's Indianapolis West Tenth Street power station which had supplied 25 hz ac power to the four abandoned lines. The plant was maintained as a standby facility to provide power for the salvage operations, then it was closed.

Public Service Company of Indiana, also on July 25, took title to the right-of-way of the interurban lines acquired by Indiana Railroad and the 999-year lease of the Terre Haute Traction & Light Company (the company's name was changed to Terre Haute Electric Company, Inc. on August 22, 1931). This former THI&E underlying company owned the electric power facilities in and near Terre Haute, the streetcar and city bus lines in Terre Haute and the interurban lines from Terre Haute east to Brazil and west to Paris, Illinois. The rail properties would be operated, as a unit, as part of the Indiana Railroad System.

For all practical purposes Indiana Railroad acquired (by deed—July 28, 1931) the rail properties that had been the property (not leased) of the THI&E. However, Indiana Railroad acquired only that part of the transmission system and other physical properties actually used for rail operations. The remainder of the transmission facilities, which included the abandoned Philadelphia (Indiana) power plant and all of the substations, now belonged to Public Service Company of Indiana. Public Service even took title to the Greenfield shops as it was expected that the line would be abandoned. Once again Sam Insull, Jr. and Robert Feustel had neatly cut loose the rail properties from the power facilities. In the approval of the transfer of the former THI&E properties Elmer Stout was directed to continue operation of the properties until all of the transfer details could be completed.

A piece of unfinished THI&E business was the Indianapolis Street Railway Company receivership. Midland United, using the services of Halsey, Stuart & Company, announced a proposed refinance and reorganization plan for the Indianapolis company in October 1930. The capital structure would be revised and the physical plant either rebuilt or replaced. A careful appraisal study was made and it was found that over twenty per cent of the trackage was completely worn out and much more needed repairs. Of the 441 streetcars owned, 100 were considered to be completely obsolete while 331 were classed as slow, outdated and inefficient.

Only ten of the newer streetcars were considered as "modern" cars. Twenty-one motor coaches were in good condition while 69 others needed replacement. New equipment proposed would include 175 one-man streetcars and 69 buses. One hundred streetcars and 29 buses would be rebuilt to round out the equipment projections. Trackage was to be renewed on those city lines that would be retained and the routes used by the interurban trains. One of the chief reasons for the rehabilitation proposal was to assure continued access to the city center for the interurban operations.

Charles W. Chase, of Midland's Gary Railways, was the man responsible for the detailed study and suggestions. It was impressive and the stock and bond holders recognized the merits of the plan to the extent that they gave it their endorsement. The proposal did call for concessions from the city and a perpetual service-at-cost franchise as a part of the Midland United involvement. The city rejected the plan at the end of the year but there were so many sound ideas in the proposals that the owners decided upon pursuing a revised plan. Midland United, however, announced they were no longer interested in participating. It would take another year and a half to get the Indianapolis system reorganized.

An early system-wide problem was the growth of paved highways. Begun at a fast pace in the mid-twenties, the roads covered the populous areas of the state, the same areas served by the interurbans. Much of the rail system's mileage was in close proximity to the new roads. Lower-priced cars, like the Ford Model-T, appeared in increasing numbers and in competition to the electric cars. They didn't have the comforts of the rail car but they could take the farmer and worker to and from nearby commercial areas, local markets and factories. The bigger automobiles quickly became the darlings of traveling salesmen and their bulky sample cases. In the era before national merchandise marketing and sales chains for distribution, these salesmen were indispensable to the local merchants. The automobile allowed more sales calls over a wider geographic area (right to the customer's door) in a shorter time and the interurban lost a good source of riding traffic.

In terms of 1931, the auto was a recognized threat but few projected the real impact on all rail passenger transportation for both short and long-haul patronage. There was good reason for the Indiana Railroad management to expect the "better than break-even" lines to continue for a number of years at the same levels. Public utilities had not been initially hurt by the Depression and few people imagined how serious things would get. All business levels were optimistically expected to recover and then hold for an indefinite period. The real impact of the world economic situation was not felt for some time. Management was being faced with outside forces the like of which they had never seen; so they proceeded on a normal course, based on what they did know, and started to modernize the railroad.

There were plenty of built-in operating problems that hampered better operations, and management had to contend with inherited restrictions and limitations. Most dated from the interurban's original concept of providing convenient access to the center of most towns. These city routes operated down the middle of the street and frequently encountered sharp curves that restricted both speed and the type of equipment that could be operated. In several cities speeds were restricted further by local streetcars operating on the same tracks. The lines, in both city and country, were largely single-track operations with low-speed, rigid-switch turnouts into sidings that were not specifically located for fast schedules.

Almost every type of railroad construction was represented on the system. The Indianapolis-Terre Haute line (built in several stages over a period of years) contained the three principal styles of roadway: 1/ adjacent to steam railroads (Indianapolis-Greencastle), 2/ cross-country with heavy cut and fill (Greencastle-Brazil) and 3/ side-of-the-road with little cut or fill work, crossing the road from side-to-side and running through the center of the street in each town (Brazil-Terre Haute). Most of the lines were of the first type and

Below The track passed from the center of the road to one side at the west edge of Cloverland. This car is heading for Terre Haute on October 7, 1939.
James F. Cook photo

Above Eastbound one-man car 428 is arriving at Boys' School siding near Plainfield. This portion of the Terre Haute line was built to heavier standards than the trackage west of Brazil. In this April 30, 1939 view the passenger load is light. Within a year buses would replace the rail line.
John F. Humiston photo

paralleled a steam railroad. Sidings of five to six-car capacity were located about every two miles. Running rail varied from 60 pounds per yard to 100-pound with the majority being 70 pound. Most trackage was ballasted with cinders or gravel although a few miles did have crushed rock ballast. As might be expected, the Indiana Railroad contained about every variable that could be imagined. Most were legacies of the very early years of interurban building and the fact that little of the system was built as part of a coordinated plan. Considering the track, route and other variables and the fact that there was little chance of any major improvements in these areas, the system did very well.

Indiana Railroad had come out of nowhere, was rapidly welded together and became a strong "super-interurban." In terms of its 800 route miles, it was the nation's longest interurban. A key factor in integrating the system was that the major companies had never been rivals. They recognized that cooperation aided their survival. The new system had unified management, financial support and integrated operations. It was rid of unprofitable lines. Now it had to exploit these advantages.

Among these advantages and/or important operating factors were Electric Power, Passenger and Freight Terminals, Freight Service and Signal Systems. These notable features, along with some of the advantages and disadvantages, are described in the following sections.

Electric Power

Electricity for the rail lines came from several generation sources and electric power distribution was the common thread of the Midland United companies. The interconnected company power lines covered more than two-thirds of the state but not the major urban centers. In Fort Wayne, the state's second largest city, ISC had about two-thirds of the commercial and residential power load with the city-owned power plant supplying the rest. Indianapolis, South Bend, Muncie, Anderson and Marion used other power company sources. Gary, Hammond, Terre Haute, Kokomo, Lafayette, and Richmond were all in the Midland orbit. The high lines, with the exception of those on the former Union Traction rail lines, all belonged to the power companies. The railroad was responsible for the maintenance of the lines along the interurban routes even though, in most cases, they owned only that portion which was directly related to operating the railroad.

The pole lines were similar on all the rail lines. The high-voltage power lines were carried high on the wooden poles with the three wires, widely separated, on one cross-arm. The overhead trolley wire was much the same on all routes. Bracket suspension from poles on 100 foot centers was the rule for rural trackage although some span wire construction was used on curves, at sidings and in some multiple track locations. Span wire was used in almost all city locations and some older mainlines (Indianapolis-Anderson). The trolley wire was largely 4/0 grooved. Feeders, phone lines and signal controls were also carried on the same pole lines.

The rail lines used alternating current (ac) transmitted at high voltage to the substations where it was converted to direct current (dc) and fed to the trolley wire. Because the dc voltage dropped at a distance from the source, it was necessary to locate a number of substations along the interurban routes to assure a constant voltage on the overhead wire. Many manually operated substations were in town station buildings where the operator also acted as the station agent.

Originally, the ac power was generated at 25 hertz (formerly known as cycles per second). Commercial power was, from an early date, generated at 60 hertz (hz) and the major power companies with traction line connections had to maintain two sets of generating equipment. The 25hz generating capacity was progressively retired as these companies modernized their power facilities and their customers replaced obsolete equipment. By 1930, ISC, NIP and Interstate had converted their rail lines to 60hz and retired their 25hz generators. They did maintain frequency converter stations which could change 60hz to 25hz to continue to supply some customers on the old frequency. The

Below An August 12, 1936 view of the huge Anderson power station, located just north of the company shops and offices. Coal was brought in on company cars as shown here and from the Pennsylvania Lines west of Meridian Street. *James P. Shuman photo*

joint ISC/Union Traction Pipe Creek (Bunker Hill) substation contained a frequency converter to act as a back-up for the Union Traction lines.

The THI&E lines were supplied by power stations at Richmond, Philadelphia, Tenth Street (Indianapolis) and Terre Haute. The first two were closed when Midland United took over, and the Tenth Street station went to Indiana Railroad. These three were 25hz plants. Richmond and Philadelphia became distribution territory for Public Service Company. The Tenth Street plant had supplied power to the four now-abandoned THI&E lines, the Indianapolis-Brazil line and the Indianapolis Street Railway. The street railway company switched to a modern power grid based on purchased 60hz power from Public Service Company's Lenore distribution station (itself retired about 1980). The Tenth Street plant had virtually no load left. After it was closed, the Indianapolis-Brazil line was supplied from Lenore station through frequency converters. The Terre Haute plant generated 60hz power for the lines west of Brazil.

Union Traction was different. It had three plants generating 25hz power located at Winchester, Eaton and Anderson. The Winchester plant was closed with the abandonment of the Union City line in early 1930. The Eaton plant had a deceivingly modern-looking exterior which housed two large reciprocating engines with each directly driving an ac generator. The engines were older than the building.

The Anderson power station was huge and, when built, was considered as an excellent example of a modern central-station power plant. Now, less than thirty years later, it was totally out of date. Five Rice-Sargent compound horizontal reciprocating engines drove five Westinghouse generators. The huge engines and whirling flywheels were a most impressive sight. A low-pressure Westinghouse turbo-generator was added in 1910 and located in the vast main engine room. Two General Electric turbo-generators were moved to Anderson from the Indianapolis & New Castle's power house with one arriving in 1918 and the second in 1923. Both were in a large bay at the north end of the power house. The Anderson plant also provided power to Traction Light & Power Company.

The Eaton power station supplied power from Muncie to Bluffton and was one of the first targets of the new Indiana Railroad management. The 25hz Eaton plant was closed in 1931 along with the 25hz manual substations at Bluffton, Montpelier, Hartford City and Eaton. These were replaced by new 60hz automatic substations and buildings at Bell and Burns and new automatic equipment in the Eaton power house building. The new installations with 500-kilowatt rotary con-

Below "Those acres and acres of reciprocating engines—I'll never forget it."—Samuel Insull, Jr. Five huge reciprocating steam engines with their great flywheels direct-drive five generators and dominate the vast floor. One of the three steam turbines can be seen through the steam-filled air at the far end of the gallery in this 1930 interior view of the Anderson power station. *Jerry D. Pruden photo*

Above The West Tenth Street power station in Indianapolis with locomotive 179 about 1925. The station's 25-hz generating equipment was already surplus in 1931 when it and the remaining THI&E lines were acquired.
George K. Bradley collection

verters cost approximately $23,000 each (less buildings). Power was purchased from the Indiana General Service Company (not a Midland United company).

Replacing the Anderson power station was a major long-range goal but not one that could be put on the plan in 1931. The Indianapolis-Peru, Tipton-Alexandria, Anderson-Marion and the Indianapolis-Muncie-New Castle-Indianapolis loop remained in the 25hz domain. A number of small towns in or near the loop were commercial customers of the Traction Light & Power Company. The plan was to quickly separate these and reassign them to Public Service Company of Indiana. It, in the meantime, left Indiana Railroad in the commercial power business. Plans were made to convert part of the Indianapolis-Peru line to 60hz with power from the NIP plant at Kokomo. The Indianapolis-Muncie rail line needed more power. The Daleville sub (between Muncie and Anderson) had an additional rotary added. This equipment was moved from the Fairmount substation. Between Anderson and Indianapolis there was a stretch of thirty miles with only one manual substation (in the Ingalls station) at about the mid-point. Indiana Railroad first proposed two new 25hz automatic substations at Tile (near Pendleton) and Bucy (near Fortville) with three 300kw rotary converters in each. This equipment could not be easily converted when the time came to change from 25hz to 60hz, so the company took a positive, new-technology step and installed two automatic 850kw Brown-Boveri mercury-arc rectifier sta-

tions. For a minimum expense, the two could be easily changed to 60hz. The new substation buildings were small while the proposed three rotaries would have required large buildings with substantial foundations. The new-technology rectifier substations represented a larger initial expense which would contribute a savings when the power supply was changed. They did boost the operating capacity of the line by an improved balance in the power. Of the twelve U. S. interurban properties operating mercury arc rectifiers at the end of 1931, only Indiana Railroad's were equipped for operation on two frequencies. The new equipment allowed the retirement of the Ingalls substation from train power use. It was retained with enough equipment to furnish energy to the railway signal system. The total cost of the 1930-31 upgrading of the power system was placed at $400,000.

Passenger and Freight Terminals

When the System took over the train operations it acquired a wide variety of passenger and freight station facilities. These ranged from the tiny shelters located at highway crossings and other remote sites to larger stations in towns and cities. In the smaller localities, the companies had an agency station in a company-owned building or rented facilities in a commercial building. The combined passenger and freight stations were, where it was practical, shared with the substation equipment. Most substations required an operator who also acted as the station agent. Local sidings could be used for train meets and for the unloading of freight cars. Under the System management, many stations were replaced by commission ticket offices or by tickets sold on the train using automated fare/ticket machines. Some passenger stations, in cities where there were separate facilities, were sold and space was allocated for a waiting room at the local freight station. This was especially true where the station building served no other function than as a passenger station.

The larger cities retained their passenger facilities because traffic volume warranted better accommodations. Trainshed terminals were located in Indianapolis, Muncie, Seymour, Louisville and Frankfort. The Louisville terminal was given up in favor of joint use of the Louisville Railway's enclosed interurban terminal. Large open multiple-track terminals were found at Fort Wayne and Terre Haute.

Street loading for freight and passengers became increasingly unpopular with local city officials especially when that activity occurred on busy streets. With more and more automobiles appearing each year, street loading became hazardous. In a few communities, clumsy train moves, which were acceptable in horse and wagon days, were not tolerable by 1931. Two typical examples could be found at Peru and Bluffton where the former ISC and Union Traction lines met and where the through Indianapolis-Fort Wayne *Hoosierlands* and *Wabash Valley Flyers* passed from one company's tracks to the other's. Crew changes were also made at these points into Indiana Railroad days.

The Peru situation was complicated by the fact that it was a branching-off point for two main lines from Fort Wayne. ISC's main line passed through the city on Main Street on its way to Logansport and Lafayette and connected with Union Traction's line to Indianapolis at Broadway. The station was on the south side of Main Street but west of Broadway. The through Indianapolis-Fort Wayne trains used Broadway and Main Street east of Broadway. The standard procedure was for a Fort Wayne-Indianapolis train to meet a Peru-Lafayette train at the Peru station and vice versa. The Lafayette-Peru cars would make several round trips in a day and, upon arrival at Peru, would unload, turn south on Broadway and then back around the wye on to Main Street. Now heading west, the car would pull through the intersection and park in the street west of the station. The southbound Fort Wayne-Indianapolis train would also cross Broadway and stop behind the Lafayette train to unload. After the station stop, the Indianapolis train had to back across the Broadway and Main intersection, clear the switch to the southbound track, reverse direction and turn south onto Broadway and the line to Indianapolis. The Lafayette car departed with no problem. A northbound through train turned east from Broadway, on a different switch, and was now facing east on Main Street. The train then had to back across Broadway to the station. Some through trains carried parlor cars when running as the *Flyer*. A further complication came from the local city cars which also used the Main Street tracks. Main and Broadway, at the corner of the Court House Square, was one of the busiest Peru intersections and was also the junction of two highways. Following the 1932 abandonment of the Lafayette line, Indiana Railroad moved the terminal to the Chesapeake & Ohio Railway Company's station where the ticket agent offered tickets for both the steam road and the interurban. This had been an advertised joint-operation connection for many years and had always been a Union Traction stop. Although the convenient C&O station was used, the official station was at the freight house, across Canal Street and to the west.

Bluffton was another meeting point. The north-south traffic was mostly through runs but Bluffton was also the eastern terminus of the Marion-Bluffton line. The company ran a number of Fort Wayne-Bluffton and return trips which required turning cars. Sunday usually meant an extra car had to be sent to Bluffton to be added to the 5:00 PM *Hoosierland* (from Indianapolis) which arrived at 8:00. The station was located at Washington and Johnson. The through trains came north on Johnson, crossed Washington and turned east on Market. At Market and Main the trains turned north. Freight trains zig-zagged east from Johnson onto Elm, north on the west side of the freight station (which faced on Washington), east on Washington and north on Main. With the abandonment of the Marion line the tracks on Washington, west of Johnson, were abandoned. This allowed the retention of the wye at the freight station. In the summer of 1932, the tracks on Johnson, from the north line of Washington Street, and on Market Street were removed. (The remaining crossing and the track to nowhere on Johnson bemused railfans in later years.) The passenger station was moved to the north end of the freight house and both freight and passenger trains then used the zig-zag route. The Johnson Street track between Elm and Washington was used for meets.

At Wabash, the old route through the city had two right-angle turns on and off Wabash Street, the main thoroughfare. The route was a serious hindrance for freight train movements and the street was shared with local streetcars. The passenger and freight stations were side-by-side on Market Street west of Wabash Street. In the summer of 1931 new tracks were built through the city and connected with the old line. This route crossed

Below A new freight terminal opened at Wabash in the summer of 1931 providing well-arranged, efficient facilities. This view to the east shows the slight rise in the main track and the depressed freight track for platform-level loading. *Jack M. Miller collection*

Above The Fort Wayne freight terminal on Commerce Drive looking west at the tracks on the north side of the building. An ample paved truck driveway on the south, loop tracks entirely around the building and even an unloading track for stone completed the facilities of this fine terminal. Too bad that it could be reached from most of the system only by difficult street running through downtown. *James P. Shuman photo*

the flood plain between the city and the river. ISC provided the fill material and local workers built the grade which was supposed to act as a flood dike to protect the river bottom section of Wabash. A new freight and passenger combination station was built near where the new line crossed Wabash Street. The station had freight house tracks to accommodate six cars and team tracks for ten more.

The larger city freight terminals merit special consideration because they were models of efficiency and were versatile enough to handle both rail and motor truck freight. The THI&E, in 1916, set up the Terminal Realty Company (a subsidiary) to purchase a former baseball park site on Kentucky Avenue in Indianapolis. THI&E's first structure was a large freight building containing office and terminal facilities for rail and local motor trucks. This facility was completed in January 1918 and, over a period of eight years, was considerably enlarged when additional buildings and tracks were added to accommodate the other interurban lines entering Indianapolis. These facilities replaced the old freight sheds at Ohio and Capitol. After the formation of the Indiana Railroad System the equity in Terminal Realty Corporation was rearranged, by contract agreement, so that Indiana Railroad had two-thirds control with the rest held by Public Service Company of Indiana and the Indianapolis & Southeastern Railroad Company.

After the consolidation, economies of space were effected and some of the Kentucky Avenue terminal facilities were leased to motor truck lines. The newer terminal building was kept as the main System freight house. This structure was 30 by 928 feet, with a granite block driveway to its north and five loading tracks immediately adjacent to the south. In addition, there were team, storage and run-around tracks. Some 12,000 square feet of the building's floor space were used for LCL transfer with the remainder for freight office, stationery storeroom, accounting office and garage space.

An even more modern rail and motor freight station was built on Commerce Drive in Fort Wayne. This facility, built in 1928, was one of the first to utilize modern skids and electric lift trucks in mechanized transfer work. The house tracks accommodated 31 cars while 14 more cars could be handled on team tracks. Storage and run-around tracks allowed easy switching movements and train make-ups.

Another modern terminal was built at Louisville. Opened in 1929, it was almost new when the System was organized. This station could load twelve cars from the building and ten on team tracks. Smaller and older freight stations of varying size, depending on local need, were located at the other principal towns on the System.

Freight Service

Freight operations were subjected to many changes throughout the company's lifetime. Initially, it was a rail service with on-line customers and the interchange with the other interurbans in the Indiana-Ohio-Michigan area. Two lines bridged the gap between the systems of Indiana and Ohio with one from Fort Wayne to Lima and the other from Richmond to Dayton. At Peru, the Winona Railroad provided a connection to South Bend, northern Indiana and the southwest corner of Michigan. At Louisville the company had a track gauge problem as all but one of the connecting lines were built to a different gauge.

Interchange with the steam railroads was limited, with one exception, to movement of steam road cars onto the interurban lines and to trackage with curves of sufficient radius to allow the passage of the rigid-drawbar cars. On the other hand, the interurban trailers, with their swing drawbars, were unacceptable to the steam railroads. From various junction points the interurban was able to handle standard railroad cars over portions of its trackage. In 1932 track connections were available at several points. On the Louisville line these were from the Pennsylvania connection at Columbus to the north city limits at Seymour, from the Pennsylvania at Scottsburg covering the territory from the south city limits of Seymour through Sellersburg. (The Baltimore and Ohio connection at Watson was added in 1934.) At Kokomo the NIPCo had connections with both the Nickel Plate and the Pennsylvania providing interchange from the east city limits of Frankfort to the west city limits of Marion. ISC had a number of connection points. On the Northern Division, the Pennsylvania connected at Conlogue (Cedar Siding) and the New York Central connected at Stoners with interchange south from both points to the Spy Run Yards in Fort Wayne. (It was claimed that cars could be moved north to Kendallville and Waterloo but that would have required getting through the junction at Garrett which was a tight-radius wye.) The NYC also connected at the Spy Run Yards (Kamm Street Yard). At Fort Wayne the Nickel Plate connected at the McKinley Yard and the steam road cars could be handled west from there to the east city limits of Logansport. The Nickel Plate also connected with the ISC at Peru. The Wabash had connections at Buck Creek and Burrows providing service from the west city limits of Logansport to the east city limits of Lafayette. On Indiana Railroad from the Indianapolis Industrial Center (sometimes listed as North Side Station) to the south city limits of Anderson there were switching connections for the Indianapolis Union and the Nickel Plate at Indianapolis and with the Big Four at Fort Benjamin Harrison, Ingalls and Reformatory. This 19th and Martindale terminal was completed in the first half of 1931. The terminal had trackage for more than 100 cars with facilities for loading or unloading direct from trucks. The Nickel Plate had a connection at Eaton that covered the territory from Bluffton to the north side of Muncie and at Alexandria from the south side of Marion to the west side of Muncie via Anderson Junction (the Pennsylvania connection at Anderson covered the same territory). At New Castle, from the Big Four connection, interchange cars could be handled westward to the Indianapolis Belt Railroad. For the Indianapolis, Indiana to Paris, Illinois territory, connections were made with the Indianapolis Union and with the Pennsylvania at Cartersburg. For a brief period a Pennsylvania connection at Philadelphia offered service from Indianapolis to Knightstown.

Coal was the most common commodity interchanged although standard box cars were delivered to on-line customers. A later connection at Limedale, on the Terre Haute line, with the Monon proved unique as the Monon would handle interurban box trailers over a short portion of their mainline, in a switch movement, to a cement factory. This was a unique operation that was not considered by the other railroads.

Freight train operation was at its peak in the early days of the system. There was good traffic over the main lines including considerable movement of livestock. The latter volume had decreased following the abandonment of the THI&E Lafayette and Crawfordsville lines and the only significant livestock volume came from the

Below The Muncie freight house on October 20, 1940. South of the passenger terminal, it was poorly arranged by 1930's standards. Most freight trains had to pass through the passenger trainshed and then turn west on Howard Street to switch cars to the freight house. Trains had to see-saw into the tight-radius lead tracks, usually blocking auto traffic on Mulberry Street and sometimes Walnut Street. *M. D. McCarter collection*

Louisville line. The greatest volume of interurban traffic was the less-than-carload (LCL) freight shipped in box trailers destined for a number of cities. It was the kind of freight service where the interurban excelled and provided much faster service (frequently overnight) than the competing steam railroads. It was also a type of traffic that could be easily lost to any more-flexible type of transport.

The former Union Traction-ISC connecting operations were continued under the new system. This included two interesting through freight runs, the *Lindbergh* and the *Aeroplane* (later known as First and Second *Aeroplane*) operating between Muncie and Fort Wayne. Those trains moved cars from central Indiana to the Toledo and Detroit area. Much of the traffic was automotive parts from the Indiana plants and suppliers of the Detroit auto makers. Loaded cars left Indianapolis at 10:45 AM on the "Day Muncie" via Anderson. At 4:30 PM, the *Lindbergh* (First *Aeroplane*) took trailers from Anderson. Muncie, Indianapolis and New Castle north to Bluffton. By 6:30 PM the train was ready to leave Bluffton after a crew change (freight train crews continued to change at Bluffton, just as they always had, until 1934) and the ISC crew now had the train still headed by a 700-series freight motor. These former Union Traction motors were disliked by the ISC crews and they sent them back, as quickly as possible, on the next train. At Fort Wayne, the train moved through the center track of the Main Street passenger terminal arriving in front of the old Pearl Street terminal at 7:40. The Fort Wayne cars were cut off and taken to the Commerce Drive freight terminal. A Fort Wayne-Lima freight motor would pull cars south from the terminal to a point south of Calhoun and Columbia and then back through Columbia and Harrison streets to reach the cars standing on Pearl Street. (If the *Lindbergh* was early the cars would have been pulled directly to the Commerce Drive terminal and then taken out by the Fort Wayne-Lima in one operation. This "early" situation was, according to the late Stanley Chausse, more the norm than the exception.) The train left the Fort Wayne terminal at 7:45 and brakeman Chausse recounted that the train was frequently 11 or 12 cars long. With this length, the train would be moving south from Main, on Clinton Street, while the last cars would still be coming off Calhoun, one block west on Main Street. The train's conductor and brakeman would have to be at the two switch locations and prepared to use hand or lantern signals to indicate any trouble. (This was especially critical at Main and Calhoun, the center point of the city streetcar operation.) The motorman could not see the train's rear cars and could only be directed by signals from the crew. The Fort Wayne-Lima frequently used ISC and Lake Shore Electric freight motors on their trains because it had only four of its own. At Lima the train was broken into several parts for forwarding north, east and south. The *Aeroplane* cars headed north from Lima at midnight, over the C&LE lines, to Toledo. Picked up at 3:00 AM, the Eastern Michigan-Toledo Railroad took the cars on to Detroit where they arrived at 7 AM. This was "next morning" delivery although it did require early morning shipment from Indianapolis for the 315-mile run. The train had an excellent record which resulted from the cooperation of all the connecting rail lines. Second morning service was available for shipments not sent out until later in the day. After the abandonment of the Fort Wayne-Lima in June 1932 some of this freight moved through the Dayton connection until the Toledo-Detroit route was abandoned in October 1932.

During these peak years the interchange of cars was heavy and the reporting marks of cars at the Indianapolis and Fort Wayne terminals showed cars from every connecting, interchange, interurban line in the three-state area. The abandonments of the early thirties quickly reduced the number of rail connections.

Below Express trailers like 391, being uncoupled on Kentucky Avenue just northeast of the Kentucky Avenue freight house grounds, were frequently used on the Terre Haute line. The one-man car is about to proceed to the Indianapolis Traction Terminal with its passengers. Car 391 was a box trailer body mounted on old passenger car trucks to permit this higher-speed "mixed train" operation. *James P. Shuman photo*

The Indiana Railroad System had many other scheduled freight movements but the number of complete schedules still available is limited. The accompanying schedules came from the former Union Traction (September 1930) and Public Service Company and former THI&E (July 1932). There are some variations in the timings due to the two different dates of these schedules. ISC timings are believed to be early 1930.

Indiana Railroad System
(Indiana Service Corporation)

LAFAYETTE DIVISION

PM	PM	AM		AM	PM	PM
6:00(1)	4:00(2)	8:30	Lv Fort Wayne Ar	4:30	10:00	6:00
7:30	5:45	10:15	Huntington	2:30	8:00	4:15
9:00	7:00	11:30	Wabash	1:30	5:00	2:30
10:00	8:00	12:15	Peru	12:30(3)	4:00	1:00
	10:00	2:00	Logansport		3:00	11:00
	10:40	2:30	Delphi		1:10	10:00
	11:30	4:45	Ar Lafayette Lv		12:30(4)	9:00(5)
PM	PM	AM		AM	AM	AM

(1) Peru Turn; Carries through cars Fort Wayne to Kokomo; Fort Wayne to South Bend; Fort Wayne to Warsaw; Wabash to South Bend.

(2) Lafayette freight. Carries through Indianapolis car via THI&E; Fort Wayne to Wabash and south on UT; Fort Wayne to Logansport and south on UT; Shipments for Monon R.R. at Lafayette.

(3) Peru Turn; Carries through cars South Bend to Fort Wayne; Kokomo to Fort Wayne; Winona Railroad short points to Fort Wayne.

(4) Carries car from Indianapolis via THI&E to various points; Logansport to Fort Wayne car; Shipments for Nickel Plate points via Fort Wayne.

(5) Carries freight from Lafayette, Delphi and Logansport for north of Peru. Next morning delivery at all points up to South Bend; Shipments from Monon R.R. at Lafayette for all points; Shipments for Detroit; Wabash to Fort Wayne car; Huntington to Fort Wayne car.

BLUFFTON DIVISION

PM	AM	AM		AM	AM	PM
4:00(1)	10:30(2)	1:30(3)	Lv Fort Wayne Ar	1:15	4:30	7:40
6:30	12:00	2:45	Ar Bluffton Lv	12:00(4)	3:00(3)	6:30(5)
PM	N'n	AM		Mid	AM	PM

(1) Carries through cars Fort Wayne to Muncie and connections; Fort Wayne to Indianapolis; Fort Wayne to Bluffton and Marion.

(2) Aeroplane

(3) Muncie Local

(4) Aeroplane; Carries through cars Indianapolis to Fort Wayne; Indianapolis to Lima; Marion to Fort Wayne.

(5) Lindbergh

NORTHERN DIVISION

PM	AM		PM	PM
4:00	9:30	Lv Fort Wayne Ar	2:00	6:00
7:00	1:00	Waterloo	1:00	
9:00	3:30	Ar Kendallville Lv	10:30	3:55
PM	PM		AM	PM

MARION & BLUFFTON DIVISION

PM		AM	
4:00	Lv Fort Wayne Ar	4:00	(next day)
7:00	Bluffton	1:00	(next day)
10:00	Ar Marion Lv	4:00	
PM		PM	

FORT WAYNE—LIMA RAILROAD COMPANY

PM	PM	PM	AM	AM		AM	AM	AM	PM	PM
7:45(1)	7:30(2)	1:00(3)	9:30(4)	1:30(5)	Lv Fort Wayne Ar	4:00	4:30	10:30	1:00	7:00
12:00	11:30	6:00	3:00	6:00	Ar Lima Lv	1:00(6)	2:00(7)	5:30(8)	8:30(1)	3:30(9)
Mid	PM	PM	PM	AM		AM	AM	AM	AM	PM

(1) Lindbergh. Through cars.

(2) Local. Carries Ft. Wayne to Toledo via C&LE; Ft. Wayne to Detroit via D&T; Ft. Wayne to Dayton via WO, D&T; Ft. Wayne to Springfield via C&LE.

(3) Cleveland freight. Ft. Wayne Western Ohio through Car south of Lima; Ft. Wayne to Cleveland.

(4) East Local. Western Ohio House car points north of Lima.

(5) Aeroplane.

(6) Local. Dayton to Ft. Wayne and Toledo to Ft. Wayne car via C&LE and car from Toledo via C&LE for local points on FW-L.

(7) Through car from Springfield via C&LE and Toledo to Ft. Wayne via WO.

(8) No Local work between Lima and Fort Wayne. West Bound Aeroplane.

(9) Lima Local WO car and connections; Cleveland, Detroit via TBG&S.

THROUGH FREIGHTS

Muncie Local	Aeroplane	Lindbergh		Muncie Local	Aeroplane	Lindbergh
7:00 PM	7:00 PM(1)	10:45 AM	Lv Indianapolis Ar		8:30 PM	4:45 AM
10:00 PM	10:00 PM	4:30 PM	Muncie	6:45 AM	5:00 PM	12:00 Mid
3:00 AM	12:00 Mid	6:30 PM	Bluffton	3:15 AM	12:00 PM	6:30 PM
4:30 AM	1:30 AM	7:45 PM	Fort Wayne	1:30 AM	10:30 AM	4:00 PM
	6:00 AM	12:00 Mid	Lima		5:30 AM	
(Next Day)	4:00 AM	3:00 AM	Toledo		1:00 AM	
	7:00 AM to 10:00 AM	7:00 AM	Ar Detroit Lv		7:00 AM	

(1) Through cars next morning delivery to Lima and second morning to Detroit from Indianapolis.

Right Looking north along the Monon main at the Limedale interchange near Greencastle. Both steam-road and interurban freight cars are on the electrified Indiana Railroad-Monon interchange track. The Monon would switch the interurban cars over its tracks to a nearby cement works.
Richard H. George photo

Indiana Railroad (Former Union Traction):

Explanation of the Work on Various Freight Runs Effective September 28, 1930.

Day Muncie

Crew reports at the Indianapolis Freight House at 10 AM. Train consists of trailers for points beyond Muncie. Trailers for intermediate points which require a special move will be pulled by this train. This freight will do way-station work in both directions.

On the return trip this freight pulls trailers for South Bend, Anderson and Indianapolis. South Bend trailer is set off at Anderson for the Anderson-Peru Freight.

South & West Aeroplane out of Bluffton

Crew takes the train at Bluffton (from the ISC crew) when it arrives from Fort Wayne. No local work is done between Bluffton and Indianapolis, except setting in and picking up trailers at Muncie. Train runs via New Castle to Indianapolis. Makes up the train in Indianapolis for the return trip via New Castle. Does no way-station work except in Muncie to pick up Cleveland freight and any cars for points beyond Fort Wayne.

North local out of Muncie

This train leaves Muncie at 11:30 PM doing way-station work between Muncie and Bluffton, arriving in Bluffton at 3:00 AM, makes up train for the return trip, leaves Bluffton at 3:30 AM doing way-station work at all stations, and arrives in Muncie at 6:30 AM. Makes up train for the west, leaves Muncie at 7:30 AM for Anderson, arrives in Anderson at 8:35 AM. Makes up train and leaves Anderson at 9 AM, arrives in Muncie at 10 AM; doing local work both ways. This crew does yard switching in Muncie and marks off at 11 AM.

First Aeroplane

This crew does yard switching and leaves Muncie for Bluffton at 4:30 PM, pulling trailers which come in on the Day Muncie from the west and all other trailers which are consigned to points beyond Fort Wayne. No local work is done on this train northbound. Returning south it leaves Bluffton at 7:20 PM doing way-station work all the way to Muncie, arriving in Muncie at 10:30 PM. Helps north local Muncie to get ready and the crew marks off at 11:00 PM.

Night Muncie

Reports at Indianapolis Freight House at 6:45 PM, makes up the train and leaves at 7:15 PM. This train does way-station work from Anderson to Muncie only, eastbound. At Anderson trailers will be picked up which are ready to go to Muncie and points beyond.

Leaves Muncie on the return trip and does way-station work all the way. This freight pulls the Anderson set-off trailers on the eastbound trip and a trailer for all points between Indianapolis and Bluffton and beyond, except the trailers for Muncie proper.

New Castle Freight

Crew reports at the Muncie freight house at 5:30 PM, makes up train taking whatever trailers are necessary to go on this division for the work and also connection trailers which are delivered to the THI&E at New Castle. This train does way-station work in both directions from Indianapolis and picks up connection trailers at New Castle on the return trip. On the return trip this freight pulls all the trailers out of Indianapolis for Muncie proper.

Marion-Indianapolis Freight

This crew reports at the Marion Freight House at 5:45 PM, makes up train, does way-station work Marion to Anderson and unloads any freight west of Anderson which has been picked up north of Anderson. Also picks up a trailer at Alexandria for Anderson and sets off one trailer at Anderson which the Marion freight house has loaded for Anderson and points east.

On the return trip the train is made up at the Indianapolis Freight Yards by the crew and will be composed of a trailer for Marion and cars for beyond Anderson. The way-station freight is loaded in the motor. At Anderson a trailer which has come from the east will be picked up for Marion. This train does way-station work from Indianapolis to Marion on the return trip, except in Anderson.

Anderson-Peru Freight

Crew reports at Anderson Freight house at 5:00 PM and makes up the train composed of a motor and all trailers destined for Kokomo, Peru and beyond. This freight does way-station work between Anderson and Peru both ways. On the return trip it receives a trailer from the Winona Railroad which has way-station freight in it for points between Peru and Muncie. At Tipton on the return trip, a trailer will be picked up which has freight in it for Elwood and Alexandria. The Elwood freight is unloaded and the trailer taken on to Alexandria where it will be set off. Delivery is made out of this trailer during the day by the Alexandria agent. This crew sets their train in at the Anderson freight house where it will be worked by the freight house crew and get ready to go east.

Indianapolis-Kokomo Freight

Crew reports for duty at 6 PM at the Indianapolis Freight House and makes up a train composed of a trailer for Elwood and the Kokomo set-off. This train helps the Cannon-Ball out of Indianapolis in case the Cannon-Ball has more trailers than it can handle. This train waits at Ripple for leaving time and does all the local work to be done between Indianapolis and Kokomo both ways. On the return, at Kokomo, this freight takes a trailer off the Anderson-Peru freight with freight for local points south of Kokomo.

Cannon-Ball Freight

This crew marks on at the Indianapolis Freight House at 6 PM, makes up train and leaves the Indianapolis Freight House at 6:30 PM for Peru, pulling all trailers for points beyond Kokomo including the trailer for Logansport. This train does local work north of Kokomo.

At Peru this train switches the yards, making up the southbound train which is composed of all trailers for points south of Kokomo and connecting lines at Indianapolis.

Public Service Company of Indiana   July, 1932 freight timetable
Indianapolis-Louisville

#1A (Through)		#2A (Local)		#3A (Local)		#4A (Through)	
New Albany	6:00 PM	New Albany	6:30 PM	Lv Indianapolis	6:30 PM	Lv Indianapolis	2:00 AM
Lv Louisville, Ky.	7:00 PM	Lv Louisville, Ky.	6:30 PM	Greenwood	8:10 PM	Greenwood	2:40 AM
Jeffersonville	7:20 PM	Jeffersonville	7:45 PM	Franklin	9:00 PM	Franklin	3:00 AM
Scottsburg	8:00 PM	Scottsburg	9:15 PM	Edinburg	10:15 PM	Edinburg	3:15 AM
Seymour	8:45 PM	Seymour	11:10 PM	Columbus	12:01 AM	Columbus	3:40 AM
Columbus	9:30 PM	Columbus	1:00 AM	Seymour	1:45 AM	Seymour	4:30 AM
Edinburg	10:00 PM	Edinburg	1:30 AM	Scottsburg	3:00 AM	Scottsburg	5:35 AM
Franklin	10:30 PM	Franklin	2:10 AM	Jeffersonville	4:30 AM	Jeffersonville	7:20 AM
Greenwood	11:01 AM	Greenwood	2:35 AM	Ar New Albany	5:30 AM	Ar Louisville, Ky.	8:00 AM
Ar Indianapolis	12:01 AM	Ar Indianapolis	3:30 AM	Ar Louisville, Ky.	5:00 AM		

Train 1A handles all cars from Louisville, Jeffersonville, New Albany and Seymour for Indianapolis and points beyond. Also picks up freight at Columbus. The New Albany car is switched to Jeffersonville by a switch motor. All freight for points between Indianapolis and Fort Wayne, New Castle or Terre Haute is transferred by the night force at the Indianapolis freight house.

Train 2A pulls a car from Louisville to Seymour and does all local work between Louisville and Indianapolis.

Train 3A handles all cars from Indianapolis to New Albany and Louisville and loads and unloads freight at all stations in between except for Columbus and Seymour. This is loaded in a car(s) and set out by Train 4A. New Albany car switched at Jeffersonville.

Train 4A handles cars from Indianapolis to Seymour and Columbus and freight for Louisville and steam road connections south and west of there. This freight is transferred at Indianapolis by the night freight house force.

Indiana Railroad (former THI&E lines)   July 1932 freight timetable

Indianapolis-Terre Haute

#8A		#9A	
Lv Terre Haute	11:00 AM	Lv Indianapolis	6:00 PM
Brazil	12:30 PM	Greencastle	7:30 PM
Greencastle	2:00 PM	Brazil	9:00 PM
Ar Indianapolis	3:30 PM	Ar Terre Haute	10:00 PM
#10A		#11A	
Lv Terre Haute	8:00 PM	Lv Indianapolis	3:00 AM
Brazil	9:15 PM	Greencastle	4:45 AM
Greencastle	10:15 PM	Brazil	5:30 AM
Ar Indianapolis	12:01 AM	Ar Terre Haute	7:00 AM

Train 8A handles all freight and cars between Terre Haute and Indianapolis and to points beyond Indianapolis. All LCL is transferred to train departing Indianapolis that same evening.

Train 9A does local work from Indianapolis to Terre Haute. Handles freight for steam road connections, at Terre Haute, for Vincennes and Evansville for next morning delivery.

Train 10A does local work between Indianapolis and Terre Haute and pulls all cars for Indianapolis and beyond (Columbus, Seymour, Fort Wayne, New Castle, Richmond and Louisville, Ky.). Also for Richmond steam road connections where rates apply. Freight is handled by Indianapolis freight house night force.

Train 11A handles all freight between Indianapolis and Terre Haute and for steam road connections routed via Terre Haute. Receives all freight for points west of Indianapolis transferred by the freight house night force.

Indianapolis-New Castle-Richmond

#15A		#16A	
Lv Indianapolis	6:15 PM	Lv Richmond	12:30 AM
New Castle	8:30 PM	New Castle	2:30 AM
Ar Richmond	11:00 PM	Ar Indianapolis	5:30 AM
#17A		#18A	
Lv Richmond	6:00 PM	Lv Indianapolis	12:01 AM
New Castle	9:00 PM	New Castle	2:30 AM
Ar Indianapolis	11:30 PM	Ar Richmond	5:30 AM

Train 15A handles the Dayton-Cincinnati car, Springfield-Columbus car, Dayton-Troy car, and Muncie car from Indianapolis. Also Muncie-Dayton car and Fort Wayne-Dayton car at New Castle.

Train 16A handles Cincinnati-Dayton, Dayton-Troy-Springfield cars for Indianapolis, unloads these cars at all points Richmond to Indianapolis. Also Dayton-Muncie and Dayton-Fort Wayne cars to New Castle.

Train 17A handles all freight from and to points between Richmond and Indianapolis and north of New Castle.

Train 18A handles all freight from and to all stations between Indianapolis and Richmond except for New Castle.

THROUGH FREIGHT

One major freight train change took place in the mid-thirties which provided 12-hour service from Louisville to Fort Wayne. These fast freight trains were called "hotshots" and were placed in service on September 9, 1935 with the following schedule:

Northbound		Southbound	
Lv Louisville	5:00 PM	Lv Fort Wayne	7:00 PM
Indianapolis	9:30 PM	Peru	11:30 PM
Peru	1:00 AM	Indianapolis	3:00 AM
Ar Fort Wayne	5:00 AM	Ar Louisville	7:30 AM

This was a fast service which carried a trailer for Peru, picked up a trailer at Indianapolis for Fort Wayne and unloaded any freight on the train at stations between Peru and Fort Wayne. The southbound hotshot handled a trailer out of Fort Wayne for Indianapolis and picked up a trailer at Peru for Louisville. The train would load freight between Fort Wayne and Peru, at all stations, for Louisville and beyond and Terre Haute and beyond only. No cars would be set off or any freight loaded or unloaded between Peru and Indianapolis. In both directions, this schedule was appreciably faster. Between Louisville and Indianapolis, according to Robert Stacy, the northbound train was a first class train and operated as a second section of a passenger train. However, on several occasions, around Greenwood, he saw the train lose its rights on account of being two hours late. White lights were put up as the train received new orders changing it to an extra train.

Above A typical Indiana Railroad freight pulls into the yards at the Kentucky Avenue freight houses (the tile-roofed buildings). This was a thriving manufacturing district; the terminal was well located. Motor 730 has been renumbered from ISC 853 and fully repainted for Indiana Railroad; trailer 671 is still in Union Traction orange with just a "patch" paint job to change the name. *George K. Bradley collection*

The Kentucky Avenue terminal daily operations reflected a number of changes through the years as motor trucks made an increasing presence. Some of this has been described by George Krambles who worked at the freight house in 1936. The typical rail line-up (1936), according to Krambles, included 28 cars, each with a definite destination. The motor cars were generally loaded with freight for transfer to connecting lines or with way freight, while the trailers were loaded not to break bulk until in the freight house at the destination.

A day's operating cycle began at Indianapolis in the afternoon with LCL shipments arriving by local truck at the freight house dock. A switching crew would be just finishing a lineup of equipment for the day, using double-door cars where extra-large shipments could be expected and the proper motor cars to handle each train to its destination.

Truckers immediately began loading cars from the LCL accumulated on the freight house floor. Shipping orders were rushed to the office upstairs where clerks rushed the preparation of waybills. First car to leave the lineup was the Terre Haute "fast" trailer, an express car with passenger trucks (usually 391, 501 or 502), which was picked up by a regular passenger car on its way out of town in the late afternoon. This car was loaded with Terre Haute "transfer" freight, destined to points in western Indiana and Illinois via rail and truck connections. Merchandise handled on this car would be at final destination early the following day.

At about 7:00 PM the loading of through freights ended, and, as soon as the waybills could be pouched and delivered to the conductors just coming on the job, trains were ready to depart. A few minutes' work coupling cars and testing brakes was followed by departure in close order of freights for Ft. Wayne (via Peru), Louisville, and Dayton. Some cars in these trains contained transfer freight which, late that night, would be hastened via some connecting line to its ultimate destination. The waybills for these cars were rushed to the passenger terminal so they could go ahead on a passenger train to give the agent at the junction point a head start on his evening's work.

There followed a lull at Indianapolis freight house until about midnight, when the way freights, having started from outlying terminals about sundown, began to arrive. A night lineup was quickly made and there would ensue a furious period of freight transfer so that these trains might turn about and start back to their terminals at about 3:00 AM.

Again there was a lull until early morning, when the through freights began arriving on their return loaded with freight for Indianapolis and Indianapolis connections. The day's cycle closed with the transfer of this freight into drays (trucks) of the railroad or consignee.

Another freight service was the Dispatch and C.O.D. Freight which was essentially an express and small freight shipment service. The shipments were handled in the baggage compartments of passenger trains insuring delivery to any station on the system in the same day. Rates were higher than regular freight but less than the company's express rates. C.O.D. carried a slight additional charge. This was a station-to-station

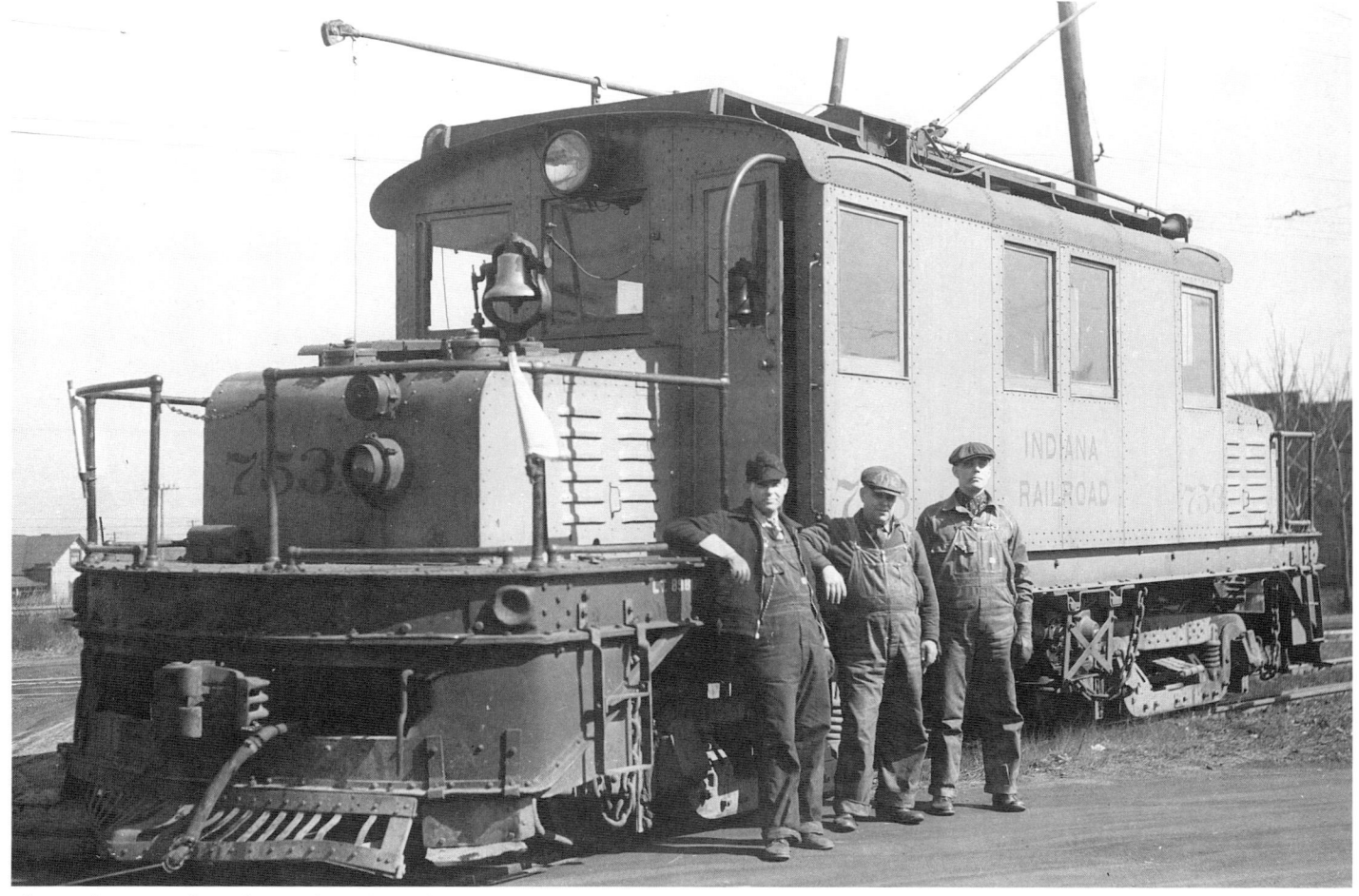

Above The 753 at the Indianapolis Industrial Center at 19th and Martindale on the city's north side. Left to right are brakeman Allen Smith, conductor Buzz Askew and motorman Russ Powell.
Glenn Niceley photo, George Krambles collection

service with no pick-up or delivery service. The company stimulated this and other LCL business when, on October 16, 1935, it began free pick-up and delivery service with twelve of its own trucks at Indianapolis. The service was expanded to the other terminals.

Closed pouch mail, baggage and dogs were also carried in the passenger car baggage compartments. The mail, in a two-man car, was in view of the motorman and considered safe by postal standards. It was a fast method for transporting mail, particularly that which went to points on the company's rail lines. The postal service for many communities was, as a result, faster in 1930 than today (1991). Up to 150 pounds of baggage was carried free for each full fare. An accompanied dog, provided with a properly fitting collar and strong chain, could be transported in the baggage compartment for a full fare charge.

There were also occasional special moves that had been made since the early days of traction freight. Although none are a matter of record in Indiana Railroad days, the interurbans had moved such diverse cargos as carnivals. Shortly before the creation of the system, ISC had moved a carnival consisting of a ten-car freight train and a passenger motor. The move was interline from Logansport to Michigan City on the tracks of the ISC, Winona and Northern Indiana lines. Another was from Bluffton to Huntington using three trailers, a motor and a passenger trailer. The company's traffic men were always looking for business.

Through Ohio River-to-Chicago coal movements have frequently been mentioned as one of the reasons for the interurban consolidation. Coal was important to Midland United's generating stations. Standard railroad coal cars were being moved over the South Shore Line which was part of the Midland holdings. The South Shore had always enjoyed a distinct advantage of not having been constructed to typical interurban rail standards. Instead, it had the advantage of approaching mainline railroad engineering standards and was in excellent physical shape following the Insull-sponsored rehabilitations. The rest of the Indiana lines were plagued with light rail, light bridges, close clearances, short sidings, sharp curves and an inordinate amount of street running in almost every city and town.

Indiana Railroad had trouble enough moving coal trains comprised of six of its own cars to an on-line generating station because of the physical limitations. The idea of linking up the interurbans into a route from the Ohio River, at Louisville, through Indiana, to Chicago was a virtual impossibility. Between Louisville and Indianapolis the Public Service Company lines had several sections of restrictive street running with tight right-angle turns. Indianapolis presented the biggest obstacle as there was no terminal railroad offering a north-south by-pass.

Construction of an interurban belt line was considered. Sam Insull, Jr. and Robert Feustel rented a Ford for two days in the summer of 1930 to drive around the

Above Freight motor 711, a reconstruction of a high-clerestory, wooden, Kentucky Traction & Terminal Company passenger car, leading six freight cars, crosses over U.S. highway 31 and a local street on the north side of Franklin. *James P. Shuman photo*

city to search for a freight route. One proposal would have made an excellent use of an existing facility and, according to what Harry Norford later told Don Walker, was actually investigated for feasibility. This route would have had cars enter the city from the south on Shelby Street, travel as far north as the Indianapolis Union Railway, and then run west over that railroad's track to a point where the line crossed a canal. Built much earlier as part of the ill-fated Indiana canal complex, it now belonged to the Indianapolis Water Company (an independent utility) and was used to bring water to the treatment plant. The canal started from a north side entrance on the White River, near Broad Ripple, ran westward crossing College Avenue (the Peru line) and continued southward to a point west of the central business district where it terminated close to the Union Railway. The canal had wide, flat-top eastern banks and the proposal was to lay tracks on them. This expensive project was never attempted.

Indiana Railroad's own tracks ran only as far north as Peru. From Peru to the South Shore connection, at South Bend, required traversing two "foreign" interurban lines. The Winona Railroad Company covered part of the gap—the 65 miles from Peru to Goshen. The Winona was a "friendly" line in Public Service Company's electric service area and a company that had been reorganized in 1924 by Martin Insull and Harry Reid at Samuel Insull's request. James P. Goodrich, the principal bondholder (and ex-governor of Indiana), had purchased it at foreclosure. He apparently approached Sam Insull for help in salvaging his investment in the old Winona Interurban Railway.

Renamed the Winona Service Corporation it was refinanced and new bond issues replaced the old ones. In the transaction Interstate acquired the company's transmission lines from Peru to Goshen. However, the Winona was never put into the Middle West Utilities or the Midland United camp. It remained a friendly independent. Refinanced in 1929 (with an increased funded debt) it was renamed Winona Railroad Company, and slipped back into receivership in 1932. But, in 1930, this potential bridge line was in place.

From Goshen to South Bend was another matter. This 26-mile segment belonged to the Northern Indiana Railway, Inc. It was the oldest portion of the company's interurban lines and had extensive street running in Goshen, Elkhart, Mishawaka and South Bend plus numerous tight curves that could not handle standard steam railroad cars. In short, the physical plant of this route was unsuited to heavy coal trains. The Northern Indiana was also a sizable independent rail system and not especially friendly to the Insull interests. From South Bend to Michigan City the Northern Indiana's route via La Porte competed with the South Shore and the Northern Indiana felt that it had been hurt by the improvements on the shorter South Shore route.

Talk of the through route dated from as early as 1926 and Samuel Insull even stated that such a service

Above Packages, newspapers, pouch mail and even dogs rode the front baggage compartment of the Indiana Railroad cars. The 428 has just arrived at Indianapolis and some of the front compartment cargo is on the baggage cart. *Glenn Niceley photo, George Krambles collection*

was "possible." Through interurban freight trains (a motor car and trailers) had been operated over most of the route for years but the movement of long, heavy coal trains was out of the question and it is doubtful that any amount of modernization money could have made it profitable. Passengers would have faced an equally slow and roundabout route which would have competed against several direct steam road connections on the Chicago-Indianapolis and Chicago-Louisville routes. (Samuel Insull, Jr., in a 1978 interview, dispelled the myth that Midland United had any plans to link its various interurban lines in the Chicago area with the Indiana Railroad System. In Insull's words such an idea "was not considered on the passenger side.")

Both passenger and freight traffic were promoted. Advertising and "word of mouth" campaigns helped the passenger side while the freight side was supported by the traffic department. The interurban traffic representatives' effort for on-line and interline business was increased after 1930. The freight effort became a very serious game as the onset of depression saw the region's overall business decrease. Weekly reports of traffic representatives' calls were sent to C. D. Hardin. Most of the business reports were optimistic, honest and offered some insight on the times. C. H. Etter, the traffic representative in Anderson, sometimes reported on non-freight items that seem silly today but were facts of life. For example, at General Motors' Anderson Delco-Remy and Guide Lamp divisions employee loyalty was demanded with a heavy hand. Etter reported, on May 23, 1931, that "Delco Remy Corp., have notified all employees who own a Ford automobile that they will either have to sell it and buy a Chevrolet or trade it in on one or leave the service of the company." Jobs were hard to come by and, no doubt, most complied.

Signal Systems

Interlocking plants, block signals and manually operated semaphores assisted the system's excellent safety record. Signaling supplemented all standard rules of operation, schedules, meet orders and train dispatcher's instructions.

Most interlocking plants were at steam railroad crossings. Usually, they were built (on a shared-cost basis) to the specifications of the "senior" road. Upper-right-hand quadrant semaphore signals were typical. A few plants had both distant and home signals as in standard railroad practice. The approach of an interurban train was under full control and prepared to stop. Split-rail or "toad" derails were used on the interurban approaches and cleared by the interlocker operator. The signals and derails were operated by lever movements, through rod connections, and the signal position was interlocked with the derail.

Several junctions were more complex, having a multiple-function lever-operated signal machine controlling home and distant signals to protect both roads. One major installation was at Clymers, where the Wabash Railroad, Vandalia Railroad and the ISC's Logansport-Lafayette line each crossed the other two. The signal machine here contained 72 functions and was maintained by the Wabash Railroad with the other lines paying part of the operating cost. Auburn Junction, a crossing of four rail lines on the Northern Division, featured an interlocking plant shared by all four companies. The interurbans avoided such complicated crossings where possible. In many cases they had resorted to bridges or underpasses especially where land contours permitted an inexpensive grade separation.

A special case existed in traversing the Big Four bridge into Louisville. Indiana Railroad operated under

Above Hiking south from Fort Wayne in October 1940, Jim Shuman encountered freight motor 738 hurrying north with one car in tow. The Nickel Plate's Fort Wayne-Muncie line is on the right. *James P. Shuman photo*

control of the Big Four, maintained the signal system and operated under the steam railroad's rules (including a second man on any one-car, one-man train).

Automatic track circuit block signals protected over 200 miles of the system's trackage. These signals resulted from the 1912 order by the Indiana Railroad Commission specifying block signal protection for treacherous or heavy-traffic areas. Most were installed by 1920. The signaled territory exceeded that ordered by the commission. Automatic block signal systems of two manufacturers were used: Union Switch and Signal Company (USS) and General Railway Signal Company (GRS). The USS "TDB" (Traffic Direction Block) system was adopted by the predecessors of Public Service Company of Indiana to protect over 25 miles of the Louisville line. Signals were not necessary in the larger towns due to the inherent safety of local speed regulations. The signals were set in pairs, one for each direction, at the sidings and used upper-left-hand quadrant semaphores on masts to the right of the track (except at Tracy siding where a street was in the way). Thus the arm extended toward the rail for better visibility, an important point where the power line poles created a wall effect. The semaphores had only two aspects: a 45-degree position with a green light and horizontal with a red light. The third lens position on the standard arm was vacant. The arms were painted yellow with a black band on the governing side and black with a white band on the back. Intermediate signals, located about midway between the sidings, used green and red color lights.

Home and intermediate signals were absolute with only "stop" and "proceed" indications. As a train passed a siding and entered a block, the signal changed to stop giving rear-end protection to the train. At the same time, the opposing signal at the next siding and the next opposing intermediate signal changed to a stop indication. As the train proceeded through the block and passed the intermediate signal, the signal at the passed siding would clear and show a proceed indication. This allowed a second train to make a following movement and still have full protection. If opposing trains passed the siding signals at the same time, they would be stopped by the intermediate signals. With no preliminaries (circuit overlaps providing an advance action), two opposing trains could approach each other at a siding because the intermediate signals indicated proceed to each train. Both siding signals would show stop indications. Because no distant indication was given, this system required (by company rule) that all signals be approached under full control and prepared to stop. Main track switches were connected to the system so that an open switch set the signals at stop. Some switches had an indicator signal (mini-semaphore or color light) showing the trainmen whether the block was clear so that a switch could be opened.

Color light signals had been installed on 175 miles of ISC, THI&E, NIP and Union Traction lines brought into the Indiana Railroad System. All but one section used the GRS "APB" (Absolute Permissive Block) system modified for electric railways. APB was considered to be less rigid than the USS "TDB" system because a third indication was used: red over yellow (proceed with caution prepared to stop if flagged by a preceding train or any other obstruction) as well as red (stop) and green (proceed). The first, or end, signal of each installation was normally lighted; the others remained dark until a train approached. As with the USS system, home signals were located at the sidings (at the middle of double-end sidings and near the switch of stub-end

Above On December 15, 1940, southbound extra 376, on a railfans' special trip, pauses at the Nickel Plate's enclosed wooden interlocking tower south of Montpelier. *John F. Humiston photo*

Below On this same trip, southbound 376 stops at the Erie Railroad crossing north of Kingsland. The levers controlling this primitive interlocker are located out in the weather. *John F. Humiston photo*

Above Southbound 78 waits at Miller siding south of Greenwood with a "clear" block. The diagonal blade was as "clear" as these semaphores could be: they had no vertical position.
Glenn Niceley photo, George Krambles collection

sidings). The light-signal heads for both directions were mounted back-to-back on the same mast.

APB signals allowed following movements, between passing sidings, through the use of permissive indications (red over yellow) while the signals governing opposing movements, between passing sidings, displayed an absolute stop indication. With no intermediate signals, it was necessary to use a preliminary or circuit overlap to prevent two trains from entering the block simultaneously. Signals were activated from a distance of 2000 feet (considered the maximum daylight viewing distance of the light indicator). If the signal showed green or red over yellow, its immediate opposing signal, on the same mast, showed red. The opposing signal at the next siding, a few miles away, was also activated by the overlap and showed red. The preliminary would assure trainmen that the track would remain clear to the next siding.

Distant signals were used in some locations where a clear view of the home signal, at the siding, was not possible due to hills or other obstructions. The distant signal allowed a train to continue at normal speed by presenting (or repeating) the aspect of the home signal. However, if there was a train between the distant and the home signal, the distant signal would show red.

Block indicators were used to expedite train meets. The block indicator signal was a single, shielded light with a metal-disc background, mounted on a line pole. The indicator, placed at the 2000 foot approach point, was connected on the overlap to the next opposing signal, several miles away. Block indicators were often installed one-way in each direction, from an approxi-

Below The ISC's valley line crossed the Wabash Railroad at grade, east of Lagro. The tower controlled the crossing. One of the semaphores, set at "clear," can be seen behind the westbound 58.
James P. Shuman photo

INDIANA RAILROAD
MUNCIE - ANDERSON - INDIANAPOLIS

Effective Sunday, September 29, 1935.
At 4:01 A. M. Central Standard Time.
Superseding Time Table No. 207.
Destroy all Time Tables of previous date.

TIME TABLE NO. 208

[Westbound timetable showing trains 37, 931, 35, 33, 929, 31, 29, 927, 925, 27, 25, 923, 23, 921, 21, 919, 19, 917, 17, Note B 915, 913, 15, 13, 911, 11, 9, 909, 7, 5, 907, 3, Note A 303, Note A 1, 905, 903 running between Muncie and Indianapolis via Shop, Hart, Russ, Yorktown, Dolby, Make, Glass, Daleville, Camp, Chesterfield, House, Pit, Cemetery, Anderson Jct., Anderson, Belt, Taft, Goul, Pendleton, Tile, Rolla, Stone, Ingalls, Dent, Mur, Fortville, Bucy, McCordsville, Oaklandon, Post, Ft. Harrison, Valley, Lawrence, Negley, Long, Indianapolis.]

Time points in HEAVY FACE TYPE denotes meeting points.

L. M. BROWN, Gen. Supt. Transportation.

Note A—Daily Except Sunday, Thanksgiving, Christmas, New Years, Decoration Day, July 4 and Labor Day.
Note B—Saturday Only.

Above Perhaps Indiana Railroad's busiest stretch of single track was the suburban service between Marion and Gas City but the Muncie-Anderson-Indianapolis line regularly carried more passenger and freight traffic than any other. It included the brisk suburban Fort Harrison service. Both the through and suburban service are shown on employees timetable 208. *George K. Bradley collection*

mate center location of the signaled territory. In almost all cases, the sidings had only one block indicator. When a distant signal was used, there was no need for a block indicator as the signal aspect served the same purpose.

All trains were scheduled, by timetable or train order, for meets at specific sidings. The company rules and regulations stated, "At double end sidings, west and southbound trains will take siding unless otherwise directed...." "At single end sidings the train facing the

Below Meeting points on Indiana Railroad's single-track lines were specified by timetables and train orders. However, signals were important aids to safety. In the diagram, signal heads are shown side-by-side so that the reader can observe the aspects for trains in both directions. In the field they were usually mounted back-to-back, as shown in the photograph on page 63. *Roy G. Benedict*

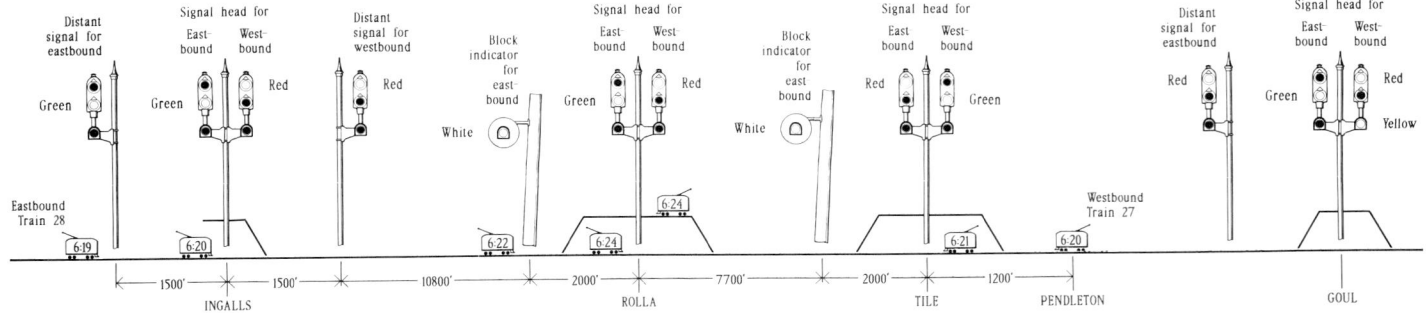

60

R OF LROAD
.POLIS DIVISION
). 208

This Time Table for the government of employees only.
Read Special Instructions and Rules Carefully.

EAST BOUND—Read Up

[Employees Timetable No. 208 — Eastbound schedule table for the Muncie-Anderson-Indianapolis Division, listing trains 2, 902, 4, 6, 300 (Note A), 8, 904, 10, 906, 12, 908, 14, 910, 16, 912 (Note B), 18, 914, 20, 916, 22, 918, 24, 920, 26, 28 (Note A), 922, 30, 924, 32, 926, 34, 928, 36, 930, with stations from Muncie (56.52 mi) through Shop, Hart (6 cars), Russ (5 cars), Yorktown (2 cars), Dolby (6 cars), Make, Glass (5 cars), Daleville (3 cars), Camp (10 cars), Chesterfield, House (5 cars), Pit, Cemetery (18 cars), Anderson Jct (DT), Anderson (DT), Belt, Taft (7 cars), Goul (7 cars), Pendleton (5 cars), Tile, Rolla (25 cars), Stone, Ingalls (3 cars), Dent (7 cars), Mur (6 cars), Fortville, Bucy (6 cars), McCordsv'le, Oaklandon (8 cars), Post (DT), Ft. Harrison (12 cars), Valley (DT), Lawrence (DT), Negley (4 cars), Long (DT), Indianapolis.]

C. C. LENTZ, Trainmaster.

---

switch points will take the siding unless otherwise directed. . . ." The illustration shows a portion of the Muncie-Anderson-Indianapolis Division's signaled territory with trains #27 and #28 in a scheduled meet at Rolla (Employees Timetable No. 208). Eastbound #28 approaching Ingalls would encounter a green distant signal, the equivalent of a "dark" (unlighted) block indicator at 6:19 PM. The Ingalls home and distant westbound signals would already be red, having been activated when the train passed Dent siding (west of

Right Over 200 miles of the Indiana Railroad System were protected by automatic track-circuit block signals which, along with an excellent train-order dispatching system, made the railroad one of the safest interurban train operations. *Roy G. Benedict*

Above A two-car *Dixie Flyer* en route to Louisville races past a clear block signal at Edinburg siding, outside the town of the same name, on July 3, 1938.
M. D. McCarter collection

Below Home Place, north of Indianapolis, had a hand-operated semaphore to assist passengers, day or night, to signal a train to stop. *James F. Cook photo*

Below This hand-operated semaphore protected the North Anderson streetcar line at the Pennsylvania Railroad switch to the power plant. *James F. Cook photo*

Above Economy and efficiency were achieved by mounting the color-light signal heads back-to-back on the same mast. This is Shop siding and wye west of Greencastle.
John F. Humiston photo

Ingalls). Passing the eastbound distant signal at Ingalls would activate the westbound siding signals at Rolla to show red. The operator of train #28 would find the signal at Ingalls to be green and, if on time, would pass at 6:20 PM. Westbound #27 would depart Pendleton at 6:20 PM heading for Tile. Approaching Rolla, #28's operator would see a block indicator which should show a white light if opposing train #27 was on time and had already passed the Tile siding signal at the scheduled 6:21 PM. Train #28 could pass the lighted indicator and approach Rolla to meet train #27 on schedule at 6:24 PM. Train #27 would take the siding at Rolla clearing the eastbound signal to green for train #28 to pass. After train #28 passed, the westbound signal would clear to green for train #27 to continue. If train #27 had been late, train #28 would have encountered a dark block indicator. The operator would have stopped short of the indicator and phoned the dispatcher. Unless the dispatcher ordered a changed meeting point, train #28 would wait for the indicator to light and then proceed to Rolla siding. If train #28 had passed the dark block indicator, it would automatically activate the westbound signal at Tile siding, stop the late train #27 and cause further delay.

The APB signals were installed on about half of the ISC Wabash Valley mileage and the Indianapolis-Terre Haute line. IR inherited the Union Traction-installed signals on most of the single track from Indianapolis to Muncie, Marion and Tipton. But no line had end-to-end protection. The Richmond line (mostly straight track along the National Road) had only a 3.2-mile segment. Perhaps the most astonishing omission was the Muncie-Fort Wayne section, a long, fast, cross-country line with no signals. Double track, such as several miles between Indianapolis and Post (near Fort Harrison), needed no signals by interurban standards. However, it was a territory of heavy traffic with suburban, local and limited passenger trains plus occasional freight trains. Within the double track, a crossover and junction, at Spring Valley, was protected.

Northern Indiana Power Company's predecessors had made two signal installations. APB signals were used for the first section of five miles. In a later seven-mile installation, USS TDB signals were used with Model 13 lights displaying red and green lenses (rather than the semaphores of the Louisville line). Indicator signals at switch locations used mini-semaphores.

No signals protected section crews because all section cars had insulated wheels which did not activate signals. Their operators had to know train scheduling, and train crews had to be advised when track workers might be on the line. Main track switches were not to be opened for section cars because a stop indication in both directions would result, possibly halting a train a few miles away. The rulebook said that section cars were to be lifted from one track to another. Because the track circuits could be activated by any piece of metal across the track, the section crews used insulated track gauges.

Right At Daleville, the station agent went out into the highway crossing to warn highway traffic of oncoming trains.
James F. Cook photo

Left A typical shelter at Kennard with a bell and light warning device. The four red lenses facing roadway traffic spelled out "STOP" while the end lights gave the motorman an indication that the crossing lights were working.
James F. Cook photo

Below At the Highway 67 crossing of the Muncie-New Castle line the modern flashers, among the last installed, were of the type still familiar today.
James F. Cook photo

Above Cartersburg station on the Terre Haute line. In Indiana, at that time, the board stenciled "DANGER" in red appeared under crossbucks. The birdhouse-like box on the pole next to car 427 contained a light for flagging trains at night. *James F. Cook photo*

The GRS main signal heads with their two lights and distinctive pointed hoods saw further use after the abandonment of the IR. Some, sold to the South Shore, served for forty years as dwarf signals or gate indicators. Later, these units appeared at the Illinois Railway Museum (Union, Illinois) where they govern the streetcar loop movements.

Nachod signals were used in several places on single-track city lines. In Terre Haute, Anderson and Muncie, Nachod signals controlled interurban movements on bi-directional city track. Some of these were installed after city car service had ceased. These signals operated from contactors on the trolley wire, were more feasible than the use of track circuits in paved streets and were less expensive. They helped avoid embarrassing meets along hilly or curved sections where sighting from one turnout to the next was impossible. Streetcar collisions were not serious factors. Trolley contactor signals counted cars in and out of signaled blocks so that following movements were possible.

Manually operated semaphores of several types had been used and a few were in place when IR assumed control. A few of them survived until the line was abandoned. Highway crossing warnings, another form of signals, ranged from a simple crossbuck to automatic crossing gates. The motorist was the greater problem at highway/railway crossings.

In general, Indiana Railroad used good, contemporary railroad practices to protect itself and its operations. In the four major areas described and others, the system was superior to almost all of the interurban rail lines.

Below Integration of the central Indiana interurbans resulted in scenes such as this view from February 17, 1934. A fine steel car, still in Union Traction's handsome deep red paint with a green roof, is found at the Terre Haute shop of the old THI&E. The euphonious–almost perfect–title is in gleaming gold leaf on the letterboard. *Glenn Niceley photo, George Krambles collection*

Chapter 4
The Highspeeds

Left Indiana Railroad's 35 new cars made an impressive appearance "coming at you" or from any other angle. At Cleve siding, north of Hartford City, on August 20, 1938, the operator's phone is plugged into the lineside jack to call the dispatcher. *George Krambles photo*

All of the Indiana Railroad System's rail rolling stock was put at the disposal of the System's management, creating one of the most intriguing melanges ever assembled. Much of the acquired Union Traction rolling stock was never used because it was already obsolete. Union Traction had a practice of retaining surplus equipment, and not even an extensive scrapping program in 1929 had eradicated the vestiges. Some open cars sitting in the yards dated from before the turn of the century. These and many similar vintage cars were quick candidates for scrapping at the Anderson Shops. The steel passenger cars from Interstate and Indiana Service Corporation joined the former Union Traction steel cars on most of the major runs and began appearing in many system-wide locations. The better wooden cars continued to work the lesser lines or plodded along on local trains.

Freight equipment was completely mixed among the lines, going wherever it was needed, without the earlier concerns that most motor cars remain on "home" trackage. Service equipment was treated in much the same way. Over the next three years, virtually all usable interurban equipment was assigned a new Indiana Railroad System number although many were never repainted, renumbered or used in System operations.

Losing services were eliminated and it was only a matter of time before the costly parlor/dining car service was eliminated. These cars were taken off on December 1, 1930 because the service was not profitable. A large part of the expense was crew cost. The Indianapolis-Louisville sleeping cars continued a little longer because they consistently had high occupancy. There were three of these ten-section sleeping cars with the unusual windows in the upper berths. One car was spotted each evening, for early boarding, at Louisville and Indianapolis on an out-of-the-way track until the departure of the last train of the evening. It was rare, if ever, that anyone boarded the sleepers outside of the two terminals. The cars were set-out (northbound at Greenwood Shops and southbound at Scottsburg Shops) and picked up by the first train in the morning so the occupants had an early arrival. The service continued until late 1932 when, long after the introduction of one-man cars, the service was ended to reduce high crew costs and release the heavy motor passenger cars, used for pulling the sleepers, for use elsewhere.

Sam Insull, Jr. and Bob Feustel reviewed the passenger cars and decided they needed to make a drastic change in the service and the type of equipment used. Insull knew of the 1924 ISC and Union Traction joint plan for medium-weight passenger equipment. Only ISC took any steps by purchasing, from St. Louis Car Company, ten cars designed by Arthur Redderson, Superintendent of Motive Power for ISC. Six of the bright red cars went to the ISC-managed Fort Wayne-Lima Railroad and the other four, after running tests on the main line, became orphans, finally finding a home on the ISC Northern Division. Later, Union Traction and ISC bought heavy steel cars that used a two-man crew. These cars were more expensive to run and provided none of the imagination needed to attract and hold riders. So the new management initiated a study of the newer interurban cars' designs. Within a few days after Indiana Railroad assumed control, a test was made using the hottest new car available. This was arranged through the friendly association between Dr. Thomas Conway and the Insull group. Conway had unified a group of Ohio interurbans into one company called the Cincinnati & Lake Erie Railroad (C&LE). A major modernization step had been a purchase of twenty fast one-man lightweight interurban cars. Conway loaned one of them to Indiana Railroad for a test.

Car 128, one of the C&LE coach-parlor units, was brought to Fort Wayne over the connecting Fort Wayne-Lima Railroad. This fast, brilliant red car, along with its sister cars, was making a spectacular showing on the Ohio system. The cars, affectionately known as "Red Devils" by employees and the public, were compact in design, offered a comfortable ride and had been an instant hit with the riding public. A careful study was made of car 128 after it arrived at ISC's Spy Run shops on August 6. The car with Feustel, Redderson and others was run to Indianapolis as an "extra" to check clearances over the route through Muncie and Anderson. At Indianapolis, Feustel was joined by Sam Insull, Jr., Henry Bucher, W. A. Sauer, Col. R. H. James (chief of traffic for all Insull properties) and some twenty other staff people.

The 128 with its special party left the Indianapolis Traction Terminal on the morning of August 7, and sped north to Noblesville, Kokomo and Peru. This line was very typical of the IR trackage. At Peru the car turned west to Logansport and Lafayette. The Logansport-Lafayette section had some of the best trackage in the state with long tangents of private right-of-way. Going and coming from Lafayette the 128 had an excellent chance to show its acceleration and speed capabilities in excess of 70 mph. On the return, the car went through Peru and up the Wabash valley to Fort Wayne, where the impressive trial ended. The car was then returned to the C&LE, but not before Feustel was interviewed. The Fort Wayne *Journal-Gazette* quoted him, "The Cincinnati & Lake Erie car yesterday proved to show the most satisfactory tests of all the new equipment tried out thus far on the ISC lines."

What had been tried? The system's principal mainline trains were being run with heavy-weight steel cars ranging from four to seventeen years old. With them, running time reductions were currently being made on the *Hoosierland* and the *Wabash Valley Flyer* (Indianapolis-Fort Wayne) and the *Dixie Flyer* and *Hoosier*

Above Car 432 with parlor cars "Purdue" and "Indiana" at Indianapolis for a special trip in 1933. In regular service, on Sundays, three-car Indianapolis-Fort Wayne trains with two heavy steel cars and a parlor trailer were the rule as late as 1931. *George K. Bradley collection*

Flyer (Indianapolis-Louisville). But heavy steel two-man cars would not be considered.

Indiana Railroad had several lightweight car philosophies to consider. Two alternative car types were already on the system; their capabilities and limitations were known. Operated by only one man, they embodied the very lightest and medium-weight cars.

The Marion & Bluffton division had two one-man interurban cars—really little more than rural streetcars. Slow and not particularly comfortable, the four-year-old cars were satisfactory for the lightly traveled route but would not be suitable for longer lines.

The ISC 323-series car were of medium weight; they were very successful, could run 55 mph, and gave travel times as quick as the traditional heavy cars. Their easy-riding trucks showed that careful design and balance of the running gear improved the marketability of travel. Riding had increased and operating costs dropped when the cars were introduced in 1924 to the ISC Northern Division. In 1928 the cars were given new interiors, new motors and remodelled for one-man service.

The Cincinnati Car Company was a leading builder of advanced lightweight cars, notably the "curved-side" design. In Indiana it was best exemplified by the Indianapolis & Southeastern's cars of 1929. The System's design and mechanical people were familiar with them. They also watched the new C&LE cars which embodied Dr. Conway's ideas and Cincinnati's best engineering. Through Conway's cooperation, the specifications were already at Fort Wayne or were brought along with the 128 on August 6. Besides the Indianapolis trip, that car was evaluated on several Fort Wayne-Bluffton runs by engineering and operating people.

The System's car design group would be at Fort Wayne, where Arthur Redderson headed the ISC engineering team. New designs for city cars as well as medium and heavy-weight interurbans had come from the ISC's engineers. The Union Traction shop was good at rebuilding but had no significant experience with lightweight interurban cars. The Interstate's main line was almost exclusively operated with very heavy steel cars which were still preferred by most of their management. The Insull companies—whose talents were often shared—used heavy cars for high-density-traffic lines around Chicago. Gary Railways had been re-equipped with lightweight city and interurban cars by the Insulls, but its short runs were comparable with the Marion & Bluffton—certainly not with the main IR routes.

By the end of August (the cover carries the penciled date), a typewritten "Specification Covering Ten (10) Single End, Double Truck De Luxe Interurban Cars Approximately 46 ft Long Overall for the Indiana Service Corporation" appeared. A two-page "addenda" described "Fifteen Single End, Double Truck De Luxe 'Local' Interurban Cars," similar but with a rear baggage compartment. The specifications called for steel sheets and steel shapes rather than the C&LE's aluminum sheets on steel structure. Staff people suggested modifications (at least nine different handwriting styles appear).

From the very start a number of modifications were made. Most obvious was the decision to give the new car design a rounded rear end as opposed to the flat, bus-style rear of the C&LE cars. The rounded rear was dictated for more than a cosmetic appearance as Indiana Railroad wanted the cars to operate in multiple unit and the specifications called for Ohio Brass Com-

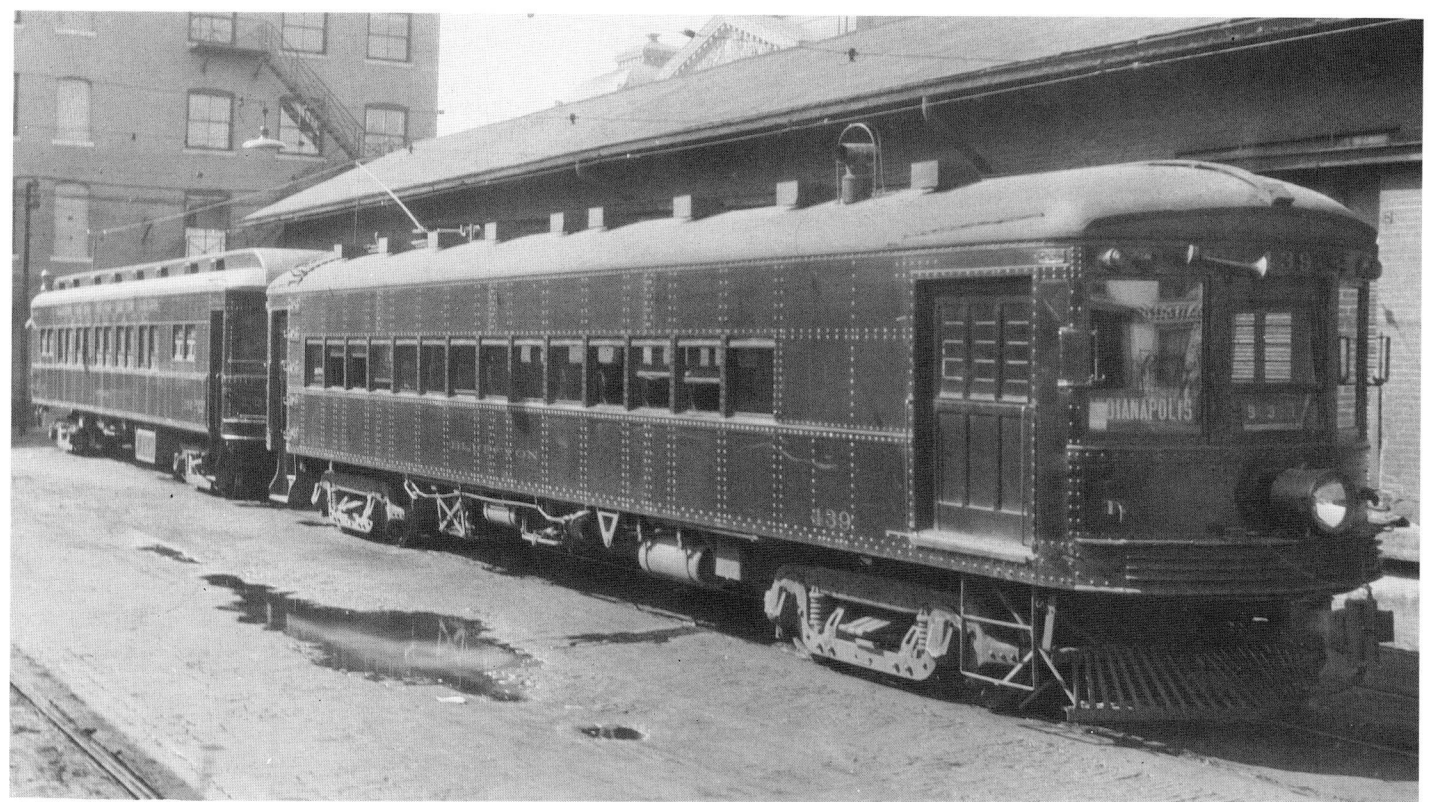

Above One of the Interstate's three sleeping cars with car 439. The Union Traction name has been painted out on the 439 but it has not been relettered. The company name on the sleeping cars was not changed as the service lasted only until late 1932. *George Krambles collection*

pany's No. 10 Tomlinson couplers with electric control and bus line circuits. The company apparently anticipated traffic at current levels which often required two- and three-car trains of the heavy cars.

Designing continued through the fall. Trucks for 35 cars, plus two spare trucks, were ordered by ISC from General Steel Castings Company on October 8, 1930. This date shows that many ideas were already firm.

Revised specifications dated December 30, 1930, for 14 de luxe coach-parlor cars and 21 de luxe coach-baggage cars incorporated most of the pencil notes on the earlier set. The December 30 cover sheets name Indiana Railroad and the builders, American Car & Foundry Company (ACF) at Jeffersonville, IN for the 14 cars and Pullman Car & Manufacturing Company at Chicago for the 21 cars. These December revisions were sent to the builders for development of their own shop specifications. Both firms were to coordinate details, making the two groups as similar in appearance and appointments as practical.

Some of the components were already proven by use on the C&LE. For example, ten of the C&LE cars (coach-baggage cars 110-119) had General Electric equipment: four 600-volt 100-horsepower 706A motors and controls. Coach-parlor cars (120-129) had Westinghouse apparatus: four 300-volt 100-horsepower 539 motors and HLF control. The car tested in Indiana during August was from the latter group. IR chose GE 706 motors and Westinghouse HLF control for all of its new cars.

Indiana Railroad's cars were considerably improved C&LE cars. Dimensions and general arrangement were similar to the Ohio line's popular "Red Devils" but the bodies varied in structure as well as in appearance. Intended for three-car multiple-unit train operation, they had center sills suitable for the resulting transmitted stresses. Four-car trains were run on several occasions with the motors of the fourth car cut out so that it was pulled as a trailer. The brakes were really not well suited for more than three-car trains. The MU operation was an important improvement over the C&LE cars, which could not be run in trains. All-aluminum body framing and sheathing avoided the C&LE cars' eventual electrolytic corrosion. Notwithstanding the aluminum construction, the newer cars weighed two tons more than the C&LE's.

Exterior and interior lighting of the IR cars was powered by a 32-volt battery charged by a motor-generator, whereas the lights on most interurban cars were energized from the trolley. Dimming of lights due to line voltage fluctuations or a loss of lights, including the headlight, if the trolley dewired was a weakness of the C&LE cars that did not occur on the IR cars.

A major difference was the use of newly designed Commonwealth trucks from General Steel Castings Company. A longer wheelbase, equalization bars and totally different springing provided improvements over the C&LE cars' Cincinnati Car Company trucks. The trucks were put to an early test. C&LE car 114 was sent to Spy Run shops on February 16, 1931. Its controls (unlike the HLF control on the C&LE) were compatible with the IR's 600-volt motors. The 114 was placed on the spare set of Commonwealth trucks. On February 22 it went to Indianapolis by way of Muncie and returned the following day on the same route. The trips were record-breaking runs. The car was then run on the ISC near Fort Wayne for several days including trips to Bluffton and return. On March 2 and 3 another Indianapolis run was made. This time a number of officials joined motorman Emory Ross. The terminal-to-terminal time was cut to 3 hours 11 minutes, several minutes faster than the previous speed run. Valuable schedule information was gained. No difficulties were noted. The officials were delighted with the performance of the new trucks and the prospect offered by the new cars. The 114, restored to its own trucks, was returned to C&LE.

Meanwhile the public perception of a super interurban was being cultivated: "$1,000,000 Order Placed for Interurban Cars." (The actual cost was $986,545.) That press release of January 10 described the 35 new cars as incorporating the most advanced features of high-speed interurban cars designed for one-man operation. Everyone connected with Indiana Railroad waited for the biggest step of the year 1931: the arrival of the cars. The ACF plant at Jeffersonville was practically on the System's tracks. The cars were run under their own power, in trains of two and three cars, starting the second week of July. Public Service Company crews took the cars to Indianapolis where IR men took over for the trip to Anderson. There the cars received a final pre-service check.

Delivering the Pullman-built cars presented a greater problem though they also came on their own wheels. There was no continuous 600-volt rail connection from Chicago. The new cars had Tomlinson couplers (similar to those on the Illinois Central Railroad suburban electric cars) providing mechanical, electrical and pneumatic connections but preventing direct coupling with standard railroad cars. Three-car trains with a combination knuckle fitted over the coupler at one end were delivered by the Pullman Railroad to the 1500-volt South Shore Line near the Pullman plant. A South Shore locomotive towed the cars to an interchange on the west side of South Bend.

From here the cars were run under their own power by John Armstrong, an Indiana Railroad (ISC) motorman, and a second IR man, sometimes Russell Powell. Powell described how the trains ran over the Northern Indiana Railway, Inc. to Goshen, then over the Winona Railroad to Peru, carrying a home road trainman as a pilot on each line. On the Winona two of each car's four motors were cut out because of chronic low voltage. At Peru the cars moved onto Indiana Service Corporation en route to Spy Run shop in Fort Wayne. Over ISC, with all the motors cut in, Armstrong ran the cars up to a good speed. Beginning the first week in July, seven trips were made to deliver the 21 cars.

The Fort Wayne visit was intended for a routine check and test running but a severe problem was found. On one of the first Fort Wayne-Bluffton test trips, some 1500 feet of rail was loosened due to oscillation in the new trucks. After that each car was carefully checked. The swing links of the trucks were modified. The problem seemed solved, but the company kept a track walker out to watch for any damage during the break-in trips. Test runs were made using a three-car train loaded with sand bags to approximate a full passenger complement. Starting on July 14, break-in runs were extended to Anderson to try new schedules, using cars 50, 65 and 66, the ones first delivered. They were run as second sections of regular trains or as extras and used two-man crews, as did the regular service.

Enhancing the new image, the cars introduced the brilliant vermillion-orange and green paint scheme. They also had a singular monogram, newly created for the company. Stylized letters "I" and "R" with an arrow

Below The lightweight, but fairly slow-speed, Marion and Bluffton 202 on Washington Street in Bluffton. This car became the property of the Indiana Service Corporation and was later used, occasionally, on the Northern Division. *Berner/Maguire collection*

passing horizontally through the center and pointing toward the front of the car appeared in the green paint with silver accents. Three trains of one coach-baggage and one observation-lounge car were displayed at strategic points along the Indianapolis-Muncie-Fort Wayne and Indianapolis-Louisville routes from July 18 to July 25. Special trips were made for the press, city officials and civic leaders. An estimated 20,000 people toured the new cars.

Nevertheless the press in 1931 was blasé. Times had changed: 25 years before, the arrival of four parlor cars for the Wabash Valley line had merited several front page columns in the Fort Wayne newspapers. Now 35 superior cars rated only an inside story, complimentary but not written with the enthusiasm of earlier years.

The Company prepared a take-one folder for its riders. *Hoosier Traveler* Number 1 (July 1931) offered a glowing description of the cars:

MODERN ELECTRIC CARS INTRODUCE NEW ERA IN SWIFT, COMFORTABLE TRANSPORTATION

". . . Nothing like these new cars has ever before been offered the traveling public in Indiana. They mark a complete new step—a new conception—in effortless, fast, safe transportation. . . .

Greater Speed

"Answering the modern demand for quick, safe transportation, the 35 new deluxe cars have been equipped with specially designed and constructed motors, capable of driving them at speeds of 70 miles an hour and more.

"In addition to the powerful motors, a streamlined exterior with rounded contours reduces wind resistance and adds to the speed of the cars. They have a remarkably rapid pickup after a stop and soon reach full speed.

A Higher Factor of Safety

"After long research and experiment, the new cars have been equipped with a number of safety devices designed to insure safe travel at increased speed.

"A new type air brake with double shoes clasping both sides of each wheel has been used. In addition each car has a system of electro-magnetic brakes, which create a magnetic field between a special shoe and the rails, thus adding to the certainty of control. . . .

"If for any reason the motorman's hand on the controller releases its tension, the current driving the car is immediately shut off, and the brakes applied automatically until the car comes to a complete stop.

Comfort in a New Sense

"No detail has been overlooked in a determined effort to make these cars express the utmost in travel comfort, attractiveness and beauty.

"Fourteen of the cars are equipped with a special observation-lounge compartment occupying the rear third of the car space. . . . The observation-lounge compartments will be available to all passengers without extra charge.

Below The 324 turning onto Pearl Street in Fort Wayne from the storage tracks at the old freight terminal. This ISC car was an extremely successful modernization and one-manning of a two-man medium-weight car.   *M. D. McCarter collection*

Above Indianapolis & Southeastern Railroad's new lightweight car 220 at the Cincinnati Car Company in 1928. Because of "nosing," improved arch-bar trucks were substituted on all 13 cars beginning in December 1930.
M. D. McCarter collection

Beauty Surrounds Traveler

"The luxury, comfort and delightful ease of the observation-lounge compartments defy description. Thick carpeting covers the floor. The pattern of the carpet blends artistically with the two-tone shading of the walls and ceiling, which varies in each car to complete an attractive, modernistic color scheme.

"A number of solid American walnut tables support reading lamps and afford convenient space for reading matter and small parcels. Deeply upholstered chairs and a pair of tapestry divans complete the furnishings in the compartment. Narrow sills and wide expanses of crystal clear glass afford an uninterrupted view of the countryside.

"In the coach compartments of both the observation-lounge and standard cars are individual easy seats of air-cushioned leather. Headrests on each chair and arm rests at the sides assure complete relaxation.

Clear Vision Afforded

"The car windows are higher and wider than those of previously used equipment. Ventilators in the cars assure a constant supply of fresh air regardless of open or closed windows. In the summer electric fans furnish cooling breezes. In the winter the cars are heated by electricity . . . .

"The new cars are 8 feet 9 inches wide by 46 feet in length, and have two four-wheel trucks. They weigh 25 tons. The passenger capacity of the observation-lounge compartments is 10, and of the coach compartment in the same type cars, 28. The passenger capacity of the standard coaches is 40."

"Fordization of the interurban lines by replacing heavy rolling stock with lightweight equipment and speeding service to 65 and 75 mph was the plan announced by Robert Feustel." That statement had appeared almost a year earlier in the August 1, 1930 Fort Wayne *News Sentinel* when the company had announced it was studying new car designs. Now the new cars entered Indianapolis-Fort Wayne service on July 27.

This route, having two maintenance points and consisting mostly of IR's own trackage, was the logical start-up point. Four trains each way, using the coach-parlor cars, carried the *Hoosierland* name and covered the route in 3 hours 5 minutes on one train and 3 hours 10 minutes on the others. The Louisville line received the new cars on August 3. As soon as enough cars were available, four southbound *Dixie Flyers* and four northbound *Hoosier Flyers* covered the distance in three hours retaining the names associated with the limited service. With all 35 cars on hand it was possible to operate all trains on the two routes with the light, low-floor cars. In turn, the higher, heavier steel cars displaced wooden cars from through runs on other lines. Very few wooden passenger cars remained active.

The new cars did not solve the long-time problem of serving local passengers. Limited trains, such as the *Hoosierland,* were scheduled to make only designated station stops. The new capabilities improved the running times between towns and boosted overall train speeds. Those who rode frequently may have known which trains made all stops. However, the occasional short-haul passenger comprised much of the traffic. He would try to flag down a limited train at a country stop only to have the car race past. Perplexed and angry, he was left to wait for the next train, perhaps more than hour behind. Without a timetable, he could only hope it was not another limited. Eventually IR responded by leaving enough slack in the schedule to allow all trains to make some extra flag stops.

After a few months the company realized that it had plenty of the coach-parlor cars. Without baggage, mail and express space the fast name trains could accommo-

Above One of the "Red Devils" in a posed publicity photo taken at the Cincinnati & Lake Erie Railroad shops near Dayton, Ohio when the car was new. The 112 was one of the coach-baggage cars. *Jack Keenan collection*

date people with hand luggage but not the commercial traveler with display trunks. The coach-baggage cars were more versatile. Later some of the coach-parlor cars were converted to that form.

The many virtues of the new equipment were not lost on the operators. "Operator" became the new job title for the drivers of the one-man cars. The "operator" title also applied to work on the second and third car of a train of the new cars: operating the doors, "lifting tickets" (collecting fares) and assisting with switches at meets. All operators received the same rate of pay. The classifications "motorman," "conductor" and "brakeman" remained in use for crews of two or more men on the old cars and freight or work trains.

Below Coach-parlor 58 north of Bluffton on August 20, 1938. Seven-year-old car was in excellent condition. *John F. Humiston photo*

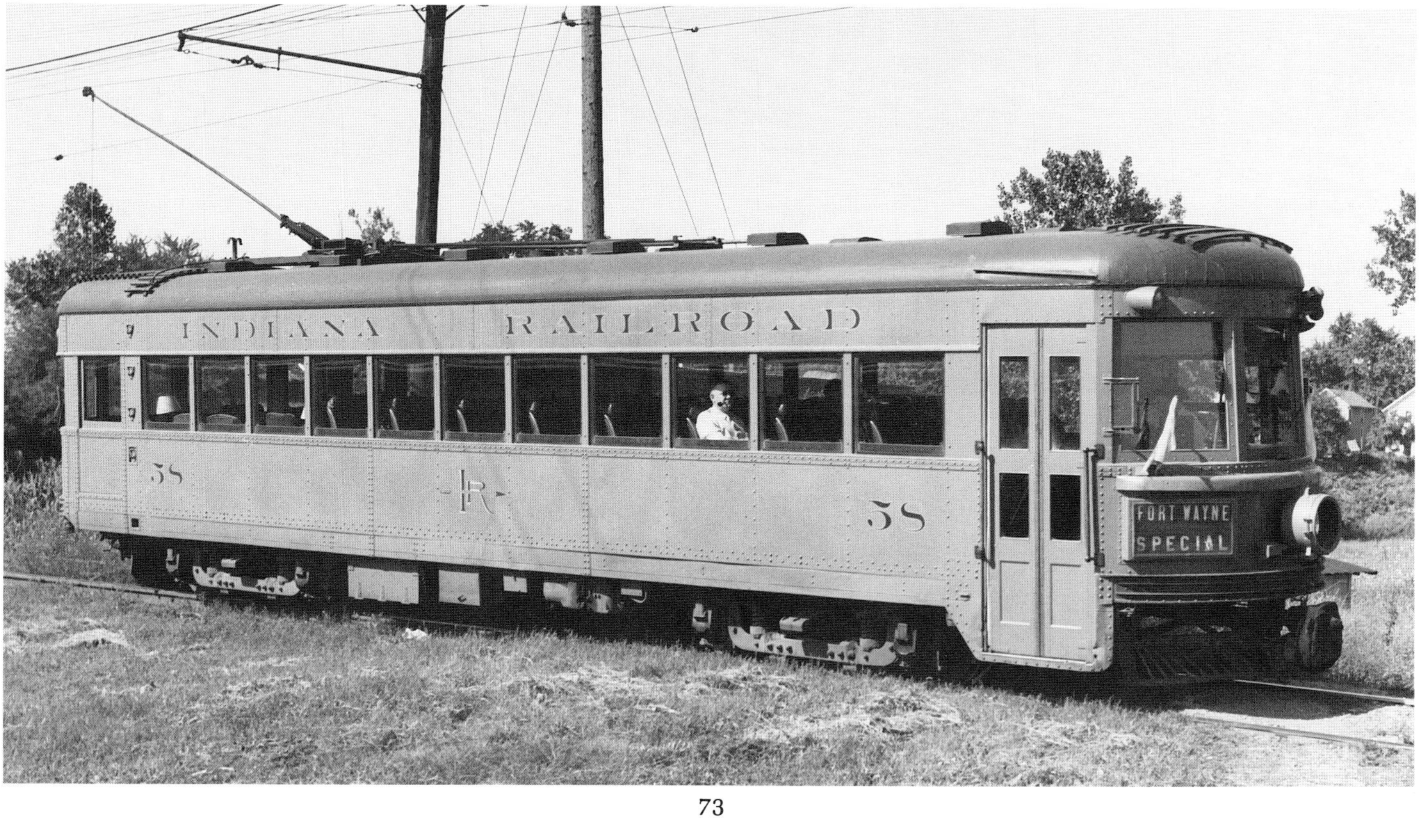

Above The well designed and placed operator's controls and the Ohmer ticket printing fare register of highspeed 59 in 1937.
John F. Humiston photo

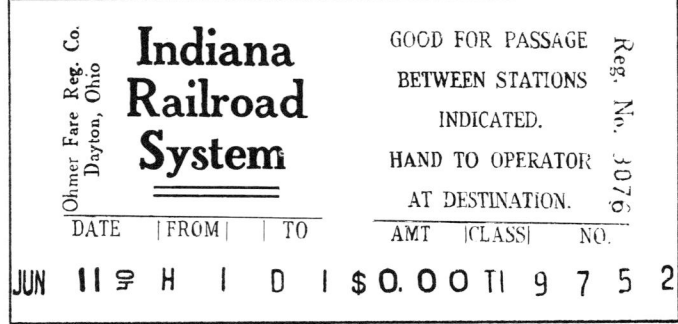

Above The Ohmer fare registers printed tickets in purple ink on goldenrod paper. This example, issued from H-1 (Fort Wayne) to D-1 (Indianapolis), was a seat check in exchange for a ticket (TI) previously bought at an agency. The same form served as a cash fare receipt for direct fare payment. *Herbert G. Harnish*

C&LE cars roamed over the IR lines. A special Toledo-Lima-Fort Wayne-Fort Harrison run was made on June 19, 1931 using three C&LE coach-parlor cars to move 125 Citizens Military Training Camp students. While on IR each car required a two-man crew because one-man operation was not instituted until the mid-July introduction of the highspeeds. The C&LE cars returned to Ohio after the trip as the students were not scheduled to return until mid-July. C&LE 129 went south from Fort Wayne, as an extra, at 4:00 AM on July 19 and returned north at 10:30 AM, probably with some of the students.

The highspeeds began to show up in the company promotional activities. Two large illuminated signs appeared in Anderson. One was on the exterior wall of the Anderson station and the other was a large billboard near the freight house. Both featured the new highspeeds. There is some indication that other billboard signs and colorful posters. similar to the successful South Shore Line's promotional activities, were

Below A company publicity view showing the new coach-parlor interior from the front platform. The passengers are employees and members of their families. Charles Lentz is the man in the straw "sailor." *George K. Bradley collection*

The new cars were lively in the hands of a good operator. They accelerated quickly, reached 80 mph and braked rapidly. Even so it took alert driving to meet the new faster schedules. The cars were so different that they soon earned the name "highspeeds," thereby placing a new word in the railway lexicon.

The highspeeds were popular for special parties. They had a chance to leave the system as IR and C&LE handled each other's charter runs. A coach-parlor car carried a party from the Muncie Gear Company to Columbus, Ohio to see the Ohio State-Northwestern football game on October 24, 1931. The car departed Muncie at 6 AM (Central Time) and arrived at Columbus at 12:15 PM (Eastern Time). A thirty-minute break for lunch, near Columbus, meant that the 170-mile trip was covered in under five hours. After the game, the car left the Columbus terminal at 4:37 PM, made a two-hour dinner stop at Springfield, arriving at Muncie at 12:15 AM. The trip over the Dayton & Western and C&LE was a nice outing for the charter group and a chance for the new highspeeds to be admired.

Right Members of the Fort Wayne city council and local newspaper men were given a special demonstration run on July 18, 1931. Train operation still required a two-man crew and they were V. F. "Vern" Ramey and H. F. "Pat" Howey.
George K. Bradley collection

Left The Anderson passenger station received a painted advertising sign. Even though the tracks were in the streets, canopies provided shelter near the northbound (at left) and southbound (foreground) loading points. These niceties were not available after the passenger terminal was moved to the nearby freight house. *George K. Bradley collection*

Below A billboard in front of the freight house a few hundred feet up the street reinforced the message. Later the passenger facilities were moved to space in this building. *George K. Bradley collection*

Above At Fort Wayne's three-track terminal on September 20, 1933, the Indianapolis via Muncie route was assigned the highspeeds while the Indianapolis via Peru route continued to use the heavy steel cars until 1935. *Clyde E. Helms photo, James P. Shuman collection*

planned. The company also sponsored an employee basketball team, the "Indiana Railroad Arrows."

Faster speeds presented a rising problem with motor vehicles. Trucks and buses were controlled as the Public Service Commission's regulations provided a reasonable containment of intercity truck and bus competitors and, in many cases, the sheer cost of operations had kept these firms small and marginal operations. Indiana Motor Transit Company, the former Union Traction and Interstate bus lines protected part of the system from further bus competition. Intercity trucks were still limited by small capacity and inadequate roads although Indiana's extensive highway building program of the late twenties now linked most larger towns and cities.

The automobile, due to these road improvements, presented the real problem as it stole passengers from both the interurban and the motor bus. Often they were dangerously operated and represented a new peril. The auto had to be registered and carry a license plate but formal training and regulation of drivers was virtually non-existent. The ability to get a car going was about all that was required. People accustomed to driving a team of horses sometimes forgot that they had to watch the road ahead at all times. In many cases drivers just became inattentive and acted as though their auto was the only one on the road. This unconscious contempt led to many one- and two-car auto accidents. Where the interurban paralleled the highway or ran in the middle of the roadway it did so at the risk of collision with a careless driver. When it came to motor traffic and interurban confrontations, the big steel interurban cars held a slight advantage over the smaller and lower highspeeds.

The interurban car operators were beyond blame in most accidents. Some operators, who did not take erratic drivers into consideration, were not prepared to avert an accident by slowing or sounding the car's air horn. The company's level rail-highway crossings took a death toll because drivers did not see the train or tried to beat it. Each accident caused damage to the rail car and usually delayed the train. Sometimes the entire line was tied up until the damaged interurban was free to move. The company, on one hand, pushed the operators to keep on schedule and, on the other hand, held safety meetings with company officials stressing that it was better to proceed with caution and be late.

Operators and motormen earned an impressive system-wide safety record under Indiana Railroad management aided by good train dispatching, the many miles of signal controlled track and the interlocking plants that protected many railroad crossings.

Two types of train-stopping derail devices were used at railroad crossings. Split-rail derails were the most common type used. When open, the trucks of a car that failed to stop would hit the ties and bring the train to an abrupt halt. The "toad" derail frog, used at some points, could tip a car or damage the car trucks. The Lagro interlocking between the ISC and the Wabash used a toad until the early thirties. Motorman Heine Trip was on a two-man car and busy talking to a crew member riding in the front cab of the car. Motormen were never supposed to converse with passengers and were to keep crew conversations to a minimum. Trip missed seeing the signal for the Lagro crossing until he saw a Wabash local freight approaching at a leisurely pace and with a clear signal. He applied the air too late and the sudden brake applications caused the brake rigging to pull tight and hold that position which jerked the trucks out straight and nearly rigid. With several sharp bumps the car wheels slid over the toad without derailing the car. It stopped before reaching the crossing. It also brought a company official out of the passenger compartment to ask some embarrassing questions.

One-man car operators had to talk to passengers but conversation was supposed to be kept minimal and to business at hand. That was a hard rule as most operators were friendly and got to know their regular passengers. Conversation could be a distraction as operator Eli Applegate learned. Talking to a passenger, he failed to notice the derail at Race siding. The Company got the car rerailed and Eli got a ten-day, no-pay vacation. Bill Frazee made an even bigger mistake at Dent siding on the Indianapolis-Anderson division. Dent had spring switches on both ends of a pull-through siding. The switches were good for 25 to 30 mph. Frazee's highspeed roared into the switch at close to 50 mph when he hit the air brakes. The trucks locked in a straightened position by the emergency application, rode over the top of the rail and sent the car, upright, into a corn field.

Once in a while those in control of the trains were surprised. Ernest Wills, the company's chief signal maintenance man, recorded the surprise of Frank Cain. Cain came on duty as the night operator at the Monon Railroad interlocker south of Carmel at midnight on October 26, 1935. It was chilly so he stoked the fire in the stove and unknown to him, on the roof as well. At 1:30 he discovered the entire roof was on fire. Except for a few papers, grabbed in a hasty exit, everything went up in flames leaving charred embers and twisted machinery. Until Wills and his crew could install a new crossing signal the company set out a flag shanty and borrowed a stove from the Monon. Flags were put out and both the Monon and Indiana Railroad trains made a positive stop at the crossing to receive clearance. The new signal was not put into service until June 25, 1936. There is little doubt that, for its time, Indiana Railroad's system operations were run with care and efficiency. Management's efforts to insure good operation met with virtually universal support from all the employees.

During the early years there was a car/dog story that made good human interest copy for a slow news day. Fresh in from a trip, a car was spotted over one of the shop pits when the car inspectors heard a plaintive wail from above one of the car trucks. To their surprise they found a terrier puppy, trembling and oil-spattered, sitting on top of the front truck. No one knew how long he had ridden in that spot or how he had survived. Rescued, he was found to be none the worse for the ride and was taken home by one of the shop workmen.

When the highspeeds arrived and the THI&E was acquired, Indiana Railroad was at its zenith as Midland United's super interurban. Before the THI&E purchase the company had owned approximately 290 route miles of interurbans and the original "system" totalled nearly 650 route miles in length. The new acquisition gained 137 new route miles plus the operation of 36 more miles west of Brazil controlled by Public Service Company. The Indiana Railroad System briefly contained over 850 route miles plus eleven city operations, in June 1931. From this pinnacle the mighty Midwestern rail system began a near-decade-long roller coaster ride.

Below The big steel cars at the Indianapolis Traction Terminal were soon joined by the highspeeds as shown in this November 1932 photo. Wooden cars were no longer seen here in regular service. *Robert V. Mehlenbeck photo*

Chapter 5
The Roller Coaster

Left Highspeed 52 as Train 8 at Anderson on July 4, 1938.
John F. Humiston photo

The second half of 1931 saw a change in Indiana Railroad but it was, for the most part, a series of controlled, orderly plans developed largely by Robert Feustel and executed by Henry Bucher and his staff. Putting the new cars into service would be the primary positive step. Along with the acquisition of the THI&E properties, it would be a wonderful summer!

The highspeeds were the last hurrah for the country interurban in the United States. And what splendid cars they were! They quickly showed that they could run fast, had remarkable acceleration, were very comfortable and were nothing like anything else that ever burnished the rails. The proportions were just right, with rounded contours and a sturdy, solid appearance. This compact design made them, in the eyes of many, the best lightweight cars ever built. A half century has not changed that opinion.

The THI&E purchase brought in more rolling stock. The cars immediately acquired from the predecessor companies came to just under 500 units. The THI&E interurban passenger cars were reasonably maintained, but ancient, wooden cars (none newer than 1908) that had had hard use and required constant attention to keep them running. Technically, all of the rolling stock (interurban passenger cars, city and suburban cars plus many freight and service cars) went into service on the Indiana Railroad. In practice, many cars saw little, if any, further service. Some were treated in the same manner as the older Union Traction cars and had the THI&E herald and car names painted over and the new company name added. Most of them remained in service on the same lines as before. By November, wooden cars had been replaced on the Indianapolis-Terre Haute run by steel passenger cars displaced from the Louisville line. A substantial amount of usable freight equipment also came into the company's fold and most of it was kept in service. The THI&E's 600 had been built as Hugh McGowan's private car shortly before his death in 1911. It was an outstanding example of the craftsmanship of the Cincinnati Car Company. Modified for charter service, it continued in use but the demand was very light and the 600 was retired in 1933.

Indiana Motor Transit Company, now an IR subsidiary, had 31 motor coaches for its routes. These, added to the 51 ex-Union Traction buses, gave IR a fleet of 82 motor coaches.

With all of the equipment available, the company could have run the system for some time. It included a number of fairly new steel cars which, with some effort, could be changed to one-man operation. Instead, new cars had been added to the system. Obviously Sam Insull, Jr. and Robert Feustel had looked ahead because the 35 new cars were more than needed for the full schedules on the two long lines they had in 1931. There were probably enough highspeeds for one more route.

Feustel's "Fordization" was also hitting the new highways, siphoning off more and more riders. The cash expenditure for the highspeeds was, in retrospect, an error–a most fortunate one for riders and railfans–based on early optimism that the highspeeds would turn the tide against declining ridership.

Sam Insull, Jr. reflected, nearly fifty years later, that his approving Feustel's purchase of the cars was wrong. "We took the route of putting new lightweight equipment on the Indiana Railroad. That was my mistake. We failed to see the effect of the swing to automobile passenger equipment." He also speculated that had this million dollars been invested in track improvements to increase coal traffic, interesting possibilities might have appeared. The Insulls had, however, taken a positive viewpoint on the interurbans they controlled. They introduced a high standard of service to their operations. Courtesy was also a hallmark of passenger service crews on the Insull lines.

The Insull companies owned a number of scattered small properties that were abandoned early because of their hopeless situation. In Indiana, Midland United decided to retain and modernize those interurban lines that were, and could remain, profitable. This optimistic viewpoint that a substantial investment should be given a full chance to prove itself was based on an assumption that the economics of the 1920's would continue. The situation by 1931 was changing much faster than Sam Insull, Jr. or Robert Feustel had expected or imagined.

Reduced ridership due to the national economy in general and the private auto in particular cost further declines in the revenue. The first loss of major consequence occurred when one of the two connections to the Ohio interurban lines went bankrupt. The Fort Wayne-Lima Railroad was under ISC supervision and coordinated with the System operations. It slipped into receivership in June 1931, largely because a complaint charged the company owed a $65,000 power bill for 1930 and had operated at a net loss in 1930. The other connection to Ohio, the 39-mile Dayton & Western (from Dayton to Richmond) had fallen into receivership on February 6, 1931. Dr. Conway recognized the value of the D&W connection between his C&LE lines and the Indiana Railroad. The D&W receiver turned the supervision of the line over to the C&LE. Conway held this interstate link with the assumption that Feustel would hold the Fort Wayne-Lima line.

The Indiana Railroad System started the anticipated paring of some previously marginal, and now definitely unprofitable, branches. The Tipton-Alexandria line terminated passenger service on June 30, 1931. Trackage on Monroe Street, in Alexandria, was removed on August 24 requiring the still operating freight service to be routed via Tipton. Freight service lasted until March 2, 1932 to allow existing freight customers at locations such as Elwood and Orestes to make other arrangements. The six miles from Elwood to Orestes probably remained somewhat longer, in serviceable

Above THI&E's fine private car went into Indiana Railroad charter service, and was one of the most handsome of the wooden interurban cars. The 600 had been built as a business car for Hugh McGowan in 1911.
George Krambles collection

condition, for the continued movement of gravel trains. Western Indiana Gravel Company's electric railroad operation at Dundee, west of Orestes, continued to move gravel from their operation to the Nickel Plate Railroad. IR closed its shop facilities at Tipton in September 1931. The Eaton shop building, used for storage of old wooden cars, remained open through 1932.

The Public Service Commission authorized the abandonment of the ISC-owned Marion & Bluffton line effective August 16, 1931. The termination of this unprofitable operation punched a hole, at least on the map, in the system's network of rail lines. Buses operated by Marion's O. E. Thomas took over the through Marion-Bluffton service although, in this case, there was no directly paralleling highway. The potential of the Marion & Bluffton had never been very good. This line had ISC's first one-man cars which, with the ISC Northern Division cars, were the System's first one-man operations. Only two cars, with an old wooden car for a spare, were needed for the regular Marion-Bluffton passenger schedule.

Below Highspeed 65 and bus 69 in the car storage area west of the old freight house, south of Ohio Street, in Indianapolis. Bus 69, a 1925 Mack model AB parlor coach, came to Union Traction in 1926 from Hoosier Stage Lines.
Ewing Dale photo

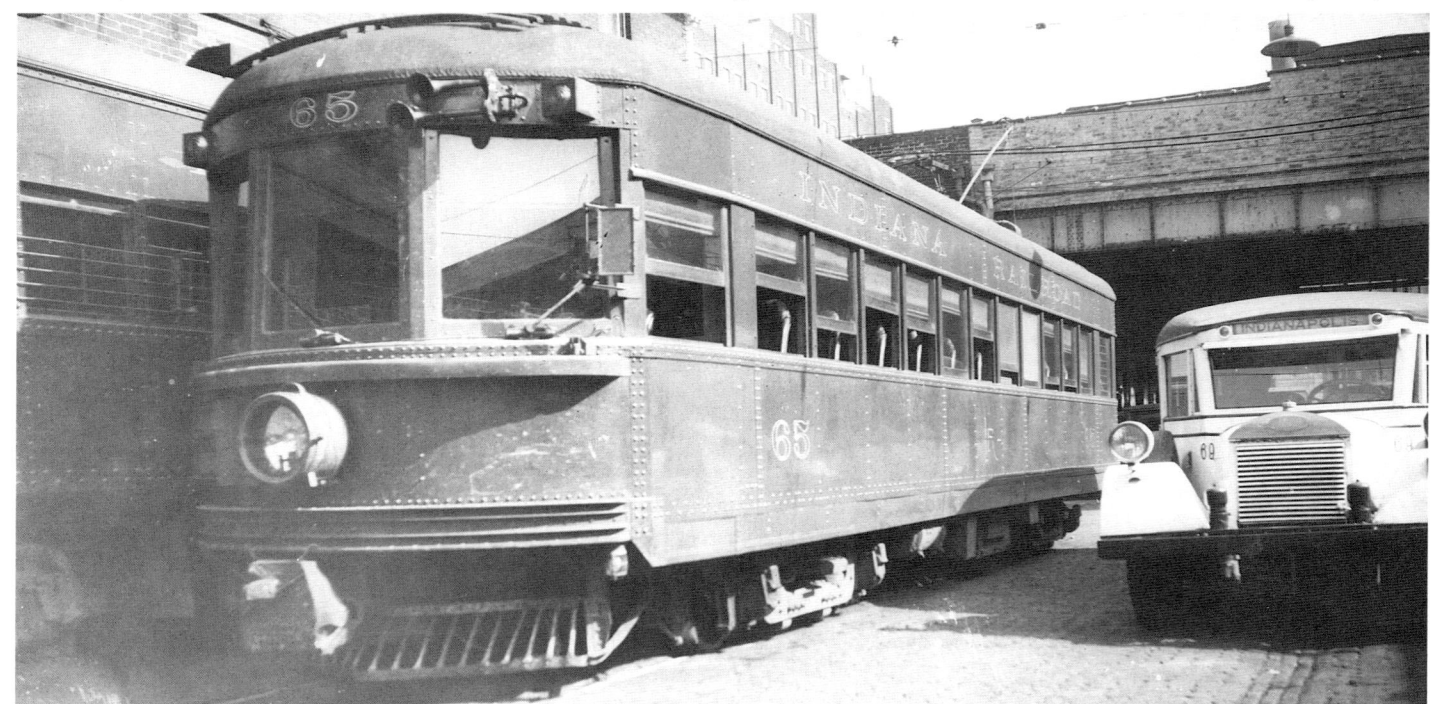

Above After August 31, 1931 the three western tracks of the Traction Terminal were allocated for intercity buses. Buses from Central Greyhound Lines and two other companies join the interurban cars.
George K. Bradley collection

The Muncie city car lines were abandoned on October 11, 1931 largely due to a continued lack of support from the city government. Virtually unregulated bus competition had been allowed in Muncie for several years. The System's management was not interested in investing money in a losing proposition. The interurban cars continued to use portions of three former city car lines to reach the downtown trainshed and the adjoining freight house. The city officials did not actively oppose the interurban lines. Removal of the city cars did allow the interurban cars to move faster.

Motor buses made their presence known in the Indianapolis Traction Terminal. The nine tracks had never been used to their fullest capacity and the demise of several lines reduced the number of daily trains. The entire trainshed track area and much of the open area to the rear, except between the rails in some sections, had always been paved. Starting on August 10, 1931, buses were assigned the three west side tracks and a number of companies immediately moved in, including the system's own Indiana Motor Transit Company. Interurban cars used the remaining six tracks. Joint terminal use produced a coordination of services.

Schedules and fares were changed again on December 1, 1931. Basic fares were 3¢ a mile but several special fare combinations were introduced for the benefit of frequent riders. The new fare structure was accompanied by an advertising campaign using newspapers, radio station broadcasts, car cards and streetcar dash cards. Posters were placed in terminals, local stations and, wherever possible, in the storefront windows or counters of the affiliated utility companies.

The Indianapolis-Richmond line had come into Indiana Railroad under petition for abandonment but it was still running at the end of 1931. The delay occurred because several cities, Greenfield in particular, had fought the rail service suspension petition. The Indianapolis-Richmond route was an example of very early interurban construction which was handicapped by too much side-of-the-road and street running especially in Indianapolis where the route entered the city and ran over the heavy trafficked East Washington Street city car line. Additionally, it followed the National Road (U.S. 40) and had lost most of the local freight business to unlicensed motor trucks.

The abandonment, once again, threatened to break the long-standing connection between the Indiana and Ohio interurban lines. Through one-car Indianapolis-Dayton passenger service dated to the Schoepf-McGowan Syndicate days. Suspended in 1920, the through limited service had been re-established in 1922 by the Dayton & Western in a joint effort with the THI&E. When the D&W went bankrupt, through service ended and passengers had to change cars at Richmond. Under the new C&LE management (beginning June 15, 1931) five second-hand lightweight cars acquired from the Cleveland & Southwestern were placed on the Dayton-Richmond route. Indiana Railroad decided to keep the eastern portion of the line and filed an amended abandonment petition with the Public Service Commission. The Company proposed rerouting Richmond trains over the "Honey Bee" line from Indianapolis to New Castle, then south to Dunreith and east to Richmond over that portion of the line to be retained in the amended petition. Although longer, the Honey Bee route had a less congested entry into Indianapolis allowing passenger and freight service to Dayton, through Richmond, on reasonably fast schedules. The route went into use on January 4, 1932 and the Indianapolis-Greenfield-Dunreith segment was abandoned. In the service change, through trains turned south at New Castle instead of continuing north to Muncie. A revised schedule of Muncie-New Castle trains was put into effect.

Coincident with this abandonment, much to the relief of operating officials, was the retirement from daily service of a group of wooden cars. The cars still carried their original THI&E numbers which were in the

Above Steel plated THI&E 67, several times rebuilt, was one of the cars continued in use by Indiana Railroad on the through Indianapolis-Dayton runs until January 1932.
George Krambles collection

thirties, sixties and seventies. These cars were segregated and the train orders carefully marked because Indiana Railroad, itself, already had two car series (highspeeds and birneys) with some of these same numbers—rare enough, but three active car series with the same numbers must have been a record in the annals of electric railway history.

A "Shipper's Guide" with a brilliant orange cover was issued to promote the new Indiana Railroad System freight services. The booklet was directed toward traffic managers. It described and illustrated the system-wide freight service and coordination plan. These routing guide books for freight shipments to over 20,000 points were distributed throughout the United States. The guide showed interconnections and routes for through shipments with more than 60 steam and 23 electric railroads. Its 141 pages formed a valuable and complete compendium of all routes between Indiana Railroad and other lines. The booklet was a widely used and very successful contribution to an increase in the freight business. Much of this interchange business was less-than-carload freight. It was another step in the planned upgrading of the freight capabilities of Indiana Railroad. The strength of Midland United and the friendly nationwide connections of the Insull utilities were contributing factors.

On January 12, 1932, B. P. Shearon purchased at "upset prices" (the lowest price prescribed by the court as a satisfactory amount) the three formerly leased and now abandoned THI&E lines. This included the Lafayette line (which sold for $75,000), the Martinsville line ($30,000) and the Crawfordsville line ($50,000). The purchase included all the physical assets of the three lines, which had been idle for over a year. Shearon bought them in the name of Midland United Company. The sale was affirmed by the court and, on March 1, 1932, Midland sold the properties to Public Service Company of Indiana. Public Service acquired all the physical assets of the three but was really interested in the pole lines and rights-of-way essential to electric power transmission and distribution. The rolling stock at the Lebanon, Crawfordsville and Mooresville barns also belonged to Public Service Company. These cars, except the eight at Mooresville and two that could not be moved, were delivered to Indiana Railroad crews at Crescent Avenue in Indianapolis.

Most of the cars were not used and were put into storage, eventually dismantled, and the scrap sold to a salvage firm. Elderly line car 191 remained active on the Indianapolis-Lebanon line, to patrol the transmission line, until the rail facilities were dismantled. Later Public Service sent this car to Indiana Railroad where it became line car 763.

The Terre Haute-Paris line of the Terre Haute Traction & Light and its sub-lessor, the Terre Haute & Western, was discontinued on January 25, 1932. This was an interstate line, crossing into Illinois, but it didn't reach any major source of traffic or connect with any other line in Illinois. *Transit Journal News,* on February 13, 1932, recited a litany of the recently abandoned Indiana lines. The publication opined that the closing of the Paris line would mark the end of the series of curtailments of the electric railway mileage in Indiana. But with these abandonments and the January termination of the Indianapolis & Southeastern's rail lines, only the Indiana Railroad System was left operating rail lines from the Indianapolis traction terminal.

The optimism expressed in the *Transit Journal News* survived all too briefly. A series of abandonments, which seemed small at first, rapidly assumed major proportions and drastically reduced the system in 1932. The system lines shrank first. Public Service Company of Indiana, on May 10, 1932, abandoned the short six-mile Watson Junction-Charlestown branch. This trackage was part of a route operated from Louisville, offering local and suburban service, using some of Public Service Company's second-best cars. Five days later city streetcar service in Jeffersonville ended. The local Louisville-Jeffersonville-New Albany operation, over the Big Four Railroad bridge, was cut back to service from Jeffersonville to New Albany. Direct service on the Public Service Company's broad-gauge line,

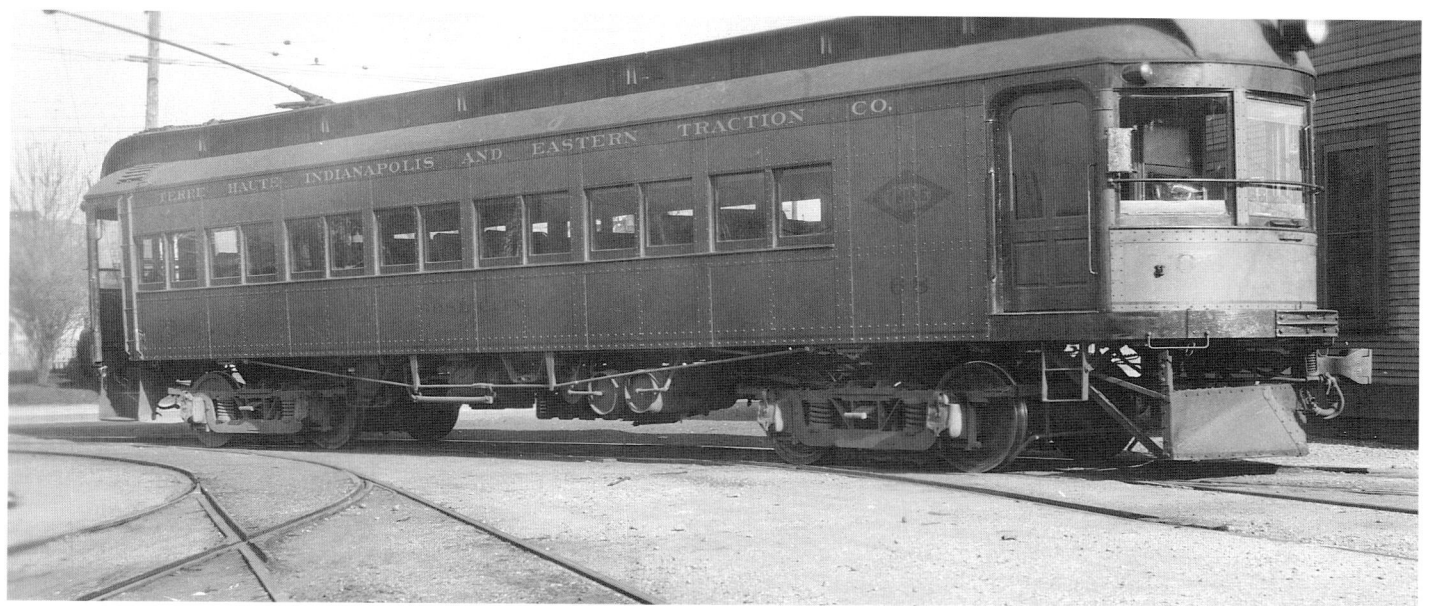

Above THI&E's Eastern Division (Indianapolis-Richmond) continued as part of Indiana Railroad until January 4, 1932 when Indianapolis-Dunreith was abandoned. The THI&E 68, shown at Greenfield shop, was representative of the cars in use. *George K. Bradley collection*

over the Kentucky & Indiana Railroad bridge, to New Albany was continued and this shorter route plus a new highway bridge to Jeffersonville made the longer route impractical. ISC ended the Logansport streetcars on April 29 as a prelude to the May 21 abandonment of the 55-mile Peru-Lafayette line. This route was not profitable. It had a low passenger potential and virtually no freight traffic. Among the last interurbans built, 26-year-old Logansport-Lafayette segment contained some of the best track and roadway in the entire Indiana Railroad System.

Earlier, the Northern Indiana Power Company's city service in Kokomo had ended on April 17, 1932. After the streetcars stopped the north-south and the east-west interurban lines continued to use the city streets. To eliminate trackage on paralleling city streets all interurban car movements were switched to Union Street and the former Union Traction station. The NIP cars were switched on the wye at Union and Markland to reach the station for the next two and half months. "Traction Line Quietly Curls Up and Quits," was the heading of the July 1 Kokomo *Tribune*. The NIP interurban line ended when the 9:20 eastbound left the station on Sunday evening June 30. "Service on the Marion-Frankfort Line Passes Unmissed and Unmourned" was the sub-head. The rail line had outlived its usefulness, at least in the eyes of the newspaper.

Part of the old east-west line on Kokomo's West Markland Avenue, from Union Street to the Belt railroad, reached the power company's large stone quarry on the city's southwest side. Indiana Railroad expected to retain the quarry and haul crushed limestone for ballast and for highway construction. Some people wanted the trackage removed. The Kokomo *Tribune*, among others, supported the track retention because it meant a few more jobs in the depressed labor situation.

With the exception of the Markland Avenue track, the Northern Indiana Power Company's involvement in the Indiana Railroad System was ended. The Frankfort-Kokomo-Marion rail passenger service was replaced by Claude G. Hines' Muncie-Kokomo Coach Lines.

On the same day that service ended on the NIP line, Indiana Railroad's own 34-mile Anderson-Marion line closed down. This and the NIP line had been operated as one through route since 1930. The Marion city system and the short Marion-Gas City line continued as an isolated operation.

All of these abandonments were victims of the original system plan that service would be retained as long as passengers and shippers patronized it. The July 1931 *Hoosier Traveler* stated:

"The active support and patronage of the public . . . will make it possible to maintain . . . the excellent service now being introduced.

"Service on some lines . . . has been discontinued, a step made necessary by lack of patronage from the various towns through which the interurbans operated.

"The lines . . . connecting principal cities of the state will be continued, developed to the utmost and operated for so long as they continue to receive whole hearted support from the communities they serve."

Midland United had gone to great lengths to assemble a self-supporting system. But "use it or lose it"! Location or length of the line was not a factor; its financial contribution was. The Peru-Lafayette line, for example, was a long route in very good physical condition but a money loser of sizable proportions.

Passenger service was reduced in May 1932 when a revised timetable was issued. The new timetable reflected the recent abandonments but did not showcase the reduction in service. Trains on the Indianapolis-Peru-Fort Wayne route, for example, were changed from every two hours to every three hours. Cutting trains probably saved operating expenses but it produced awkward and often inconvenient schedules. Travelers to intermediate and terminal cities found that a working or shopping day was either cut short or made much longer. For the business rider, unproductive time created a loss.

Another severe blow came on May 8, 1932. Midland United and Indiana Railroad lost a giant when 47-year-old Robert Max Feustel died after a brief illness, first

Above January 25, 1932 saw the end of the interstate route from Terre Haute to Paris, Illinois and the retirement of the 118. Behind the 118 is the 119 which had been used on the already-abandoned Clinton and Sullivan lines. *George K. Bradley collection*

Below Purdue University Christmas specials at Lafayette in December 1930. Cars like wooden 354 and steel 378 carried heavy student loads from Lafayette to Fort Wayne and intermediate points on a schedule faster than limited trains. *Richard H. George collection*

Above Northern Indiana Power Company 104 at the Kokomo shops. This company's cars saw little service for Indiana Railroad as they were quickly replaced by bigger cars which had been displaced by the highspeeds.
George Krambles photo

diagnosed as acute nephritis, which turned out to be a virulent, fast-spreading cancer. At the time of his death he was president of Midland United (estimated value $300,000,000), Indiana Railroad, Indiana Service Corporation, Public Service Company of Indiana, Chicago South Shore & South Bend Railroad and vice-chairman of Northern Indiana Public Service Company.

Feustel could not have stopped what was happening to the interurbans. The Fort Wayne-Lima interstate route might have survived a bit longer but the receiver recognized the hopeless situation and suspended the operation of this rail-only property on June 30, 1932 following the total collapse of the Michigan connections in 1931 and 1932. Only the Richmond-Dayton line remained to connect the Indiana and Ohio interurbans.

The roller coaster had started down fast and the Indiana Railroad System was reduced to approximately 575 miles of main lines plus the city lines. The roller coaster car might slow and momentarily hesitate as it came to the top of each rise—but it always continued downhill.

IR was reeling from two shock waves of epic proportions but the real trouble had just begun. Brewing since before the company was formed, it now began to boil over and two more blows were delivered within the next year.

In the fall of 1929 Samuel Insull's self-confidence had been matched only by his financial strength and prestige. He was surprised but not paralyzed by the great October crash of the stock market as he had weathered his share of financial crises. Following the crash he went to the aid of some of his associates, using his own apparently secure position, rescuing those who were caught with marginal brokerage accounts. In many cases he was helping them hold on to stocks of the Insull companies. All employees of the companies had been encouraged to become stockholders. Contests were held to attract employee investment and most employees put some of their money into stocks. The Indiana employees bought Midland United common stock. Customers were approached to buy stock with the idea of involving a large number of people in company investment.

Utility stocks held up after the 1929 crash. There was some depreciation in value during 1930 and the overall value of the Insull companies slipped. The operating companies experienced record earnings in 1930 and this situation continued into 1931. The utility business seemed calm while Wall Street financial matters during this period were, at times, nearly insane. For those with money it was an excellent time to enter the market providing they could move with complete assurance that their line of capital was sound.

The Morgan-related banks in New York grouped their electric and gas utilities under the United Corporation. United gained control of a sizable number of major utilities including some where the late Randal Morgan (no relation to the New York Morgan group) had held substantial ownership. (The Federal Trade Commission's extensive study of utility corporations, made over several years in the 1930's, required more than 70 volumes. Midland United is covered in Volume 60. The Morgan companies are in Volume 52 and others.)

Insull and his associates made several financial moves aimed at strengthening their control which ended in seriously weakening their position. They were put in a borrowing situation and they used the stock of several major companies as collateral.

This placed the banking group in a strong position to give or withhold money when the Insull companies needed it. Several loans, one large note in particular, were coming due and would have to be refinanced. Using the stocks which were held as collateral, the banking interests were able to gain leverage to achieve repayment of their loans. The bankers' next act had a devastating effect on the Insull-controlled companies—especially Indiana Railroad. What was happening in

Above Cars like the 442 and the 446-449 series cars were put in service on the Anderson-Marion-Frankfort run which combined the Northern Indiana Power Company's route with the former Union Traction Marion branch. *George K. Bradley collection*

New York must have seemed light-years removed from most IR employees. Even the system management would not have predicted what happened next.

Sam Insull and a number of his business associates held a meeting in Insull's office in the Edison Building in Chicago, on February 27, 1932, to hear a proposal from Owen D. Young, chairman of the General Electric Company and the New York Federal Reserve Bank. Young said he had been asked to act as a mediator for the New York banks who expressed concern about the value of the stock held as collateral and they wanted to appoint an individual acceptable to both groups to approve any major expenditures. The first person suggested refused the responsibility. Other candidates were not acceptable to either the New York or Chicago banking interests which held loans due from the Insull companies. According to Insull (in his memoirs) someone suggested Arthur Andersen, of the firm of Arthur Andersen & Co.—Certified Public Accountants, to act in this capacity. (In 1978, Sam Insull, Jr. claimed he was that "someone.") Young was agreeable to the idea and returned to New York where he confirmed the appointment on February 29.

Arthur Andersen and his partner, John Jirgal, convened a meeting on April 5 at Andersen's office where they advised Insull that Middle West Utilities Company was in difficulty, had a huge note maturing on June 1, and should be reorganized. The same people later met in New York. According to Harold L. Stuart, of Halsey, Stuart & Co., Owen Young stated that everything possible should be done to save Middle West. Andersen then pulled Stuart aside and said that he didn't understand because, the day before, Young had agreed with Andersen that Middle West must be reorganized and could not be saved. On April 8, another meeting was held, this time in Young's office, which was attended by several members of the Morgan banks. Young then advised Insull and Stuart that the New York banks refused to put up any more money and that Middle West would go into receivership. It was the beginning of the end for Insull.

Samuel Insull was put in the position where he resigned from all of his companies on June 6, 1932. The resignation extended down through Midland United and Indiana Railroad. Sam Insull, Jr. was allowed to remain for a period of months until he, too, resigned. The presidency of Midland United, vacant since Feustel's death, remained unoccupied until further decisions could be made. The influence of the key men who had created, enlarged and nurtured the Indiana Railroad was swept away. The value of the common stock in the companies, including Midland United, collapsed and swept away the employee savings/investment hopes. The long, downhill roller coaster ride was over. The character of the railroad would now be different and the positive influence swept away.

Below Car 405, as southbound train 57, just north of the School Street loop, end of the North Anderson city line, on June 30, 1932. This was the last day of service on the Anderson-Marion-Frankfort line. *James F. Cook photo*

Above A quiet moment on a cold 1932 day at the Indianapolis Traction Terminal with cars 84, 379 and 433, but no people in sight.
Tony Chase photo, Richard H. George collection

 **Left and Right** Indiana Railroad's familiar "arrow" monogram designs appeared in green, edged with aluminum, on both sides of new and repainted cars. There were two variations, one for each side, so the arrow always pointed toward the front of the car.

Below After the parlor cars were taken out of regular service, the "Purdue" and "Indiana" remained available for special trips. At the Anderson shops, the 438 and "Purdue" prepare for a charter trip on September 8, 1934.
M. D. McCarter collection

Chapter 6
Politics and Bowman Elder

Left Public Service Company's very heavy 153 was transferred to the Terre Haute line where the 150 series cars were used not only on the *Highlander*, which stopped only at town stations, but also on local trains. *W. B. Cox photo, George K. Bradley collection*

At the bottom of the corporate pile of former Insull companies, Indiana Railroad was ignored by the bankers—at least for the moment. Regardless of what happened, Henry Bucher, L. M. Brown, J. A. Greenland and the other Indiana Railroad managers had plenty to do. Their task—a way to retain their jobs—was to keep the system profitable. They had to get rid of the losers and move ahead. The Insull empire's failure was surely a deciding factor in the rash of abandonments in the second half of 1932. On the positive side freight solicitation was stepped up by using representatives to seek additional business. Special passenger services were promoted for events such as the Indianapolis "500" race at Speedway, the Kentucky Derby, the Indiana State Fair and other gatherings at any point on the line.

Publicity campaigns made extensive use of radio broadcasting facilities. Street car dasher cards and inside car cards promoted the service. Theaters, movie houses, restaurants and hotels were all solicited for advertising business that could be tied to the interurban services.

Mainline track and roadway was improved. Rolling stock was kept clean and neat to present an attractive appearance. A lot of paint was used to keep the company's own cars looking their best. Some of the system freight equipment needed paint but that was a question of which company should apply the paint. The same went for much of the service fleet.

By late 1932 the system had virtually eliminated the wooden passenger car fleet. The wooden cars had been the mainstays of the lines that were abandoned in 1932 and even these lines had some steel cars after the highspeeds had arrived. The wooden cars could be relegated to dead storage at inactive car barns. ISC and Public Service Company kept a few of their wooden cars as semi-active spares for several years and then retired them. Excluding the wooden cars, the system boasted 43 heavy steel two-man-operated cars, two medium-weight two-man cars, five medium-weight one-man cars, two lightweight one-man cars, six trailer coaches and the 35 highspeeds for a total of 87 motor passenger cars and six trail coaches. Indiana Railroad also had in its own reserve two parlor cars and car 600, the business/party car. Both ISC and Public Service Company had good steel "retired" cars in storage that were available if needed. There was also an abundance of city and suburban passenger cars for the city routes.

Indiana Railroad kept spare cars at a number of locations on the system, especially at major terminals, always ready to fill in for regular cars or special services. This was an anomaly because the system's top operating men came from ISC and Public Service Company and both of these companies had always operated a rather full schedule with a minimum of interurban cars.

The highspeeds held down the Indianapolis-Fort Wayne via Bluffton and the Indianapolis-Louisville regular service. Whenever the big cars were also on these lines, the company motto, brought from ISC by Feustel, Bucher and Lentz was indelibly imprinted into the crews' mind: "Be sure you are right, then go ahead." (That phrase is believed to have originated following the Wabash Valley's disastrous 1910 Kingsland wreck as a reminder to leave nothing, particularly train operations, to chance.) Day-to-day planning and actual train operations always took the different cars into consideration. It was the kind of care that would give the system an impressive passenger service safety record.

In the May 1932 schedule reductions, trains were taken off several routes. The service cuts made enough highspeeds available to consider using them on a third route and the 72-mile Terre Haute line was selected. Service on the Terre Haute line had been cut with one Highlander limited train and three locals eliminated. One highspeed was sent to Terre Haute on a trial trip on June 1. It covered the route thirty minutes faster than the two-man steel cars but made only three stops as opposed to the limited's eleven station stops. Pleased with the trial run, L. M. Brown announced that the highspeeds, with the observation-lounge section, would be used for the Highlander runs. Several of the cars were placed on display in cities along the route and a "special" was run for the benefit of city officials and the press. This eastbound car was delayed because of photographers, but it impressively made up the lost time. In the process, operator A. W. "Heavy" Moore had a close call with a negligent motorist near Plainfield. The car brakes made an efficient and rapid stop which impressed the slightly shaken audience.

On June 20 the highspeeds went into regular service on the Indianapolis-Terre Haute line. Two weeks later, on July 5, the highspeeds were replaced by the two-man steel cars they had relegated to the sidetrack. These were Public Service Company's 150-series cars which were among the system's heaviest cars. Terre Haute Division Trainmaster C. D. "Gib" Harmon was pleased because he particularly liked these big cars.

The Terre Haute line highspeed trial was the victim of stringent times as company officials stated the operation of the highspeeds had demonstrated that the right-of-way would have to be rebuilt for their continued operation. Such an expenditure was not justifiable under the current economic conditions. The trackage on the line was not suited for fast running due to the lack of any elevation on the curves but the real culprit was the trolley wire. Between Greencastle and Plainfield the trolley wire was higher than normal because steam railroad cars were handled on some of this trackage to move coal. The highspeeds sat lower than the other cars and their trolley pole and retriever did not allow proper contact with the overhead wire. At speed all the rope would run out of the retriever, as the pole reached for the high wire, and the wind drag pulled the rope back in an arc. In truth, the trolley pole springs couldn't compensate against the short rope and the drag which allowed the trolley pole to fall below the wire and break contact. Loss of power meant the car slowed and the pole would go back up. If it missed the trolley wire, it could get caught and tear down the overhead. Longer poles and more rope might have solved the dewirement problem but it was an expenditure that was not considered necessary in the summer of 1932.

The return of the big cars failed to intimidate motorists and it was carnage as usual along the National Road. In early 1932 the Public Service Commission ordered the installation of automatic crossing gates for high-accident rail/highway crossings. A set was installed at the entrance to Rose Polytechnic Institute (now Rose-Hulman Institute of Technology) to protect the main entrance drive to the school. The cost was borne by the railroad as it was determined that the highway commission was not required to contribute. The reasoning was given that the crossing gates were installed "to protect electric trains operated by Indiana Railroad." The trains also needed protection from truck drivers. A vehicle described by the Brazil *Daily Times* as an enormous, six-wheeled truck turned over and landed on the interurban tracks. In 1932 a truck of this size, in over-the-road use, was a rarity. The next year a big car demolished an auto and killed three. The crossing, west of Plainfield, was protected by red flasher lights. The same motorman several months later, had the misfortune of being the motorman in two fatal heavy-car vs. auto accidents in 24 hours and within one mile of each other on the outskirts of Terre Haute. The auto drivers were at fault and all of the fatalities were in the flimsy autos and not the big interurban cars.

Even with the surplus of cars one special movement involved the use of city cars. Although Fort Benjamin Harrison was a regular suburban run for Indiana Railroad (using standard interurban cars) it required twenty Indianapolis Railways city cars to transport 1600 students, attending a civilian summer training camp, from there to the west side of Indianapolis for a ball game using the tracks of both the city and interurban company. The twenty-car caravan made the trip to the baseball grounds and return.

Public Service Company of Indiana took its leased subsidiary, Terre Haute Electric Company, Inc., out of the transportation business when it sublet the Terre Haute street railway and bus system and the interurban from Terre Haute to Brazil to the Indiana Railroad, on June 12, 1932, for a term of fifty years (retroactive to

Below Car 407, all lighted and signed for New Castle, awaits as a spare car on Track 5 north of the Indianapolis terminal trainshed in October 1932.
Robert V. Mehlenbeck photo

Above In the days of one-man operation, westbound car 438 actuated Indiana Railroad's only set of automatic crossing gates. They protected the main entrance road to Rose Polytechnic (now Rose-Hulman) Institute.
James F. Cook photo

January 1, 1932) at an annual rental of $100 per year. All of the equipment, franchises, etc. were included in the lease. This made the operation of the Terre Haute Division less complicated and simplified the operations of the city properties.

All capital expenditures, improvements and renewals were to be at the expense of Public Service Company although they might be done by Indiana Railroad at the direction or on orders from the Public Service Company. Repairs and maintenance, to keep the property in good order, were the responsibility of Indiana Railroad. Insurance for or the replacement of any of the subleased property was also in the hands of Indiana Railroad.

L. M. Brown was promoted to general superintendent of transportation in charge of all interurban, street railway and bus operations for the Indiana Railroad System. J. Allen Greenland was moved to Terre Haute as manager of the city system.

Charles W. Chase was a longtime associate of the Insulls and had been president of the Gary Railways as well as an officer and director of the South Shore and Indiana Railroad. Soon after Gary Railways was sold, in 1932, Chase severed his relationship with Midland United to become president of the newly reorganized Indianapolis Railways, Inc. Earlier Chase had submitted a plan for rehabilitating the Indianapolis company as part of a proposal submitted by Midland United in connection with the purchase of the THI&E. Within the next few years Chase took the nearly moribund Indianapolis property in a leap ahead to be one of the outstanding city transit properties in the nation. Track rehabilitation, the purchase of 90 new streetcars, starting a trolley coach system and modern motor coaches were all in the extensive program. Chase was an important friend for Indiana Railroad because the system's interurbans entered Indianapolis from five directions and used local streetcar tracks to reach the Traction Terminal.

Public Service Company disposed of one more piece of the overall system. The local buses at Columbus, which had replaced the streetcars in 1929, were sold to James W. Leppert. Leppert Bus Lines, Inc. took over the three local bus routes on November 20, 1932.

Indiana Railroad drastically reduced its motor bus operations during 1932 retaining only the city bus services at Anderson and Terre Haute plus some inactive franchises. The company reported an abandonment of 167 bus route miles. All of the former Union Traction runs had already ended. Indiana Motor Transit Company ceased all of its bus operations on August 31, 1932. The lines involved ran from Indianapolis to Terre Haute and Richmond and along the Danville Road. Some of the route certificates were sold to Pennsylvania Greyhound Lines, Inc. for $115,951. Public Service Company abandoned 121 miles of bus routes. This included the Indianapolis-Louisville route, the sale of the Columbus city lines and some services in the Terre

Above Massachusetts Avenue in Indianapolis on June 28, 1935 with Indiana Railroad 440 bound for Fort Harrison. Two of the new Indianapolis city cars are also at this six-street intersection.
George K. Bradley collection

Haute area which had replaced earlier, now abandoned, interurban routes. The Indianapolis-Greenwood service, which belonged to Public Service Company, and not part of the System, was the only remaining intercity bus operation.

The company had a large surplus of used motor buses. Some of them were transferred to city operations at Terre Haute, some were sold to other bus companies and some were stored. The stored vehicles were further reduced by random scrappings. Periodically a few were put into use to haul equipment and track crews.

Indiana Railroad coped with what was described as a thirty-year record for snowfall during November 1932. Practically all trains arrived at the Indianapolis Traction Terminal within an hour of their scheduled times. The only serious problem had been at Richmond where sleet brought down part of the overhead lines. The dependability of the electric railway vehicle was effectively demonstrated. Highway and street snow removal was, in those years, almost non-existent whereas the electric lines were well equipped with sweepers and plows to clear the streets and open the trackage. Snow storms usually played havoc with train dispatching because many scheduled meets were missed requiring dispatchers and operators to be creative and careful in continuing service.

Another kind of storm hit Indiana and the United States in November 1932. The Democrats swept elections throughout the country thrusting Franklin D. Roosevelt into the White House and Paul V. McNutt, former Dean of the Indiana University Law School, into the Indiana governor's chair. McNutt was a man of considerable charm and great ambition who was good at using issues to his advantage and one who recognized his political supporters.

On January 1, 1933, John N. Shannahan was named president of Midland United. He succeeded to the Feustel vacancies in all of the subsidiary companies, including Indiana Railroad. He was also a man with an excellent record. Shannahan, who was nearly 60 years old, was president of the Omaha & Council Bluffs Street Railway, had been in the electric power, interurban and street railway business for many years, with no previous ties to the Insull companies. He was considered to be a fine manager and had served as president of the American Electric Railway Association. He stated his interest in preserving the subsidiary electric railways but his primary concern and efforts would be on behalf of the electric and gas utilities.

Indiana Railroad reduced fares to 2¢ per mile for one-way fares and 1.5¢ per mile for round-trip tickets. Ten-ride commutation tickets were sold at 1.35¢ per mile and 500-penny mileage coupon books were sold for $3.75. Shannahan announced the fares as effective April 27 and said, "This is an experiment to ascertain whether the people of Indiana wish to maintain . . . electric

Service Commission. All members now served at the will of the governor instead of fixed four-year terms. The three members had to represent the two major political parties. A public counselor was also added and the first one was Sherman Minton, later named to the United States Supreme Court.

On June 27, 1933, General Electric Company filed in the Marion County Superior Court for receivership of the Indiana Railroad over a $328 debt. It was soon revealed that the line owed current obligations of over $210,000 and, for legal purposes, General Electric was selected to file a "friendly" suit on behalf of all the creditors. This was a familiar procedure but the next action may have surprised some of the players.

In most electric railway receivership cases the president or general manager was usually named as the receiver by the court. That may have been what was expected in the case of the Indiana Railroad. If it was, then a number of people were shocked.

Judge Russell Ryan, of Marion County Superior Court 5, was also involved in Indiana Democratic Party activities and along with Governor McNutt had special plans for Indiana Railroad. Judge Ryan appointed Bowman V. Elder as receiver for Indiana Railroad. Elder was an Indianapolis real estate manager and one of the

railways. . . .(We) are willing to speculate on the willingness of the people to cooperate with us by using our facilities." This statement would tend to indicate that Shannahan was pro-rail, but only if the rail lines were profitable. He also had to know that reduced rates, by themselves, would only reduce the net operating income. It would take the lines into a negative income position which might ease justification should it become policy to abandon the lines. What had not been considered was the action taken by C. D. Hardin. As Hardin later related, no one told him he could not operate a promotion campaign to attract riders. It was not part of the original plan but Hardin used all news media to let the public know about the very attractive, low fares. Signs appeared at all on-line locations and employees supported him by word of mouth. Even the freight motors carried painted metal signs highlighting the 1-1/2¢ per mile fare. Ridership did increase and revenues held fairly firm. The fare and promotion were a success from Hardin's viewpoint. What Shannahan thought is not recorded.

Shannahan was up against some other forces that he could not control. The Democrats had control of the Indiana General Assembly before they gained the governor's chair. Now that legislative combination introduced a series of reforms against the supposed ills of the utility companies. On March 2, 1933, Governor McNutt signed into law a reorganization of the Public

Above A few passengers stand in the late afternoon sun as they wait to board their trains in the last months of 1932. The chilly day has most people already in a warm car or inside the terminal building.
Tony Chase photo, Richard H. George collection

founders of the American Legion, headquartered in Indianapolis. He was also involved in state politics and the number two Democrat in the state behind Frank McHale, the party's state chairman. The two made a powerful combination and had actively supported McNutt. Elder's appointment became effective on June 28, 1933. Frank McHale acted as attorney for the receiver. The surprising court appointment may have been very fortunate for the company as, for all practical purposes, Indiana Railroad was removed from the hands of Midland United. It was also instantly changed from a very private organization (with precious little financial information made available) to a very public organization with all major steps noted in the Superior Court record books.

Had it not been for the receivership Shannahan could, no doubt, have filed for the termination of the interurban lines at the earliest opportunity, either at his own volition or at the command of the new people in financial control. The Midland corporate records were

Below Westbound highspeed 64, coming from Anderson, has just crossed Keystone Avenue on the north side of Indianapolis. Paralleling 38th Street, this was IR's principal section of rural double track.
Robert V. Mehlenbeck photo

being revised, to conform with the new accounting procedure and a corresponding rearrangement of the debt structure, in a manner that would be unfavorable to Indiana Railroad. Shannahan was still the company president but his power was practically eliminated by the receivership. This did not mean that the receiver and the court totally ignored the corporate officers but it did mean that the officers were not the active managers. Changes were not in order as the utility companies were not enjoying the best reputation and the newly revised Public Service Commission would be very reluctant to eliminate any services, at some utility company's request, especially if that service was provided to any local area where voters might be adversely affected by a loss of service. This was 1933; "New Deal" Democrats were sitting in Washington and many state capitals tinkering with economic matters and promising to champion the cause of the "common man." That Bowman Elder became receiver may not have been such a surprise.

Chester D. Porter, vice president and general manager of Public Service Company of Indiana, was named as manager for the receiver although Henry Bucher would stay on for several years as general manager for the company. Eventually both were replaced. Other people, such as L. M. Brown and Charley Lentz, remained in their management/operations positions. Elder had no intention of eliminating the excellent and competent management talent. The operating force reported to the receiver who was, in effect, the chief operating officer. The court was told, and agreed, that Elder's compensation would be $12,000 per year, a substantial sum in 1933. Although it took several months, Elder soon became very familiar with his charge and its strengths and weaknesses. The top management people actually ran the day-to-day operations but only those who viewed the operation in a positive way were welcome.

During the rest of 1933 it was business as usual for the company except that an effort was made to dispose of all surplus lands, material and equipment to generate much-needed cash. Western Indiana Sand & Gravel Company at Orestes, on the Tipton-Alexandria line, bought part of the trackage for $800 in 1933. The next year they bought line car 775 for $500. Most of the huge collection of old rolling stock on the Indiana Railroad property was stored at Eaton and Anderson. These cars had little, if any, operational value and, in a time of negligible prices for scrap, little salvage value. S. Solotkin, of Greenfield, purchased most of the company's scrap lots after the useless wooden passenger and freight car bodies were stripped of usable parts and then sold or burned. The scrapped cars provided the company with an inventory of usable spare parts that could be used on the active equipment. By 1936, 440 old cars were removed from the equipment list.

The scrapping procedure, which had been going on at a slow pace for several years, was heartbreaking for many longtime employees. A number of them had turned out, at an earlier date, to see the end of Union Traction's fine private car "Martha" which had had no place in the no-nonsense, no-private-car scheme of Insull and Feustel. The Martha was pulled outside from its long-standing berth, tipped from its trucks, landing with a twisting of wood and breaking glass, and set on fire.

Above Bowman Elder (circa 1930) *William L. Elder collection*

There were tears in the eyes of many as the flames consumed the most visible symbol of the old Union Traction Company.

Some more promotional zest appeared in late 1933 when Indiana Railroad announced a plan to link the interurban services with airlines for travel outside the state. Connections were made at Indianapolis, Terre Haute and Louisville with "high speed, distance flying planes of American Airways, Inc." The low fares in effect and C. D. Hardin's promotional campaign were continued under the receivership and were important in holding riders. At that price it was the most attractive

Below Frank McHale (circa 1930) *William L. Elder collection*

and cheapest transportation. Newspaper ads stressed the low fare and compared it against the cost of operating an auto.

Earlier in the year, on February 15, an agreement was reached to sell the isolated street railway property at Marion, solving an Indiana Railroad problem and assuring continued local service. The sale to the new Marion Railways, Inc. became official on April 1, 1933. The company also acquired 17 Birney cars and a large supply of spare parts. The abandoned Anderson-Marion line had been left intact so that cars and equipment could be moved to the Marion lines. The Marion-Gas City operation was abandoned as the new Marion company did not want the short intercity line which included the long steel Deer Creek trestle and a multiple-span bridge over the Mississinewa River. That line also required the use of double-truck cars and had been using cars from Anderson with two painted in the same color scheme as the highspeeds. The Marion rail lines continued as a successful company.

As 1934 opened, Public Service Company planned to resolve its local rail operations in the Falls City area. The company owned the local rail and bus lines in New Albany and the intercity rail link between New Albany and Jeffersonville. It also owned the five-foot-gauge "Daisy Line" across the Kentucky & Indiana Terminal Railroad Company's Ohio River bridge from New Albany to Louisville.

Two companies were organized to purchase the properties because of the nature of the owned and leased properties. The Home Transit Company and the New Albany & Louisville Electric Railroad Corporation were owned by the same people and they took over on April 22, 1934. The New Albany operation bought the streetcars then in use while the new bridge operation leased cars from the Louisville Railway Company. It also moved the terminal to the Louisville & Interurban's Jefferson Street station. The interurban rail line between New Albany and Jeffersonville was abandoned at midnight on April 21 to coincide with the sale. The new company substituted bus service. Indiana Railroad offered freight customers a truck connection to New Albany from the Jeffersonville freight house.

Some things did go right. Business increased when citizens realized the interurban was in trouble. Usage of the cars was up and the overall losses decreased. The results of increased traffic were reflected in the addition of more trains to the schedules in the first half of 1934. No one could complain when the fares were so low. Most of this passenger traffic was short-haul business into the various commercial centers served by the interurban. Long-distance travel was more of the exception than the norm.

At the end of regular service on June 1, 1934, the Northern Indiana Railway, Inc. interurban rail lines ceased operations. Almost immediately afterwards, the Winona Railroad ended its interurban passenger service and abandoned its route north of New Paris. This broke the interurban link between central Indiana and the Chicago area. The passenger loss was negligible but the two lines had provided some valuable freight connections. Interurban freight could still go east, by way of Dayton, to Columbus and Cleveland, Ohio via the C&LE and its connections. As the interurban systems shrank so did the options for shippers.

Above Private car "Martha," a proud symbol of Union Traction, had no place in Indiana Railroad's scheme of things and was among the wooden cars destroyed. *George K. Bradley collection*

Attempts were made to improve the package freight and less-than-carload shipments. At Fort Wayne, Store Door Delivery Corporation, an independent company, began handling pick-up and delivery of shipments to points that could be reached through Indiana Railroad's Indianapolis terminal facilities. This service was an added extra but introducing a motor truck firm into the picture could lead to further erosion of business through this highly mobile form of competition.

On June 9, 1934, Midland United Company filed petitions in the Federal Court at Wilmington, Delaware. Midland filed in Delaware because the company was incorporated in that state. The filing was a petition to the court to reorganize the company under the new Federal Corporate Bankruptcy Act. This action complicated an existing muddled state of corporate affairs within Midland United. This petition, however, worked to Indiana Railroad's benefit as Public Service Company of Indiana and Indiana Service Corporation had to take some steps to resolve their own corporate affairs. When Indiana Railroad started operations in 1930, there was a "gentlemen's agreement" between IR, Public Service's predecessor, ISC and Northern Indiana Power Company that a single management team would coordinate the railway operations of all four companies. No leases or other contracts formalized this arrangement.

Midland United's petition for reorganization and Indiana Railroad's receivership combined to present a problem for the "gentlemen's agreements" which existed between the several companies. It was a clear possibility, under the reorganization, that each of these companies might become free-standing and the "family relationship" would be broken. The central supervision of the interurban lines had proven successful and it was the only way they could approach profitability. Besides,

Above Steel suburban cars 207-212 were used for Indianapolis-Broad Ripple service until the mid-twenties when they were reassigned to other lines. All had the heavy anti-climbers to protect them in collisions with higher-floor interurban cars. The 208 and one other were given pilots instead of "city car" fenders and painted in the new Indiana Railroad colors in early 1932 for the Marion-Gas City run. *M.D.McCarter collection*

neither Public Service or ISC was very excited about going back into the interurban railway business. The entire system idea had sat dormant for over a year as the Midland United subsidiaries sorted out their problems. However, it was now time for Bowman Elder, as receiver for Indiana Railroad, to take action to preserve the system concept.

Public Service Company was financially pressed and wanted to escape from the costly liability of its 999-year lease of the Indianapolis Columbus & Southern Traction Company or, at least, to cut its losses to the minimum. In September 1934, Public Service Company filed for abandonment of its own trackage from Seymour to Louisville and for a reduction in service on the leased IC&S line from Seymour to Indianapolis to one train a day each way. However, the chance of the Public Service Commission's approving the action at this time was quite remote because the Superior Court had stated that a considerable part of the revenue of Indiana Railroad was derived from the interchange of freight and passengers over the route of the Public Service Company of Indiana, from Louisville to Indianapolis, and the routes of Indiana Service Corporation from Indianapolis to Fort Wayne.

The court also directed that, "in order to avoid any material decrease in the income and earnings of . . . Indiana Railroad . . . it is desirable, necessary and in the public interest that the petition . . . not be pressed." That order left only one clear path for Public Service to limit its losses. They would have to lease the Indianapolis-Louisville line to Indiana Railroad and did so on October 1, 1934. The single evident point was that the future of the total railway properties was linked. Without the System, the lines were fragmented and could not stand alone. Bowman Elder used this fact to the railroad's advantage. By the gain of a formal lease of the Indianapolis-to-Louisville line he maintained the flow of traffic on the south end of the system.

The lease included the use of the railroad and that portion of the overhead system used for the railroad's operations. The rest of the power distribution system remained with Public Service Company. Usable passenger, freight and service motor cars were also included. Necessary stations, buildings, etc., but not the substations were also leased. The rental for all of this was $1.00 per year. Indiana Railroad was responsible for the operations and maintenance of the line plus insurance and other similar expenses. Indiana Railroad presented a monthly statement of revenues and operating expenses to Public Service Company. Any surplus was to be paid to reimburse the company for previous deficits incurred. The underlying Public Service-IC&S lease continued as in the past. This resulted in continuing losses on the lease. Public Service was relieved of the day-to-day operating problems of its interurban lines. However, Public Service Company's continued objective was to be out of the railway business—completely—and as soon as possible.

If a lease of the Public Service Company's lines was necessary it was mandatory to do the same with the Indiana Service Corporation's lines. The fortunes of the interurban operations of ISC and Union Traction, the Indiana Railroad predecessor, had been inextricably linked since the early 1900's. Trains of the two companies had operated through Peru and Bluffton, the two principal connecting points between the two companies, for years. The October 1934 ISC lease was different and more complicated because ISC did not lease all of its rail facilities to Indiana Railroad. Indeed, some of these facilities had never been a part of the "system." The Fort

Above The Louisville Railway Company's interurban terminal on Jefferson Street had only two through tracks. Indiana Railroad highspeeds are on the left, dual-gauge track. The rear of a New Albany and Louisville broad-gauge car is on the right in this 1936 photo.

James P. Shuman photo

Wayne streetcar lines had been kept separate and now that it was time to spell out "system," the ISC Northern Division and the Peru streetcars were also excluded. ISC leased the trackage from the end of the Broadway city line to Bluffton and from the end of the Taylor city line to the center of the curve at Broadway and Main in Peru. All cars in use on the leased lines or those that might be expected to be used were included. The Fort Wayne passenger station, the Commerce Drive freight terminal and other stations and necessary buildings became Indiana Railroad's responsibility. The power system was treated in the same manner as the Public Service Company lease with the exception that the substation equipment became Indiana Railroad's problem. Responsibility for the maintenance of the interurban line and leased property, conformity with any laws, ordinances or franchises covering the operations and insuring the operations went to Indiana Railroad. ISC insured the physical property.

Excluded were all "passenger, freight and service motor cars and trailer cars required by Lessor in the operation of its interurban lines known as the Northern Division." Also, all of the property of the ". . . local street railroad systems located in the Cities of Peru and Fort Wayne, Indiana." This meant that approximately 1.5 miles of track from the center of Peru to the west side of the city was retained for local street cars. ISC also kept rights to operate over the interurban tracks to the east side of Peru because the local car line's route was on Main Street, east and west, and from city limit to city limit. The Peru-to-Lafayette interurban, although abandoned in 1932, was not sold for scrap until September 1936 so this small portion in the streets of Peru was no problem.

ISC retained the Northern Division for several reasons. Technically, it was a separate company which, although no meetings of Board of Directors had been held since 1924, was not dissolved until September 2, 1936. Retention removed any question of sub-lease complications and allowed ISC to haul coal and other freight from Stoners (a New York Central System interchange) or Cedar (a Pennsylvania Lines interchange) to the Spy Run generating plant and other customers. Passenger service continued to operate with the 323-series lightweight cars painted and lettered for Indiana Railroad.

Indiana Railroad took care of local switching to other customers such as the Centlivre Brewery, State

School and Filtration Plant even though it meant extending trackage rights over the private right-of-way of the Northern Division from Wells Street through the power house/shops complex to and over Spy Run Avenue. Trackage rights were also extended over Spy Run Avenue, Superior Street and the downtown loops for the movement of cars to and from the shops. Cars could be stored at the old Pearl Street freight terminal or at Spy Run shop yards. ISC agreed to do repairs at the cost of parts and labor plus 25%.

For all practical purposes Indiana Railroad operated the leased ISC lines as if they were its own. IR was responsible for that which was leased to it and for keeping it in good repair. Taxes, franchise payments or any assessments became the lessee's problem. All electric power was to be purchased from ISC. Where electric substation equipment was in shared or adjacent quarters with rail stations or facilities, the Indiana Railroad employees (if so qualified) took care of the substation and transmission business for the lessor. ISC paid Indiana Railroad for these services.

Differing from the Public Service Company lease, Indiana Railroad received all revenues, paid all expenses and kept any surplus. IR also had to absorb the losses. Indiana Railroad paid ISC an annual rent of $5,000 for the use of the properties.

Rolling stock was sorted out with the receiver's staff deciding what they needed from the two utilities for the operation of the leased lines. Originally most of these "system" cars had been assigned to Indiana Railroad but, in many cases, they were never used. Because of the maintenance responsibility assumed with the cars taken in the lease, Indiana Railroad took no more than necessary. These included the steel passenger cars and the usable power and trailer freight equipment. The cars that were not selected were then put in storage and eventually scrapped by the power company owners.

From the October, 1934 lease date forward, Indiana Railroad and Indiana Railroad System were one and the same with one organization in control through ownership or lease. The only exception was the ISC Northern Division passenger service which was included in the Indiana Railroad timetables and ticketing. A revenue division was made but a passenger could ride from Louisville, KY to Kendallville, IN on the Indiana Railroad.

Simple survival was now the key object and keeping the system intact was important to all the companies. Freight continued to move although one of the largest and most consistent carload movements was coal from the Terre Haute area to system power plants and other on-line customers. It had to be hauled in the company's own "high-side" gondolas which could take the many twisting turns on the routes through the cities. Terre Haute Division crews delivered the loaded coal cars to Indianapolis at the Kentucky Avenue freight terminal during the day to be picked up for forwarding to points on the two lines to Fort Wayne.

Coal trains moved up Capitol Avenue, past the Indiana State Capitol, turned east on Ohio to Massachusetts and then over two routes. Fort Wayne-bound coal trains left the city over College Avenue, went north to Peru and then to Fort Wayne with coal for the ISC's Spy Run power plant. Russell Powell states that the normal delivery point for the six-car coal trains was Ardmore siding on the west side of Fort Wayne. A working day rarely allowed sufficient time to deliver the cars to the power plant. One of the typical drawbacks of traction freight was the slow street running and the Fort Wayne street operation was long and twisting with a special

Below ISC ran its Northern Division (north of Fort Wayne) as part of the system. Even on such "lesser branches" as this, the interurban railway business went on all day and well into the night—about 18 hours a day seven days a week. *Ralph A. Perkin photo*

Above An empty coal train, led by motor 711, passes through Plainfield in March 1939. Substantial brick buildings combining the power substation with the passenger station were found in several towns on the Terre Haute line. *James F. Cook photo*

problem at Calhoun and Superior Streets where the street railway tracks split into east and west branches only 200 feet north of the level crossing of the Nickel Plate railroad's main line. Due to a constant concern about a derailment or other hang-up on the Calhoun and Superior tongue switches, no more than two coal cars or freight trailers were allowed north of the railroad crossing at one time which slowed the movement considerably. Trains could be taken to Pearl Street and broken up there for movement to Spy Run Shop, the power house and Commerce Street freight terminal.

Powell was also motorman on coal trains to the State Reformatory, near Pendleton, where Indiana Railroad had a track connection into the prison rail yard. These trains came out of Indianapolis over the Massachusetts route to the Belt Line connection and then north and northeast toward Anderson. On one trip, with Vern Ramey as conductor and Bob Evans as brakeman, they made an untimely arrival at the reformatory. On hot days some of the prison trusties, who were allowed to work outside the wall, knew if they happened to be close to the prison's beehives a good way to get out of work would be to stir up the bees. Hitting a hive could send a cloud of bees on a rampage and the trusties and guards would have to clear the area. This had happened shortly before the coal train worked its way up to the switch and when Evans dropped down to throw the switch some of the bees went after him. Ramey, not knowing that an entire hive was on the loose, dropped down to show Evans how to avoid the bees. They went after Ramey who ran for cover ducking into a nearby shed for cover. The shed contained the hives and beekeeping equipment. From there he ran for a water-filled gravel pit where, in the process of falling down the steep sides, he broke his leg. The guards saw what was happening and sent men wrapped in burlap to rescue the crew.

Normal entrance into the state reformatory was made at 8:00 AM when the guard force was at maximum strength. The Superintendent would come down to let the train through the two sets of gates that provided access to the tracks in the prison yard and then oversee the operation. Prisoners were kept clear of the railroad area of the yard and any outside of the lock-up were made to stand against the wall. According to Powell, it was a pretty good shove to get the cars rolling and into the yard. The empties had to be taken out and then the loaded cars shoved in. On one occasion a guard, who was a former railroader, gave conductor Al Grossman the OK to come ahead. Grossman gave Powell the signal and he sent the six cars rolling briskly ahead right over the derail, which the guard had forgotten, putting all of the coal cars on the ground. Since the cars were inside the gate, all Powell could do was uncouple and back out leaving the derailed cars inside for the convicts to unload and rerail by the next night.

On another occasion Powell's freight motor was heading six side-dump cars westbound along the Wabash Valley trackage east of Rich Valley. At Rich Valley the signal maintenance man, for this signaled territory, had stepped from his "speeder" (motor section car) and was talking on the trackside phone to Indianapolis. The speeder's wheels were insulated and had not activated the signal so Powell did not know the track was occupied. Vern Ramey was riding in the front and saw the speeder around a curve well ahead of its coming into Powell's view. Ramey spluttered and stuttered but couldn't get the words out until it was too late. The signal man was listening to a description of a new style speeder the company had just purchased when the train, braking hard, roared by and totally destroyed his speeder. Indianapolis was then given the suggestion that they buy another of the new model speeders.

On October 16, 1934, Indiana Railroad moved to the Louisville & Interurban Company's interurban terminal on Jefferson Street between Third and Fourth Streets in Louisville using existing dual (broad and standard) gauge tracks. This allowed the old terminal, about a block away, at 428 South Third Street, to be closed. This provided a joint terminal operation with the Louisville & Interurban's trains for the next year until the L&I abandoned its remaining lines. After that Indiana Railroad and the New Albany & Louisville Railroad were the only companies operating through the terminal. As 1934 drew to a close, the Indiana Railroad System seemed, momentarily at least, in a secure survival position.

Above Line car 767 and two motorized section cars, along with the line and maintenance crews, covered the areas east and west of Wabash. *Jack M. Miller collection*

Below Nick Ross on one of the company's motorized section cars at the Wabash station. The company had 22 motor cars in service as late as 1938. *Jack M. Miller collection*

Chapter 7

1935-1936 – The Good Years

Left Out of its normal territory, car 93 fills in for a highspeed on a Columbus local of September 4, 1937. Lacking proper signs for the Louisville line, the operator has displayed the destination of the return trip. Here he's still southbound, passing Greenwood shops.
John F. Humiston photo

By the end of 1934 a number of economic matters slammed into the Indiana Railroad with a smashing effect that could have leveled the railroad and certainly given the controlling interests of Midland United cause to consider disposing of the entire property. But once again, the receiver, and not the owners, would chart the course. He would do his job of running the rail lines, and the company would survive.

The original Indiana Railroad concept as planned by Samuel Insull, Jr. and Robert Feustel, was shifted beginning in mid-1932. The shift had revised the premise that was basic to the creation of the Indiana Railroad: an essentially debt-free railroad that would rise or fall on its own operating performance. Overnight Indiana Railroad found itself operating at a loss as a result of depreciation charges and interest expense and was millions in debt!

Discovering what happened is not readily apparent until one looks at the Indiana Railroad's financial statements. First, Indiana Railroad was mandated to record depreciation expense. Previously, no depreciation of its property and equipment was recorded. This accounting change converted previously reported operating income to an operating loss. (As a utility company subsidiary, Indiana Railroad had adopted the accounting procedures of the parent holding company. At that time, railroads were, generally, using betterment accounting. Under betterment accounting there is no depreciation charged while the equipment or property is in service. However, any like-kind replacements, such as poles, rails, wires and similar items, are expensed. In 1932, straight line depreciation accounting procedures were mandated. Straight line depreciation is based on original cost and assumes that each piece of property and equipment has an estimated useful life. Property is depreciated on the books as soon as it is placed in service.) Second, Midland United carried certain assets and liabilities of its subsidiaries, such as Indiana Railroad, on its own books. Beginning in 1932, these assets and liabilities were "pushed down" to the respective subsidiary company's books. For Indiana Railroad the amount of this "advance of funds," as of December 31, 1932, was $3,660,495. This was the amount of money that Midland United had spent to acquire the Union Traction, THI&E and other interurban properties. In addition, Midland United held a 6% demand note for $1,750,000 in cash advanced to Indiana Railroad. This money apparently represented the cash needed to buy the new highspeed cars and the new power distribution equipment. The interest expense was yet another burden on the Indiana Railroad's expense ledgers. However, in the financial world it is acceptable to charge a subsidiary with the investment in its assets. In reality these audit revisions provided a truer economic picture of the railroad.

In April 1932, two professional firms had been retained. Day & Zimmerman, Inc., was to render an engineering evaluation report (fair market value appraisal) and Arthur Andersen & Co. was to make an independent audit of the Insull companies. The audit and evaluation are considered in the Federal Trade Commission (FTC) study of utility corporations. (There is some bias in the multiple-year FTC hearings and some "favorable" material may have been overlooked, but the basics are factual. Volume 60 of this series deals with Midland United Company, its chief subsidiary Midland Utilities company and the subsidiaries of both.)

The FTC record showed that the auditor's report consisted of two statements, one based on the financial books of the company and the other on a pro-forma basis giving effect to the engineer's report. The engineering firm's report was necessary as the value of the plant and property was important as collateral for future borrowings and established the rate base in the eyes of the Public Service Commission.

The engineers valued certain properties on the basis of the much higher cost of reproduction whereas Midland United had acquired the assets at low foreclosure costs. This produced, in the case of Indiana Railroad, a huge difference between the book value and the appraisal value. As of April 30, 1932, the book value, as audited, was $4,553,321, while the cost of reproduction was estimated, by the engineers, at $11,451,449. The practical effect of this difference is that the earnings of the railroad were simply not adequate to replace property as it wore out. Another assumption was that the owners could realize more from selling the property than operating the railroad. As there were few (if any) buyers for an interurban railroad, the most viable alternative was abandonment and selling the assets for scrap.

During the 1933 FTC hearings, Ray Garrett, of Chicago, attorney for Midland United Company and subsidiaries, one of the witnesses on behalf of Midland United, noted that holding companies were victims of the depression and reduced earnings, as were all public utilities. Garrett, a specialist in corporate law and railroad reorganizations, also referred to "unprofitable properties" which did not earn operating expenses. The elimination of these properties, particularly the railways, would, in Garrett's mind (and therefore Midland's) have a positive effect on the earnings of the other properties.

The interurban rail property losses were doing serious financial damage to several of the power companies. Public Service Company of Indiana had recorded losses on the Indianapolis-Louisville line starting in 1928. This increased to over $400,000 annually by 1932. ISC's interurban lines were money losers but the Fort Wayne city lines made enough to offset that loss and keep positive net railway earnings. The Indiana Railroad net operating earnings were negatives. The current (1933) controlling interests at Midland United were not interested in negative earnings figures. The 1933 Midland management was considerably changed from 1930 and the accounting policies had also been substantially modified. The auditors, as instructed, had changed the depreciation system to straight line with adequate reserves. This meant the auditors had to sort through the financial records and arrangements of Midland United Company. This quickly proved the interurban lines were "unprofitable operations" and continuation of operations was not desirable. The new management of Midland United assumed a position whereby they would prefer to abandon the rail operations and salvage the property.

The 1933 court appointment of Bowman Elder, an outsider, to be receiver of Indiana Railroad broke the link with Midland United. He could liquidate the company or try to restore it to a solvent position. Elder, with Judge Ryan's approval, had decided to keep the company operating if for no other reason than the employees. Elder could take such actions as he deemed necessary to try to restore the company to a solvent position. Judge Ryan, later succeeded by Judge Herbert Wilson, in charge of the receivership did not object to spending money if it produced savings and kept the lines operating. For that matter, the court offered virtually no objections to the actions of the receiver as long as they were reasonable and presented in the best interests of the company and its owners. Indiana Railroad continued to operate and provided employment for over a thousand people at a time when work was very scarce. Pursuing this path would be a plus for Governor McNutt and the state Democratic party, also of interest to Bowman Elder and Frank McHale.

Help continued to come from the State House. Governor McNutt, in a radio address, spoke out on the plight of the interurban systems and their future. The sharp decline in business was recognized as a product of the new concrete roads in the State Highway system which now radiated from Indianapolis. The passenger and freight losses by the interurbans had resulted in large scale abandonments of trackage along some of these same general routes. Many cities no longer had electric railway service. The competing truck companies were restricted by law but the Governor commented that these restrictions were useless unless accompanied by adequate enforcement to insure that rates and competition were kept within the limits of the regulations.

McNutt noted that the Indiana Railroad was a greatly improved and modernized interurban, combined from several companies, and operated with modern and fast passenger equipment. He did not elaborate on how the Indiana Railroad came to be modernized, who was responsible and made no mention of the fact that the company was in receivership. Faster and more convenient freight service was cited as another positive factor for the Indiana Railroad. He spoke of the possibilities of a plan for combined services between Indiana Railroad and a group of truck operators using joint tariffs as an economically sound and practical plan. McNutt stated, "Unlike competitive transportation agencies, the electric roads are not in a position to increase the scope of their operations. Their mushroom and subsequent decline proved the need for such a service on a large scale was only temporary."

The Governor, from an employment and tax return basis, wanted the electric roads to survive and operate at a profit through cooperative rail-truck efforts and through modern passenger equipment coupled to low fares. His public support of the Hoosier State interurbans and Indiana Railroad in particular is interesting. His positive influence would prove to be very helpful to the receiver and, of course, the Elder and McHale political power was very helpful to the governor.

Bowman Elder, although functioning as the receiver. acted largely through another former Midland United man, Louis Rappeport, the general auditor. Rappeport had come from the South Shore Line and, typical of many officials of the company, was highly professional in his dealings. The characteristic quality level of Indiana Railroad management continued. This was reflected down through the ranks to all employees. Some management individuals were more popular than others but all had a job to do. Rappeport was necessarily close with the company's money (on Elder's behalf) and was not a popular person among the employees.

Above Louis Rappeport (circa 1932) came to Indiana Railroad from the South Shore Line. After leaving the company in 1941 he went on active duty in the U.S. Army. Captain Rappeport was killed April 17, 1943 in action in North Africa. *George K. Bradley collection*

It may have been Rappeport who suggested that all usable passenger equipment should be considered for conversion to one-man operation to effect savings in labor costs. Most of the steel cars would be worth converting. However, anticipating a need for usable and economic cars Elder went into the second-hand market to look for good one-man cars. The Indianapolis & Southeastern's fairly new (1928) cars had been stored at Indianapolis since 1932 but these available, low capacity coach-parlor cars were passed over by Elder. Instead, he decided upon some other displaced Indiana interurban cars.

Northern Indiana Railway, Inc. had operated three mainline interurban routes and in 1930 introduced ten

Above Newly delivered from Cummings Car and Coach Company in the spring of 1935, a former Northern Indiana Railway, Inc. car, is now Indiana Railroad 94.
George K. Bradley collection

lightweight cars built by Cummings Car & Coach Company. The ten cars were idled in June 1934 when the Northern Indiana retreated to a city streetcar system. The cars, purchased on an equipment trust, remained in storage at South Bend. Initially, Cummings wanted to convert the cars for city operation to get the Northern Indiana to retain them. The idea was practical but the continued burden of paying the equipment trust notes was not and the cars were shipped to the Cummings plant at Paris, Illinois. These lightweight cars had the virtue of a seating configuration similar to the Indiana Railroad highspeeds with a smoking section and baggage area in the rear. The seating capacity was fifty which was comparable to the large two-man steel cars in service on the Indiana Railroad. At only 42,500 pounds, they were considerably lighter than any interurban cars operating on the Indiana Railroad. The ten cars were fairly fast and economical power users but were not the best-riding cars if they were compared with the highspeeds. Overlooking this comparison with some of the best interurban cars ever built, the Northern Indiana's cars have to be considered as good, durable and practical cars.

Elder, if he was not aware of the fact, was probably advised that the Northern Indiana had originally proposed to use these cars on a fairly fast South Bend-to-Indianapolis through run—similar to the long distance service that he might have in mind. Elder leased the ten cars, which required only a few minor changes, from Cummings on April 4, 1935. The cars were to be shipped ready to run and already repainted in the tangerine orange and green paint. They were given numbers 90-99.

Overlooking the financial burden of the debt "pushed down" on the company, 1935 saw the positive effects of pruning the unprofitable rail routes, bus routes and other services which resulted in a reduction of the deficits. The losses had mounted from 1930 but operations were now coming close to break even. Business in central Indiana was somewhat better and prospects for Indiana Railroad did look better. Cutting the operating labor force was another factor and helped keep the total wage costs down.

Under the controversial National Recovery Act (NRA), minimum wages, hourly work regulations and many other labor-related actions were imposed on all industries. The NRA was invalidated by a Supreme Court decision on May 27, 1935, but the pattern of labor regulation thus established continued. By petition, Indiana Railroad had obtained, in April 1935, a complete exemption from compliance with maximum hour and minimum wage provisions of the NRA Transit Code in the operation of the company's buses. At this point Indiana Railroad-owned bus service was confined to Anderson and Terre Haute city bus routes. According to *Transit Journal News* bringing the bus hours and wages up to the NRA code would cost the company $6,800 per year. The rail lines were not subject to the NRA code, but had compliance been ordered, the rules would have been applied to all employees. That action would have increased the payroll by nearly $100,000 annually. No sooner did the NRA fall than Congress passed the Wagner Act with the National Labor Relations Board (NLRB) requiring employers and unions to bargain in good faith.

A new service was begun in September 1935 when the Indiana Railroad began running railway post office cars over two routes. The service succeeded earlier steam railroad trains that had carried RPO cars over the Nickel Plate Road between Indianapolis and Michigan City and between Fort Wayne and Connersville. The interurban company had carried, and continued to carry, closed-pouch mail bags on regularly scheduled passenger runs. These mail bags were in the charge of the car's motorman and the bags were frequently kept

Above Early morning of September 1, 1935: the first trip of Railway Post Office car 375 on the Indianapolis-Peru run. Although the car is signed for Fort Wayne, the RPO car terminated its run at Peru. Later, in regular schedules, riders had to change cars for the Peru-Fort Wayne leg of the trip.
Bass Photo Company

near the front of one-man cars, where they could be watched, rather than in the rear baggage compartment where they might be tampered with. A specific amount of space was contracted for the mail on each of the interurban routes and a price for the use of the space was established by the company and the U.S. Post Office. Local mail trucks picked up and delivered the mail bags at each terminal.

The two Railway Post Office (RPO) routes did not directly succeed or duplicate the former steam railroad services as the Indianapolis-Michigan City route had been dropped in 1932 and the Fort Wayne-Connersville run in 1929. Apparently the volume of mail handled warranted a review of the policy and it was expedient to provide sorting facilities over part of these routes.

Three of the ISC-owned heavy steel cars were rebuilt for the RPO service. These big 375-series cars had an additional bulkhead that separated the motorman's compartment from the baggage section. The former baggage area was enlarged to over 18 feet in length, up to a new steel bulkhead with a 24-inch "dog house" door separating it from the passenger area. The mail section interior was equipped in regulation RPO fashion and was placed in charge of a railway mail clerk. The 375 series cars had an added advantage of battery-powered interior and exterior lights, as in the new highspeeds, and offered continuous lighting even if the trolley left the wire. The service required only one car for each route but, because of the special requirements, a third car was also altered and kept available on a rotating basis as a spare. The three cars, 375-377, carried a two-man crew because the cars also operated as scheduled passenger runs. The mail service contract was a valuable asset for the rail line because it provided a guaranteed return on the runs.

Indiana Railroad would not allow the Indianapolis-Peru RPO car to exceed the assigned route and make the complete Indianapolis-Fort Wayne run because the car had to be available for the return Peru-Indianapolis run. A separate car covered the Fort Wayne-Peru territory and a crew imbalance occurred because of the two-man crew on the RPO cars. Detailed orders were issued to move both personnel and cars around to meet the schedule. Operators deadheaded—with pay—to odd locations (even country sidings where train meets were scheduled) to cover the crew changes. The newly acquired 90-series cars were operated as empty extras at odd times to balance the equipment. South of Fort Wayne, the full existing schedule was retained in addition to the RPO runs. This resulted in having two trains only about 25 minutes apart over portions of the run.

The Indianapolis-Peru run began on September 1, 1935 and the Fort Wayne-New Castle run began on September 13, 1935. Because of the way the postal service designated some runs, many people believed the second route actually ran from Waterloo to Dunreith. The RPO car run never exceeded Fort Wayne to New Castle with the outer ends covered as closed-pouch mail.

Cummings Car & Coach had delivered all the 90-series lightweights by the end of April 1935. The ten were in use by early May on the Indianapolis-Fort Wayne via Peru route and they produced desirable results. More people were riding and the increase was attributed, in part, to the newer cars with most of the increase being recorded at city stations. Their arrival also allowed the retirement of the oldest steel cars in the 400 series, which were seriously deteriorating from rust.

Above Changing from a southbound coach-baggage car to an RPO at Peru. One-man 447 has completed the first leg of train 213 from Fort Wayne to Peru; two-man RPO 377 will continue to Indianapolis. Both cars are on Broadway just north of the Chesapeake & Ohio Railway tracks on June 30, 1938.

John F. Humiston photo

The 90's were not without their problems. Their previous service, for which they had been designed, was out of South Bend and the operating conditions were very similar to those encountered in their new environment. Northern Indiana Railway, however, ran the cars at fairly slow speeds with the fastest line (South Bend-La Porte-Michigan City) averaging 27.5 mph. On their new run the cars ran at an average of 31.5 mph over a longer route. No reason was given in a February 1936 report from Westinghouse, but it shows that the 90's developed plenty of electrical problems. Part of the reason may lie in the operators' treating the lightweights in the same manner as they did the heavy cars. Broken armature leads were very common on the 90's' Westinghouse motors. Then the winter of 1935-1936 was very severe and the problems became compounded with operators running long distances on only two of the cars' four motors. Westinghouse suggested that the cars never be run on less than three motors. The harsh weather and the too-frequent operation of the cars with only half of the motors working produced severe overloading of the cars' switches and control equipment. The results could be disastrous.

Above Railway Post Offices used a distinctive identifying postmark for each scheduled route. This postmark is from the northbound Fort Wayne-New Castle run in the latter days of RPO service.

Philip E. Buchert collection

February 1, 1936 had just begun, it was 12:50 AM and Scott Armstrong was operating car 99 on the last run into Fort Wayne. Train 34 was already twenty minutes late as it hurried north on Broadway on the way to the Main Street station. The streets were practically deserted at that early hour and the temperature was near zero. The train never reached the terminal. At the General Electric Company complex the car started its descent into the long subway under the Pennsylvania Railroad. Armstrong eased back on the controller and the warm, brightly lighted car started down the grade and drifted between the steel upright supports. The rumble of the car wheels echoed from the walls of the cavern and as it moved into the upgrade, Armstrong advanced the controller handle and a surge of power flowed through the control equipment. The motors took hold and drove the car ahead. Moments later an apparent ground in the controller caused a massive short circuit. The controller literally blew up, sending flaming debris all over the front end of the car. Continuing arcs and flashes of electricity, plus the first explosion engulfed the front of the car in smoke and flames. The surprised, startled, but unhurt Armstrong had to flee his position with no chance of opening the front doors or doing much else beyond a quick escape.

The flames and smoke spread with almost incredible speed and Armstrong along with the suddenly wide-awake five men and two women passengers fled to the rear of the car. The closed door separating the rear smoker and baggage section from the forward passenger area provided a moment of safety. The rear baggage door was also controlled from the front and could not be opened. Some of the side windows without protective bars were broken and all escaped. No one was hurt beyond their dignity.

Above One-manning 30 heavy steel cars exemplifies the competence and skill of the Anderson shop force. The 433, on May 30, 1936, swings from Capitol to Kentucky Avenue in Indianapolis on a Terre Haute run.
William C. Janssen photo

With no power, the fiercely burning 99 had rolled to a stop just beyond the north end of the subway grade and practically in the lap of Engine House No. 5 of the Fort Wayne Fire Department. Fire engines from No. 5, and soon after from No. 3, responded and put out the fire but not before the interior fittings and the roof were totally destroyed. The metal sides were buckled beyond repair. Below the floor there was little damage. An ISC work motor was called to tow the burned-out hulk to the Spy Run shop. A work crew cleared the debris from the tracks so city streetcars could start their early morning runs on schedule.

The wreck of the 99 was purchased from Cummings (the ten cars had been secured on a lease basis) for the insurance and scrap value. Arthur Redderson noted the trucks, motors and the rear controller unit could be used as spares.

The nine surviving 90-series cars were more than were needed for the requirements of the Fort Wayne-Indianapolis via Peru line even with one or more kept as spares at the two terminal cities. This car group moved about and was used elsewhere on the system as the needs changed. When they were removed from the Fort Wayne via Peru route they were replaced by newly remodeled one-man heavy cars. The 90's were used on the Richmond line and then were moved to the Fort Harrison and Muncie-New Castle runs. Although not as advanced as the highspeeds, the 90's were good passenger cars and proved their worth in increased traffic wherever they were assigned. All in all, this group of cars proved to be one of Bowman Elder's better investments.

Fires were more common on freight equipment. Although these cars were well maintained, the freight motors were subject to abuse in regular service as crews sought to get their runs over the road in the allotted operating time. Russ Powell and Al Grossman were hustling along in an ex-THI&E freight motor, with passenger gearing, and two hopper cars when the 707's controller burst into flames. The train coasted to Oaklandon where the 707 burned to the trucks.

Powell also had an unpleasant winter experience with another old 700-series freight motor. The car was at the Kentucky Avenue freight terminal when the L-4 controller shorted and set the car on fire. The crew made a quick departure—so quick that Powell forgot his new coat and lost it to the flames.

From late 1935 through the early months of 1937 the better owned and leased steel cars were converted to one-man operations. Heber LaMonte, the former Union Traction Superintendent of Motive Power, was replaced by Arthur Redderson early in 1935. Redderson, in a dual capacity with both Indiana Railroad and ISC, commuted, for hours each day, from Fort Wayne to Anderson to handle his responsibilities. He may have been "on loan" to Indiana Railroad, with IR paying part of or all of his salary, as it had a need for his talents at a time when there was very little reconstruction activity at Spy Run shops in Fort Wayne. Redderson had a superior background in designing, building, operating and maintaining electric railway equipment. Recently, he had been in charge of the acquisition of the 90-series lightweight cars. Earlier, before the design of the highspeeds, the ISC's 323 series of medium-weight

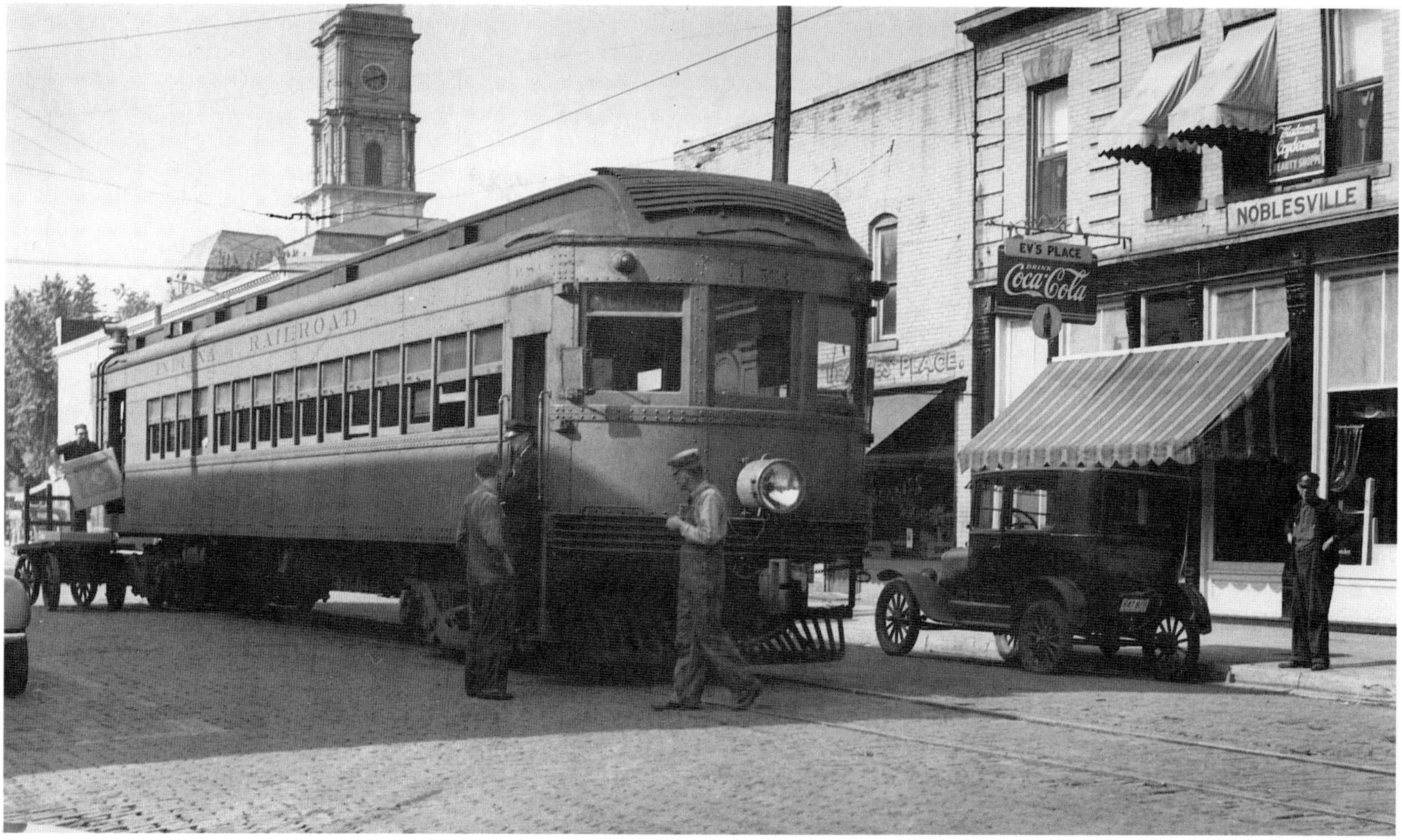

Above Northbound train 204, with one-man car 453, unloads some express at Noblesville station on July 2, 1938. Even the smaller cities had station help in the days of low wages. *John F. Humiston photo*

Below It's August 14, 1936 and recently one-manned 458 is at the Indianapolis Traction Terminal taking on closed-pouch mail for towns eastward to Dayton, Ohio – a long through run. *James P. Shuman photo*

two-man cars had been turned end-for-end, the interiors rebuilt and changed to one-man operation. Redderson now brought his experience, talents and high personal standards for quality to the task of converting the steel cars. Each car was reconstructed with the perfection of a builder's shop. Seating was reversed and a new and larger lavatory facility was placed in front of the bulkhead dividing the non-smoking and smoking sections. The former right rear door was blanked out and replaced by the operator's position and controls with a window where the upper half of the door had been. The former left rear door became the entrance with modified steps and a folding door. The reconstruction kept the shops busy (and men employed) plus creating an operating labor reduction through the elimination of a need for a conductor on all regular passenger trains. Only the RPO cars required the conductor's service in passenger operation.

One-man operation brought on the last major change in the company's rules and regulations which had been evolving since the new system took control. Interurban rule books had been in use on Indiana lines for many years. They were fairly standard in format and, in most respects, followed steam railroad practice with variations for electric line operation. The company also had a rule book for bus operations. One of the first changes, made on April 26, 1931, was the elimination of train classes. The only designations were "Regular" and "Extra" trains. Regular trains were trains authorized by a timetable schedule. Extra was broken in two groups with "Extra" for all freight trains and passenger specials and "Work Extra" for work trains. Trains were also broken by "right" and "class" with class meaning the train was given precedence by the timetable while right was conferred by train order. Right was superior to class. All trains not in the timetable were considered as extras. The employee timetable, the company's official governing document for train operation, indicated meeting points and the trains that were to be met at that point. The reverse side carried a variety of specific rules and information for governing train operation. Most of Indiana Railroad was single track so there were specifics for meets. At double-end sidings, west- and southbound trains took the siding unless otherwise directed by train order. At single-end sidings, the train facing the switch points took the siding unless otherwise directed. Trains consisting of two or more trainmen were to take the siding for an opposing one-man car in normal operation and, if the one-man car took the siding (in the case of single-end sidings), the two-man crew was to assist the one-man car in and out of the siding. Under normal operating circumstances and when time was available, the one-man car operators helped each other by throwing the switch.

The rule book covered train order methods, in detail, since many orders were passed from the dispatcher to car operators by telephone with all facts carefully written and read back by the operator to the dispatcher who kept the master train-order book for dispatching. The rules were clear that, if there was any doubt, the dispatcher was to be contacted and no movement should be made without permission. At meets or register points, trainmen were instructed to be certain that the train met or passed was the train specified in the timetable or train order. Trainmen adhered to the rules and regulations and produced an outstanding record of safe operation.

The overall change to one-man operation kept the operator a very busy person with a variety of duties to perform beyond the responsibility of operating the interurban cars on a tight time schedule. The operator became conductor as well although he was now aided

Below Having connected with an Indiana Railroad train at the Richmond station, Dayton & Western Traction Company's 1209 turns from South Eighth Street to East Main Street in downtown Richmond on May 31, 1936. *William C. Janssen photo*

Above Northern Division 325 at Fort Wayne has been turned end-for-end and changed from two-man to one-man. This car group served as the model for one-manning of usable two-man steel cars. The 325, on August 21, 1934, is riding on a test pair of Standard C-50-P trucks.
Clyde E. Helms photo, John A. Rehor collection

Below From the exterior it was hard to tell that the newly one-manned 445 was among the oldest cars in use. It had been built 23 years earlier for an interurban line in Michigan. The Dayton-bound car is near Wood (Westwood) siding on the Indianapolis-New Castle line on September 7, 1936. *Robert V. Mehlenbeck photo*

Above At the ramshackle Dayton station in 1936, C&LE "Red Devil" 125 shares the loading track in Kenton Street with a 450-series car. Indiana Railroad's highspeeds, not used on the Dayton line, never regularly met the C&LE cars after which they were modeled. *James P. Shuman photo*

by a special ticket-dispensing fare machine. In signaled territory, introduction of the one-man car produced a change that required greater intervals between trains. Where a red over yellow signal had allowed a car, closely following another car, to proceed with caution, now only the red (stop) and green (proceed) indications could be observed.

County seat towns were busy places on most Saturdays. With the resulting passenger loads and street traffic congestion, it was hard to make scheduled running times even with the lively capabilities of the highspeeds. The operator always had to push. George Krambles recalls a Saturday afternoon trip with Walter Fidler operating one of the highspeeds. Fidler was running out of Fort Wayne on first train 27 (the first of two sections of this *Hoosierland)* at 4:00 PM and was due in Indianapolis at 7:10. On the return he would leave Indianapolis on train 34 (a fast local) at 9:15 and get back to Fort Wayne at midnight. The afternoon trip would be a tough one and on this day he was determined to be on time. Going through Waynedale, Yoder and Ossian, which were really just crossroads flag stops for the limiteds, he was running as fast as possible. He had one foot on the deadman pedal and the other on the air gong valve. One hand held the whistle cord and the other reached into the switch cabinet overhead to flash the car's front green classification lights on and off. With their attention thus called to the green, second-section, signals, the people waiting at the country stops would instantly know that the next car was right behind this one rather than a couple of hours behind as scheduled. At least, that was what Fidler supposed.

In Bluffton the downtown station was bracketed by four right-angle turns in city streets that couldn't be run at more than 10 mph. Fidler took them as fast as he could, all the while flashing the green and ringing the air gong. About ten people, hearing the gong, came out of the waiting room and scurried across the track to be on the right side to board. One might suppose that they, too, would understand they were to board the second section or that a second section was even in the offing.

At Hartford City, Fidler had to call the dispatcher for a train order. To save time, he hit the ground running while Krambles loaded passengers and "lifted" the tickets. Soon after, Fidler returned at a trot and Krambles relinquished his seat, asking, "Did he give you any orders?" "No orders," Fidler replied, "but he wanted to know if we picked up all the passengers at Bluffton. I told him, 'all but ten!'"

Indiana Motor Transit Company had been inactive since the intercity bus routes had been sold. It came back to life on October 16, 1935 when the company resumed operations by providing a general pick-up and delivery trucking service presumably to all potential customers. Actually, it was for Indiana Railroad and in February 1936, owner Indiana Railroad executed contracts with the company for its services. Indiana Motor Transit Company, as a solvent subsidiary, could borrow money for trucks and equipment and operate on an independent basis. It could provide the needed pick-up and delivery service link in the railroad's less-than-carload (LCL) freight service. The trucks all carried the Indiana Railroad name. The firm's name was modified to Indiana Motor Transit, Inc. on December 28, 1936.

In 1931 the Cincinnati & Lake Erie preserved the Indiana-Ohio traction connection by executing a supervisory contract to manage the Dayton & Western's operations. By 1936 the D&W receiver decided the company could not be successfully reorganized.

Bowman Elder, coming off a fairly successful year, felt that retaining the connection would be important for a profitable 1936. He was still working to bring the company back to being a strong electric railroad. In February 1936, the trade press carried a news item indicating that Elder was proposing the purchase of the D&W. In March, another report indicated the sale would take place. However, Elder could not purchase the line without risking being challenged in court.

The matter was resolved when P. A. Hommel, the receiver of the D&W, sold the railroad property to the Fidelity Trust Company of Indianapolis on June 30, 1936. According to Hommel, the sale did not even bring enough to pay off the outstanding bonds. No equity was left for the stockholders. There is some question about the C&LE's lease (supervisory contract) for the line as a new agreement with the new owner would be needed. Jack Keenan in his book, *Cincinnati & Lake Erie Railroad, Ohio's Great Interurban System,* says the supervisory contract was terminated on June 30. Elder leased the property from Fidelity Trust on August 12, Indiana Railroad's first operating timetable for this portion was issued on August 9, even before the

Above The spacious Terre Haute terminal had four tracks. Loading in the center of the August 14, 1936 photo is one-man car 428 towing an express trailer. One man 446 is temporarily equipped for double-end operation on Brazil locals. With no wye at Brazil, the car was simply run backwards. *James P. Shuman photo*

Below The company's local delivery truck 4 is next to the Indiana Railroad freight house. The truck and the freight motor 712, turning from Cherry to Ninth Street, on August 19, 1938, represent the freight side of the business at Terre Haute. The four station tracks served both passenger and freight trains. *John F. Humiston photo*

lease was signed. According to Bob Stacy, Indiana Railroad had operated the line since August 2. Who ran it from June 30 until August 2 is not known at this time, but we conjecture that the C&LE continued on a day-to-day basis, anticipating Elder's takeover.

The lease is interesting as Indiana Railroad did not lease the Dayton & Western Traction Company – only the physical properties of the 39-mile interurban line from Richmond eastward to Dayton, with certain exclusions. The D&W barn at West Alexandria with yard tracks, 26 cars (including the five lightweight passenger cars), the stations at Eaton and New Lebanon (Ohio), and all the spare parts and materials were specifically excluded from the lease. Included were one manual and three automatic substations. Not mentioned in the lease, but later acquired, was one D&W freight motor. Elder did include a contract option to purchase the Richmond-Dayton interurban line for $66,000 less the total of all the $625 monthly lease payments made.

The lease contains no mention of the D&W (except for exclusions) as it was a defunct company undergoing liquidation. However, the Dayton-Richmond line was commonly, although incorrectly, called by the old name.

As lessee, Elder ordered the rehabilitation of the deteriorated line. Basic construction was similar to the rest of the system with the exception of ten miles from the state line to Eaton, Ohio, rebuilt in 1927, which used simple catenary overhead wire. The pole line was shared with the Dayton Power & Light Company who provided the 33,000-volt three-phase 60hz power.

Indianapolis-Dayton one-car (no changing at Richmond) passenger service was faster with the new timing at 4 hours and 25 minutes over the 124-mile line. This was fairly fast as earlier limited trains, using the shorter 109-mile route, were only a half hour faster.

Indiana Railroad and C&LE cars shared the Dayton passenger terminal. The passenger service used most of the rebuilt heavy car groups and the 90-series lightweights with the entire group of the later type transferred from the Peru route in late 1936. Several people who rode the line during this period described both the 90's and heavy cars as riding well over the rebuilt trackage. Passenger volume actually increased.

Each fall, Trainmaster Charles Lentz issued a trainmen's bulletin about "slick track" caused by leaves and weeds on the rails in the early part of frosty mornings which could leave the operator nearly helpless in need of quick stops. Sanding the rail helped but Lentz suggested playing it safe and allowing extra stopping distance.

An accident of this type occurred at Germantown siding, near Cambridge City on the Dayton line. Bill Grandison stopped his car to await the arrival of westbound car 440 with operator Vern Ramey. Ramey should have slowed down, stopped, got out, thrown the switch and moved his car into the siding so the 434 could proceed. Throwing the switches was the job of the car operator who took the siding. Ramey couldn't stop and his car slid on the slippery rails into the 434 killing Grandison.

The Dayton extension was a positive step to keep the Indiana Railroad in a profitable or, at least, break-even position. It appeared they might make the grade– a super-human effort when it had been considered a near-hopeless task only three years earlier. Now they were on the way to being a survivor. The idea could be upset–it was fragile. Much too soon it was apparent the idea would be short-lived.

Left Bill Grandison's eastbound train 612, car 434, stopped at Germantown siding near Cambridge City on the Richmond line at 7:00 AM with orders to hold the main. It was a frosty November 13, 1936 and westbound train 603 was to take the siding. Vern Ramey, according to the Richmond *Palladium*, tried his brakes, with little success, nearly a quarter mile from the switch. With the brakes in full emergency application the car slid the last 220 feet. Arch Jackson, a company employee, ran back into the car warning passengers. In the impact, the 434 was knocked backwards about 250 feet. Grandison was thrown through the front window and killed. Ramey and ten passengers had minor injuries. The cars had the same floor height so the anticlimber device worked, locking the floors (so that one would not slide up over the floor of the other). The 434's front end may have been weakened as the anticlimber was pushed back separating from the underframe which was bent down.

The Public Service Commission investigation blamed frosty rails.

George K. Bradley collection

Accidents—Was It the Inflexible Flyer?

The interurban lines had had accident problems since the first car turned a wheel. Derailments, caused by a variety of circumstances, were the most common irritant. These rarely did more than shake or bruise a few passengers but they could tie up the line for hours and riders had to tolerate the resulting delay. After good highways were built, the bus and truck operators were able to show their flexibility when they easily detoured around an obstacle.

By chance, the Dispatcher's Record of Movement of Trains for Wednesday, January 29, 1936, for the ISC Northern Division exists. At the time, this line used the four medium-weight 323-series cars. Three cars were required to maintain normal schedules on this "Y" shaped route with the fourth kept as a spare. About every two hours, one of the three cars left each of the three terminals. On some occasions there was a three-way meet on the Garrett wye, but usually the trains to and from Fort Wayne met on a siding south of Garrett. At Garrett, one of the two cars coming from the two north terminals would proceed to Fort Wayne with the other laying over to await the arrival and transfer passengers from the northbound car. The same procedure continued throughout the day.

January 29 was a cold (14 degrees) morning and train 502 (car 326) headed north from the Fort Wayne terminal at 6:03 AM. Meanwhile, at 6:10, Train 501 (car 323) started south from Waterloo for Fort Wayne and train 503 (car 325) left Kendallville for Waterloo. The southbound cars had been the last cars into the two terminals the night before. They now rolled through a light snowfall, carefully picking their way over the rails and brushing away the night's snow. Both, having started a few minutes late, managed to make Garrett on time. The 323, after a brief stop, went south to Fort Wayne meeting the northbound 326 at Wagoner. The 326 rolled onto the west leg of the Garrett wye, transferred passengers that were ticketed for Waterloo to car 325, and headed for Kendallville. The 325, now train 504, proceeded east and north to Auburn and Waterloo.

From Home Siding, in Fort Wayne, ISC's 202 (the former Marion & Bluffton 202) deadheaded north at 6:35 AM. With no turning facilities south of Garrett, the single-end 202 backed the eight miles to Green siding where it waited for southbound 323 to pass at about 7:00. Extra 202's operator called for orders and, at 7:15, headed back to Fort Wayne in revenue service, as a school tripper and making local pick-ups at the Sanitarium, Children's Home and other stops. Stopping short of the switch onto Wells Street, the car's passengers transferred to an inbound Third Street line streetcar. At 7:40 Extra 202 then backed to Home Siding and returned to the Spy Run yards. As it cleared the switch, car 323 passed by heading north as Train 506.

Other morning activity would see switch motor 817 northbound to Cedar to bring back two interchange steam railroad cars. Freight motor 848 picked up trailer

Below The 323 entering Waterloo with the Fort Wayne-Jackson (Michigan) line of the New York Central in the background. It's only two blocks to the Waterloo station. *Ralph A. Perkin photo*

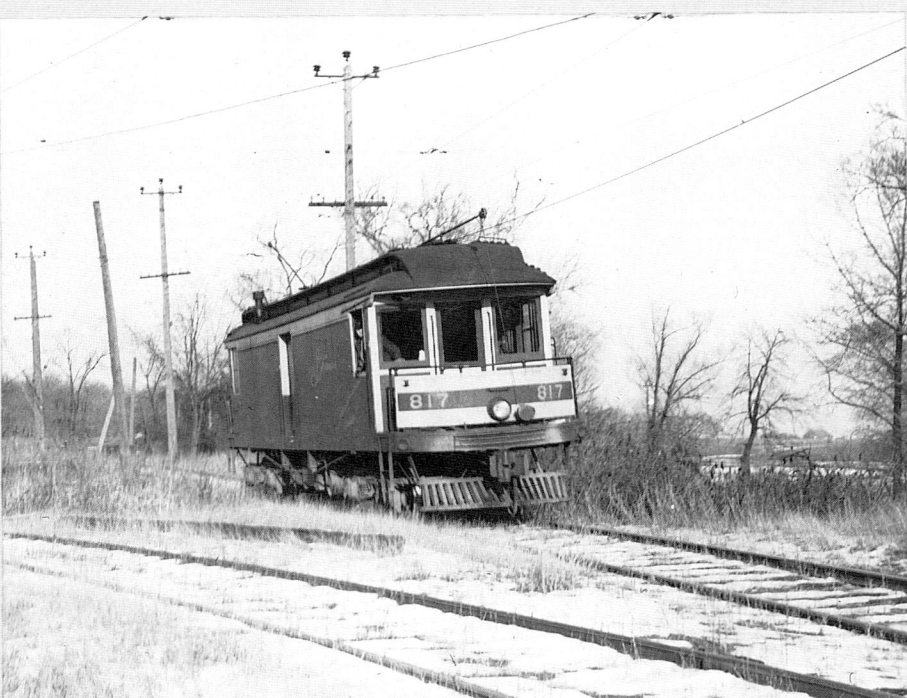

Above Switch motor 817 southbound at Pit siding on a snowy December 6, 1940. By this date the only purpose of the Northern Division is to switch coal from two railroad interchanges to the Spy Run generating plant in Fort Wayne. *James F. Cook photo*

Effective Sunday, September 29, 1935,
At 4:01 A. M. Central Standard Time.
Superseding Time Table No. 53.
Destroy all Time Tables of previous date.

FORT WAYNE TO WATERLOO AND K

STATIONS AND SIDINGS	DAILY							
	540	538	536	534	532	530	528	526
	Loc	Loc	Loc	Loc	Loc	Loc	Loc	Loc
	P M	P M	P M	P M	P M	P M	P M	P M
FORT WAYNE	......	10.45	......	8.20	......	5.45	......	4.30
HOME	......	10.53	......	(533) **8.28**	......	5.53	......	4.38
McAFFEE	......	10.54	......	8.29	......	5.54	......	4.39
ADAMS	......	10.58	......	8.33	......	5.58	......	4.43
WALLEN	......	11.03	......	8.38	......	6.03	......	4.48
ROOT	......	11.05	......	8.40	......	6.05	......	4.50
GREEN	......	11.08	......	8.43	......	6.08	......	4.53
HUNTERTOWN	......	11.11	......	8.46	......	6.11	......	4.56
SHOAF	......	11.15	......	8.49	......	(529) **6.15**	......	(525) **5.00**
STONERS (NYC CON.)	......	11.16	......	8.50	......	6.16	......	5.01
PIT	......	11.20	......	8.53	......	6.20	......	5.05
ENSLEY	......	11.21	......	8.54	......	6.21	......	5.06
HESS	......	11.23	......	8.56	......	6.23	......	5.09
CEDAR (PRR CON.)	......	......	......	......	......	......	......	......
WAGONER	......	11.25	......	8.58	......	6.25	......	5.10
GARRETT	......	11.27	......	9.00	......	6.27	......	5.12
GARRETT	......	(537) **11.27**	(533) **9.00**	......	......	(531) **6.27**	(525) **5.12**	......
ALTONA	......	11.30	9.04	......	......	6.31	5.16	......
AVILLA	......	11.36	9.10	......	......	6.37	5.22	......
CONLOG	......	11.40	9.14	......	......	6.42	5.27	......
BIX	......	11.44	9.18	......	......	6.46	5.31	......
KENDALLVILLE	......	11.50	9.20	......	......	6.50	5.35	......
GARRETT	(539) **11.27**	......	......	(535) **9.00**	(529) **6.27**	......	......	(527) **5.12**
HOLMAN	11.35	......	......	9.10	6.35	......	......	5.20
AUBURN	11.39	......	......	9.14	6.39	......	......	5.24
WATERLOO	11.50	......	......	9.25	6.50	......	......	5.35
	P M	P M	P M	P M	P M	P M	P M	P M
	Loc	Loc	Loc	Loc	Loc	Loc	Loc	Loc
	540	538	536	534	532	530	528	526

HEAVY FACED TYPE denotes meeting point.

Note A—Daily except Sundays, Thanksgiving, Christmas, New Year's, Decor

Below The 324, headed to Kendallville, and the 325, for Auburn and Waterloo, occupy two legs of the wye in the town street at Garrett station. The southbound car has already left for Fort Wayne. This is the same situation and maybe the same trains—certainly the same cars—as on January 29, 1936. *Glenn Niceley photo, George Krambles collection*

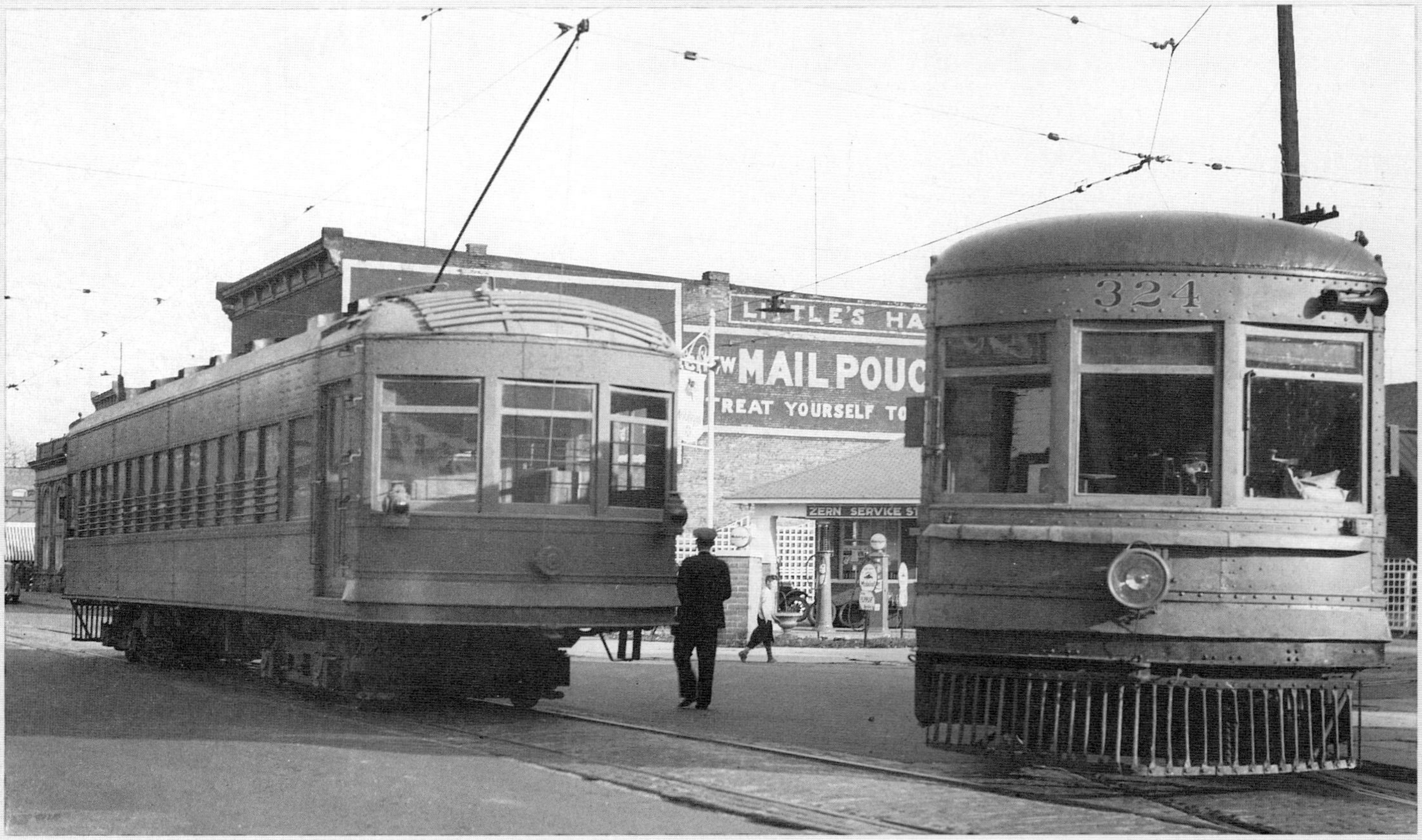

INDIANA SERVICE CORPORATION
NORTHERN DIVISION
TIME TABLE NO. 54

KENDALLVILLE—NORTH BOUND—READ DOWN · WATERLOO AND KENDALLVILLE TO FORT WAYNE— SOUTH BOUND—READ UP

This Time Table for the government of employees only. Read Special Instructions and Rules Carefully.

FIRST CLASS										DAILY			STATIONS AND SIDINGS	Mileage from Waterloo and Kendallville at Garrett	Distance from FORT WAYNE	DAILY					FIRST CLASS					DAILY						STATIONS AND SIDINGS
524	522	520	518	516	514	512	510	508	506	Note A 504	Note A 502				501 Note A	503 Note A	505	507	509	511	513	515	517	519	521	523	525	527	529	531	533	535	537	539	
PM	PM	PM	PM	AM	AM	AM	AM	AM	AM	AM	AM				AM	AM	AM	AM	AM	AM	AM	AM	AM	PM	PM	PM	PM	PM	PM	PM	PM	PM	PM	PM	
	2.20		12.30		10.30		8.30		7.30		6.00	FORT WAYNE	20.4	0.0	7.15			8.20		9.55	11.30		1.30		3.45		5.30		6.45		8.35			10.30	FORT WAYNE
	2.28		12.38		10.38		8.38		7.38		6.07	HOME	19.2	1.2	7.07			8.12		9.47	11.21		1.21		3.36		5.21		6.36	534 8.25			10.24	HOME
	2.29		12.39		10.39		8.39		7.39		6.08	McAFFEE	18.8	1.6	7.06			8.11		9.46	11.20		1.20		3.35		5.20		6.35		8.24			10.23	McAFFEE
	2.33		12.43		10.43		8.43		7.43		6.12	ADAMS	16.2	4.2	7.01			8.07		9.42	11.16		1.16		3.31		5.16		6.31		8.20			10.19	ADAMS
	2.38		12.48		10.48		8.48		7.46		6.15	WALLEN	13.8	6.6	6.57			8.03		9.37	11.11		1.11		3.26		5.11		6.26		8.15			10.15	WALLEN
	2.40		12.50		10.50		8.50		7.48		6.17	ROOT	12.6	7.8	6.55			8.01		9.35	11.09		1.09		3.24		5.09		6.24		8.13			10.13	ROOT
	2.43		12.53		10.53		8.53		7.51		6.20	GREEN	10.7	9.7	6.52			7.58		9.32	11.06		1.06		3.21		5.06		6.21		8.10			10.10	GREEN
	2.46		12.56		10.56		8.56		507 7.55		6.24	HUNTERTOWN	9.1	11.3	6.49			7.55 506		9.29	11.03		1.03		3.18		5.03		6.18		8.07			10.07	HUNTERTOWN
	2.50		517 1.00		513 11.00		9.00		7.58		6.27	SHOAF	7.5	12.9	6.46			7.49		9.25 514 11.00			518 1.00		3.15		526 5.00		530 6.15		8.04			10.04	SHOAF
	2.51		1.01		11.01		9.01		7.59		6.28	STONERS (NYC CON)	6.9	13.3	6.45			7.48		9.23	10.58		12.58		3.13		4.58		6.13		8.03			10.03	STONERS (NYC CON)
	2.55		1.05		11.05		9.05		8.03		6.32	PIT	4.4	16.0	6.40			7.43		9.19	10.54		12.54		3.09		4.54		6.09		7.59			9.59	PIT
	2.56		1.06		11.06		9.06		8.04		6.33	ENSLEY	3.7	16.7	6.39			7.42		9.18	10.53		12.53		3.08		4.53		6.08		7.58			9.58	ENSLEY
	2.58		1.08		11.08		9.08		8.07		501 6.36	HESS	2.4	18.0	6.36 502			6.41		9.16	10.51		12.51		3.06		4.51		6.06		7.56			9.56	HESS
												CEDAR (PRR CON)	2.1	18.3																					CEDAR (PRR CON)
	3.00		1.10		11.10		9.10		8.09		6.38	WAGONER	0.7	19.7	6.34			7.39		9.14	10.49		12.49		3.04		4.49		6.04		7.54			9.54	WAGONER
	521 3.02		1.12		11.12		511 9.12		8.12		6.42	GARRETT	0.0	20.4	6.32			7.37		510 9.12	10.47		12.47		522 3.02		4.47		6.02		7.52			9.52	GARRETT
523 3.02	1.12			515 11.12	9.12				8.12		503 6.42	GARRETT	11.6	20.4	6.32 502			7.37		9.12	10.47 514	12.47			3.02 522	4.47			6.02 530	7.52		9.52 538		GARRETT
	3.06	1.16			11.16	9.16			8.16		6.46	ALTONA	11.1	20.9	6.27			7.32		9.07	10.44	12.43			2.58	4.43			5.58	7.48		9.48		ALTONA
	3.12	1.22			11.22	9.22			8.22		6.52	AVILLA	6.0	26.0	6.21			7.26		9.01	10.38	12.37			2.52	4.37			5.52	7.42		9.42		AVILLA
	3.17	1.27			11.27	9.27			8.26		6.56	CONLOG	2.8	29.2	6.16			7.21		8.56	10.33	12.32			2.47	4.32			5.47	7.37		9.37		CONLOG
	3.21	1.31			11.31	9.31			8.29		6.59	BIX	0.5	31.5	6.13			7.18		8.53	10.28	12.28			2.43	4.28			5.43	7.33		9.33		BIX
	3.25	1.35			11.35	9.35			8.35		7.05	KENDALLVILLE	0.0	32.0	6.10			7.15		8.50	10.25	12.25			2.40	4.25			5.40	7.30		9.30		KENDALLVILLE
521 3.02		519 1.12		513 11.12			509 9.12	505 8.12		501 6.42		GARRETT	9.8	20.4	6.32 504		7.37 508		9.12 510		10.47 516			12.47 518	3.02 524		4.47 526	6.02 532			7.52 534		9.52 540		GARRETT
3.10		1.20		11.20			9.20	8.20		6.50		HOLMAN	6.4	23.8	6.24		7.29		9.04		10.30			12.39	2.54		4.39	5.54			7.44		9.44		HOLMAN
3.14		1.24		11.24			9.24	8.24		6.54		AUBURN	5.0	25.2	6.20		7.25		9.00		10.35			12.35	2.50		4.35	5.50			7.40		9.40		AUBURN
3.25		1.35		11.35			9.35	8.35		7.05		WATERLOO	0.0	30.2	6.10		7.15		8.50		10.25			12.25	2.40		4.25	5.40			7.30		9.30		WATERLOO

L. M. BROWN, Gen. Supt. Transportation.   C. C. LENTZ, Trainmaster.

Above Northern Division employee timetable no. 54 was in use at the time of the January 29, 1936 activity. The scheduled trains described in the text can be found on this timetable. Train number changes at Garrett are shown as are the numbers of trains met. *George Krambles collection*

---

164 (to set out at Auburn) and went north to do the daily LCL chores. Southbound car 326 came into Fort Wayne a bit late because something was wrong with the car which would take it out of service. Spare car 324 had already left the terminal at 8:30. The two cars met on Wells Street's double track and exchanged operators so the regular man could pick up his run and keep on schedule. It appeared to be just another routine winter day.

The "routine" day ended about 3:20 PM when southbound train No. 521 (car 324) derailed on the switch at Pit siding, some four miles south of Garrett. The reason is unknown but it created instant confusion. Wreck motor 828 was sent north from Spy Run as a follower to Extra 202 which, after picking up its passengers at Wells Street, was on its afternoon northbound school tripper run to Green siding. The inflexibility of the interurban line was now apparent: 324 was off the track blocking the line until the 828's crew could get things clear while cars 323 and 325 plus freight motor 848 were north of the 324. With the 326 out of service, only the slow 202 was to the south. After the 828 passed Green, at 4:25, Extra 202 ran backwards and returned to the Spy Run yards.

When word came that the track was clear, Indiana Railroad's car 96 (a reserve held for the Indianapolis via Peru line) was pressed into service. It was still cold (18 degrees) but the snow had ended as 96 left the Fort Wayne terminal at 5:50 PM. With the 324 rerailed, the 848 and three loaded steam railroad cars rattled by Pit at 5:58. Southbound 324 left at 6:08. The 828 left Pit after car 325 passed at 6:20.

Northbound car 96 had taken the siding at Shoaf to let the 848 and the 324 pass with the 325 following on a few minutes later. The 324 was picking up passengers which slowed its progress. The 325, with virtually no stops, rapidly closed the gap on the 324 pulling into the Fort Wayne terminal at 7:16 only two minutes behind the 324. The 828, returning to Spy Run, also met the 96 at Shoaf. When the line had cleared, the 96 hustled north to Garrett and Kendallville. Turning around, the 96 immediately headed back to Fort Wayne. By the time it arrived the schedules and cars had been sorted out and car 96 slipped back into reserve.

The mishap had occurred during hours of light traffic so few passengers were inconvenienced. But the derailment isolated rolling stock, stranded some passengers and delayed the LCL freight. The wreck car had to be called into service. It required an extra operating and wreck crew which made it a fairly costly operation even in the days of low wages. From these viewpoints, the interurban lines were expensive to operate and inflexible—points that were remembered when bus conversion was considered.

Chapter 8
1937—Strike!

Left Northbound car 82 descends from the Ohio River bridge of the Big Four Route (Cleveland, Cincinnati, Chicago and St. Louis Railway) on April 23, 1939. After wrapping around the camera position, the tracks entered a Jeffersonville city street behind the photographer and passed under the steam railroad's bridge approach.
Richard H. George photo

The last few months of 1936 began a period of labor strife which seriously hurt the rail system. As might be expected, the handiwork that started this action was well-intentioned but the end result didn't benefit the company and hurt some employees. "Strike" in reality spelled "disaster."

Labor difficulties went back over two years but little had happened because no serious system-wide organizing had taken place. At the time of the NRA Transit Code exemption, Indiana Railroad claimed to operate nearly 400 miles of interurban rail lines, approximately 60 miles of city street railway, and 14 miles of city bus routes (Anderson and Terre Haute). This excluded the non-leased Public Service Company's Indianapolis-Greenwood bus service. In 1935 the Amalgamated Association of Street, Electric Railway and Motor Coach Employees (Amalgamated) began to organize some Indiana Railroad employees. The Brotherhood of Railroad Trainmen (BRT) also began organizing some rail crewmen. Neither was immediately successful but the Amalgamated did succeed in unionizing the Anderson shops and power house plus the Anderson and Terre Haute city operators. The company's wages were low especially in comparison with the General Motors-owned Delco-Remy plants in the Anderson vicinity. Jobs were still hard to find and most people were happy to be working. At the same time management was trying to trim the costs of operation (labor costs in particular) and the effort had brought several months of profitable operations. Put these forces together and a collision was bound to occur.

On November 18, 1936 an NLRB arbitration board ordered the wages of the Amalgamated union members, excluding other employees, increased by 20 percent. The arbitration was the result of a May 8, 1936 action filed by Amalgamated's officials.

In the interim a 5% increase had been granted by the company on August 1. Louis Rappeport pointed out that the arbitration demand would convert the company's precarious profit picture to a serious loss. Elder's team had nursed the line back to uncertain health—he was justly proud of this—and he was not about to see a small victory converted to defeat by a labor union.

Bowman Elder had taken his responsibility as receiver far more seriously than many anticipated. Most expected him to preside over a relatively quick liquidation of the rail system to meet the growing demands of creditors. However, assisted by an able and loyal staff, Elder had turned the system around and on a year-to-year basis it was now a break-even operation. This encouraging situation had prompted the 1936 takeover of the Richmond-Dayton line. The rail system still held together and in maintaining the status quo, Indiana Railroad remained a viable property. Elder had also stated that continuing employment for many of these people was doubly important because some were too old to secure new positions. The arrival of a militant Amalgamated union group seeking higher wages had not been in the plan, and it changed the future of Indiana Railroad.

Elder and Rappeport determined they could pay a 12.5% increase to all employees and maintain a precarious "profit" picture. The Amalgamated officials were adamant, refused to accept the lower amount, and demanded the full 20% arbitration award.

On December 31, 1936 Judge Wilson issued a Superior Court ruling that the NLRB arbitration award was excessive and unfair. Because the Amalgamated continued to demand the full 20%, Wilson ordered that the receivership be closed with the entire Indiana Railroad System to be abandoned on January 9, 1937. Immediately following that news 1106 of the total 1205 employees signed petitions accepting the 12.5% pay increase. This included 446 of the nearly 600 union members. The NLRB, based only on the Amalgamated's complaint and with little or no investigation of its own, ruled the petitions had been signed under threats from company management (which is what the Amalgamated told the NLRB) notwithstanding the fact that the court, and not the company, had ordered the abandonment. Fair or foul the petitions did exist and the only threat was in the mind of the signer who, after hearing Wilson's order, thought, "Will I have a job or not?" The union and the NLRB actions were very confusing for the next few months.

The Amalgamated represented employees at two widely separated locations—Terre Haute and Anderson. Communication between the two locals was poor and to some extent they were unrelated. The BRT members, on the other hand, were all over the system and their communication was much better. The two unions were bitter rivals on a national level. The national Amalgamated wanted to represent all hourly employees and it was the national group that told the locals what to do. The trainmen members of the BRT accepted the 12.5% award, further angering the Amalgamated. The union then charged Elder with "union-busting" activities and, through the NLRB, filed complaints against Elder, as receiver, and the Indiana Railroad corporate officials. Filing against the latter group displayed union and NLRB ignorance because, as Indiana Railroad's corporate attorneys (the Midland United attorneys) quickly responded, the corporate officers had had no hand in the management of the company since it was placed in receivership in 1933.

Judge Wilson's December 31 order had been issued with some reluctance. There were over 1200 jobs at stake. On January 2, 1937, because of the petitions, Wilson allowed Elder to continue operations and to pay some increases. Trouble followed soon afterwards at Terre Haute when Local 1064 of the Amalgamated called a meeting on the night of January 16 to discuss the 20% increase. A national union officer was present and he apparently approved waiving a charter requirement for a secret ballot. Instead, following some fiery rhetoric, a voice strike vote was declared passed and, at five in the morning of January 19, the Terre Haute city lines were strikebound. To avoid any unpleasant confrontations, interurban cars came into the city only as far as the car barn on Wabash Avenue. Passengers had to find their own transportation downtown.

On January 25 Judge Wilson called a conference at Terre Haute of the union heads, company officials, the mayor and local business leaders. The union was adamant on the arbitration award total of 20% in wage increases. They did not care how the arbitration had been achieved or decided nor whether it was fair or not. The city and business officials recognized that the Terre Haute lines and employees were a Terre Haute problem that could be solved with a local-service fare increase. That increase was for city car and bus operators only and a one-cent fare advance could cover those employees. Service was to be restored on January 27.

The Anderson area employees held a meeting on January 25. This assembly was described by the Anderson Amalgamated officers as a "hostile" company-sponsored meeting. An uneasy peace seemed to prevail for the moment.

While combating the human element, the company found itself attacked by natural elements. There had been plenty of cold weather and snow but this had been accompanied by some warm periods and rapid thaws. While snow and ice made the reopening of the Terre Haute rail lines difficult, a series of thaws had created high-water problems on the Louisville line. Between Columbus and Seymour the interurban ran east of the East Fork of the White River to avoid bridging the river twice. The route was through a low area prone to flooding. High water closed the line on January 15 disrupting service. That was only a mild problem to nature's next act.

The Falls City area was bracing for high water on the Ohio River but it was totally unprepared for what happened. For several days the Louisville, New Albany and Jeffersonville newspapers predicted high water based on up-river reports. At Jeffersonville, *The Evening News* reported on the rising waters and on January 21 predicted the river would crest at the flood stage of 38 feet. The newspaper did not reflect alarm. It was the last issue until February 20. What happened came as a monstrous surprise to everyone. The river went to 39.3 feet on the 21st and over the banks. The following day the river stood at 45.6 feet and had invaded every low area in the three cities. The peak was on January 27, at 57.1 feet, and virtually all of the three cities was underwater. So was the Indiana Railroad. It was the worst flood of record and did incalculable damage to business and individuals. Many people lost all of their personal belongings while many business owners saw their buildings, stocks and equipment damaged or destroyed by the water. Indiana Railroad was caught with the rest. The company's biggest problem was joining the task of digging out as all streets were buried in a thick, gooey mud after the river receded. Poles, wires, tracks and buildings had to be checked and repaired. Cold weather that followed the flood added to the hardship. Service was not restored until the first week of March.

On the operations side, Indiana Service Corporation lopped off the northernmost rail lines in the system. The Northern Division of ISC, although not part of the leased lines system, was for all practical purposes part of the system. ISC had petitioned to abandon the operation in February 1935 but, following a Public Service Commission hearing, agreed to a continued operation. Citizen groups from the communities served by the line offered to try and gain more business for the railroad. ISC was willing to go along for six months but seeing an honest effort was being made to increase the patronage the rail lines continued the service longer. The time extension gave the company more financial loss ammunition in a new appeal to the Public Service Commission. W. Marshall Dale, ISC vice president and general manager, publicly thanked the citizens.

Below Freight motor 717 descends on the Louisville side of the Big Four bridge with the last southbound freight train into Louisville. The date is October 31, 1939. *Dr. Howard R. Blackburn photo*

Below A westbound highspeed whips across the White River bridge west of Chesterfield on April 10, 1938 gaining speed for the steep grade to Jackson's Crossing. *James F. Cook photo*

Above Highspeed car 70 leaving the Louisville Railway Company's interurban terminal on the dual-gauge track. Now turning east into Jefferson Street the car will follow a tortuous route over Third Street, Prospect Alley, Brook Street, Madison Street and Wenzel Street before climbing to the Ohio River bridge. Bridge operation required a two-man crew and the second crew member is standing in the car door on this July 3, 1938. *John F. Humiston photo*

Below Indiana Railroad's Jeffersonville station and yard on July 3, 1938. The station was the drop-off point for the second crew member, who rode the next car back to Louisville. An eight-track car barn stood here until the early 1930's and these six tracks were originally under roof. The station building extended to the street, enclosing two more tracks. The entire area was under 10 to 15 feet of water in the 1937 flood. *John F. Humiston photo*

Left ISC 817 southbound at the Wallen substation on the Northern Division. December 6, 1940 is a chilly day and the crew has a good fire in the 817's heater. *James F. Cook photo*

On January 29, 1937 the Public Service Commission ruled that the ISC lines north of the south edge of Garrett would be abandoned for freight and passenger service at 12:01 AM February 15, 1937. ISC retained freight-only service on the Fort Wayne-Garrett portion after that date.

Short Way Lines of Indiana, Inc. which already ran highway bus service from Fort Wayne to Waterloo and on to Lansing, Michigan added a new leg to its service to include Garrett, Auburn and Waterloo. Short Way also picked up the pouch mail contract between Fort Wayne and Waterloo.

The uneasy labor peace ended without warning. The Amalgamated, apparently not understanding or appreciating the reasons for the comparatively easy victory at Terre Haute, did not compare situations and began discussions about a strike action at Anderson. In an abrupt move, the Amalgamated's officials showed up at 4 o'clock in the morning of March 19 and took the Anderson shop, power house and city lines employees on strike, surprising the company and most of the local employees. No notice had been given until the actual pulling of the power house switches. The local streetcar and bus operators had no advance warning with some totally surprised employees showing up for work and finding they were on strike. Even more surprised were the riders who were suddenly and without warning left with no public transportation. The strikers cut the power to those rail lines served with 25hz power by throwing the switches at the feed-line panels. The engines and turbines were shut down. Immediately affected were the Indianapolis-Anderson-Muncie (including the Fort Harrison line) and the Indianapolis-New Castle-Muncie (the old "Honey Bee" line) service. The power shutoff also darkened eleven small towns along the Honey Bee route creating confusion and angering the residents. There was no violence—a pleasant surprise because Anderson and much of central Indiana had just experienced labor strife of unpleasant proportions. Among those voicing complaints about the local transit strike were General Motors unionized employees who now had to walk or drive their car to work.

Bowman Elder met with representatives of the union, in Indianapolis, but stated that he would take no action until the electric power was restored. He expressed great concern about the strikers' shutting off the

Left Striking employees parked loaded coal cars, a city car and a couple of work motors on the entrance track to the Anderson shops and power house. With no electric power the line was blocked as shown in this March 25, 1937 view.
James F. Cook photo

Above Burcutt siding was the south-end layover point for the Fort Wayne-New Castle RPO car as there was no available space in New Castle. Although this photo dates from July 22, 1939, the setting was much the same during the 1937 strike. *John F. Humiston photo*

power without warning to the eleven communities and leaving a small town like Mt. Summit without electricity to operate its local waterworks. Unimpressed and angry, the Amalgamated representatives drove back to Anderson. They did not appear to appreciate that cutting the power to several towns was not in their favor.

Union officials met again with Elder on the 22nd but no agreement could be reached. Following the meeting, the company announced that the supervisors had pulled the boiler fires at the North Anderson power house. Elder also said the Anderson strike problems could not be resolved as easily as had the recent strike at Terre Haute. There the penny fare increase created enough direct revenue to pay an increase in wages to a relatively small group of local operators. A similar increase in Anderson city fares would not cover the additional 7.5% increase demanded for well over 100 employees.

Several days later, on March 26, an effort was made to break the strike as employees from other divisions journeyed to Anderson to encourage the local workers to go back on the job. The power house boilers were lit in hopes that line might start. The Amalgamated's representative intervened and the police were called in to assure that order would be maintained. To everyone's credit there were no incidents beyond a few shouts. The deadlock continued and the boilers went cold. To assure that 25hz power would not be brought in over the two-circuit high line between Anderson and Bunker Hill (Pipe Creek), striking linemen threw heavy chains over the high line wires near the power house.

In the meantime, Public Service Company of Indiana provided 25hz power to Mt. Summit, Sulphur Springs, Oakville, Cowan, Honey Creek and Springport along or near the Muncie-New Castle route and some power for the rail line. Their New Castle steam generating plant had a limited 25hz capacity. Later the towns of Mt. Comfort, Mohawk, Willow Branch, Maxwell and Eden on the Indianapolis-New Castle route also received power from Public Service Company.

Only a limited portion of Indiana Railroad was shut down. The lines from Indianapolis to Louisville, Terre Haute and Fort Wayne (via Peru) were not affected at all. These lines, the Fort Wayne-Muncie route and Dayton-Richmond-Cambridge City (where a convenient wye was located), continued to offer a modified passenger service. There was not enough traffic from Cambridge City to Dunreith to make it worthwhile. All of these lines used purchased power.

During the strike the Muncie dispatchers dutifully wrote annulment orders for all through trains on the Indianapolis-Richmond-Dayton line and for those through runs that came through Muncie on either of the two Indianapolis lines. A re-bidding of the runs between Fort Wayne and Muncie and the short-turns in between

Left Highspeed 79, at 16th and Arrow streets in Anderson, makes the first trip after the strike. It's late in the morning of May 22, 1937 after the power house boilers got up steam. The car had not been washed as everyone was just returning to work. *James F. Cook photo*

Below One of the temporary independent bus operations in Anderson during the 1937 strike. This bus is turning south onto North Meridian Street. *James F. Cook photo*

was made on March 21. The dispatchers acted in a normal manner and recorded the scheduled trains but simply annulled the movement or revised the orders to cover the modified operation set-up for the strike period. Train orders were issued for the Cambridge City-Dayton operation where the runs had also been rebid in accordance with the restricted service.

There was enough power on the Muncie-New Castle line to let the RPO car through as well as some other cars that made only the short run to maintain the service link between the two cities. Periodic freight motor movements were also made. Frequently these moves were late due to the low voltage on the line. Power was available south of New Castle but the company must not have believed the territory provided enough potential to continue operations during the restricted power period. Cars could move between the two segments and the Richmond line was not totally isolated. Surplus cars and work equipment were moved from the Richmond end of the line to the main system by a round-about route. Some of the 90-series cars from Richmond were moved to Indianapolis through Muncie, Fort Wayne and Peru. They came north, one at a time, with some going through the south side of Muncie at a bare crawl due to the low power.

The strike period produced an interesting opportunity for Indiana Railroad passengers. The company would sell and honor Indianapolis-Muncie tickets allowing passengers to travel via Peru and Fort Wayne. This was a roundabout way to travel but it gave a fantastic amount of mileage, almost 200, for the price of a ticket over a route of only 57 miles.

In mid-April 1937 Elder returned to the court and asked Judge Wilson for an order allowing him to proceed with the liquidation of unprofitable units of the Indiana Railroad System. He said: "As receiver I cannot permit the assets of the trust to be dissipated. For nearly four years, every effort was made to continue operation, and so long as there was cooperation from all parties concerned, we made considerable progress. There are only two alternatives: To sit by and watch the assets drain away, or to plug the leaks by abandoning unprofitable operations. The latter course is the only logical one.

"During the closing period of 1936, labor troubles developed, which, together with other unforeseen factors, beyond the control of the receiver, have rendered

operation of the system as a whole unprofitable and created a situation which, regardless of any effort the receiver may make, offers no reasonable prospects for future improvements.

"The wage demands of the strikers have been the final straw that broke the camel's back. The previous wage increases, which amounted to nearly the entire operation profit of 1936, coupled with loss of revenue and extraordinary expense occasioned by floods, strikes and other conditions beyond the receiver's control, have made the outgo exceed the income for 1937."

On April 28 Judge Wilson signed an order granting court permission to abandon the Indianapolis-Dayton division at midnight on May 8 and to sell its assets. Louis Rappeport testified that the division had lost $87,896 in the eight months from July 1, 1936 to February 28, 1937. The Honey Bee line and the former D&W rails were going and no attempt was made to replace the service with either buses or trucks. The Fidelity Trust Company petitioned the Indiana Public Service Commission on May 4 to abandon their Dayton-Richmond line because it had no potential operator for the property. The Indiana-Ohio freight connection went with the abandonment. The existing interurban service between Cambridge City and Dayton ended on May 8. The Richmond city streetcar lines continued as an isolated piece of the rail system.

On May 3 another attempt had been made to solve the strike. Frank McHale acted for the company. No progress was made, but it was now clear to the union that 150 to 200 employees would lose their jobs follow-

Above Westbound 81 at the Spring Valley crossover on July 7, 1938. In one-man days, eastbound Fort Harrison cars backed through the spring switch on the right to the westbound main, then ran forward (against traffic) to the junction in the distance. The overhead pan was aligned so a trolley pole pushed by a backing car would move to the crossover wire.
M. D. McCarter collection

Right Southbound car 56 as Train 411 in a sea of Queen Anne's Lace at Bundy siding on the Muncie-New Castle shuttle on July 29, 1939. This was normally the territory of the lightweight 90-series cars. *James F. Cook photo, M. D. McCarter collection*

ing the Dayton line abandonment. This was a stark reality, not the receiver's rhetoric. It could not fail to make an impression on the Anderson strikers.

The strike was finally settled on May 21 after nine weeks. The Amalgamated won the full 20% but didn't gain its demand for a closed shop and dues check-off. The Anderson city operators, who wanted to go back to work, may have been one reason for the settlement. They were worried because the city, partly at the request of other local unions, was considering handing the franchise over to another bus company. This could cost the Indiana Railroad city line employees their jobs and the thought of the unemployed former workers of the Dayton line was terrifyingly recent.

The boilers at North Anderson were fired and the old engines creaked back into motion on the morning of May 22. Indiana Railroad power house employees were not running the plant. These union members lost their jobs as Elder contracted with Indiana General Service Company to provide electric power needs. The

Above In the late afternoon, a southbound, two-car *Hoosierland* with cars 80 and 56 meets car 57, a northbound *Hoosierland*, at Mason siding, 19 miles north of Bluffton, in 1940. The operators exchange trains and return to their home terminals. *Richard H. George photo*

employees of that company were running the power station as part of a change from 25 to 60hz current.

Interurban passenger service started on the morning of the 22nd as energy flowed back into the lines. The Anderson city routes were restarted on the 23rd and the freight trains were able to roll on the 24th. The threat to the Anderson city routes ended with the return to work. Also, Liberty Transit, a legitimate competitor in some parts of the city, had joined Indiana Railroad in opposition to any new operator.

With the restoration of full power, Indiana Railroad brought the remaining rolling stock in from the Indianapolis-Dayton line. Only the streetcars and local work equipment were left behind at Richmond. Some of the company employees continued to work, for a short period, in the unpleasant duty of tearing up the Indianapolis-New Castle-Richmond line. (Fidelity Trust sold the Richmond-Dayton line for salvage.) It was sad work, the first abandonment in several years, and meant further limitations on the company's rail freight service. It was readily apparent that the Amalgamated union might have won the battle, but many employees, including some who had made the union's action a success, were now without a job. A hollow victory for them!

On June 3, 1937, the court formally authorized Elder's petition to close the North Anderson power house, sell the equipment and contract for commercial power. The small communities, formerly served from the power house, were now the customers of Public Service Company or Indiana General Service Company. The remaining railway load required only part of the Anderson power house capacity. Power distribution was changed to 60hz purchased power as soon as the equipment could be modified. Used 60hz substation equipment was brought in from the Richmond-Dayton line and from some of the system's power company affiliates who had retired converters on hand. Automatic rotaries were installed, as replacements, at Muncie, Springport, Daleville and Lawrence. One manual rotary was put in the Orchard substation and two manual rotaries were placed in the Anderson power house building. The two rectifier substations, at Bucy and Tile, were changed from 25 to 60hz current as a follow-through of the 1931 modernization plan.

The change was completed by the end of the year and the North Anderson generators coasted to a halt for the last time. In January 1938, all of the power house boilers, engines, turbines, generators and all of the related equipment from the old generating station were offered for sale to salvage dealers. Over the next few months all of this scrap was removed from the building. Beginning in August, the building and smoke stacks came down and the one-time showpiece was no more.

Elder had also received court permission to substitute 60hz replacement equipment at the Broad Ripple, Noblesville and Tipton substations on the Peru line. These were 25hz installations and were, since the time of the strike, supplied from Public Service Company of Indiana through the use of frequency converters. Elder may have been under some pressure to relieve Public Service Company of the added load. The receiver's ledger of annual expenses shows over $11,000 was expended toward these conversions during the calendar years 1937-1938. On the other hand, Robert Stacy reports seeing no replacement apparatus in these substations. He was an active Indianapolis railfan at that time and visited these sites following the strike.

In addition to the Amalgamated's settlement, the BRT and Indiana Railroad signed a new agreement effective June 24, 1937. It did not call for increases to the 20% level. This agreement covered only trainmen.

The next to go was the Anderson streetcar service. The company's bus replacement had been planned earlier in an agreement reached between the city and the company. The strike delayed the retirement of the local streetcars until the night of November 13, 1937. Interurban cars were switched from Meridian to Main streets so that they used only Nichol, Arrow and Main streets.

That 1937 was a major turning point for the Indiana Railroad is now evident even though it may not have been apparent to the casual observer of the time. The events of 1937 made it clear to Elder that the company could not continue as a rail line. A drastic change would be required for Elder to preserve and perpetuate the company. For the old order, the pattern had been set: it was the beginning of the end.

Winter's Punch

Left On the wye at the Spring Valley station on a chilly November 25, 1938, the 91 comes off the Fort Harrison branch and heads toward Indianapolis. *Glenn Niceley photo*

Right On January 15, 1939 highspeed 57 makes the station stop at Anderson before a long, cold, snowy run to Muncie and Fort Wayne. *James F. Cook photo*

Below Ninth and Main at Anderson's courthouse square on November 23, 1938 with a snow-covered 52 running as a *Hoosierland*. Chances are that train 15 will arrive Indianapolis "on time." *James F. Cook photo, M. D. McCarter collection*

Above Anderson passengers board car 67 on a cold, blustery and snowy January 25, 1938. *James F. Cook photo*

Below A heavy car breaks through fresh snow in the streets of Plainfield on January 7, 1940. *James F. Cook photo*

Right Entering Anderson, highspeed 63 crosses the Belt Line after making a trip from Indianapolis through the snow-covered countryside on February 21, 1938. *James F. Cook photo, M. D. McCarter collection*

In Hoosierland a winter day can range from a mild temperature, bright and sunny, to the boiling gray clouds of a roaring blizzard. Weather variables could create havoc for a system with an east-west line from one side of the state to the other and a north-south territory of nearly 225 miles. (The north-south portion spread from the Ohio River to the northeast corner of the state.) Shifting weather patterns could produce a variety of weather conditions throughout that area and snow and ice created interesting operations situations.

White wings of snow flew from the interurban car's pilot as it sped through the countryside, the noise muted by the soft snow. Much of the Indiana interurban territory was flat, open country and just windswept enough to see much of the snow blown clear. But blowing snow causes drifts and quickly fills cuts. Where the snow was deep or drifted, wedge plows were used. The company had several such plows that could be pushed by a freight motor or fitted directly to one of the cars. These plows made an impressive sight when they made a hard run at the snow and sent huge snow clouds flying to the right and left.

Interurban cars were well equipped for winter weather. Many of the older passenger cars had storm windows and were heated with efficient, coal-fired, hot-water heaters. The newer cars had electric heaters while the freight and work motors were usually equipped with a good-heating. railroad-caboose stove.

Winter brought out the best in the operating crews as they had to know every turn and twist of the line and, unless conditions were unduly severe, they managed to maintain the already tight schedules. At the same time the company marshalled its forces and put extra cars on the line to keep the track clear. alerted the line crews and kept track crews busy clearing clogged switches and ice-filled flangeways.

"Old Man Winter's" worst punch came from extremely cold temperatures, ice or sleet storms. Any of them could create havoc disrupting phone lines, the high lines or the trolley wire singly or, if a line pole snapped, all at once. Low temperatures caused the overhead trolley wire, already stretched taut, to contract and break. Sleet and ice could cause breaks at several points. The public took the good service as a matter of course and expected trains to continue on time—or at least close to schedule. They seldom thought or, for that matter, realized what it took to maintain that quality service.

Broken wires were dangerous and the standard procedure required that they be cleared from the ground and secured, out of harm's way, to a line pole. The cars would have to try to coast past the gap in the wire. Dispatchers were notified and swift action was taken. It meant long hours for trainmen, linemen and others working under unfavorable conditions. Trainmen on the car roof ruined uniforms changing broken trolley poles. Linemen repairing the broken lines were wet to the skin but on the job until trains were moving.

Sleet could encase the trolley wire in an icy sheath which the trolley shoe might break but, more often than not. caused a series of wire-damaging electric arcs. Sleet cutters (fitted over the trolley shoe) had sharp edges for biting into the ice and producing a good wire contact. But the most spectacular bit of winter was a car passing under icy wires, highlighting the night sky with flashing electric arcs brilliantly illuminating the countryside.

Below Crippled car 441 sits at the west end of the Dunreith wye as the 435 swings east to Richmond on January 20, 1936. Bucking the snow had caused the 441 to burn out its motors. *Robert M. Stacy photo*

Chapter 9
Rolling Downhill (1938-1940)

Left Near the start of its trip, northbound RPO 377 as train 304 pounds through Mount Summit on the afternoon of October 21, 1938. *John F. Humiston photo*

Indiana Railroad struggled out of 1937 in a battered condition. After partial recovery from the 1929 "Hoover Depression," the bottom dropped out of the national economy in October 1937, bringing on the "Roosevelt Depression." By early 1938 some ten million were unemployed. Business in Hoosierland suffered a sickening drop and the Indiana Railroad was among those feeling the decline.

Although in receivership, Indiana Railroad was still one of Midland United's properties. The United States Congress deemed holding companies—utility holding companies in particular—to be contrary to the public interest. The result was the Public Utility Holding Company Act of 1935. The Securities and Exchange Commission (SEC) interpreted the act and ruled that pyramided holding companies, such as Midland United, must be dissolved and that all public utilities (usually electric power companies), if they intended to remain in the gas and electric business, would have to divest themselves of their transportation affiliates. In most cases these affiliates were motor bus and electric railway companies. By 1937 it appeared that the SEC would survive any U.S. Supreme Court test of its basic commission premise. The final implications of the act and any resolution of the long-range aspects were yet to be determined. However, the threat was there and it did not make the future brighter for railway utilities.

The isolated Richmond streetcar lines were the first casualty of 1938. The city government had been pressuring the company to replace the streetcars with buses since March 1937. When the fleet of replacement buses arrived the streetcars bowed out at 11:00 PM on April 23, 1938.

The company's four main lines remained at the beginning of 1938. Rail freight continued but was confined to the company's own lines and interline truck routes beyond. Unfortunately, LCL business was extremely vulnerable to motor truck competition. To a limited extent the company was already in the motor freight business but mostly on a local terminal pickup and delivery basis. Some customers started specifying that their goods be shipped by truck but the company sent them by whichever method it felt was quickest and that was usually via its own rail freight. It was apparent that just remaining in the freight business would require some drastic changes to hold existing business and try to expand. Indiana Railroad was becoming a lonely interurban survivor. The simple fact of survival was unique as most of the midwest interurban systems were gone or were rapidly breaking up. The Michigan lines were long since gone and the last pieces of the Ohio systems would be gone within a year.

Indiana Railroad continued to differ from the other, still operating, midwest lines in its basic character, especially in the manner of operation and type of equipment operated. The highspeeds were the principal feature: they served as a magnetic attraction bringing interested people, especially those interested in railroads, to the land of this enchanting interurban. The company and its congenial employees—plus a precise, meticulous and clean operation—cast a spell over all who saw or rode *Hoosierlands, Hoosier Flyers* or *Dixie Flyers*. That spell, once cast, was never broken. For the midwestern "railfan" and many others, the Indiana Railroad was *the* interurban, one that was better and different. For them, this was the magic interurban!

The phenomenon of the "railfan" was just appearing and the term was newly coined. Individuals interested in railroads had been around since the turn of the first metal wheel on a fixed track. Over the years several societies had been developed to learn more and share information about steam railroads. Only a few paid serious attention to the streetcars and interurbans until the early 1930's. The electric line interest, first seen in the east, moved to the midwest and began to formalize into a group activity. That interest was limited by how much cash was available. Most of the concerned individuals were young men with limited finances. Those that could travel and those that lived in or near electric railway centers began to organize trips.

The Indianapolis Railfans' Club was among the first groups to charter special cars over the long routes of the Indiana Railroad—just to take a ride. These were usually one day jaunts. The trips gave the operators a chance to make the cars dart and the highspeeds were true flyers. The November 7, 1937 trip was a loop operation: Indianapolis to Fort Wayne via Muncie and return via Peru with a stopover in Fort Wayne for the fans to visit Fort Wayne steam and electric railway shops. The operator on the lead car of the two-car train (cars 60 and 55) was Russell Powell with Ralph Ellis in the second car's operator seat. Powell was qualified to operate both Fort Wayne routes. Also on board were Charley Lentz, the Indiana Railroad trainmaster, and his son Bob, riding the first car. Carmel to Indianapolis was considered "fast track" and there was plenty of power on that stretch. Once the car cleared the Monon Railroad crossing south of Carmel there was a fairly clear 7.5 mile slightly downgrade run into Broad Ripple. Powell told Robert Stacy and some others that he would give them a real show. He put the controller on the "post" and held it there until the cars hit the White River bridge just north of Broad Ripple (Indianapolis). Everyone in the cars was up and looking to see what kind of a show the two-car highspeed train provided. They were not disappointed and both Powell and Stacy maintain that the cars were hitting over 90 mph when they ran onto the White River bridge. Lentz was noticed to have

Above The three views on this page show some action along the Indiana Service Corporation leg of the Fort Wayne via Peru line. Once a scene of much activity, by Indiana Railroad days the remote Boyd Park barn only housed surplus cars. Train 208, car 455, has taken the siding for train 211, car 427, to pass in this August 15, 1938 view.
James F. Cook photo

Left Earlier, on April 22, 1936, lightweights were nearing the end of a year's service on this route. Eastbound car 91 enters Coss siding east of Lagro. The signal soon will clear to green. The 91's operator will call the dispatcher using the phone jack on the pole. To the left is the site of the Wabash and Erie canal.
Ralph A. Perkin photo

Left Small-city activity at Wabash with waiting passengers ready to board the westbound car, which is just crossing Wabash Street. With one-man cars, like this 446 type, passenger loading had to be on the right side of the train, but the local agent with the baggage cart loaded either side depending on the station arrangement. *James F. Cook photo*

Above Trip Number 3 posed southbound car 58 on the bridge over the highway and White River north of Noblesville. *John F. Humiston photo*

slumped down in his seat and pulling his hat down over his ears was heard to mumble, "I'll fire that SOB." Lentz didn't fire Powell and, in fact, they were good friends. Lentz was not a speed fan although he knew the motormen and the desire of the fans to see the cars go.

Normal maximum highspeed train length was three cars but, on occasion, a fourth car would be run with the motors cut out and pulled as a trailer. Lentz went along on many special runs and one was a four-car train on an Indianapolis-Montpelier round trip. Powell was called to ride the fourth car and found Lentz there trying to stay out of the way. Operator Clarence Wilson in the lead car took advantage of the good power on the Anderson Division and was flying. Lentz, riding with Powell, expressed his disapproval by asking Russell if the speed bothered *him*!

Members of Central Electric Railfans' Association (CERA) came from Chicago and other places for their trip No. 3 on August 20, 1938 over both Indianapolis-Fort Wayne routes. The group chartered one of the high-speeds for the day-long trip. This riding and photographing of the Indianapolis-Fort Wayne via Peru route was fortunate as the rail line would not survive the year. The Peru line was considered as marginal, at best, with the RPO car being the only guaranteed paying run. Nearly half of the route was leased from the ISC and all of the repair and maintenance costs were borne by Indiana Railroad. The CERA trip was one of the few times that the highspeeds had been used on the route down the Wabash Valley. On August 21, the fans made a second trip. This was a round trip to Louisville using one of the heavy cars (car 458) and one of the old trailers (car 302).

Indiana Railroad made an abrupt turn in 1938. Since its formation, there had been a continual reduction of operating services through the abandonment of rail lines. The service was not replaced with trucks or buses.

The policy was simple attrition and, predictably, all operations would eventually cease—something that had already happened to many interurban companies.

The Peru line was selected for a test program which would preserve the transportation services by using public highways. This was a progressive survival step taken by the receiver and his managers and one which might not have been attempted by the current owners of Midland United. Elder obtained the court's approval, in early 1938, to substitute buses for the passenger cars and the additional approval to introduce intercity motor truck service. Elimination of the expenses of maintaining the railroad physical plant would contribute to manageable operating costs. A viable transportation route would, if the plan worked, be preserved and strengthened and a number of jobs would be retained.

Ten 18-passenger Model 800-M buses were ordered from White Motor Company in June 1938. They were numbered 401-410 using the series used by some recently scrapped steel passenger cars. The company still had its 427 series of one-manned steel cars in active use but overlapping and duplicating numbers had been a common practice for Indiana Railroad and eventually led to a minor embarrassment. In 1937, when the Anderson streetcar service was about to be replaced with buses, a work order was issued at the Anderson shop to "paint car 53." There were two cars numbered 53. One of these was a highspeed and the other an Anderson city birney car. The highspeed needed new paint, and eventually got it, but the birney went to the scrap heap a few months later wearing a fresh coat of paint.

There was no serious opposition to the petition to abandon all rail service on the Indianapolis-Peru-Fort Wayne line. Indiana Service Corporation joined Indiana Railroad and petitioned to abandon all service on the

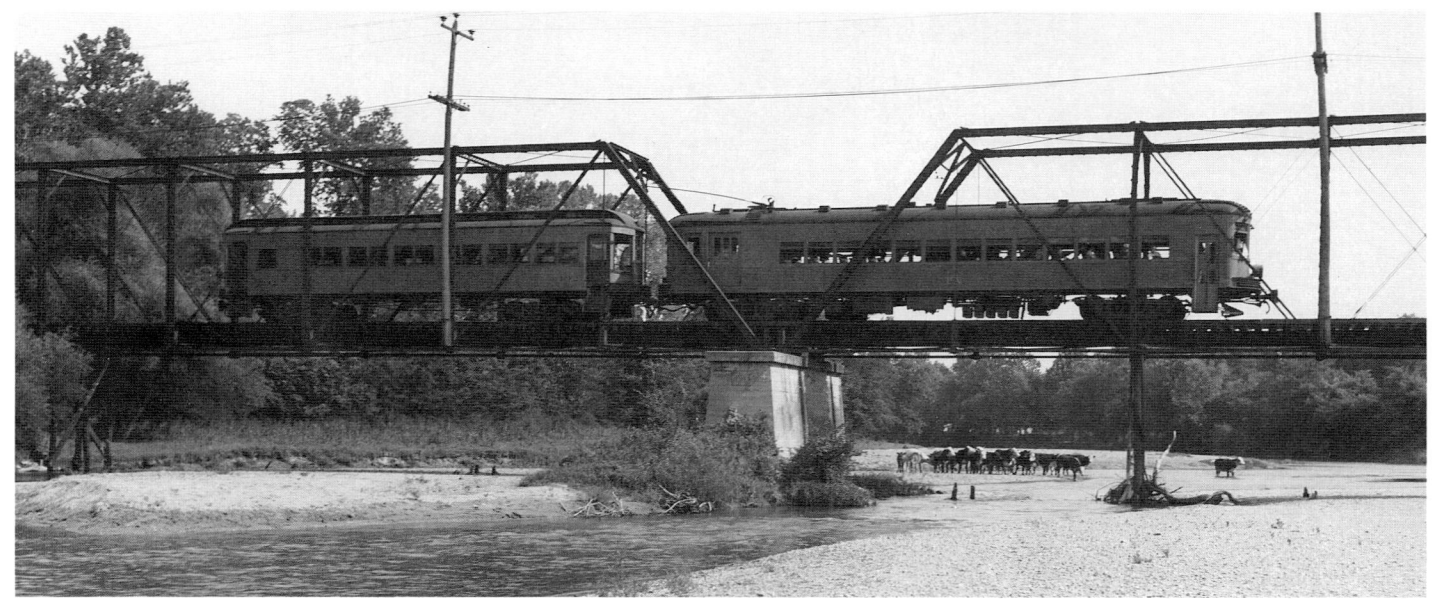

Above Pastoral scene at Flatrock River north of Columbus with the special of August 21, 1938 using cars 458 and 302. Timber bents like the one under the motor car's front truck bolstered the load capacity of the bridge. *John F. Humiston photo*

Left At Bubbling Springs, east of Chesterfield, the line crossed the highway at a poor angle for eastbound motorists. ABC Coach Lines bus 40 waits at the warning flashers for the 68 to pass. *James F. Cook photo*

Below Eastbound 430 meets westbound 435 at Huntington (formerly Diamond) siding on the west side of town on August 20, 1938. Motor 792 with a cut of steamroad interchange cars is hidden beyond the 430. Completing the four-train meet is Extra 58 West, on whose roof the photographer is standing. *James P. Shuman photo*

Above At 10:15 PM on September 10, 1938 car 435 pulled to a stop under the Traction Terminal shed alongside RPO car 375, ending all rail service on the Indianapolis-Peru line.
Richard H. George photo

Fort Wayne-Peru segment operated under the lease. ISC hired a professional engineering firm to conduct a study of the line for the benefit of the banks holding certain company securities that would be affected. Through passenger service was ended on September 5 but three trains remained in operation to carry mail until the end of the contract period. The RPO's trains (202 and 213) remained on the same schedule between Indianapolis and Peru. A steel one-man car handled pouch mail north from Indianapolis leaving at 3:15 PM on the time of former train 214 but running only as far as Kokomo. It came back as a deadhead run at 8:15 on the time of the former 219. Both the Peru and Kokomo cars, although not advertised, would carry regular passengers. The 3:15 departure got most of the passengers from the 3:15 bus departure. The mail runs continued through Saturday, September 10. The 10:15 PM arrival of the deadhead return from Kokomo with local railfans Glenn Niceley, Dick George and Bob Stacy ended the rail service. The 435, in charge of Clifford Crum, pulled into the Traction Terminal and with its white flags still fluttering stopped alongside RPO 375.

The Peru route passenger bus replacement service was accepted with few complaints. Ridership was reported to be at about the same level. However, the choice of bus models left something to be desired. The model selected was the same as the city buses that had replaced the Richmond streetcars. The Peru route buses were modified for suburban services with better seating and a baggage rack on the roof. The long intercity haul was a severe test of the Whites' endurance as well as that of the riders. Any informed Indiana Railroad patron going to Fort Wayne from Indianapolis rode the rail cars through Muncie with an assured fast, comfortable and smooth ride. The buses were noisy, drafty and, in the winter months, very cold. They provided good operating experience and information for the company management on what to order in the future. The motor freight was an improvement because it could be handled faster, with fewer transfers, and larger shippers could have door-to-door service. Ten Fruehauf trailers pulled by ten International Harvester truck tractors handled the intercity freight. This successful conversion produced impressive savings and cost reductions. Over-the-road service meant paying highway and fuel taxes but the maintenance costs for the fixed rail facilities and the expense of purchased electric power were removed. Overall, the conversion of the Peru line to buses and trucks was a success.

Indiana Motor Bus Company (IMB), an old competitor, and Indiana Railroad found that, with both in the intercity bus business over paralleling routes, they could combine their service between Indianapolis and Peru. IMB had been operating from Indianapolis to South Bend, via Peru, since the mid-twenties. Starting in April 1939, by operating alternate schedules, both companies eliminated run duplications.

In 1939 the railfans took advantage of some of Indiana Railroad's unique rail services while they were still available. These trips were spurred on by the court order of December 8, 1938 for the company to cancel its leases with the Public Service Company and Elder's announcement of plans to petition for abandonment of the Terre Haute Division and part of the Louisville Division.

The Indianapolis Railfans' Club operated a special train of three highspeeds on the Terre Haute Division on April 30, 1939. Besides scenic stops, the trip would cover the Limedale cement spur, the Binkley Mine spur, a forty-minute stop at the Terre Haute shops plus a two hour and forty-five minute lunch break at the Terre Haute terminal. The long lunch allowed time to view the Terre Haute streetcars which were to be replaced by buses. Then the group would make a fast return trip to Indianapolis. The round-trip train fare for this outing was $1.45. The trip was a success and another trip, to the Anderson shops, was made on May 14.

Hearings were held by the Public Service Commission and the Interstate Commerce Commission for the substitution of buses and trucks for the Terre Haute route and truck service only for the interstate Louisville route. Rail passenger service would continue between

Above Small buses replaced big cars on the Indianapolis-Peru-Fort Wayne route in September 1938. Two of the White buses and RPO 376 are at Fort Wayne on a wintry 1939 day. *Ed Frank, Jr. photo*

Below The three-car (66, 56 and 59) Indianapolis Railfans' special at Rock Cut west of Greencastle on April 30, 1939. The train is westbound for Terre Haute. *Philip E. Buchert photo*

Indianapolis and Seymour. The parallel Indianapolis-Franklin bus service, a separate operation, was not included in the petition. According to Louis Rappeport, the Terre Haute route lost $40,972 and the Louisville route lost $338,628 in 1938. Terre Haute Electric Company, Inc. and Public Service Company of Indiana were involved in the hearings as portions of both routes were leased from them. Hearings were virtually complete by mid-May 1939.

The last of the public hearings were held in Greencastle at the end of May. The results and comments on the hearing brought back memories of the original Insull-Feustel concept for the Indiana Railroad published in the July 1931 *Hoosier Traveler:* "The active support and patronage of the public along these lines will make it possible to maintain... the excellent service now being introduced." But the public forgot, or just didn't care in sufficient numbers.

Indiana Railroad's employee publication, *Selling System Service,* in the June 1939 issue, quoted an editorial from the Danville (Ind.) *Gazette.* "Greencastle and other towns along the Indianapolis-Terre Haute traction line are trying to 'save' it from folding up. But they can't save it by protesting and sending representatives to public officials. The only way they can save it is by patronizing the service. They can't save it by protesting in order that it will be in running condition if their automobiles break down. When any public utility starts losing money there is only one answer, just as there is with a private individual."

The Plainfield (Ind.) *The Friday Caller,* a weekly paper, reported: "Although there is some concerted activity at points along the line to have it retained interest here is apathetic, almost to the vanishing point. Local people seem to have no interest whatever except that they would be satisfied with a bus service instead of rail.

"Ironically enough, it is reported that most of the people who attended the Greencastle hearing traveled in automobiles and did not patronize the traction line they are attempting to 'save.'"

The Terre Haute local streetcar and bus system was sold to Terre Haute City Lines, Inc., a new subsidiary of National City Lines, Inc. (NCL) of Chicago on June 4, 1939. In the agreement, all streetcar operations ceased at the end of service on June 3 and the new firm began

Below On April 1, 1939, birney 460 waits at Fruitridge Avenue, east end of Terre Haute's Wabash Avenue line, as an interurban car passes. The city operator is going to take a chance by pushing the pole a few feet onto single track before heading downtown.

Richard H. George photo

Above and Below Two of the three 3-car Columbus-to-Louisville 4-H specials at Columbus in September 1939. The interurban was still an economical and practical way to handle a large crowd.

Richard H. George photo

Above Two miles north of Austin on the Louisville line, Indianapolis Railfans' special cars 458 and 302 paused on the Muscatatuck River bridge. *James P. Shuman photo*

Below "High-side" hopper cars of crushed rock are being switched on the curve at 38th Street and Orchard Avenue in Indianapolis in July 1936. *George K. Bradley collection*

Above Activity at Greencastle with westbound 427 unloading the daily Indianapolis newspapers, some packages and a few passengers on September 2, 1939.
John F. Humiston photo

as an all-motor bus operation. The NCL bus operations were from the Wabash Avenue car barn where the buses continued to share space with the interurban cars. Electric operations were continued on Wabash Avenue to reach the downtown station.

This was a fast-paced year for Indiana Railroad. Louis Rappeport continued as Elder's key person in overall company management. Rappeport through the years was criticized by some rank-and-file employees who did not like him. They felt that he was very direct and could be quite brusque, perhaps to the point of being tactless in an argument, and made no attempt to foster any popular sentiment. Others found him to be considerate and very perceptive. Rappeport's interest was the company's interest—and he did a very good job during this critical and transitional period.

One key factor in the continuing success of the railroad was the teamwork of the employees. Charter trips were part of this effort. For example: in July, August and September of 1939, there were ten rail and eight bus special movements. This included a diverse lot such as the American Legion Junior Band, several fraternal orders, women's clubs, Boy Scouts, sports groups, railfans, etc. The size of the groups ranged from 24 to 341. The largest was a 4-H group traveling from Columbus to Louisville. The operation required three three-car trains including two three-car highspeed trains and one made up of a heavy car and two trailers. On September 3, 235 baseball fans rode six cars (two trains) from Louisville to Indianapolis. On September 3 and 4 CERA

Right On October 31, 1939, the 77 closed out the Louisville line with the last departure from the Kentucky city. It carried railfans Ed Belknap (top), Dick George and Howard Blackburn. The operator, H. O. "Shorty" Harrington, holds the wreath sent by CERA to mark the sad occasion.
Dr. Howard R. Blackburn collection

Above In 1939 a two-car train which had brought a group to the Indiana State Fairgrounds has been turned and is in Negley siding along 38th Street awaiting the time to return to the fairgrounds (38th Street west of Fall Creek). *Richard H. George photo*

Below The 439 on a September 4, 1939 Terre Haute-Indianapolis run at Boys' School siding in the automatic block signal territory near Plainfield. It was the autumn of the line and of these heavy cars. *John F. Humiston photo*

Above The 93 on a Fort Harrison local turns northeast from Ohio Street onto Massachusetts Avenue on July 3, 1938. The Indianapolis Federal Building is in the background.
M. D. McCarter collection

ran two fan trips from Indianapolis. The first covered the Louisville line in car 55 and the second was a round trip to Terre Haute in RPO car 375. The bus movements were usually smaller except for the Brotherhood of Railroad Trainmen tour of Indianapolis. This group of 225 required nine buses. L. M. Brown followed all of these trips closely but when a choice was available he rode with the railfans.

By late summer 1939, abandonment of the Terre Haute and Seymour-Louisville lines received approval. Service south of Seymour ended at 1:15 AM on November 1 when the last northbound train pulled into Seymour. This last *Hoosier Flyer* was decorated with a wreath supplied by CERA. Motor trucks took over on the same day as part of a coordinated and expanding freight service. There was no replacement bus service.

Elder may have erred in the ending of the Indianapolis-Dayton passenger service without any company-owned bus replacement which could have established the company's position as an interstate motor bus operator. Now, in 1939, the company petitioned the ICC for permission to run interstate charter bus service to the four adjoining states and was denied.

In December 1939, a joint petition was filed with the Public Service Commission by Public Service Company of Indiana and a new independent corporation called Suburban Lines, Inc. for the latter to purchase the 21-mile Indianapolis-Greenwood-Franklin bus route. Service was operated by Indiana Railroad but the route and the nine buses belonged to Public Service Company. The sale was completed on May 16, 1940.

The end of through service to Louisville raised an old problem. The remaining 62-mile Indianapolis-Seymour portion was in passenger service only. It continued because it comprised the line of the Indianapolis, Columbus & Southern Traction Company (IC&S) leased to Public Service Company and sub-leased to Indiana Railroad. Public Service, much as it would like to, had not come up with a plan to escape from the 999-year lease of the IC&S. On weekdays 16 trains continued to roll from Indianapolis on the truncated line under Indiana Railroad management for Public Service Company.

When Public Service Company of Indiana petitioned for permission to abandon service south of Seymour a decision had to be made about the Louisville Cement Company at Speed. Special sidings had been built to provide that company an interchange with the B&O, via the interurban, at Watson. The cement company shipped carloads of cement in standard railroad box cars. The connection was a profitable one but an operation that Public Service Company could not continue as part of its compliance with the regulations to get out of the transportation business.

The rail operation was sold to a new corporation, Southern Indiana Railway, Inc., an independent company set up by Bowman Elder and Frank McHale. The new firm officially took over on March 18, 1940 although it had been operating since November 1, 1939.

January 7, 1940 was the scheduled date for the end of the 72-mile Terre Haute line. The new White buses, of a considerably improved design from those used on the Peru line, were delayed in delivery so the electric cars kept running. Except for some clean-up operations, all rail freight had been transferred to trucks on January 2.

The first buses arrived on the seventh and management expected to have enough on hand and ready by the eleventh. The winter weather was terrible and the

Above On July 3, 1938 the 83 eases downgrade into the curve that will carry it over the Nickel Plate Railroad to the Eaton station one-half mile south of this rolling country setting. *James F. Cook photo*

Below The May 19, 1940 railfans' special train with the 65, 57 and 58 at the station on the Fort Harrison loop. The 59, running as the regular car, follows the train. *M. D. McCarter collection*

Above On July 3, 1939, cars 95, 91 and 376 rest under the Muncie trainshed. Some of the 90's, though in use on the Muncie-New Castle shuttle at this time, would be surplus cars before the end of the year.
M. D. McCarter collection

last interurban car left Terre Haute on Thursday morning, the 11th, at 12:35 AM (some fifty minutes late) and arrived at Indianapolis at 2:45 AM. On board were Louis Rappeport, L. M. Brown, Charley Lentz, Ed Belknap (from the Indianapolis ticket office) and a number of railfans. The buses went out in the morning on the 11th, navigating nasty, ice-covered roads. The poor driving conditions and the start of a new schedule created havoc and all the runs were late. This disappointing start was compounded by the fact that the route closely followed the old line which meant that it ran over county roads as well as main highways.

An orphan operation remained east of Terre Haute. The Binkley Mine was served by Indiana Railroad who, in 1935, built trackage into the mine, interchange tracks with the CMStP&P RR (The Milwaukee Road), and used the mainline interurban in between. The switching service was the mine's only connection with other railroads so it could not be abandoned. Indiana Railroad, to keep the operation going, had to purchase the connecting mainline trackage from Terre Haute Electric Company.

The company management faced problems that had not been apparent, a decade earlier, when that company had been created by Insull and Feustel. Many of the company's business and industry customers were gone, displaced or rearranged. The auto had been seen as a threat but never on the vast scale that emerged during the 1930's. Not only was it a short-haul rival, taking the country and town people into the cities, but as the state highway system expanded and improved the personal auto took away more and more intercity passengers. The family auto was convenient: one could come and go as he pleased—when he wanted to go—without consulting a schedule or waiting for the interurban car. Ridership had been falling and the Peru and Terre Haute route conversions clearly showed that buses, with a smaller capacity than the rail cars, could easily handle the existing traffic. The highway motor coach sacrificed some of the speed and better riding qualities of the highspeeds and bigger cars, but the motor coach had a variety of virtues including simple economics. The lower operating cost and flexibility of the motor coach made it an easy winner over the expensive fixed plant of the rail-bound interurban.

Since Indiana Railroad lost its interurban connections and had never been able to develop much carload interchange steam railroad freight it was left with the highly vulnerable LCL freight business. This part of the overall rail operation was possibly 20% of the total revenue. Motor trucks had improved even more dramatically than motor buses during the 1930's and now had more powerful tractors pulling longer trailers over better highways. (The trailers were forty feet in length, small by 1991 standards but not smaller than many of the interurban box cars.)

The highway freight business brought an increasing need for more equipment and a radical change in the Indiana Railroad operations. The first ten truck tractors and trailers had been joined by seven more International tractors plus six used and fourteen new Fruehauf semi-trailers and a fleet (over thirty) of smaller, local trucks.

By the end of 1939, Indiana Railroad had become a party to all motor freight tariffs, thereby putting itself

Below A group of Detroit railfans chartered highspeed 59 on May 14, 1939. The 59 is at Anderson Junction and will proceed north to the shops.
Richard H. George photo

Above In late 1940 the 705 and three trailers are ready to depart from the Fort Wayne freight terminal. *Philip E. Buchert photo*

Left Eastbound 57, on May 26, 1940, makes the mandatory stop at Lawrence phone booth where all trains reported to the dispatcher. *James F. Cook photo*

Below It's January 12, 1941. Though facing toward Anderson, 772 and train on Ohio Street behind the Indianapolis Traction Terminal carry spare wheel sets, motors and other parts for use at the Columbus shop. *John F. Humiston photo*

Above A number of fantrips were run in the last few months using the highspeeds, the RPO cars, work motor 1150 and box motor 716. Indiana Railroad's L. M. Brown, in the dark coat, chats with several railfans at Indianapolis prior to the last such trip: on January 1, 1941 with 716.

Richard H. George photo

in a position to handle both truckload and LTL (less than truck load lot) service to any point in the United States served by a truck line. An interchange agreement with cooperating connecting companies sent the orange and green Indiana Railroad truck trailers to Chicago as well as points in Illinois and Ohio. At Indianapolis, the Kentucky Avenue freight terminal changed along with the switch to highways. Only the northern freight house continued in use by Indiana Railroad for rail and motor freight. The second building was leased to other truck lines. The terminals were 24-hour-a-day operations because the trucks did not have any of the street restrictions and limitations of rail freight. Indiana Railroad's new trucks were able to handle all of the LCL business as well as truckload lots. Where the interurban substituted trucks the freight business actually increased, producing good revenues. Speed and the door-to-door service were plus factors that held long-time shippers and attracted new ones.

During 1940, with the shift to highway trucks and buses becoming more apparent with each day, Indiana Railroad completely took over the local delivery services. Indiana Motor Transit, Inc. was liquidated during 1940. Its remaining assets were taken over by Indiana Railroad. The subsidiary corporation had been profitable. The closing of the company generated a $24,500 dividend for the parent.

Conversion to trucks and buses had an even more attractive plus in the elimination of track, overhead wire, power distribution and other fixed rail facilities. This resulted in cost reductions in labor, maintenance and taxes. In the short view, quick income was realized from the sale of scrap and unused real estate. The Peru line conversion had generated this sort of return and it was expected that the Terre Haute line would be the same.

Following the end of the Peru line the number of rail cars was reduced. The first step was to return most of the leased ISC and Public Service Company cars. The ISC's McKinley Avenue yards in Fort Wayne as well as the Scottsburg and Columbus Public Service Company yards were filled with surplus equipment and much of it was quickly scrapped.

On February 25, 1939, the remaining eight 90-series cars were purchased from Cummings Car and Coach Company to cancel the lease agreement. These cars were now in use on the Fort Harrison and the Muncie-New Castle runs. With the end of the Terre Haute and Louisville lines a rapid reduction of passenger cars took place. The one-man steel cars were considered by the Illinois Terminal Railroad. No action was taken and they were sold for scrap along with the 90 series in April 1940. The highspeeds held down all of the runs with the exception of the Fort Wayne-New Castle mail runs which used the leased RPO cars. The company's freight and service rail equipment inventory fell as the requirements dwindled. Many of the company's cars were sold to a salvage company and scrapped in the yards behind the Anderson shop. The sudden increase in scrapping had to remind employees of the brighter days of 1931 when the scrapping of old cars meant new equipment. Now "new" meant trucks and buses.

Indiana Railroad continued to promote rail and motor coach passenger service. Even the Seymour line was promoted with testimonial newspaper ads featuring frequent riders who used ten-trip tickets on a regular basis. The interurban's virtue of inexpensive and dependable transportation was still worth selling.

Bowman Elder, under court order and Midland United pressure to end the receivership, made a final decision that the quickest way to solvency was through the abandonment of the remaining rail lines. In November 1939 the court authorized Elder to give notice of termination of the lease of the ISC-owned Fort Wayne-Bluffton line. The rail service would continue until the appropriate agencies approved the abandonment.

Chapter 10
Death Comes for the Railroad

Left It's January 12, 1941 and sun would rise on the passenger service only six more times. The 71 is passing Dent siding with a morning local to Muncie. It holds the main while spring switches would route a westbound car through the siding, hence the block signal by the switch rather than at mid-siding. *John F. Humiston photo*

The death sentence for the railroad operation was passed on February 15, 1940. Separate petitions were filed with the Public Service Commission and the Interstate Commerce Commission to substitute buses and trucks for the remaining rail service. The I.C.C. was involved because of the freight services which extended beyond the state borders. Indiana Service Corporation acted jointly with Elder in the petition to cover the abandonment of all service on the ISC-owned Fort Wayne-Bluffton line following the end of the Indiana Railroad lease.

According to the company, the Indianapolis-Fort Wayne line lost $51,322 and the Muncie-New Castle line lost $17,883 in the first nine months of 1939. The company also revealed that, in an attempt to reduce costs, there had been a substantial deferral of maintenance in recent months. Elder maintained serious doubts that he could secure funds or credit for a rehabilitation program that would be needed to extend the life of the two rail routes.

Indiana Railroad was still fast and appeared in the January 1940 *Railroad Magazine* "Speed Survey" with four regularly scheduled runs at better than a start-to-stop average of 60 mph. Between Poneto and Keystone, on the Fort Wayne Division, 6.65 miles were covered in 6.5 minutes (a time determination made by the magazine) for an average speed of 61.4 mph. On the Indianapolis-Seymour line, a 9.1-mile stretch, between Columbus and Azalia, was covered in exactly 9 minutes for an average speed of 60.6 mph. This performance meant speeds in excess of 70 mph had to be achieved. The snappy acceleration of the highspeeds still made such schedules possible.

Some might question how a railroad with admitted deferred maintenance could allow such speedy operation to continue. The railroad physical plant was safe and the operating procedures were not slackened. The company had an abundance of reliable rolling stock. There were 30 mechanically sound highspeeds, more than needed, and as a result, four badly damaged units were never repaired. Elder's concern was that little, if any, money was spent on improvements and that most of the actual railroad physical plant was old and rapidly wearing out. However, actual track and other maintenance continued as always.

In 1940 the back page of Indiana Railroad public timetables boasted frequent trips and low fares. Services emphasized included (in both directions) twenty trains between Indianapolis and Seymour; 32 trains between Indianapolis and Muncie; 19 trains between Indianapolis and Fort Wayne and 18 buses between Indianapolis and Terre Haute.

Even though the company was listed in annual train speed surveys, train speeds had slowed since the 1931 introduction of the highspeeds. Fort Wayne-Indianapolis *Hoosierland* trains had been scheduled at 3 hours and 10 minutes. By 1940, the time had been lengthened to 3 hours and 25 minutes. Times of the Indianapolis-Seymour trains had remained much the same since 1936.

One reason for slower schedules was the additional stops for limited trains. The *Hoosierland* trains had only eight city stops in the early system schedules but over the years, to accommodate more passengers, 12 flag stops were added at smaller towns. There were some passengers at most of these stations and the extra time was needed. At Spring Valley westbound trains would discharge passengers and eastbound trains would pick up passengers for the benefit of Fort Harrison riders. The extra stops were popular with riders who frequently expected all trains to make all stops.

Motor bus schedules were ten minutes slower than the earlier trains on the Terre Haute-Indianapolis through runs. Indianapolis-Fort Wayne through buses took 4 hours as opposed to 4 hours and 15 minutes for the interurban cars. However, through buses used "Route 1," a designation for the shorter U.S. 31 highway route. "Route 2," which ran from Indianapolis to Kokomo by way of Tipton and Noblesville was closer to the longer interurban route. The line to Terre Haute, by use of county roads and highways, kept closer to the older interurban route.

By mid-1940, abandonment was approved but a final date was not set as permission to substitute buses had to be obtained. The court moved a step at a time and, with abandonment approval secured, authorized the receiver to borrow money and arrange for the purchase of the necessary trucks and buses.

Facilities were changed to accommodate the change to highway operations. A new Terre Haute bus depot was established near the center of the business district. The principal change was the lease of a two-story headquarters building in Indianapolis on the northeast corner of Ohio and Senate. All of the Indianapolis offices, drivers' recreation rooms, and service facilities for the truck and bus fleet were consolidated at the new location. This change meant vacating space in the Traction Terminal building and the Indianapolis freight terminal and the movement of garage and service equipment from Greenwood. It also set the stage to move the maintenance center to a system-center location from the aging Anderson railroad shops. (The local Anderson buses had their own service facility.)

In anticipation of the end of rail service, the 30 highspeeds were offered for sale in September 1940 through Transit Equipment Company of New York, a used equipment dealer. The C&LE lightweights had been

Above Good maintenance continued even though abandonment was only a month away. Line car 763 is at Eagleville north of Bluffton in December 1940 not just doing a temporary splice but fixing the line as if it would continue indefinitely. *James F. Cook photo*

Above Cars also received good mechanical care as shown in this summer 1940 interior view of the Anderson shops. By then highspeeds and RPO cars handled the passenger work. All active cars were kept in ready-to-run condition through the very last day. *James F. Cook photo*

successfully sold in the secondhand market and Elder hoped for the same results. The highspeeds were well-known and considered well-designed, good-looking, versatile cars. But the C&LE cars had become available first following the collapse of the Ohio line and had found their way into the small secondhand market for such cars. Reportedly, several inquires were received and some people supposedly came to see the highspeeds. A couple of the better prospects used heavy, large passenger cars and were reasonably satisfied with them. They, and others, may not have had nor wished to spend the money. Sadly, no one offered to buy all or a portion of these finest-ever highspeed cars.

On October 5, Indiana Railroad received final authorization to substitute buses for the two rail lines. Seventeen new 29-passenger buses and 28 trucks were on order for the expected January 1 change (postponed until January 18). The stage curtain was ready to fall on the rail operations and, for all practical purposes, the true interurban in Indiana. The news brought the railfans for a last look and CERA operated a special trip on October 20.

The Securities and Exchange Commission, on November 1, 1940, initiated proceedings under the Public Utility Holding Company Act to simplify Midland United's corporate structure. This official action, al-

Below On the east side of Yorktown, the state highway swerved in from the north on its way from Muncie. On October 19, 1940, car 81 enters the street posing a traffic hazard for any eastbound motorists. The "turn" arrow warns the motorists—not the trains. *John F. Humiston photo*

Above It's December 1940 and a westbound highspeed racing through the early morning haze has its air horns blaring a warning as it crosses one of the White River bridges, east of Anderson Junction, on its way from Muncie. *James F. Cook photo*

Above Westbound highspeed 72, in January 1941, runs up the long grade from another White River bridge to Jackson's Crossing west of Chesterfield. This open-country tangent offered some fast running opportunities. *James F. Cook photo, M. D. McCarter collection*

though anticipated, actually came too late to be considered as the cause for the end of the rail service. It did accelerate Midland United's interest in the recapture and disposal of the subsidiary company to comply with the SEC demand. The 1940 Midland United management was much different than the original organization. They wanted to divest themselves of transportation subsidiaries and had already disposed of their interest in the South Shore Line. Elder and Rappeport were urged to get the Indiana Railroad house in order to end the receivership. The parent was willing to work out agreements and terms that could help speed the return to solvency.

In the last quarter of 1940 arrangements were started to close down the rail system. The company began to sell a variety of equipment including the four damaged highspeeds and the mercury arc rectifiers at Bucy and Tile substations. In the case of equipment such as the substations, the effective date for removal was set as following the end of rail service. The Indianapolis-Seymour line would also cease to be an Indiana Railroad operation and the line would be returned to Public Service Company of Indiana at midnight on January 18. Public Service Company had not been able to join with Indiana Railroad and Indiana Service Corporation in the abandonment petitions because of

Below Car 53 as eastbound train 16 pauses at the Yorktown station on January 12, 1941. The station, located on the left side of the street, was maintained as part of Eli Applegate's store. Applegate was also an Indiana Railroad operator. *John F. Humiston photo*

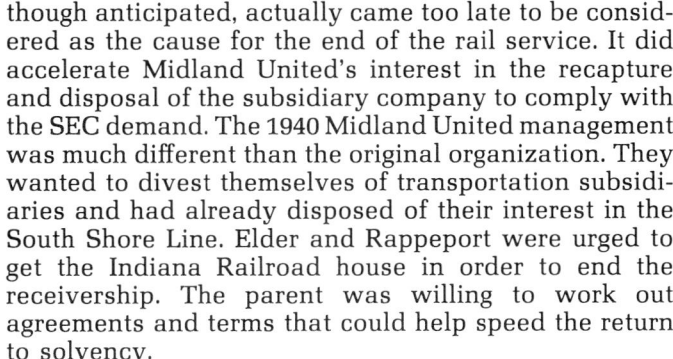

Above On October 10, 1940 highspeed 68 passes one of the company's local delivery trucks. Both have just left the Anderson station, in the distance, and are slowing for the Pennsylvania Railroad crossing. The 68 will then continue south on Main Street.
John F. Humiston photo

Below Train 15, car 52, southbound on Anderson's Main Street, rumbles past the abandoned city car track on Ninth Street. This is the last Sunday for the Indiana Railroad, January 12, 1941. Not likely you would find so little traffic here on a weekday!
John F. Humiston photo

the IC&S lease agreement requiring Public Service Company to have passenger service operated.

Formal notices were posted on all lines indicating the termination of passenger operations at the end of the scheduled service on January 18. The two freight routes had notices indicating the end of rail freight on January 14. Motor trucks would take over the freight chores. The advanced date allowed the company to collect its freight cars and bring them into the Anderson shop area, the Kentucky Avenue freight terminal and McKinley Avenue. The later two were the gathering points for the few remaining pieces of Public Service Company and ISC equipment.

Three of the new buses and one of the new trucks were taken on a caravan tour of the principal cities on January 15 and 16. The new bus schedules and routes were explained and publicized but the timings were a bit embarrassing following the extravagant press notices about the many bus virtues. The fastest timing was four hours, over one half hour longer than the high-speeds' current timing. The publicity conveniently avoided any schedule comparison. The problem was one of long standing as there still was no direct highway between Fort Wayne and Indianapolis.

The suburban Fort Harrison line would also be converted using five new buses. There was one less run but the schedules were almost the same.

The Last Day

Saturday, January 18, 1941, was an unpleasant day. Even the weather was bad. It had been cold and somewhat foggy, with occasional snow, for several days but that didn't stop any trains. This was a busy day because, besides the regular Saturday traffic, there had been plenty of advance notice and publicity on the passing of the electric railroad service. It was a "business as usual" day with the 376 making the round-trip Fort Wayne-New Castle mail run for the last time. Two cars (64 and 74) were cleaned up for special "last run" trains to accommodate those people from the Anderson area with a special interest in the line. The two special cars were run to Indianapolis early in the evening and lined up to follow the last regular through car to Muncie. There were no multiple-unit train operations on the last day so Voyle V. Vandevender and Marion Harman ran these "last" cars and kept them as close together as possible within safe operating rules on the slow run. When they reached Anderson the distance was closed to a safe visual distance. When they reached the home of the late H. A. Nichol, the former Union Traction general manager, they were greeted by track torpedos and railroad flares and the cars made a brief stop. At the Anderson station the two cars unloaded their passengers and moved to the shops. The last regular car, Train 36, had left Indianapolis at 11:40 PM in advance of the two specials. It waited at Anderson long enough to pick up some passengers, from the specials, who wished to continue to Muncie. The train arrived at 1:35 AM, some 15 minutes late, and was considered to be the last regularly scheduled train on the Indiana Railroad. Earlier, at 11:00 PM, car 71 left on the last run to New Castle where the car usually laid-over for the night to make the first morning run into Muncie.

Below At Anderson, many passengers boarded trains in the vibrant business district rather than at the station further north. Westbound on 11th Street, car 68 crosses Meridian Street where a commission ticket agency was maintained in a drug store. *John F. Humiston photo*

Above At the New Castle station, narrow Race Street featured curb loading, where RPO 377 sits facing west on July 22, 1939. Track in the foreground in 14th Street, the former main line to Dunreith, provided access to the freight tracks on the south side of the station.
John F. Humiston photo

Below The 79 eases around the curve and turns eastward, paralleling 38th Street, as it crosses Orchard Avenue in Indianapolis after the 20-minute run from the center of the city. This lightly loaded local carries several soldiers and children on the Fort Harrison run.
John F. Humiston photo

Fort Harrison traffic had been heavy all evening. The 11:30 departure from Indianapolis (run on weekends and shown in the public timetable though it was an extra) operated as two cars to carry soldiers who had to be on the post about midnight. The daily regular train 932, car 53, in charge of Arthur "Red" Thompson, left the Traction Terminal at 12:01 AM on the 19th, two minutes late, and met Extra 61 West and Extra 82 West at Long Siding. The 53 made a quick run to Fort Harrison arriving at about 12:35 AM and departed, as train 903, at 12:45 AM. Train 903 would make a lonely return run, stop at Lawrence to register (as all trains were required to do) and then continue on its timetable scheduled run to arrive at the Traction Terminal at 1:10 AM.

Train 903 was a daily car but on Sunday and Monday (actually late Saturday and Sunday night) there was a "clean-up" car that left the Traction Terminal at 1:30 AM and arrived at Fort Harrison at 2:00 AM. The car was usually filled with sleeping servicemen returning with late passes. The run back to Indianapolis was almost a "ghost" run and rarely carried any revenue passengers. This 1:30 AM extra departure is apparently the car operated by Oda Lynch. Rather than return to Indianapolis, Lynch was allowed to proceed from Fort Harrison to Oaklandon Siding where he left the car overnight.

In the wee hours of the morning of the 19th all scheduled and extra runs had been completed. The trains had carried their last revenue passengers. Indiana Railroad was now a bus and motor freight company.

Closing Down

Sunday morning, January 19, 1941, started the final clean-up of the passenger rail facilities. Within the next 48 hours the main line would be history and only the isolated Binkley Mine switching operation would remain of the one-time huge rail system operated under the Indiana Railroad banner.

The 18th had been handled as a normal day so there were a number of cars at different locations following the end of the day's operation. Some of them were at terminals, as normal layovers, for the first car out on the next day's schedule—which would never come. These cars had to come home to Anderson and the concluding trek began on Sunday morning. Oda Lynch started his run in the morning moving a car that was now minus several pieces of the parlor car furniture. At Indianapolis, seven cars sat on the storage tracks and, one by one, they moved out of the Traction Terminal property towards Anderson with Lynch's car ahead of them. Car 53 led this procession followed by 59, 82, 61, 56 and two others. They ran within visual contact and all operators were warned to be alert as the public had been notified of the abandonment of rail service and would not be expecting to see any trains at rail/highway crossings. Train orders were issued for each car in the parade as they had an actual meet with the line car moving westward. All of the cars were run as extras but with the same operating precision as on any normal day. The line car went to Indianapolis and then returned shutting off connections and other electric facilities along the return route.

The situation at Fort Wayne and Muncie was a bit different. Clifford Tobias, a Fort Wayne-based operator, had brought highspeed 63 into Fort Wayne at 1:20 AM on the 19th. Later that morning he reboarded the car and, accompanied by Chester Warren (another operator) and William Minch (McKinley Ave. Yardmaster), started south on a quiet last trip of a highspeed car to Muncie. There were already four other highspeeds at Muncie. Ray Moppin had brought in the 71 as the last car off the New Castle line. Eli Applegate had made the last Fort Wayne-Bluffton run the night before but, instead of tying up for the night, he had taken the empty car 58 south through the lonely and empty dark night and spotted it at the Muncie terminal. Bill Frazee had been at the controls of the 77 which had been the most publicized

Below Early on January 19 the cars from Indianapolis head due east toward Anderson. The 59, 82 and 61 stand at Long "siding" (end of a substantial length of double track alongside 38th Street) waiting for a meet. Each car carries white flags as they are all "extra" trains. Anderson line car 773, now coming west, will shut down the power facilities on its return trip. *Richard H. George photo*

Above Muncie terminal on the morning of January 19, 1941 with (left to right) trainmaster Wilbur Ireland, dispatcher Jimmy Vance, and operators Harry Clapp, Marion Harman, Bill Frazee and Eli Applegate ready to take the 58, 63, 71 and 77 to Anderson.
James F. Cook photo

"last run" from Indianapolis to Muncie. The 80 was also at Muncie as a spare car. Harry Clapp, the senior operator on the line, was an Anderson resident and had to come to Muncie on one of the new buses. He had to pay his fare because all passes were cancelled with the end of rail service. Clapp and three other operators (Harman, Frazee and Applegate) took four of the five cars over the line to Anderson. Jim Cook, from Anderson, and Glenn Niceley, from Indianapolis, had driven to Muncie to photograph the round-up of cars. They were invited to ride on the lead car, the 77, with Harry Clapp.

At the Anderson shop, Tobias, Minch and Warren, who had also ridden over from Muncie, climbed aboard reserve RPO car 377. The 377 belonged to the ISC and was the south-end relief and protection car for the mail service. Now the three Fort Wayne men would take it back to its owner. Clapp also offered Cook and Niceley a ride back as he was returning to Muncie with Tobias on the 377. Although probably at their own risk, Cook and Niceley were the last non-employee rail passengers over the main line of the Indiana Railroad.

Stopping at Muncie terminal for a few minutes, the 377's crew discharged the riders, picked up orders and then Tobias, as motorman, and Minch as conductor, headed north closing out electric car operations over the Muncie-Fort Wayne route. The run was in the classic interurban tradition with a heavy car and two-man crew. The car made a brief stop in Hartford City long enough for Floyd Pruden and his son Jerry to go out to the car and bid farewell. The car shifted to ISC tracks at Bluffton and headed into Fort Wayne, through the terminal and north to Spy Run Shop. When the car entered the shop yard the passenger interurban era ended for many Indiana cities and towns.

Harry Clapp, following the 377's departure boarded car 80 and made the final passenger car run to Anderson arriving in the late afternoon. The Anderson shop and yard was now filled with an array of 61 cars. One more came home on Monday the 20th. This was the Muncie line car in charge of conductor Albert Leard and motorman Carl Pendergast. Precise in operation to the end, veteran Muncie dispatcher, James Vance, issued the final train order to the line car. At Powers Street and Kilgore Avenue the car stopped and line foreman Lester Cortner threw the switch killing the power on the New Castle line as a symbolic gesture of shutting down the system. Running west, the elderly 763 made the ultimate run to Anderson Junction and then rattled over the bridge to the shop yard.

Was passenger service ended? Observant individuals in Indianapolis might notice a highspeed enter and leave the city. The car was orange, had a green roof and carried the Indiana Railroad name. It was not a ghost. Starting January 19, Public Service Company of Indiana Train 1 left Seymour at 8:00 AM. Arriving at Indianapolis at 10:10, the car entered an electrified spur track off Ohio Street and discharged a few passengers. The car remained on the storage track (soon to be the only track with an overhead wire) until 3:30 PM when, as Train 2, it headed back to Seymour, arriving at 5:40. This fragment operation was unadvertised, remote and known to only a few people. It was the way Public Service Company wanted it.

Below Clifford Tobias, with Chester Warren behind him, climbs aboard 377 at Anderson shops. The 377, property of ISC, had to be returned to Fort Wayne. It was the last Indiana Railroad car operated north of Muncie.
Gene Bock photo

Below When Indiana Railroad shut down, cars like the 82 could no longer be photographed streaking past Cleve siding north of Hartford City. But Jerry Pruden's son created this scene, a line sketch, for his father.
Jay D. Pruden

Above Decorated with a wreath, line car 763 stops at Anderson Junction on its last trip. Lester Cortner, head lineman, stands in the doorway. *Jerry D. Pruden collection*

Below Finished? Highspeeds filled Anderson shops waiting in vain for a buyer who never came. A sad, sad end for a fleet of over 25 of the finest electric interurban cars ever built. *Gene Bock photo*

Chapter 11
Aftermath

Left Until September 1941, the two surviving passenger cars 65 and 78 took turns covering a single round trip a day to Seymour. This 1940 view, on Capitol Avenue, Indianapolis could have been the afternoon departure. Actually it was taken a year earlier when the line ran every hour or two all day. *John F. Humiston photo*

There was no happy ending at Anderson as, under pressure from Midland United and the officers of Indiana Railroad (R. A. Gallagher, of Public Service Company of Indiana, was also president of the railroad), Elder and Rappeport moved to end the receivership. The quickest method to return the company to solvency and to silence the owners was to convert all rail properties to fast cash via the salvage route.

The Indianapolis-Muncie-Fort Wayne and Muncie-New Castle rail lines were sold to companies who used motor trucks and a Plymouth locomotive to take down the wire and tear out the rails. Other obsolete and non-useful property was sold to salvage firms. The deal was for cash—in advance.

The same thing happened to the rolling stock. It was sold for $36,000, as a package deal, to Simon Solotkin & Son's salvage company who was given a limited time to get the cars off the railroad's property. These sales saved a drawn-out involvement in scrapping the rail facilities, eliminated several legal/time problems about removal of trackwork and allowed an immediate reduction in the company work force.

Most of the freight and other wooden cars went, one by one, to a funeral pyre as each was burned for easy recovery of the metal. No one came to buy the highspeeds and all but three were quickly destroyed in a terrible short-sighted action. They were dragged from the shop building (also for sale) to the outside area by salvage company employees and quickly broken up for the valuable metals in the bodies. Piles of motors, truck frames, castings of all kinds, etc. were stacked in the yard. It was a tragic waste. The downward pressure upon Elder had forced this action. The Midland United officials should have seen the resale value of these excellent cars. War winds were very evident and had the cars been retained for a few months their value would have increased.

Elder had ordered two highspeeds held out for operation on Public Service Company's Indianapolis-Seymour line. The 77 and 78 were set aside but somehow the 65 was on the Seymour run on January 18 so the 77 made the last revenue run to Muncie and went to the torch. The 65 became the "lucky" car.

Car 55 was the special car, rebuilt as a business car for use by Bowman Elder, though it was available for charters. Modified to a complete parlor car, the regular seats were removed and it was outfitted with surplus furnishings from the lounge sections of several highspeeds converted from coach-lounge to coach-baggage configuration. It was among the cars sold to Solotkin.

Lehigh Valley Transit Company had purchased 13 of the C&LE lightweights (including the 114 and 128 used in the test runs) during 1938 and 1939. One of these cars was accidentally burned on December 20, 1940 and LVT decided to replace it with one of the Indiana Railroad cars. The unique 55 was purchased from the scrap company. It was loaded at the Anderson yard in late January 1941, the only car saved from those awaiting the torch. An interesting twist resulted from this sale. LVT modified the car body to conform with the C&LE cars and placed it on the Cincinnati ABC 74 trucks from the burned car. Ten years before, C&LE 114 had been placed on the superior Commonwealth trucks for testing purposes; and now the 55 was on the Cincinnati trucks. (The 55 survives in a museum but it is as modified by LVT.)

In some legal hopscotch during April, Midland was able to have Bowman Elder removed as receiver and Ray Garrett installed as trustee. The action resulted from shifting the court proceedings from Marion County Superior Court in Indianapolis to the Federal Court in Wilmington, Delaware where the Midland United bankruptcy case was being handled. The reasoning behind this move is not known but the Federal Court dismissed the action and sent it back to Marion County with Elder in control.

On May 19, Elder announced that Midland United had agreed to a settlement that, with court approval, would terminate the receivership. In the agreement, Midland United waived certain rights and claims. Under this plan, creditors would be paid 100 cents on the dollar and property would have assets of approximately $15,000,000 with about $200,000 in cash. Elder said this was possible due to the sale of the rolling stock, rails and other non-useful equipment from the abandonment of the interurban lines.

The eight-year-old receivership was terminated on June 22, 1941 and the company was returned to Midland free, clear and unencumbered by any debt except for the bookkeeping entry of $7,928,000 (listed as "other unadjusted credits") indicated as predating 1933. Elder and Rappeport, plus the excellent and dedicated Indiana Railroad management, deserved considerable praise for rescuing the company, making it solvent, and returning it as a viable, going concern. The new interests now in charge of Midland United were publicly, at least, short on any praise, appreciation or rewards.

Midland United immediately installed new officers and shuffled some of the managers of the Indiana Railroad. Ray Garrett, long associated with Midland United Company as an attorney, became the new president. Garrett's appointment as president (and earlier as the momentary trustee) is interesting because he had spoken of the elimination of this "unprofitable property" during the FTC hearings nine years before. Bowman Elder and Frank McHale were now able to devote full time to their normal business which included the Southern Indiana Railway. Earlier, Louis Rappeport, who had been announced as the prospective Indiana Railroad general manager, found himself on the outside and no longer employed (His involvement with the U.S. Army may have been part of the reason. Although not exactly clear, Rappeport may have been a reserve officer called to active duty.) John T. Martin became operations manager in addition to maintenance supervisor. A. E. Jost, from Midland United, was named vice president and comptroller.

On September 1, 1942 the Federal Court authorized the sale of Indiana Railroad as part of the Midland bankruptcy simplification. The bus and truck firm was purchased by Wesson Company, a Chicago-based machine tool manufacturing firm, for $650,000. Wesson Company owned all of the outstanding stock of Wesson Tool Company and on September 19, 1942 all of this stock was donated to Indiana Railroad. Earlier on September 9 the trustee of the Midland United Estate made a capital contribution to Indiana Railroad of $7,208,206 to forgive the company's indebtedness to Midland United.

Wesson Tool was liquidated and its assets and liabilities were absorbed by Indiana Railroad on September 21, 1942. On the same date Wesson Company changed its name to Wesson Illinois Company and Indiana Railroad became Wesson Company headed by Ray Garrett. Indiana Railroad Division of Wesson Company was the new name used for the operating transportation facilities. The post receivership management group remained in charge.

The other Midland subsidiaries resolved their interurban rail problems. Indiana Service Corporation tore up its Fort Wayne-Bluffton trackage, using its own crews, in the spring of 1941. Public Service Company was left with operating the leased Indianapolis, Columbus & Southern Traction Company. That problem was far more complicated than the ISC situation.

Robert A. Gallagher had been sent to Public Service by Midland to arrange a reorganization program resulting (on September 6, 1941) in a new Public Service Company of Indiana, Inc., an affiliate of Midland United. The stock in the new company was later dispersed among Midland's preferred stockholders as part of the holding company's dissolution. (The Indiana Railroad employees and others who had loyally purchased

Above ISC sold the three railway post office cars to the Chicago South Shore and South Bend Railroad. The 376, in the South Shore's Michigan City yards, survives today (1991) as line car 1100, one of the oldest cars on a commercial electric railway in America.
M. D. McCarter collection

Below A salvage firm bought the retired highspeeds. In turn, the scrapper sold Elder's special car 55 to the Lehigh Valley Transit Company in January 1941. Loaded on a flat car, the 55 was the only highspeed at Anderson to survive.
James F. Cook photo

Above Indiana Railroad moved its offices and maintenance facilities to Senate and Ohio Streets in Indianapolis. Its two-story building is to the left of Hotel Roosevelt. Most of these buildings have since been razed for further Indiana state office building expansions.
Philip E. Buchert photo

Midland's common stock were given no consideration in the dissolution. The common stock was declared worthless.)

By mid-1940, Gallagher put together a recapitalization plan, arranged a retirement of the current long-term debt and was trying to get out of the transportation business. No reorganization plan would be approved by the Securities and Exchange Commission unless it complied with the Public Utility Holding Company Act. For compliance, the transportation properties had to go. The leased IC&S, from Indianapolis to Seymour, was an embarrassment and a problem because Public Service Company was paying the Irwin, Miller and Sweeney families of Columbus (the owners) over $150,000 each year under the 999-year lease—at a rate of five percent on capital stock and the interest on all of the bonds of the lessee.

On January 18, 1941, Indiana Railroad as the sub-lease holder was operating a full schedule of 16 round trips daily on the Seymour line. However, the sub-lease was terminated at the end of the day with the last car arriving at 1:00 AM on the 19th. Public Service Company's attorneys had previously determined that the lease agreement with IC&S could be met by running the barest minimum of service: one daily round trip starting on January 19. (This has been described by some as a "franchise" run but in the true sense, there were no franchises involved. If anything it was a "lease" run.) All of Public Service Company's own passenger cars had been sold or scrapped. Two Indiana Railroad highspeeds had been left behind for the Seymour line. As negotiations with IC&S dragged on, Public Service Company, on March 18, 1941, was forced to purchase cars 65 and 78 from the receiver, paying the ridiculously low price of $1500 each. They were not repainted nor was the company name painted out and the public thought that Indiana Railroad still owned and operated them. Although no attempt was made to publicize the daily service, Trains 1 and 2 regularly carried a few passengers.

The two-train operation continued in an uneventful manner until September 8, 1941 when the "impossible" accident happened. It was of the stuff that might be discarded by a good fiction writer as implausible, so implausible that it merits retelling. The safe operations reputation of Indiana Railroad had been excellent. No passenger died as a result of a rail collision. With the rail operations ended, it was a completed record. Now, a twist of fate would have people believe otherwise, and it happened on what should have been as safe an operation as anyone could imagine.

Below Both of Public Service's highspeeds continued to carry the Indiana Railroad name. Here, at Second and Washington in Columbus on an August day in 1941, it's time to change cars. In this early morning view, 65 has just come in from Seymour and 78 will relieve it for the balance of the journey to Indianapolis while 65 goes into the Columbus barn for servicing. *John P. Scharle photo, George K. Bradley collection*

The line used one car for the daily run and, unless there was some need for the single, service/line car to do some maintenance, no other car ventured onto the line. The two highspeeds were rotated in service with a periodic change of cars at Columbus. The active car remained overnight in the Seymour train shed. Operator duties were shared by two senior trainmen: George Stephens and 6'3" George "Shorty" McLean. Each had nearly forty years of service.

The September 8 morning car left Seymour in charge of McLean. Five passengers were on board the northbound car and the trip was uneventful until the car reached Azalia Siding where the trolley pole flipped, tangled in the wire, broke the pole, ripped the trolley-rope retriever from its mounting bracket and smashed it. McLean surveyed the damage, climbed to the roof and replaced the broken pole with the spare pole carried on the roof. With no retriever, he allowed the trolley rope to dangle in easy reach in case the pole dewired again. He then called the Columbus barn and reported what had happened. He also said that he would bring the car northward to Columbus and that some help and a new retreiver would be needed. His choice to proceed was probably prompted because two young women, regular passengers, would be late for their business school classes. Car 78 moved north toward Columbus.

At the Columbus car barn the message was misinterpreted and the crew of line car 772 was given the impression that Shorty and the 78 were sitting, crippled, at Azalia Siding and awaiting help. The 772 hustled south from Columbus and, as fate would have it, met car 78 on a blind curve two miles south of Columbus. It was early and the rails were wet with the September morning dew. With brakes set both cars slid, beyond control, into a head-on collision. The line car crew jumped and McLean ran back into his car. The front ends of both cars were demolished. The "impossible" accident had happened!

Three people were critically injured. Mary Droege, one of the two 20-year-old students, died of her injuries four days later. Shorty McLean succumbed from his injuries on September 25. The others recovered. Indiana Railroad got a black eye.

The newspapers were confused. The wrecked 78 carried the Indiana Railroad name and for the past decade all traction promotion and advertising had carried that company's name. The reversion of the line to Public Service Company had not been major news. In the few days following the wreck all of the Columbus-originated stories, some of which went out on the national wire-news services, referred to the Indiana Railroad as the operating company. Public Service Company of Indiana, understandably, kept a low profile.

The accident stopped service on September 8 and nothing, absolutely nothing, ran the whole line again. L. M. Brown had arranged for a clean-up of the wreck and the two smashed cars were brought to the Columbus car barn. No attempt was made to repair either car. The 65 was left in the Columbus barn. Public Service Company's representatives would not make any comment. The accident attracted attention which the power company did not want. The traction line crash was the first in years and received continued front page coverage in Columbus' *The Evening Republican*. Interestingly enough, when a highway accident killed two men on U.S. 31, near Seymour, the story received about two front-page column inches. Next to it was a wreck follow-up story of nearly twelve column inches.

Below In late afternoon, George D. "Shorty" McLean is with train 2—the only southbound train—at its destination. *Philip E. Buchert photo*

Brown and others stated they were investigating the accident but were non-committal about restoring passenger service. *The Evening Republican* reporters were told that an old freight car would be converted to a line car. They also quoted an unnamed source who had indicated that two passenger cars were absolutely necessary because the "mechanism of a passenger interurban is so intricate that it requires thorough servicing every few days." This "servicing" comment was questionable since the cars were only lightly used and there was plenty of idle time for any service work at the Columbus barn. More than likely the company was following the long-time practice of always having a spare car.

The collision presented Gallagher with two options. One choice would be to obtain more cars and restore service. The second choice meant expediting the lease buy-out and getting out of the transportation business. The latter was closer to the intent of a plan filed with the SEC a year earlier and which had become effective on September 6, only two days before the crash.

A final agreement was made with the current owners of the IC&S (the Disciples of Christ Church through an endowment from W. G. Irwin) to sell the line for an approximate net cost of $1,200,000. By February 1942, both the state and federal regulatory bodies had approved the sale and authorized the issuance of notes covering the sale. The $1,520,000 in twenty-year notes plus other costs was a financial burden for Public Service Company. On March 11, the company took title to the rail line and offered the rails and overhead wires for salvage. During the transfer of property titles from the IC&S to the South Construction Company, a Public Service Company real estate subsidiary, the Bartholomew County officials at Columbus discovered that most of the property in the county had never been properly recorded, as traction company property, and that in most cases the traction company and the previous owners had been paying property taxes for the same pieces of property since 1902.

One last attempt was made to keep the line in operation. In January 1942, the U.S. government had announced that a huge new army installation, Camp Atterbury, would be constructed south of Indianapolis. The interurban line paralleled the camp boundary for 12 miles and this was noticed by the Indiana 9th District Congressman, Earl Wilson of Columbus. His congressional subcommittee suggested that Public Service Company should restore service over the line to handle the huge number of civilians and military travelers and help conserve gasoline and rubber tires. A restored interurban would be one of several passenger services available. All the company had by January was an operable rail line and no desire to operate it. The two damaged cars had been scrapped and only the last highspeed, the 65, remained. The idea of restored service was dropped. The Cedar Rapids & Iowa City Railway purchased the 65 and in June it was moved from the Columbus carbarn to the switching tracks at the Columbus Creosoting Company where it was loaded for the trip to Iowa. The Seymour line contained tons of re-usable materials and it was dismantled for salvage. By the end of August 1942, nearly a year after the collision, the curtain closed on this last portion of the mainline Indiana Railroad System.

Gallagher's effort produced an even greater utility consolidation than Insull and Feustel had planned. In territory size, Public Service Indiana, the name commonly used, is by far the largest electric utility in Indiana today (1991).

By 1943 only the rail access to the Binkley Mine operation remained. This rail line belonged to Indiana Railroad Division of Wesson Company. Because rail was only a small portion of the overall bus and truck operation, the Public Service Commission authorized the company to change its status to a "motor carrier." The mine rail line was considered as an "auxiliary" operation, a profitable venture netting over $42,000 in 1942. The mine was the rail line's only customer and when the mine officially closed on April 26, 1943, the company petitioned for abandonment. Permission was granted and all operations, mostly stand-by and clean-up, ceased on July 20, 1943.

Indiana Railroad was no longer a railroad.

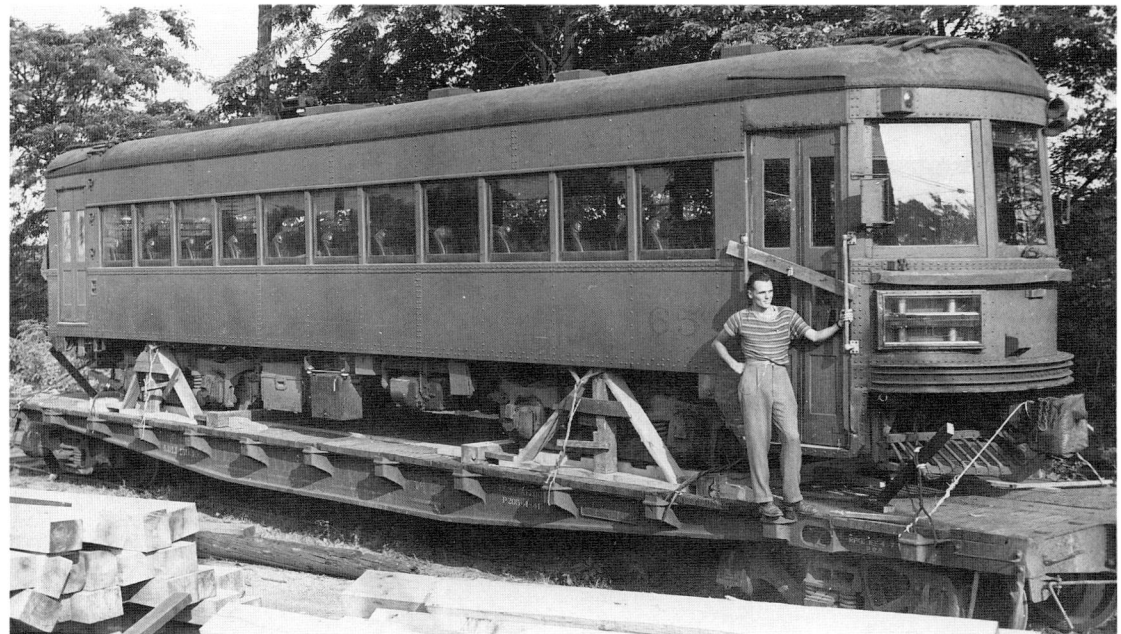

Right The 65 with Howard Blackburn at the Columbus Creosoting Company in June 1942 is loaded and ready for the trip to Cedar Rapids, Iowa. The Indiana Railroad name has nearly weathered off. *Dr. Howard R. Blackburn collection*

Chapter 12
The Motor Bus Era

Left Southeastern Trailways' bus 602, a newly arrived GMC model PD 4103, runs south along Capitol Avenue in Indianapolis on June 20, 1952. *Motor Bus Society, Inc. Library*

On the morning of January 19, 1941, all Indiana Railroad schedules were operated over the public highways. The company had bus routes from Indianapolis to Fort Wayne via both Peru and Muncie, Indianapolis to Terre Haute, the Muncie-New Castle connector, the suburban Ft. Harrison route and the city operations at Anderson and Richmond. Over 90 buses were listed as being in use for these divisions. The change saw personnel reductions as a number of rail-related employees lost their jobs. The Anderson shop was closed so those employees and the line crews were among those terminated. Rail car operators under age 50 were eligible to transfer to the bus operation. According to the news reports, some employees were eligible for a retirement benefit while some others were given jobs for a period of time until they could reach retirement.

Following the switch to buses the Amalgamated became the sole bargaining union for company employees and their presence was extended systemwide. The BRT, which restricted its membership to properties in the railroad business, withdrew from representation. The change was carried out smoothly with all employees being welcomed by the Amalgamated. A positive side of this change meant uniform wages for comparable jobs throughout the company were established and many employees received pay increases.

During 1941 the world war situation became more critical, climaxed by the United States entry in the war in December. Travel restrictions and military needs produced a huge demand for bus service on all routes with the Fort Harrison route seeing the greatest jump in ridership. The demand was followed by an equipment and fuel shortage. Suddenly, the all-too-recently-abandoned Indianapolis-Muncie rail line, with its fast cars and high capacity—to say nothing of the gas and tire savings—was sorely missed.

A new bus route was introduced, on a trial basis, in late 1942. This route, which ran from Greenfield to Anderson, was not profitable and after several months it was terminated so that the much-needed buses could be transferred to more important routes. In May 1942, the Muncie-New Castle route was sold to ABC Coach Lines and the released buses pressed into service on the heavy traffic lines.

When the war came, new bus production was limited and placed under government control. Buses were obtained from any available source and the company, as did most others, looked into every garage for serviceable vehicles. They even rescued and restored some long-retired company buses that had been used for work crews, to regular service. At the same time ten new Ford transits, already on order and approved, were delivered for use in Anderson. By the end of 1942 the company fleet contained 53 intercity buses and 64 city buses.

In December of 1942 the company was approached to sell the motor freight division. The Indiana Railroad Division of Wesson Company owned 38 truck tractors, 74 trailers and 48 local delivery trucks plus a solid freight business as a profitable complement to the large fleet of city and intercity passenger motor buses. Then, as today, it was unusual for a medium-sized highway transportation firm to carry both freight and passengers. Therefore, it was logical for the company to sell one of the two branches of service.

Indiana Railroad Division of Wesson Company sold the freight operations. Inter-State Motor Freight Systems was the buyer and took over at the end of 1942. The purchase price suggests that Wesson Company had acquired, at low cost, a considerably undervalued company as the cash from the truck operation sale was nearly enough to pay off the debt owed to Midland United for Indiana Railroad. (The dollar amount is not known but the equivalency is noted in the corporate minute books.)

After the truck division had been sold, an additional order of trucks arrived that had not been a part of the sale. Three of these were converted into tractor-trailer buses in January 1943. Corporate records indicate the company considered converting five more but sold them instead. These make-shifts helped handle the greatly increased short-haul loads on the Fort Harrison route which required a multiple of buses to be dispatched to handle the loads for some of the scheduled runs. Garrett reported that the service required at least 19 buses in peak service and as many as nine of them had been broken down at one time. On one of these bus shortage occasions Army trucks had to come to the Traction Terminal to haul 24 loads of soldiers to Fort Harrison. By mid-1943, employment fell to 272 after nearly 300 employees were transferred in the sale of the motor freight business.

Ten more Ford buses were acquired in October 1943 from a large group built on an authorization from the War Production Board. These helped solve the military post overload problem and ease the chronic equipment shortage. By the end of 1943, twenty-five buses were in use on the Fort Harrison run.

Terminal facilities were also changed. In most localities the buses now used a union bus terminal instead of a company-owned station. At Fort Wayne, for example, the buses moved from the Main Street Station (which was then razed) to the Greyhound Terminal on Jefferson. When Greyhound had no room for other companies, Indiana Railroad and the other independents moved to their own spot next to the Greyhound station. At Indianapolis the huge trainshed terminal was now designated as the bus terminal at Illinois and Market Streets. This Indianapolis facility actually belonged to the local Indianapolis Railways Company. It had been acquired as part of the final break-up of the old THI&E. At Muncie, the company used part of the old station but not the trainshed. Bus loading was moved to the north end of freight terminal,

Above Built by White, the 412 was one of eight buses purchased to replace the interurban cars on the Terre Haute line. *Motor Bus Society, Inc. Library*

Left The highspeeds were replaced by the 29-passenger 432 and its sisters. Both views were taken in August 1946 under the Indianapolis trainshed. *Motor Bus Society, Inc. Library*

Below Indiana Railroad's fleet of orange and green tractor-trailers ranged over a wide territory. In 1939, the equipment was modern, equal in size to that of all major motor truck lines. *George K. Bradley collection*

Above Following World War II the company bought larger 37-passenger Aerocoach buses. The 449 holds a charter run at Columbus (Ohio) in August 1947. *Motor Bus Society, Inc. Library*

Right When Indiana Railroad ended rail service, Ed Belknap left his ticket window to drive the new White suburban buses on the Fort Harrison route. *George K. Bradley collection*

south of Howard Street at Mulberry. The building was modified for bus use and put in use in November 1942. The sale of the truck lines caused an almost immediate move back across Howard Street. The express terminal, at the rear of the old Charles and Mulberry Streets building, was razed and replaced with a covered walkway with buses entering the terminal from Mulberry Street. The waiting room in the old terminal was again used but the trainshed area became a parking lot.

As the war emergency eased, the company began making plans for peacetime operations. John Martin suggested an equipment standardization instead of continuing the hodge-podge bus fleet. New buses began to arrive in 1945, and 21 older buses were sold. Garrett advised the company directors they would face strong postwar competition and that much of the inflated wartime traffic, particularly the military personnel, would disappear. He recommended purchasing the Indiana Motor Bus Company but no arrangements could be made.

In the spring of 1945, Ray Garrett, a partner in the Chicago law firm of Sidney, Austin, Burgess & Harper, wanted to rejoin the firm on a full-time basis and asked that he be relieved of the day-to-day chores of bus management. A suggestion was made that Wesson Company buy out Henry P. Bruner's Wisconsin bus and rail operations and secure the service of Mr. Bruner for the Indiana properties. Bruner was known in Indiana, as in the early 1930's he had managed Coordinated Transport, Inc., another Insull affiliate. A formal offer was made but no agreement was reached. With this rejection in mind, the Board appointed John T. Martin to be vice president and general manager relieving Garrett of many day-to-day duties.

In 1945, the Denny and Hines Bus Company, owner of the Muncie transit system, offered the bus lines to Indiana Railroad Division of Wesson Company. The Muncie company was taken over on October 2, 1945.

In March 1946, Ray Garrett repeated his advice that the Board consider expanding or selling. Indiana Motor Bus Company was being considered again when Henry Bruner approached Wesson Company with a suggestion that he buy the company's operation. Apparently a contract was submitted but, according to the company

Above In 1949 Aerocoach built a group of seven handsome T-361-C city-type buses, similar to the GMC bus design, for the Anderson city routes and the Fort Harrison suburban run.
Motor Bus Society, Inc. Library

Above By 1952, bus 84 resembled a GMC 40-passenger unit. Built for use in Muncie in 1948 as a TDH-3207 (32 passengers), it was one of several stretched for Fort Harrison service.
Motor Bus Society, Inc. Library

minute books, none of the Bruner terms were really firm and no guarantee could be obtained. The matter was then dropped. However, the key to the matter was Garrett's sound advice and repeated warning that the company should expand or sell. In partial response, in 1947 the company did establish a schedule south from Muncie through a number of small cities to Jeffersonville. Soon it was extended to Louisville. The route was not very successful but it provided access to new territory and became a useful route item.

During the war and postwar years, the Anderson and Richmond city lines were kept in good shape. Many of the city buses were nearly worn out by the end of the war. In a replacement program old Beaver, Indiana, White and Yellow buses were replaced with new GMC diesel buses which joined the newer Ford buses.

The intercity fleet was modernized with repeat orders for 37-passenger Aerocoach intercity motor coaches. Aerocoach also built a group of city-type buses for the Fort Harrison route. All service was operated with a clean, modern and well-maintained fleet of buses.

An important parallel to the motor coach story began in January 1932 when the Indianapolis & Southeastern Railroad Company, already operating connecting buses from Greensburg to Cincinnati, abandoned its rail operations and substituted motor buses over the entire route. The corporate name was modified to Indianapolis & Southeastern Lines, Inc. (I&SE). The motor bus and other business operations were moderately successful but, following the end of the war, the owners decided to dispose of the bus business rather than consider any expansion.

Benjamin D. Kramer and Clement J. Villeneuve entered into an agreement with the I&SE, on February 16, 1945, for the sale of the motor transportation business portion of the corporation. These two men owned several bus companies including De Luxe Motor Stages, Inc. (De Luxe Trailways), with a Chicago-St. Louis bus route, and Empire Trailways, operating from Chicago to Wanatah, Ind., where it connected with Victory Coach Lines, Inc. operating from Wanatah through Lafayette to Indianapolis. The agreement was completed on October 29, 1945 and the sale included the Indianapolis & Southeastern Lines company name.

As a result, the older Indianapolis & Southeastern Lines, Inc. changed its name to Southeastern Properties Corporation (as it was now a real estate company) and later became part of Public Service Company of Indiana.

Below Three of Indianapolis & Southeastern Railroad Company's ten straight-eight Studebaker parlor coaches used on the extension to Cincinnati, Ohio.
Bus Transportation, George K. Bradley collection

Right The 37-passenger 507, in 1952, carries the shorter "Wesson Company-Owner" name.
Motor Bus Society, Inc. Library

Above A charter run of Indiana Railroad in June 1951 carries the company name to New York City. Aerocoach 508 signals a right turn off West 41st Street.
Motor Bus Society, Inc. Library

Right Anderson's bus station in May 1945 with the 466 loading and a bus from the Hines Coach Line in the background.
George K. Bradley collection

Left Southeastern Trailways (SET) 601, a General Motors PD4103, calls at the old interurban station at Greencastle on June 17, 1952—and even cuts across the corner of the block as the rail cars had done.
Motor Bus Society, Inc. Library

Below The 224, a 1968 Eagle 05, at Cincinnati in April 1982.
Motor Bus Society, Inc. Library

Kramer and Villeneuve set up a new Indianapolis & Southeastern Trailways, Inc. to take over the routes and equipment. Victory Coach Lines was purchased in May 1946. In order to establish a through Chicago-Cincinnati route under one name, the three companies (De Luxe, Victory and I&SE) were merged into Indianapolis & Southeasten Trailways, Inc., one unified company, in October 1947. The route was extended, in late 1949, to Knoxville, Tennessee.

Ray Garrett's recommendation to expand or sell was implemented in June 1950 when Indiana Railroad, Division of Wesson Company (all that was left of the Wesson Company) and its equipment were sold to Kramer and Villeneuve. Operations of both companies were consolidated at the Senate and Ohio location in Indianapolis. Predictably, there were personnel changes and mergers of services. Trailways people assumed most of the management and operating positions. Intercity bus operations now went under the Trailways name and the old name was changed as each bus came in for routine painting.

For tax purposes, Anderson City Lines, Inc., Muncie City Lines, Inc. and Richmond City Lines, Inc. were set up as separate corporations owned by Indiana Railroad, Division of Wesson Company. The control continued for a number of years. However, the three systems fell victim to the malady hitting all local transit companies: rising cost and declining revenues. Systems of this size were particularly vulnerable and the Anderson operation was discontinued in June 1969.

The corporate name of the Indiana Railroad, Division of Wesson Company was shortened to Wesson Company. In September 1971, all of the companies, including Indianapolis & Southeastern Trailways, Inc., were merged in Wesson Company as it had the broader corporate charter of the two principal firms. The surviving corporation was then renamed Southeastern Trailways, Inc.

The Richmond city system was turned over to the city of Richmond in April 1973. The one-time suburban Fort Harrison bus line was turned over to Indianapolis Metro, the city's public transportation corporation. Muncie's bus lines were sold to the city to become a municipal operation on June 28, 1981.

Southeastern Trailways, Inc. moved its offices from the Ohio and Senate location to a new location on West 16th Street. This was precipitated by the state government's purchasing the property for future government office buildings (the property is across the street from the Indiana State Capitol).

Martin Kramer, son of B. D. Kramer, is currently president of Southeastern Trailways, Inc. which is an independent in the family of companies operating under the Trailways banner. The intercity bus fleet has undergone progressive changes and continues to operate the most modern intercity motorcoaches. The company remains as a strong survivor in the rapidly changing world of deregulation as well as the changed character of the intercity highway systems. Services have been expanded with runs south from Louisville to

Birmingham, Alabama in a pool with Trailways, Inc. None of the former Indiana Railroad routes has Southeastern Trailways bus service today (1991). The bulk of the current service is based on the Indianapolis & Southeastern routes and their extensions.

The changes in the bus services show the need for constant modifications to continue a viable city and intercity public transportation operation. The building of the national Interstate Highway System displaced the motor bus from the local, rural stops. The Interstates in Indiana follow the general routes of commercial transportation that have stood for well over one hundred years, but buses on them don't pass through crossroads communities. Many small cities have no intercity transportation as they, too long ago, chose to depend on the private automobile and eventually lost the rail and bus services. It goes back to Robert Feustel's basic "use it or lose it" philosophy.

Many evidences of the Indiana Railroad can be seen in the state, but each passing year reduces the physical features until one day little more than some vacant cuts, fills and bridge abutments will remain. The train terminals and city streets have seen vast changes brought on by urban renewal.

The huge Indianapolis Traction Terminal building and trainshed were vacated in the 1960's when the bus companies moved to the new Greyhound Terminal Building in the one-time freight and car yards at Ohio Street and Capitol Avenue. An insurance company acquired and razed the traction terminal in 1968. The insurance company's building sits where the trainshed covered the nine-track heart of the Indiana interurban empire while the former site of the great Burnham & Root office/terminal building is a company-owned park at Illinois and Market Streets. No marker indicates this significant location.

There is always room for thought about "what might have been" had the Indiana Railroad interurban rail operation survived into the war years. The company's premise was to operate in a modern and efficient manner—that was what the Insull modernization had brought to the property. It was this same premise spurred by the survival factor that led Bowman Elder to the less labor-intensive and lower-cost intercity motor bus conversions of the rail routes. Yet, Indiana Railroad lives on in the memories of thousands as the magic interurban, the last great hurrah for the traditional electric intercity rail concept first seen in the 1890's.

Left Silver Eagle SET 252 is the company's special Executive Coach for charter service.
Robert Redden photo

Below The 73279, at the Indianapolis terminal in April 1990, is one of Southeastern Trailways' 47-passenger 1988 model Eagle buses. The "73" prefix was added in 1989 to the numbers of all active Southeastern Trailways buses.
Southeastern Trailways, Inc. photo

Chapter 13
City Service

Left Marion Railways car 24 southbound alongside River Drive on the Matter Park line (a summertime extension of the North Marion service) on August 11, 1946. Different than the other local streetcars, the 24 was not an operating success in Marion though it was popular for fan trips. *Gordon E. Lloyd photo*

Indiana Railroad, in 1930, controlled ten city streetcar and bus operations. All were placed under the supervision of J. Allen Greenland, former Superintendent of Transportation for the ISC's city lines. ISC's large Fort Wayne City Lines, originally to be included, were withdrawn and remained in charge of J. R. McKay. Greenland had to concentrate on too many widely scattered properties and would not have time to provide the full-time supervision required at Fort Wayne.

Union Traction had streetcar systems at Anderson, Muncie and Marion. Northern Indiana Power Company had streetcar and bus lines at Kokomo while ISC ran Logansport, Peru and Wabash. Public Service Company cities included the New Albany and Jeffersonville streetcar lines plus the Columbus bus lines. The THI&E acquisition added the city systems at Richmond and Terre Haute. All but the three ISC properties used single-truck safety cars built to the design originally developed by Charles O. Birney and usually known as birney cars. ISC used cars of its own design.

The city properties did not do well under Indiana Railroad System management. This was more the fault of the times than of Greenland and his associates. In 1930 all small-city rail lines had common problems: they were wearing out or already worn out; they were inflexibly limited in the areas served; and a fixed layout restricted the number of cars that could be operated. Modifying and/or modernizing rail facilities would require large cash outlays. The birneys, a 1916 design, were seven or more years old, a poor second when compared to new buses. "Modern" buses were considered the way of the future. Most of the city properties were abandoned, sold, or converted to buses run by other companies by the end of 1934. By then the Terre Haute, Anderson and Richmond car lines were still in existence but on borrowed time.

Each of the city operations had its own story. The events that followed the Indiana Railroad System operation were governed by prior events as well as the prevailing policies of the system company owner and the current political climate. The properties are dealt with here in varying detail based upon their importance to the System, size and longevity.

Kokomo

Northern Indiana Power Company had a city operation in Kokomo using birney cars on five lines plus one bus line. The ten birney cars (numbers 51-60) had been purchased in 1920 to modernize the system. Several older cars were kept in serviceable condition to meet any special needs. Growth of the city's population dictated adding a new line in 1925. The need was met through the purchase of two International Harvester buses in that year. These were augmented by one additional bus in 1928 and two more in 1929. Clearly, the extension or future support of the rail system was not in the power company's plans.

The city trackage was shared by the Northern Indiana Power Company's Frankfort-Kokomo-Marion interurban, an east-west route along Markland Avenue but diverted north on Main Street to the NIPCo passenger station at Sycamore Street. Having no city cars in town, Union Traction had built its own tracks in Kokomo on Union, Taylor, Kennedy and Wabash Streets with a station near Walnut and Union. The two companies were connected by a switch at Markland Avenue and Union Street. All other crossings were straight through with no switches. When the former Union Traction line to Logansport ended in 1930, the Wabash Street and part of the Taylor Street trackage was abandoned. The wye at Union and Taylor remained for turning cars.

By the end of 1931, NIPCo and the System management agreed to abandon the city service without any replacement. Before they could gain approval from the Public Service Commission, the city had to find an independent bus operator to provide a replacement service. The power company also agreed to a cash payment to be used for street repairs and to deed a 13-acre park to the city.

Shortly after 11 PM on Sunday, April 17, 1932, birney car 56 (the first of the Kokomo birney cars to go into service) made the last run. Tippecanoe Coach Lines, the new bus company, started service the next day. The NIPCo interurban line was still in operation although under a petition to abandon. The interurban cars on this line were moved from Main Street to Union Street and to the former Union Traction station. The cars were turned on the wye at Union and Markland and then reversed on the wye at Taylor and Union. This situation did not continue for long as the east-west line was abandoned on June 30, 1932. Track and wire remained on West Markland Street to reach the Kokomo Stone Company and the NIPCo car barn. Besides these 14 blocks, which remained active for several years, part of the line east may have remained in service to reach a stone quarry near Greentown.

Street railway trackage was rapidly pulled up in Kokomo and the Kokomo *Tribune* published an article on how much better the city streets looked with the rails gone and the wire taken down. (Indiana Railroad continued to use Union, Taylor and Kennedy Streets for the Peru interurban route until September 1938.) The successor bus company was soon followed by Kokomo City Service, Inc. That company went bankrupt and, according to *Bus Transportation*, a mad scramble ensued for the bus rights.

The ISC properties are covered in less detail as a comprehensive history of each appears in CERA Bulletin 122, *Fort Wayne and Wabash Valley Trolleys*.

Logansport

The Logansport City Lines' four lines used ISC's own single-truck cars. The system had slipped into the red ink. The decision to abandon the unprofitable interurban line west of Peru sealed the fate of Logansport's lines. The last streetcars and buses ran on April 29, 1932. The interurban line was not abandoned until May 21.

Wabash

Wabash had a streetcar line which ran north and south and crossed over the Wabash River. The single line had a number of twists and turns on the south side and encountered stiff grades on both sides of the river. In 1930 the interurban line from Marion was abandoned and in 1931 the east-west bypass was completed taking all interurban traffic off the city line. The city was willing to allow the company to abandon the car line if it would substitute bus service. Streetcars made their last run on August 31, 1931.

ISC bought three Fargo Model 80 25-passenger buses and had them painted and lettered for Indiana Railroad. The service was successful but not profitable and ISC asked to give it up. Another operator was found to take over the line. The Indiana Railroad buses ended on April 1, 1933. Some patrons had to be told that the announcement was no April Fool's joke.

Peru

Peru is another valley city stretching for several miles along the north side of the Wabash River. Because the ISC's Wabash Valley line passed through the city there was an ideal east-west streetcar line. A variety of single-truck cars were used over the years. The Winona Railroad, which entered from the north, once had a city car operation over its interurban trackage. Crossing the Wabash River from the south, the Kokomo-Peru line of the Union Traction Company had minimal city street running.

The abandonment of the System's line west of Peru meant that the Main Street trackage west of Broadway would be used exclusively for streetcars. The change meant newer cars for Peru because the 291-299 series cars from Logansport were available. City cars were kept overnight at the Indiana Railroad freight house on Canal Street. Surplus cars for the small ISC cities were stored at Boyd Park barn along the interurban between Peru and Wabash. If one of the cars in use broke down, the motorman was sent to Boyd Park barn to get another from the cars stored there. These stored cars were dirty inside and out. The motorman had to clean the car before it could be put into use.

After Indiana Railroad went into receivership, in 1933, ISC re-assumed control of the Peru City Lines. The streetcar operation was not a money maker and ISC petitioned for abandonment of the service. The last streetcar ran on December 8, 1934. The city considered taking over the car line. Another company took over the line using its buses. At the same time ISC abandoned the trackage on West Main Street.

Below The two Wabash city cars, 220 and 214, meet on the double track in Wabash Street just north of the new interurban route shortly before streetcar service ended on August 31, 1931. *M. D. McCarter collection*

Above On the south side of Wabash, ISC 214 makes the turn west onto Pike Street after the long climb out of the Wabash River valley on Columbus and Vernon streets.
M. D. McCarter collection

Public Service Company of Indiana owned three city transit properties with Columbus converted to motor buses before the System was created. Shortly after the System took over, it was apparent that Public Service did not want the three properties.

Jeffersonville

Jeffersonville had three relatively short city lines which were extensions of the older horsecar lines. These had been electrified and became a part of the properties that made up Public Service Company of Indiana. Besides the car lines, trackage was added for the interurbans. Westward, on Court Street, the trackage crossed under the elevated approaches to the Big Four's Ohio River bridge to Louisville. Further to the west the line turned in a southerly direction paralleling the Big Four and climbed to its grade so that the interurban cars could use the steam road tracks into Louisville. Indianapolis cars and the Louisville-Jeffersonville-New Albany suburban line used this route. The local station was a triangular-shaped building in a triangle block bounded by Court, Kentucky and Sixth Streets. The New Albany cars had turned north at Spring Street while the others proceeded east on Court and north on Meigs.

A Jeffersonville local car line had physical connections with the American Car & Foundry Company tracks. Many interurban and city cars were built in this plant including the deluxe version of the Indiana Railroad highspeeds.

Each day many electric cars passed through Jeffersonville and, with the exception of some of the through Indianapolis trains, made local stops. The location on the Ohio River directly across from Louisville meant a lot of suburban and intercity traffic. The interurban had a joint trackage agreement on the Big Four bridge. On the Kentucky side, the Indiana cars had their own route using their own and dual-gauge tracks in the city streets (Louisville Railways used a broad track gauge) to reach the interurban terminal. All trains crossing the bridge carried a flagman from station to station. Suburban Louisville-Jeffersonville-New Albany cars over the bridge and local Jeffersonville lines were ended on Sunday, May 15, 1932. Public Service Company had petitioned to abandon the entire Louisville-Jeffersonville-New Albany line but had to retain the frequent-service Jeffersonville-New Albany portion of the route. This route was seriously hurt by the construction of a new Ohio River highway bridge from Louisville to Jeffersonville. The Public Service Commission felt that only the bridge portion of the electric line was hurt. This route, which connected with the company's city lines in New Albany, had six of Public Service Company's newest passenger cars, only five years old.

Following the end of Jeffersonville's local streetcars, the interurban cars were routed via Spring and Tenth streets. To ease the right-angle turn, new trackage was laid on Kentucky from Court to Spring and Seventh Streets. The freight station and car barns were located there. The passenger facilities were moved to the freight station as part of the cost reduction and consolidation of station facilities. The Seventh Street carbarn was torn down before 1935 and the area used as a storage yard. Only that portion that contained the freight house was rebuilt. During the 1937 flood, the station, the car yard and most of the rail property in Jeffersonville was under as much as 25 feet of water.

Columbus

At Columbus the interurbans ran through the city on Washington Street, which had been part of the local car lines. Leppert Bus Lines, Inc. assumed ownership of the Columbus bus system of Public Service Company on November 20, 1932.

Above At New Albany's Monon railroad station on July 23, 1939, Home Transit's birney 95 is eastbound on Market Street. Birneys handled all the base service before the war. *John F. Humiston photo*

New Albany

The New Albany situation offered different circumstances. There was room for complications with two separate operations and two different track gauges. On May 15, 1932, at midnight, Public Service Company had abandoned part of the standard-gauge city car lines (Silver Hills, Main Street and West Spring Street between W. First and W. Eighth) because of anticipated track renewals. Public Service had just reconstructed several portions of the track work and retained the State-Vincennes and Ekin lines. The company also petitioned to abandon the line to Jeffersonville. There was also the "Daisy Line," a broad-gauge operation over the Kentucky & Indiana Terminal Railroad Company's bridge using gauntlet tracks to compensate for the gauge difference. In Louisville, the cars used the broad-gauge Louisville Railway Company's track to reach the Third Street interurban terminal. Both operations were offered for sale as modestly profitable companies.

Two directly related companies were organized to purchase the properties. Robert R. Kelso and Raymond E. Korte formed Home Transit, Inc., first known as New Albany Transit, Inc., and bought the standard-gauge city lines on April 22, 1934. Service to Silver Hills and on Main Street was already replaced with bus service, leaving the State-Vincennes and Ekin rail lines. The earlier abandonment of some trackage caused an odd operation on Spring Street. The single track on East Fourth had originally crossed Spring to reach Market Street. A car coming south on Fourth (Ekin line) was now routed west to the double track of Spring Street but there was no switch to the westbound track. There was a switch from Fourth to the eastbound Spring Street track and a crossover in Spring Street west of Fourth. Southbound cars turned from Fourth to the eastbound Spring Street track and then crossed over to the westbound track. At West First Street they crossed over again, reversed ends and went east. This time the movement to Fourth was in a normal manner. A car coming south on State Street confronted a similar problem turning first onto the eastbound Spring Street track and then crossing over on a switch just east of

Below Home Transit bought curved-side cars 253 and 255 from Public Service Company of Indiana. The 253 is at the car barn on July 15, 1940. Then reserved for trippers, it was brought into the sun after photographer Korkes asked Mr. Kelso for that favor! During the war it saw regular service. *George Yater collection*

Below In July 1942 birneys 81 (facing camera) westbound to State Street and 93 eastbound to Vincennes work the major route. Cars took a short layover here to make connections with bridge trains to and from Louisville, whose station is along the Monon railroad to the right of the photographer. *George Yater photo*

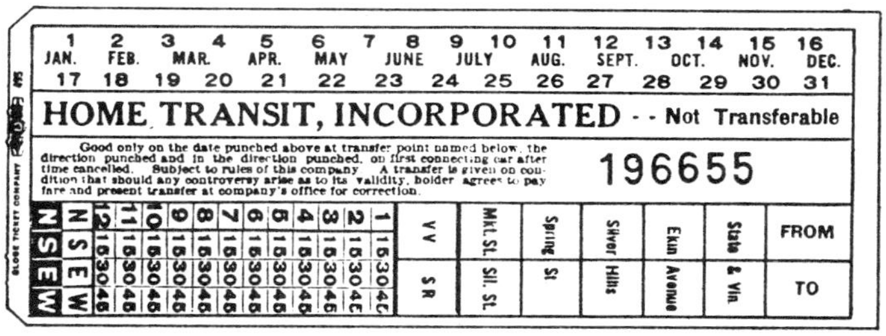

1 2 3 4 5 6 7 8 9 10 11 12 13 14 15 16
JAN. FEB. MAR. APR. MAY JUNE JULY AUG. SEPT. OCT. NOV. DEC.
17 18 19 20 21 22 23 24 25 26 27 28 29 30 31

HOME TRANSIT, INCORPORATED - - Not Transferable

Good only on the date punched above at transfer point named below, the direction punched and in the direction punched, on first connecting car after time cancelled. Subject to rules of this company. A transfer is given on condition that should any controversy arise as to its validity, holder agrees to pay fare and present transfer at company's office for correction.

196655

N S E W
1 2 3 4 5 6 7 8 9 10 11 12
15 30 45

VV / SR — Mkt. St. / Sil. St. — Spring St — Silver Hills — Ekin Avenue — State & Vin. — FROM / TO

Globe Ticket Company

Above A 1949 bus transfer. *Thomas H. Desnoyers collection*

the turn. On Spring, just west of 13th, where the double track originally extended to the Jeffersonville line, the track crossed over to the eastbound track and turned onto the single track on 13th. The operation meant that the city cars at several places regularly had to do a little dance back and forth and in the face of opposing auto traffic. This sort of operation was acceptable in the 1930's when auto traffic was light.

The new company bought a number of birney cars and two double-truck curved-side cars from Public Service. The latter cars were used for school tripper service in the early days and, for many years, only one was repainted to the blue and yellow company paint scheme. During the war years these cars and another spare birney were put into active use. The system remained little changed (with the exception of added bus service) until January 31, 1946 when the streetcars were replaced by Home Transit's buses.

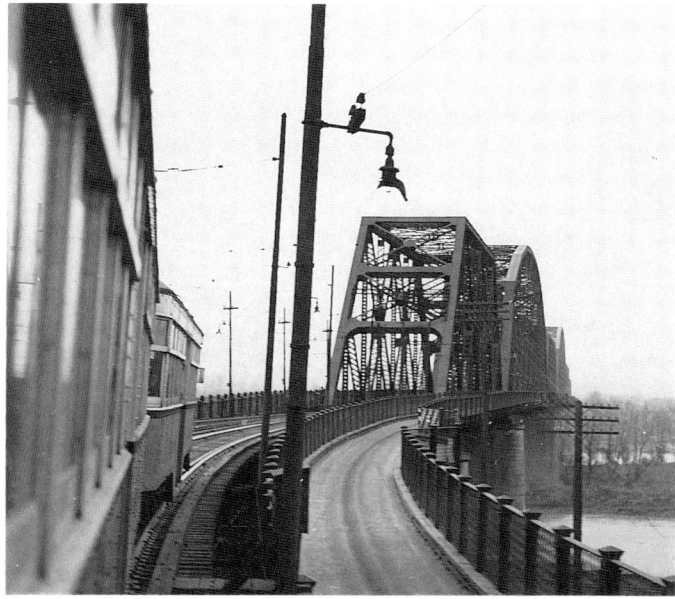

Above Heading toward New Albany, a two-car train climbs to the Kentucky & Indiana Terminal Railroad Company bridge. It's running on the broad-gauge gauntlet track, which looks like a guard rail in the photo. The nearest rail is for the standard-gauge steam trains. *Dr. Howard R. Blackburn photo*

Below Inbound New Albany & Louisville 774 turns from Jefferson onto Sixth Street. The Louisville city hall is in the immediate background. *Dr. Howard R. Blackburn photo*

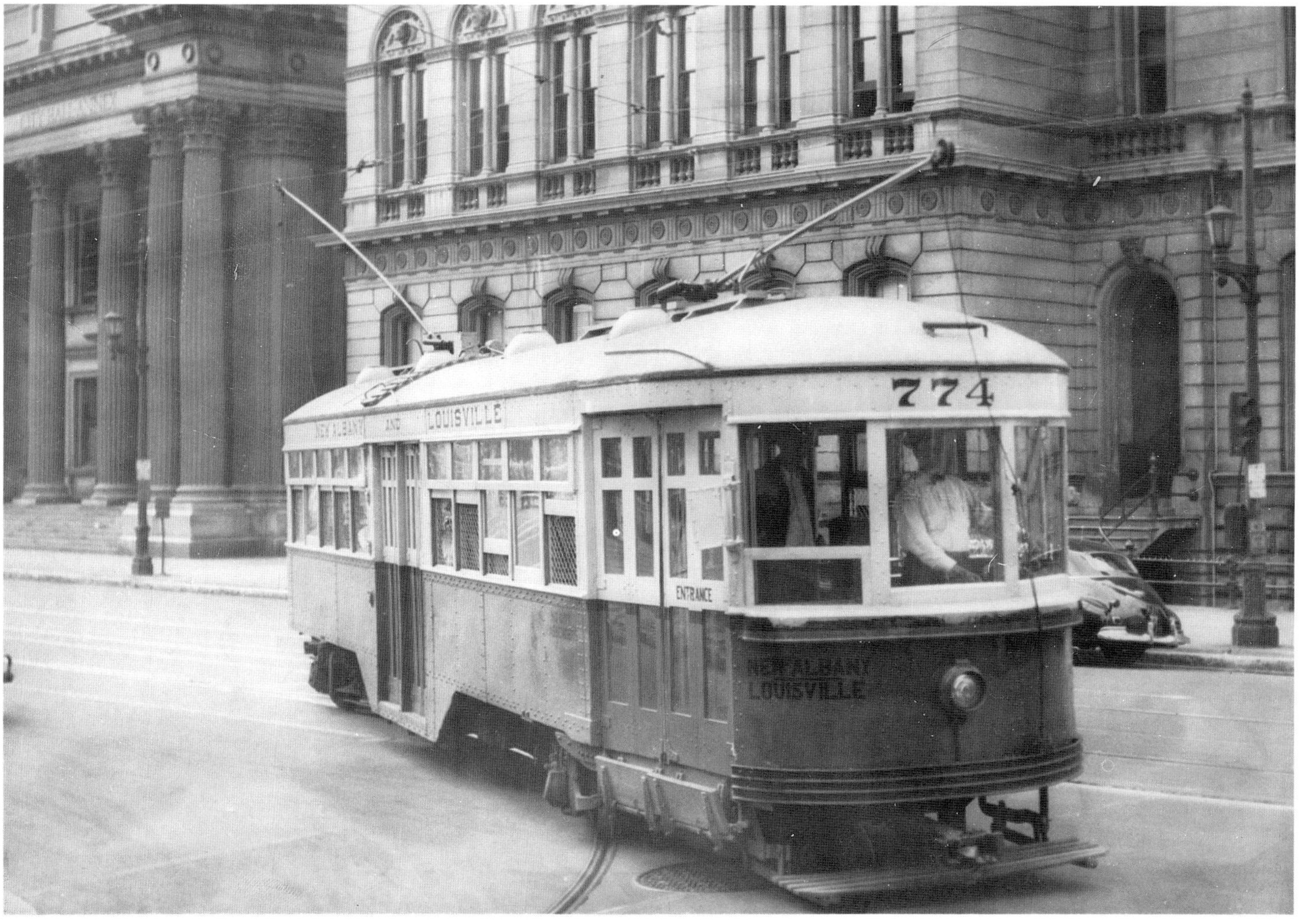

Above A New Albany & Louisville train monopolizes the street space in turning at 7th and Market Streets. Trailer trains were the usual operating format for NA&L. Such big units were no strangers to the streets of Louisville. This equipment, after all, had been "promoted" from the city lines of Louisville Railway.   *Dr. Howard R. Blackburn collection*

Home Transit did not operate the rail service between New Albany and Jeffersonville. They did start a bus line over the public roads following the midnight April 21, 1934 end of the Indiana Railroad service. The six modern rail cars were sent to the Scottsburg shop for possible sale and were later sent to Terre Haute. The new Home Transit buses didn't arrive until after the cars had stopped at midnight. Barely cleaned and serviced, the buses went into service at 5:30 on Sunday morning with no trial runs or opportunity to train the drivers.

Kelso and Korte's New Albany & Louisville Railroad Corporation (NA&L) on April 22, 1934 was the purchaser of the other New Albany-based property and acquired the right to operate into Louisville over the K&I bridge. The NA&L instituted several immediate changes. The new company did not take over the operation of ancient wooden cars that had been in use for many years. Instead it leased six Peter Witt style motor cars (#770-775) and four matching trailers (#355-358), all built in 1924, from Louisville Railway. The cars were repainted for the lessee and were immediately popular. At the same time the company moved from the Third Street interurban station to the Louisville & Interurban's station on Jefferson Street. The company operated on a thirty-minute headway with fifteen-minute rush hour service. A new station was built in New Albany, close to Market Street and the Vincennes car line.

Indiana Railroad also moved to the L&I station. The NA&L cars and the Indiana Railroad cars loaded on adjoining tracks since the terminal was equipped for dual-gauge operation. The K&I bridge operation, similar to the Big Four Bridge, required the cars to carry railroad style markers and an extra man to serve as a flagman. In the rush hour, when trailers were used, a conductor was needed for the second car and he could act as flagman. It is believed that the regular flagman was also a conductor for the rush hour period. Conductors did not wear a special uniform.

After 1939, the NA&L canary yellow cars were the only cars in the L&I terminal and still passed through on the west track from Jefferson (north) to Liberty (south). In November 1941, the cars began operating through from south to north and on the east side trackage formerly used by the Indiana Railroad cars. At the same time, the storage area on the Liberty Street side of the terminal was re-activated for use as the off-peak storage point for the NA&L cars. By this time the cars had been painted orange and cream.

Service continued virtually the same throughout the war years. Cars carried heavier-than-ever loads. The war's end saw riding drop and the NA&L quickly got out of the rail business, abandoning its service on December 31, 1945. Repainted, the motor cars went back to Louisville Railway who used them until 1948.

Public transportation in the New Albany area is now (1991) provided by the Transit Authority of River City, the Louisville bus system.

Below A two-car train for New Albany heads west on Liberty Street. The 1941 Christmas decorations are in place. A Louisville city car approaches in the distance.   *Dr. Howard R. Blackburn photo*

Above On Charles Street by the Muncie Traction Terminal, a birney turns north into Mulberry Street and will go east and south to the Industry line. *E. Y. Pattison photo, George K. Bradley collection*

Muncie

Indiana Railroad acquired the three remaining Union Traction city street railway operations located at Anderson, Muncie and Marion. The three properties should have been as alike as peas in a pod as they were similar size cities, relatively close together, parallel in their make-up and all were "Gas Belt" cities. Muncie was even considered, by some sociologists, to be *the* typical small American city and gained long-term fame in *Middletown*, by Robert S. Lynd and Helen Merrell Lynd. There have been those that disagreed with the selection but the social study covered most aspects of the community as it was in the mid-twenties. The streetcars and interurbans were considered to be so much of the normal fabric of a city this size that they rated only two text lines in a book of over 500 pages. For all of the attention of "typical" Middletown, Muncie turned out to be somewhat unique as a street railway property: a thorn in the side of the Union Traction Company as well as a two-time opportunity for the Indiana Railroad.

The Muncie streetcar system operated twelve miles of track, covered most of the city and provided an entrance for five interurban rail lines. It should have been as stable as any other well-regulated and soundly managed public transportation company. In 1925, Arthur Brady, as receiver for Union Traction, attempted to claim exclusive rights for his company, as the only legitimate operator, in the face of unregulated jitney bus operators. Unlike all the other Hoosier cities, the Muncie city government did the "atypical" thing and turned its back on the legitimate operator and actually—sometimes unofficially—encouraged the jitney bus operators. The only choice for Brady was to go to court. The legal actions continued into 1929 with the bus operators trying to place the authority for local regulation firmly in the hands of the Muncie city government, which was presumed to be far more sympathetic to the local jitney operators than to the Anderson-based Union Traction. Using a clause in a 1925 Indiana law, the jitney operators maintained the regulation authority was in the hands of the city government and that, even though Union Traction operated a local bus line, the competition was legal. The state supreme court upheld the jitney bus operators' position on a technicality but the situation was still not clear. At this point the city government might have acted or taken a stand but, for reasons still unknown, it did not.

By mid-1931, two of the five interurban routes using the Muncie local tracks had been abandoned and Indiana Railroad was now in charge. The State Legislature had become involved in the state-versus-city control of local transit and was trying to enact legislation to place all control in the state Public Service Commission. The street railway lines in Muncie had begun to shrink with the Avondale and West Side lines already abandoned. The five jitney bus operators with the city's implied consent, through no action at all, continued to pick up passengers in every area served by the streetcars. Indiana Railroad petitioned, on August 17, for complete abandonment of all its Muncie city service. Neither the morning or evening newspaper appeared surprised nor did they seem to care. Local hearings were held on September 14 with a representative of the Public Service Commission present to take testimony. Henry Bucher testified for Indiana Railroad and claimed the Muncie property lost in excess of $15,000 in each of the preceding six years. The Mayor and several city officials were present but they came only for the show with none making any comment for the record. The company said that it would consider substituting buses if the jitney bus operators were restrained. The city government hid behind the fact that a bill was proposed in the state legislature and it shouldn't take any action.

Both the Muncie *Morning Star* and the Muncie *Evening Press* carried stories on the September 25th approval for abandonment of the city streetcars effective on October 11, 1931 at the end of the daily service. The *Morning Star*, in an editorial, asked if anyone could drive an auto for 5¢ per mile and speculated that none of the Muncie bus operators were making any money if they were setting aside a depreciation amount to pay for replacement buses. Later the same paper stated, "Muncie

Below Muncie had the older birneys, including some purchased from Aberdeen, South Dakota and rebodied by St. Louis. The 78 is signed for Congerville-Industry. *George K. Bradley collection*

is going to regret its loss of streetcars." That comment was silently seconded when none of the bus operators came before the city council (as that body seemed to expect) for changes and extensions of their routes. Only local business owners showed up asking how their stores would be conveniently reached when the cars were gone and the buses didn't serve the area. The Council still pursued a "hands-off" policy until October 9 when the state legislature defeated the Public Service Commission control bill.

On October 12, 1931, the *Evening Press* stated, "Streetcar service on the Whitely, Riverside, Congerville, Industry and Heekin Park lines, all those that have been in operation for some years was discontinued by Indiana Railroad . . . ." The twelfth was a Monday and the cars had stopped on Sunday, October 11 at 11:10 PM with birney car 55 doing the honors on the Heekin Park line. Local manager Henry Engle, who along with 14 other men, lost his job when Indiana Railroad ended all its Muncie city service, said the seven cars in normal use and the three in reserve would be sent elsewhere. According to the *Morning Star*, Engle said, "[he] only wished that the folks would have given the new company a chance to prove its worthiness because it looks like [he], and the others hadn't done their job."

Indiana Railroad retained some trackage for passage of the interurban cars and portions of the uptown loop to provide access to the passenger and freight terminal. The abandonment of the city rail operation was quiet but the local transportation system with one less player was a chaotic mess. There was no city-wide plan for bus service on October 12. The five highly independent jitney bus operators continued to operate as before, as the city government failed, completely, to take a strong role in the process. They were the S. B. Denny Bus Company, the John R. Hines Bus Company, Liberty Transit Lines (Troxler brothers), White City Lines (Lon. F. Payne) and Congerville line (John R. Schisler). Each had one bus route. By 1935 the same, but now somewhat regulated, situation still existed. A City Council inspection of the buses revealed that most were in very poor condition with some unfit to be on the street. Some "new" buses were acquired. The situation echoed an April 1933 *Evening Press* editorial, "We in Muncie now realize, too late, what it meant to permit our city street cars and two of our interurban lines to slip away from us." The fractured service and ownership continued.

Order returned in October 1941 when Denny and Hines plus Juvia M. Gaylor set up a new partnership called Denny and Hines Bus Company to take over all of the local bus operations. On August 25, 1945, the three partners agreed to sell their system to Indiana Railroad Division of Wesson Company for $225,000. It is not known why the partners approached Indiana Railroad to sell what was a profitable operation. On October 2, 1945, after city approval was obtained, Indiana Railroad took over the operation. It was almost 14 years since the company had been pushed off the same streets.

Muncie City Lines was set up as a separate wholly-owned subsidiary corporation as part of the corporate reorganization of the parent company. Muncie City Lines continued to run through the 1960's but was losing money. In 1970 the city subsidized the operation to make up the deficit. Eight GMC buses (25-32) were purchased by the city in June 1972. By 1979 the Urban Mass Transit Administration (UMTA) urged the city to assume the operation. At the time Muncie City Lines owned 18 buses with none newer than 1957. These were operated with the newer city-owned buses. Southeastern Trailways agreed to sell its operation to Muncie in June 1981. It was succeeded at the time by Muncie Public Transportation Corporation's Muncie Indiana Transit System (MITS). The older buses were replaced by MITS' fleet of GMC 40-passenger RTS buses (1-16). Four Flxible buses (17-20) were added. These four, sold to Lafayette, Indiana in 1989, were replaced with three RTS buses (21-23). Nineteen buses now (1991) provide the Muncie base bus service.

Left Indiana Railroad bought the TDH-3207, the smallest version of the General Motors diesel bus, for its three city properties. On June 19, 1952, the 90 is southbound on Walnut Street at Howard Street, Muncie.
Motor Bus Society, Inc. Library

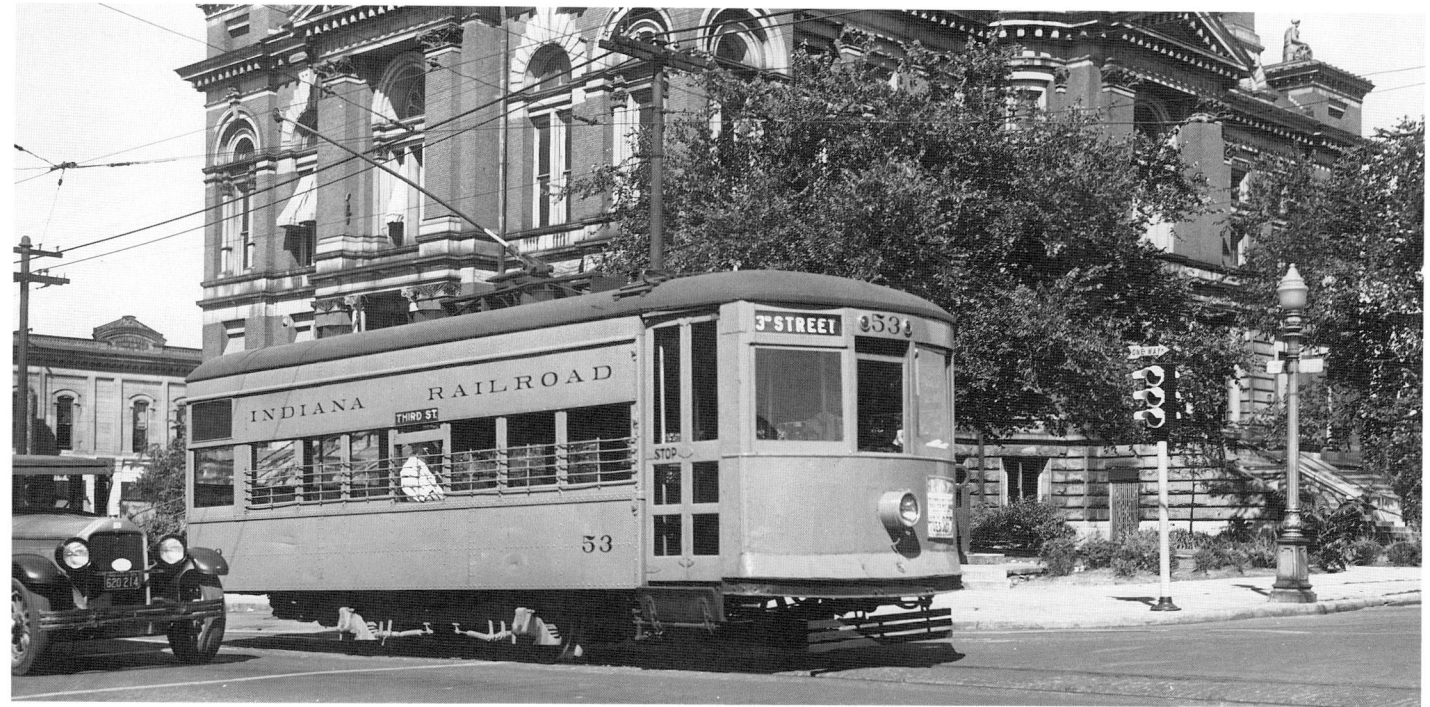

Above A misunderstanding of a work order to "paint car 53" made this view possible. Instead of highspeed 53, the shop painted soon-to-be-retired Anderson birney 53. On September 6, 1937 it is southbound on Meridian Street at 9th Street by the courthouse. *William C. Janssen photo*

Anderson

Indiana Railroad's Anderson city operation consisted of five rail lines (South Meridian, Third Street, Ohio Avenue, Hazelwood and North Anderson). Birney cars and several older double-truck cars provided the rail service. One bus line was also operated. The city service was good and it was considered as a break-even proposition. The relationship between the city and company was very cordial.

By 1936 the track work was worn and the lines no longer served the outer edges of a growing city. The chief problem was stated as one of a smooth flow of streetcars during the rush hour which created congestion and traffic jams. By mid-November it was apparent that the city and company would soon reach an accord to replace the streetcars with buses. Hearings were being held for the abandonment of the North Anderson line. Company buses had been running on the line for some time. New street construction speeded the change in a cooperative effort between city and company.

As 1937 opened it was anticipated that the city car lines would be ended early in the year. However the

Right With its pole reaching for high trolley wire across a Big Four branch line, the 57 is running along 23rd Street on Anderson's South Meridian line to the Delco-Remy plant and to a terminal loop at 34th and Lynn. *James F. Cook photo*

Above The South Meridian Street birney has just crossed the Big Four's main line. Gasoline is selling for 17 cents per gallon on November 13, 1937, the last day for the Anderson streetcars.
James F. Cook photo

company's attention was diverted to labor problems. The March 19 power house strike took everyone by surprise including the streetcar and bus operators. At this point the Amalgamated did an excellent job of alienating almost every segment of the community and had little sympathy from the city government or local labor groups. All service was suspended until May 23. It was during this period that some city officials suggested obtaining a new company to run the bus service. Anderson had a large, recently unionized automotive-manufacturing labor force. This segment of the community had been among those who suffered from the streetcar strike. To some politicians, a restored transit service might find them new friends. John Rock, active in the city politics, promoted the bus idea. It may

Below Big 212 runs along the double track in the unpaved center of Meridian Street. The North Anderson line was abandoned before 1936 was over.
James F. Cook photo

also have been part of the effort to get the city car operators back to work. Rock ran some buses, briefly, over Indiana Railroad lines for a few days and then quit. Liberty Transit, a competitor of the city streetcars for many years, operated several bus lines in Anderson. Liberty Transit opposed any new bus operator being allowed on the streets.

Indiana Railroad already had 14 older buses in use. Most of these dated from the late 1920's. The company promised a fleet of new buses if the Anderson streetcar lines were abandoned. Thirteen new 22-passenger buses built by Indiana Truck Company began arriving in November 1937. They were delayed in delivery because the company could not place a firm order until after the settlement of the strike. The Ohio Avenue car line was replaced on October 4, 1937 due to repaving and because enough buses were available for service. With a great amount of promotion and publicity advertising the new buses and modified lines, the remaining streetcars were removed from service on the night of Saturday, November 13. The interurbans continued to use the tracks on Arrow, Nichol, Eleventh, Main and Third plus the shop access tracks. A sad accident marred the Anderson operation on Sunday, January 9, 1938 when a Pennsylvania Railroad passenger train smashed bus 202 killing five passengers.

The bus system was expanded on July 5, 1939 when Liberty Transit, operating four lines, was purchased. The Liberty Transit drivers went to work for Indiana Railroad and eight of the purchased buses were reported as being reconditioned for further service. Earlier, on March 29, another small local competitor, Daily Transit, was reported as sold to Indiana Railroad although the sale was not approved until February 13, 1940. Anderson city transit was now under one company management with 11 lines and 37 buses.

More buses were added during the war years because of a large number of defense industries located

Above Action on the Hazelwood line. After the 58 passes on Nichol Avenue, the eastbound car will back out of the John Street spur. It's the last day for city cars, but interurbans to Indianapolis will continue. *James F. Cook photo*

in Anderson. The Office of Defense Transportation allocated a number of new Ford transit buses to Indiana Railroad for Anderson use. Some old buses were recalled for Anderson service and elsewhere on the system.

Following the war a number of General Motors TDH-3207 transit buses were added to the fleet. The Anderson system suffered a rapid decline in ridership as new autos became available and many local people, employed by General Motors Corporation's major subsidiary plants at Anderson, felt it was fashionable to have their own cars. Set up as a separate wholly-owned corporation, Anderson City Lines was eventually discontinued in June 1969. It was later succeeded by the City of Anderson Transportation System that runs the city buses in Anderson today (1991).

Below Indiana Model 16 buses replaced the Anderson birneys. In August 1947 the baby-sized 204 is followed south on Meridian Street at 11th by two Ford buses. *Motor Bus Society, Inc. Library*

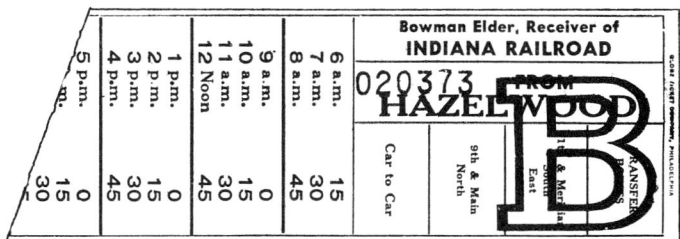

Above This 1934 Hazelwood transfer took you to 11th Street for an Ohio Avenue or South Meridian car or to the courthouse for a North Anderson or Third Street car. *Joseph M. Canfield collection*

Right In 1948 IR inaugurated 23-millimeter tokens for city bus fares. *Roy G. Benedict collection*

Below Like many city transit properties, Indiana Railroad had several groups of Ford-built buses. The 233 is on the North Anderson run in August 1947. *Motor Bus Society, Inc. Library*

Above The Soldiers Home (Veterans Hospital) is on Marion's southeast side. Car 1 is northbound through the attractively landscaped area that surrounded the car tracks and station loop on March 25, 1939. *John F. Humiston photo*

Marion
by Jerry D. Pruden

The abandonment of the Indiana Railroad interurban lines into Marion presented a problem by isolating the company-owned local streetcar lines. The last two interurbans were abandoned June 30, 1932. The System's owners were not interested in a separated operation, especially outside of their own utility business territory.

However, the 14-mile Marion streetcar system was in fairly good condition with a fleet of streetcars barely ten years old. The rail lines offered

Below In northwest Marion single-end birneys 1 and 4 meet on North D Street. Union Traction's birneys had double-end bodies, but some lacked equipment on one end such as controls and a door engine. The Soldiers Home-West Marion line was using some single-enders at the time of the sale, so Marion Railways purchased nine. *Jerry D. Pruden collection*

Above Along the College line on the southwest side, car 17 turns into a short spur track in Nebraska Street so the 10 can go downtown. A short double-end passing siding in Washington Street would have been better—but expensive to build. *Jerry D. Pruden collection*

comprehensive coverage of the city. There were no problems with the local city government. Abandonment of the lines would only create ill will.

Indiana Railroad continued to run the streetcars through 1932 and offered to sell them and the suburban Gas City line. The latter had been built as a part of the Marion system and was a line with reasonable patronage. The price was low, somewhere between scrap and book value, to encourage a buyer.

The answer came from two Marion bankers and Fred Baum, an Alexandria newspaper publisher, with their agreement of February 15, 1933 to purchase

Below On March 25, 1939, car 3 is northbound toward downtown on the Soldiers Home line. Passing the distinctive architecture of the former Union Traction powerhouse, it turns west onto 30th Street from the side-of-road double track on Home Avenue. The Marion Railways car barns are behind the photographer. *John F. Humiston photo*

Above Northbound on Adams Street, the east side of the Grant County Court House square, car 19 is between 3rd and 4th streets at 11:30 AM on August 10, 1946.
John F. Humiston photo

Left Four cars were bought from Springfield, Illinois in 1937. The 22 is at the square five years later. On this Independence Day it was one of two cars needed to maintain the 30-minute headway of the West Point-Cemetery line.
Gordon E. Lloyd photo

effective April 1. They incorporated the Marion Railways, Inc. with Baum as president. The Gas City line was not purchased because of high maintenance costs of the Deer Creek trestle and the bridge over the Mississinewa River into Gas City. Both had a high scrap value and the line required the use of double-truck cars. Avoiding the line saved on purchase costs and future operating expenses.

The company acquired all city trackage, overhead wires, power distribution system, car barn, shop, substation equipment, 18 streetcars, one line car and one snow sweeper. Before the Marion-Anderson line was dismantled, surplus supplies and spare parts were shipped from the Anderson shops (purchased from or contributed by Indiana Railroad). Power was purchased from Indiana General Service Company.

Current employees who wished to stay with the new company had preference before more people were hired. Baum met with them to determine a unique wage agreement. All except the shop foreman chose to stay.

Wages were to be based on total weekly revenue. At the end of the week, all fare receipts were to be totaled and, after a predetermined amount was set aside for operating expenses and mortgage payments, the rest was divided by man-hours worked for the amount per hour. The only differential was that shop men and motormen were paid more than section men. The wages averaged 35 cents per hour with the average work day being nine hours for a six-day week. In the early years the company lost money. Thus, in order to pay the wages, the "set asides" for loan repayments were not made.

Marion Railways operated three through routes with nine single-end (numbers 1-9) and nine double-end (numbers 10-12 and 14-19) well-maintained birney cars. In 1937 more parts were purchased from Indiana Railroad. Also, in 1937, the company bought four double-end birneys from Springfield, Illinois (numbers 20-23).

For several years, Marion Railways car 12 was painted white, covered with lights and had a figure of Santa Claus climbing up the side. This was the well-known "Christmas Car." Since there were enough cars for regular operations, the Christmas Car remained the same all year around and was used only for a few weeks. It was last used for Christmas 1941 as, by the end of 1942, the Office of Defense Transportation had called for all available transit vehicles to be pressed into service and Marion needed more cars. Car 12 went back to regular work and was joined by three more cars.

In 1942, car 24 was added to the roster along with cars 25-26. The 24 was unique. It had been rebuilt by Grand Rapids (Michigan) Railways as a deluxe car with enclosed entrance steps and leather-covered cushioned seats. Sold to Hershey (Pennsylvania) Transit, it was surplus by 1942. At Marion the car did not have any regular assignments because it caused accidents. All of the standard birney cars had an entrance step that folded down, outside of the car. Patrons were so used to this step that on the 24, out of habit, they tried to put a foot on a step that wasn't there. Falls and bruised shins made the 24 unpopular with the management and it was used as a spare car.

Two body shells were bought from St. Petersburg, Florida. Each was equipped with a truck, electrical controls, motors, seats and some body hardware before it could be placed in service. Seats in these two were of the rattan-covered, padded type, so the 24-26 provided a seating contrast from the typical wooden-slat seats found in the other cars. At this date the company had nine single-end and 16 double-end cars. Marion was an all-streetcar, all-birney city.

Marion Railways was a friendly operation and the cars would stop at almost any location for a passenger.

Below Popular Christmas car 12 in downtown Marion in December 1940. Until World War II it remained in white holiday garb all year. Then it was painted in standard orange and put into regular service. *Jerry D. Pruden collection*

Below Car 1 at the Marion Railways car barn. The motorman is Jerry Pruden and the sailor is M. D. "Mac" McCarter. *Chester Case photo*

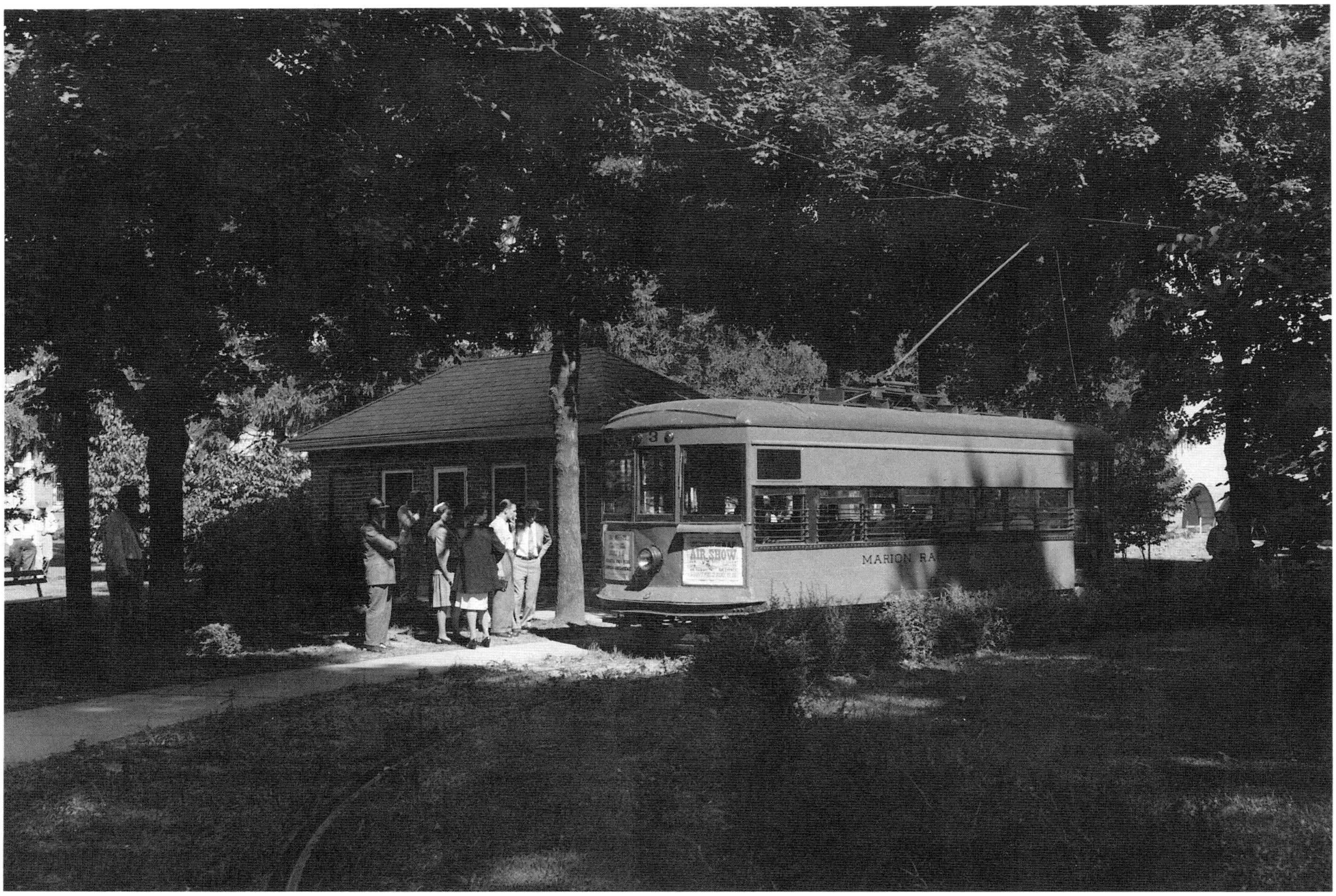

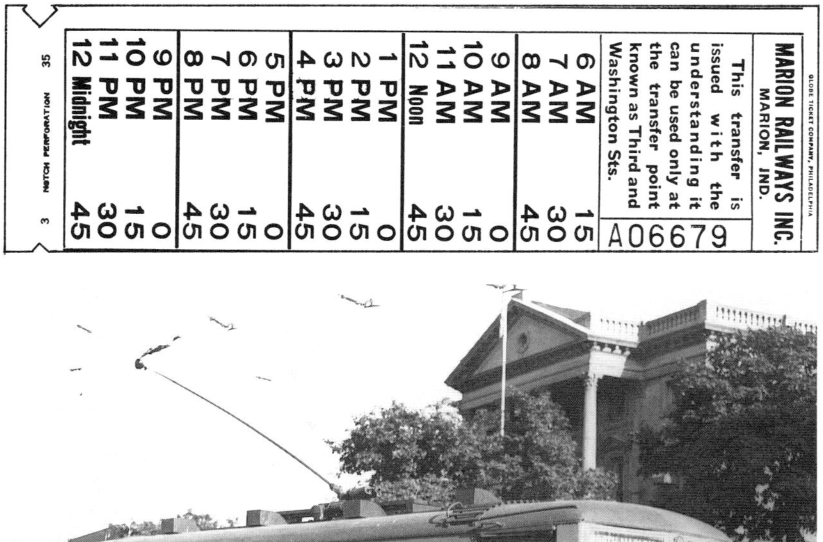
GLOBE TICKET COMPANY, PHILADELPHIA

MARION RAILWAYS INC.
MARION, IND.

This transfer is issued with the understanding it can be used only at the transfer point known as Third and Washington Sts.

A06679

6 AM	15
7 AM	30
8 AM	45
9 AM	0
10 AM	15
11 AM	30
12 Noon	45
1 PM	0
2 PM	15
3 PM	30
4 PM	45
5 PM	0
6 PM	15
7 PM	30
8 PM	45
9 PM	0
10 PM	15
11 PM	30
12 Midnight	45

35 NOTCH PERFORATION 3

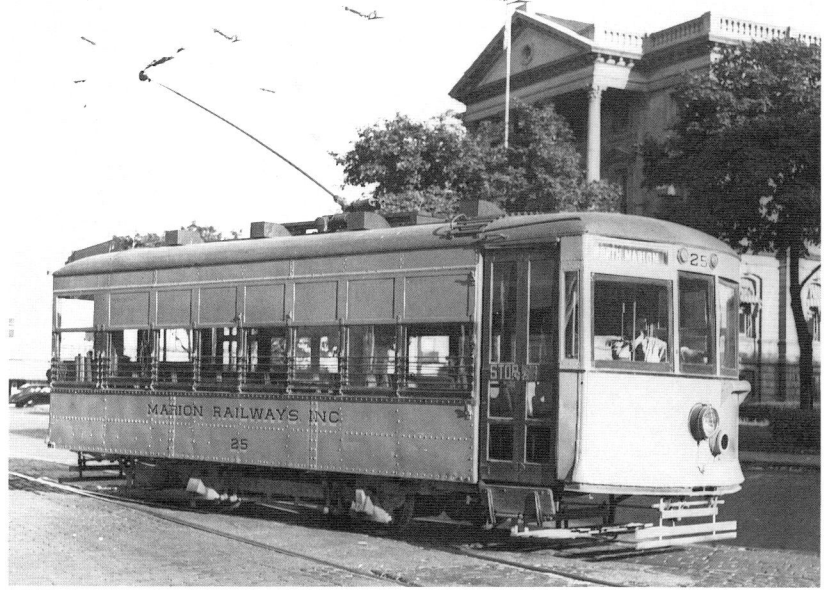

Above On August 11, 1946 car 3 takes on passengers at the Soldiers Home station. The scenic, well-maintained loop and station was a favorite railfan photo spot.
John F. Humiston photo

Left This transfer form was produced in 1935. At other times the system used transfers printed specifically from each terminus with a list of the transfer points on the back. *Roy G. Benedict collection*

Left Cars 25 and 26 were assembled in Marion. Their body shells had been trucked in from St. Petersburg, Florida. On the afternoon of August 11, 1946, the 25 is en route to the North Marion line. Northbound cars looped around three sides of the courthouse square on 4th, Adams and 3rd streets. *Gordon E. Lloyd photo*

Above Marion Railways 11 westbound on 10th Street at the C&O station on August 11, 1946. The inclined approaches to the crossing diamond gave the four-wheel birneys and West Point passengers a good bouncing. *John F. Humiston photo*

Railfans were welcomed and the company hosted special trips.

Fred Baum's death in January 1947 was a major loss. He had nursed the business into the profit column. Even if he had lived, the company had to face postwar realities. The tracks and cars were worn and near the end of their useful life. Motorists and city officials saw the streetcars as old-fashioned traffic hazards. With the city growing, there was pressure to change the operations to buses. Ten Ford buses arrived in early 1947. The West Point-Cemetery line was converted with two buses in February. On April 1, the West Marion-Soldiers Home (Veterans Hospital) line was converted with eight buses. The College-North Marion (Matter Park) line remained in operation longer because the street railway furnished the lighting (dc power) to Matter Park at no charge to the city. The city changed the lighting to ac on June 25, 1947 and the last line was converted with five additional Ford buses.

Marion Railways, Inc. continued operating the local service for several years. Faced with declining patronage and revenues the owners decided to sell. In 1956, Miller Bus Lines of Kokomo bought the company. It has since gone out of business. In 1991, Marion is served by the City of Marion Transportation Department.

Right "The morning after" showing birney car 10, the last car from the College-North Marion line. In the early hours of June 26, 1947, car 10's lights shine bright for the last time. One of the new Ford buses is ready to start Marion's first all-bus day. *Jerry D. Pruden collection*

Above Behind the brick wall along North "E" Street is Richmond's Pennsylvania Railroad station. Westbound car 41 passes on September 6, 1937. *John F. Humiston photo*

Below The 42 is signed for "E. Main." *James F. Cook photo*

Above In spring 1937, Richmond birney 31 runs east on East Main Street. Its sign, displaying "N. 5 & Car Barn," shows where it started and how it was routed to get here. Along this street was busy double track. Almost everywhere else in town the old and worn trackage was single, restricting schedule changes. *James F. Cook photo*

Two city operations came with the 1931 purchase of the THI&E. They served as the east and west anchors of the THI&E mainline. In the THI&E break-up the Richmond property became part of Indiana Railroad. The Terre Haute property was transferred to Public Service Company and leased to Indiana Railroad.

Richmond

The Richmond streetcar lines were in fair condition when Indiana Railroad took over. Most of the trackwork was sound although some was in need of replacement. The equipment consisted of 15 birneys acquired in 1923 in an unexpected "modernization" following a fire which destroyed all but one of the city streetcars. Although not new, the cars had been reconditioned at the time of the purchase and had had good maintenance since then. As in the other cities, the greatest drawback was the failure of the car lines to grow with the community so that many areas of the city did not have public transportation. By early 1937 the city was urging Indiana Railroad to replace the streetcars with buses. While the city government officials were pondering the change the municipal light and power quietly reminded them that their plant furnished power for the streetcars and it was a major load. Elder, however, let it be known that he would substitute buses if the city made a request.

At first the Anderson power house strike appeared to have no effect at Richmond. The Richmond car operators were not then members of the Amalgamated. Because power was purchased for this end of the system, the city cars as well as the interurbans eastward to Dayton and westward to Cambridge City continued after the power was cut at Anderson. Service, interrupted by the strike, beyond

Below Near East Haven Junction in August 1937, birney 37 operates alongside the National Road. *James F. Cook photo*

Above The last Richmond streetcar has run, but the car tracks and the trolley wires remain in place. Metropolitan crowds still throng the corner of Eighth and Main. White-built 310, one of thirteen new buses, loads northbound passengers in front of the predecessor of today's K-Mart. *Southeastern Trailways, Inc. collection*

Below Richmond received General Motors TDH-3207 buses after World War II to replace older, smaller buses. Eastbound on Main Street at Eighth Street, the 325 was photographed on June 19, 1952, fifteen years after the view opposite of a streetcar at the same corner serving the same route. *Motor Bus Society, Inc. Library*

Cambridge City to Indianapolis was never restored because the entire line was abandoned on May 8, 1937 before the Anderson strike was settled. The strike had certainly hastened the end of the interurban operation. Over the following weeks all of the interurban cars were taken from Richmond. The city system was left behind as an isolated rail property.

In 1938 arrangements were made to replace the streetcars with 13 buses which were ordered in February. New comprehensive lines would extend the service.

Streetcar service ended at 11 PM on Saturday, April 23, 1938—at least regular schedules were ended and buses took over. "Thousands lined Main Street..." according to the Richmond *Palladium* when, on Monday, April 25, the city retail merchants sponsored a "Parade of Progress" to bid farewell to the streetcars and welcome the new buses. Richmond Motor Bus Day was climaxed with a large parade which included the new buses and twelve streetcars (plus two city work cars) followed by new and old police cars, fire trucks, and other historic vehicles plus the Morton High School Band. Free rides were given on both the buses and streetcars during the parade and celebration. It was a mighty last hurrah for the streetcars. They went out in style and in a manner that was certainly different than at Muncie, Kokomo or Anderson. Birney car 42 became the only survivor of the local fleet when it was given to Richmond Historical Society on May 13, 1938.

In the years following the bus conversion, the fleet at Richmond was enlarged and kept up to date. During the war a number of second-hand buses were acquired and some buses were transferred from other locations. Following the war the fleet was modernized with GMC TDH-3207 diesel buses. The older buses were then retired. The last birney was also "retired" a

second time. It had been stored out of doors alongside the historical society's building and deteriorated so badly that it was scrapped.

Richmond City Lines was set up and operated as a separate wholly-owned subsidiary corporation.

Richmond's transit system was vulnerable to the rising costs and declining revenue malady and became a losing operation. In September 1971, the company was merged back into Southeastern Trailways, Inc. Anxious to maintain a profitable position, the corporation started actions to rid itself of the losing city and suburban operations. In April 1973 arrangements were completed to turn the Richmond operation over to the city. A municipal operation, Rose View Transit System, provides city transportation in 1991.

Left Terre Haute birneys appeared to be in the worst physical condition of all Indiana Railroad city cars, but at least the 490 is repainted and lettered for IR. It makes an eastbound Wabash Avenue-Fruitridge trip at Ninth Street, across from the interurban station, on April 30, 1939.
James F. Cook photo

Terre Haute

The Terre Haute system was the largest city property operated by Indiana Railroad. It had been built over a number of years, having started as a horsecar line in 1867. The car lines eventually became the property of the Terre Haute Traction & Light Company and, along with that company's power business, were leased to the THI&E. By the time of the lease the company owned the interurbans to Sullivan, Clinton, Brazil and to the state line, the Brazil segment being an integral part of the Indianapolis-Terre Haute interurban route. When Midland United acquired the THI&E, the Terre Haute property lease went to Public Service Company of Indiana and was renamed the Terre Haute Electric Company. Indiana Railroad then assumed the operation of the rail and bus system of the electric company for Public Service Company of Indiana.

Ten streetcar and five bus lines (buses had begun in city service on February 9, 1925) came into the system's city operations. A sizable fleet of over 60 Birney Safety Cars and 19 buses came with the lease. Change was imperative because much of the existing trackwork was inadequate or in need of replacement. There was little chance, even in the early days of Indiana Railroad's supervision, of any capital investment in fixed rail facilities by Public Service Company of Indiana. Rail renewal would not eliminate the numerous steam rail crossings which presented added operating costs as most required a full-time guard to protect the cars. This labor expense was not required for a bus line. Changes were made as soon as it proved practical. "Practical" meant buses and several surplus motor coaches were transferred from Indiana Motor Transit Company. The first changes occurred when the West Terre Haute to Second Street line was changed to motor buses on August 6, 1933. In the change the West Terre Haute bus line was connected with the existing Southeastern bus line, terminating at

Left In March 1936, car 266, one of the former Louisville-Jeffersonville-New Albany cars, was sent to Terre Haute. The "Interstate" name was painted out and the car tried on the South 3rd and South 7th Street lines. The trial was a success!
William C. Janssen photo

Right Still lettered "Terre Haute, Indianapolis and Eastern Traction Company," birney 471 rolls along. Most of the sixty-plus Terre Haute birneys were quickly retired in the early thirties. Scrapped cars provided operating parts, but many cars still running had badly deteriorated bodies. *M. D. McCarter collection*

25th and Hulman and serving an area not reached by the 17th Street car line. The Southeastern line was one of the city's early bus lines (the other was the Twelve Points line).

The 17th Street car line was a problem operation because it was a single-track line operating over three streets and had only three turnouts for passing with none of these in visual sight lines with the others. Nachod signals were used to indicate clear passage but these only helped to maintain a rigid schedule and limited the number of cars that could be operated at any given time.

In January 1934, the South Seventh Street line was shortened by discontinuing service south of the north line of The Milwaukee Road (CMStP&PRR) southward to the switch entering the Davis Gardens property. Later, in April, permission was granted to cut back service from Highland Lawn Cemetery to Fruitridge Avenue and change the double track over this portion to a single track for use by the interurbans. This shortened the Wabash Avenue line by about 3600 feet. These two changes had little effect on the overall city operation but the Depression-induced decline in ridership produced a surplus of streetcars and the company began to reduce the number of birney cars, retiring all those that needed major repairs, stripping them of usable parts and then selling the bodies. Spare parts were shipped in from elsewhere on the system. Three similar cars from the New Albany-Jeffersonville area were also brought in.

Below August 14, 1936 and the 203 has been in Terre Haute for just one month. After going through Anderson shop for minor changes, new paint and new numbers (200-205) the six cars looked so shiny and bright that people thought they were brand new. *James P. Shuman photo*

Above The 205 runs west on Wabash Avenue, Terre Haute's main street, at Sixth Street on August 19, 1938. The rear doors were closed and the marker lights were lowered to be stop lights. Still carrying couplers, the cars could be run in multiple-unit trains, an ability not needed in city service.

John F. Humiston photo

A major change came at the end of 1934 when the company petitioned to suspend service over North 6th Street and the outer end of North 13th Street. Both had multiple railroad crossings. This would end the North 4th Street, North 8th Street and North 13th Street car lines and change some of the through routing. North 4th had run with South 17th and North 8th went to the Union Station. Indiana Railroad, as lessee, could not buy new buses and there were no more surplus buses available. Public Service Company of Indiana, the lessor, bought five Yellow Coach 21-passenger buses. They were leased to Indiana Railroad in June 1935 completing the conversion of the three lines.

In July 1936, major improvements were announced to further "modernize" the city service. Elder, with court approval, was able to issue receivers certificates, secured by a general lien, through American National Bank. The money was used to purchase twenty 21-passenger buses from Beaver Transit Company. The new Beavers, which looked much like the Yellows, were able to replace all of the antiquated buses in use on the Twelve Points, Southeast, West Terre Haute, South Ninth and East Locust (a former streetcar shuttle on Locust from 19th to 25th Streets) lines.

Six large double-truck streetcars also appeared in early July. These cars were the former Louisville-Jeffersonville-New Albany suburban cars that had been idled in 1934. After a period of storage the cars were taken to Anderson shops where they were thoroughly reconditioned and repainted before being sent to Terre Haute in two trains of three cars each. Although not new they were considered as "new" in Terre Haute and were, easily, the best city cars anywhere on the system. The six cars were assigned to the South Seventh Street line.

Throughout the second half of 1936 labor unrest and government interference bothered the entire system. One of the trouble areas was the Amalgamated's local in Terre Haute. Judge Wilson's order of January 2, 1937 limiting the raises was not well taken. The union leaders balked and at a January 16 meeting (where there was a question later raised about the number in attendance) with only a voice vote, and no formal ballot, the local decided to strike the city lines the next morning by not taking out any buses or streetcars at 5:00 AM. The system closed down on January 17 and idled 25 buses, 23 birney cars and 6 double-truck cars.

During the strike the Indianapolis-Terre Haute interurban crews, who were not idled by the strike, continued to run cars but not into the city. Passengers were discharged at Highland Lawn and had to find their own way by taxi or other means into the city.

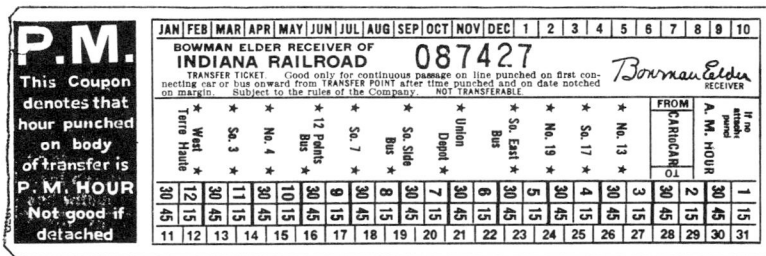

Left For a while one transfer form, on violet paper, met all of Terre Haute's needs. At another time the city used tear-offs like the one shown for Anderson — at least 12 different forms for this larger system.

George K. Bradley collection

Above In January 1937 the surprise strike of the Terre Haute employees stopped all the city buses and streetcars. The twenty new, temporarily idled Beaver buses were either parked in this facing position for normal storage or posed making possible this multiple-flash exposure in the fresh snow.
Indiana Historical Society Library

On January 26, Judge Wilson convened a meeting in Terre Haute which included the Mayor, company representatives, the Union and business leaders to settle the strike. The Union had had national Amalgamated help and refused to accept less than the full arbitration award of 20%. To achieve this the local fares would have to be raised a penny to 6¢. All parties agreed to this solution.

With the strike settled, restarting the city car lines on the 27th presented a problem due to several snowfalls since the 17th. Starting the buses was not a problem. However, the streets had been plowed by city trucks and snow and ice clogged the streetcar tracks. By late in the day, the tracks were cleared and all service was back to normal.

Seven more buses arrived in the fall of 1937. Only three car lines remained and it was no secret that Public Service Company was anxious to dispose of the leased transit facilities. Early in December 1938 Indiana Railroad was authorized by the court to cancel its leases with Public Service Company for the Seymour-Louisville and Brazil-Terre Haute interurban trackage as a first step toward abandonment.

On December 23, 1938, an agreement was signed with National City Lines (NCL) for the purchase of the Terre Haute city system. They also agreed to purchase most of the buses. NCL was not interested in taking over the streetcars and Elder secured permission to abandon the North 19th Street, South 7th Street and Wabash Avenue (from the Court House to Fruitridge) local services concurrent with the takeover by the new NCL subsidiary, Terre Haute City Lines. In June, with enough new Yellow Coach 24- and 28-passenger buses on hand to equip all lines, NCL was ready to take over. Saturday, June 3, 1939 was the last full day of streetcar operation in Terre Haute. The last car pulled into the barn at 1:00 AM on Sunday. Interurban cars continued to use Wabash Avenue until the following year.

Terre Haute City Lines used the car barn on Wabash Avenue for several years. Indiana Railroad also remained on the property to store and service interurban cars. The birneys were scrapped as Terre Haute was the last city operation in the Indiana Railroad System. The six double-truck cars were sent back to Public Service Company's Scottsburg shop. The seven newest buses had not been part of the sale and they were sent to Anderson and Richmond.

In later years National City Lines sold or abandoned a number of smaller city properties which had become unprofitable. Terre Haute was one such. Local bus service is now (1991) provided by the City of Terre Haute Transit Authority.

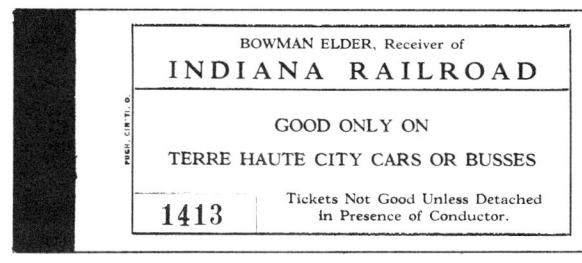

Right City fare tickets were sold in books of one hundred. *George K. Bradley collection*

Chapter 14
Isolated Freight Operations

Left From 1935 to 1943, Indiana Railroad enjoyed a concentrated source of freight traffic. The Binkley Mining Company of Indiana's huge Bucyrus-Erie mobile shovel and smaller ones worked in the strip mine pit. The coal was trucked to the company's tipple on the site. From there the haul belonged to the railroads, Indiana Railroad for the first few miles. *Southeastern Trailways, Inc. photo*

The Binkley Mine
by William A. Steventon

Indiana Railroad's most successful interchange freight operation was a one-customer installation. In 1935, the Binkley Mining Company decided to open a new strip mine south of Seelyville, a town on the Terre Haute line seven and one-half miles east of Terre Haute. The mine could have been served by the Pennsylvania Railroad so there may have been some competition for the rail connection. The operation was designated as the Bob-O-Link Mine (sometimes written as Bob O'Link in later coal company correspondence) of the Binkley Mining Company of Indiana. The railroad employees always referred to the mine as the "Binkley Mine."

Two track extensions were constructed in 1935 and consisted of two separate sections connected to the Indianapolis-Terre Haute line at two different locations. The construction was in charge of Donald H. Walker. The first extension was with The Milwaukee Road (CMStP&P RR) at Vigo, located at the eastern edge of Terre Haute. This spur turned south from the main line, located in the middle of U. S. 40, just east of the Milwaukee Road underpass and entered a two-track yard adjacent to the steam railroad tracks. The second segment left the main line 2.53 miles east of Vigo, near the overpass with the Pennsylvania. The tracks crossed U. S. 40 from the north side of the highway to reach Kuhn Yard, Glenn, Snowberger Yard and the mine tipple tracks. A connection with the Pennsylvania was located at Glenn.

Interchange service consisted entirely of delivering empty coal cars to the mine and the return of loaded coal cars to the Milwaukee Road at Vigo and the delivery of mine supplies and machinery to the mine. Empty and loaded cars from and for the New York Central and the Chicago & Eastern Illinois lines were handled through the Milwaukee Road at Vigo. At Glenn, the connection was considered as a switching service for the Pennsylvania.

As long as the main line lasted the company also moved coal, in its own cars, to points on the company lines. Binkley Mine coal went as far as Fort Wayne. There were no other customers served by these two extensions—and none to serve. When the Terre Haute line was abandoned, Indiana Railroad had to purchase over two miles of the former main line from the Terre Haute Electric Company, the former lessor. The sale was arranged on January 18, 1940 and approved by the Interstate Commerce Commission on April 18.

Prior to abandonment of interurban service on the main line, various motive power units, based at the Terre Haute car barn, were assigned to the mine run. Freight operation was sandwiched between the daily passenger trains. One of the motormen remarked how difficult it was to clear passenger trains since there could be up to 13 interurban trains during the normal working hours of the mine run.

When passenger service to Indianapolis was abandoned in 1940 the road assigned motors (electric locomotives) 752, 753, 786 and 787 to the operation together with line car 762. Glenn was established as the storage and service facility for the line. The four locomotives were reconditioned and re-equipped before being sent to the isolated trackage. Wreck motor 1151 sat on a small section of isolated track at Glenn. It was used for parts storage. Later the trucks were removed from this unit and the car body placed on a foundation. This equipment collection was more than might be needed for the operation, but it was surplus and would have been scrapped.

Thirteen employees were retained for the operation of the mine line. There were three section men, one line foreman, one substation operator, one car inspector, one yard clerk, two combination brakemen/conductors, two conductors and two motormen. Motive power was available for two regular crews. One crew worked the Milwaukee interchange at Vigo to Snowberger Yard. The second crew worked Snowberger Yard and the mine tipple. The 786 and 787 were normally assigned the run between Vigo and Snowberger and were operated in multiple unit. The 752 was assigned to the second crew at Snowberger, while the 753 was a standby unit. A work day started at the Milwaukee interchange where the motors for the two crews had been left overnight. The first to leave was the 752 with a cut of empties for Snowberger. The 786 and 787 would take another cut to Kuhn Yard, leave it and return to Vigo for a second cut. Train length down the center of U. S. Highway 40, east of Vigo, was officially limited to (but sometimes exceeded) 7 cars, making shuttle runs between Vigo and Kuhn a frequent occurrence. Once a drag of empties had been assembled at Kuhn it was pulled to Snowberger and left for the 752 to break up and move to the mine tipple tracks. The 786 and 787 would then take loaded cars back to Kuhn, break up the drag and shuttle it to Vigo, bringing back empties in turn.

Large trucks, filled by the shovels at the pit, were unloaded at the mine tipple where the coal was graded and stored or emptied into cars as ordered. The mine tipple tracks were not electrified. Cars were shoved up the hill tracks and then dropped by gravity to the tipple, loaded, dropped across the scale, weighed and then allowed to drift down to the pit tracks where they were picked up by the 752 and hauled back to Snowberger. This general pattern continued for the working day.

Above Glenn yard on the Binkley Mine line served as mid-point storage and work area. Motor 753 is on the left with line car 762 behind it. The open platform 1151 was a former THI&E wreck car containing all the normal tools required for the line. *William A. Steventon photo*

At quitting time the 786 and 787 would take a cut of seven cars from Kuhn to Vigo, while the 752 would bring a drag from Snowberger, leaving any cars for the Pennsylvania interchange resting on the Indiana Railroad main line at Glenn, and taking the rest to Kuhn. Here seven cars were cut off and taken to Vigo where both crews tied up for the night. The Pennsylvania Railroad picked up and set out their cars during the night.

There were two steep grades on the coal train route. One was eastbound out of Vigo where the tracks ran down the center of the paved highway. This was an unusual traffic hazard. The other was a westbound grade out of the Kuhn Yard. Locomotives 786 and 787 operating together in multiple unit could handle a cut of loaded cars. When the 753 was used alone, as a substitute, it was taxed to its capacity.

By late 1942 the Pyramid Coal Corporation owned the Bob-O-Link mine and made a decision to close the operation. The huge shovel was dismantled and shipped out in February and March 1943. The remaining coal was loaded out of the tipple during April and, on April 23,

Pyramid formally notified Indiana Railroad that the mine operation would cease on the 26th or 27th. Shipment of some machinery and equipment to other locations would be completed by May 1. The mine was the only customer served and permission to abandon was easily obtained. The last train rolled to a stop on July 20, 1943.

The four locomotives were moved to the Pennsylvania's Glenn siding. Three, the 752, 753 and 787, were sold to the Bevier & Southern and the fourth, 786, was sold to St. Louis Car Company. Line car 762 had burned in an accidental fire. The rest of the equipment and track was sold for scrap. The final sale ended the Indiana Railroad's rail operations.

Available records indicate that this isolated section of the Indiana Railroad did a brisk business.

Year	Cars Handled	Tonnage Carried
1941	9,186	496,335
1942	9,911	536,844
1943 (to April 24th)	2,621	141,410

Below Empty cars were brought from the left, shoved up the "hill track" where 1061 stands, dropped by gravity to the five-track tipple for loading, and then allowed to coast into the "pit track" beyond the tipple. *George K. Bradley collection*

Below The 753 with its four 125 hp motors was normally a stand-by locomotive. This single unit was powerful but "slippery" on grades. It is switching loaded interchange cars to the Pennsylvania Railroad at Glenn yard. *William A. Steventon photo*

Above Motors 787 and 786 are eastbound down the center of U. S. Highway 40 with 11 empty cars in tow. It must have been a surprise for motorists to encounter passenger and freight trains in a rural area and in the center of this major highway. *William A. Steventon photo*

Southern Indiana Railway, Inc.

Indiana Railroad hauled cement from the Louisville Cement Company at Speed, Indiana, for years but there had been no direct connection to the plant. The cement plant was east of the Indiana Railroad with the Pennsylvania Railroad and U. S. 31 in between.

A tunnel, with a screw conveyor, ran under the railroad and highway to a building located on the Indiana Railroad where the cement was bagged and loaded into rail cars for delivery to many points on the System's lines.

In 1934, a track connection was established east of Watson where the interurban ran along the north side of the Baltimore & Ohio Railroad. Since there was no other on-line industry of interest to the steam railroad, the main reason must have been moving standard railroad box cars over the electric line to the bagging/loading dock. Having connections with two steam railroads would be to the cement company's advantage.

In 1938, the situation was improved when Public Service Company built Pass "siding," which turned

Below Southern Indiana Railway's 751, a 50-ton Baldwin-Westinghouse locomotive, is coming off the mainline leg of the wye at Watson Junction. The former Charlestown line and the interchange with the Baltimore & Ohio Railroad is to the left rear. *M. D. McCarter collection*

Above In new black paint, the 750 and 714 are at Speed yard. The 751 was completely reconstructed and the 714 was thoroughly reconditioned at the Anderson shop before being sent to the Southern Indiana Railway in 1940. *M. D. McCarter collection*

northward from the main line just east of the Pennsylvania Railroad underpass south of Sellersburg. Pass siding extended two miles to the Louisville Cement Company, where a small yard (Speed yard) was built for handling and loading cars. This trackage was built to handle standard interchange cars from the steam railroads.

When Public Service Company obtained approval to abandon the electric lines south of Seymour it had no interest in this freight operation. Public Service Company was complying with federal government directives to divest itself of its transportation properties. An arrangement was made to sell this portion of the interurban lines to the newly organized Southern Indiana Railway, Inc. (SI), a creation of Bowman Elder and Frank McHale. Elder became president of the new company. A valuation study was made as of August 29, 1939. The company began operations on November 1 although the official date when all transactions were completed is March 18, 1940.

The SI acquired the new Pass siding, the 3.3-mile main line from Pass siding to Watson Junction plus 1 mile of track from Watson Junction to the B&O interchange on the former Charlestown line. The Watson Junction wye was kept as two legs of the wye could be used for storage and service (outdoors). The

Left Dieselization in 1946-47 brought some changes to the Southern Indiana Railway. Two General Electric diesels replaced the electrics, and a two-bay service building was built at Sellersburg. The 100 rests alongside the building. *Donald J. Heimburger photo*

Above Southern Indiana's 100 is delivering boxcars to the B&O (now CSX) interchange east of the former Watson Junction. These tracks are the remnants of the old Charlestown branch of the Public Service Company's interurban lines. *Donald J. Heimburger photo*

only building was the Watson Junction station which housed one Westinghouse rotary converter and had room for some office space and equipment storage. There were three mainline sidings named Dix, Bridge and Belknap.

Three pieces of rolling stock were sold to SI, but not until they had been thoroughly reconditioned at the Anderson shops. The 751 was a Baldwin-Westinghouse 50-ton locomotive built in 1923. Locomotive 750 was practically new as it had just been completely reconstructed with only the cab and part of the frame salvaged from the original unit. Work motor 714 was a recent Indiana Railroad rebuild from a steel baggage car. It was equipped with a roof platform so that it could double as a line car. All three pieces arrived with new IR paint and lettering. Later, they were painted a shiny black and lettered in white for SI.

G. L. Harmon left Indiana Railroad to be superintendent of the new line. Harmon spent much of his time on the SI but also had office space at the company's official headquarters in Indianapolis.

The Southern Indiana has been a success and keeps busy handling interchange cars from the B&O. The major change occurred in 1946 and 1947 when two bright orange General Electric diesels (100-101) replaced the electric operations. The Watson Junction station building and sidings were removed soon afterwards. Local offices are now (1991) located at Speed and the two-bay service building is in Sellersburg. Headquarters are in Indianapolis and William L. Elder is president, succeeding to position following the death of his father.

Western Indiana Gravel Company

Western Indiana Gravel Company had two gravel pit operations that were connected to Indiana Railroad's former Union Traction lines. One was located on the southeast side of Anderson and had rail connections with the Big Four and the end of the Ohio Street car line. Steam road interchange was moved directly to the Big Four by an elderly work motor which probably came from the Union Traction Company at some date before 1930. Some interurban interchange was handled for company use. The pit remained active in the 1950's. The other operation was larger. The Stillwell Brothers Gravel Company owned both of the pits and sold them to Western Indiana about 1930.

The company's larger location consisted of a branch line south from the Alexandria-Tipton line at a point west of Orestes. The track crossed the Nickel Plate at Dundee station and extended south approximately 1.75 miles to the pit. While the Stillwells owned the line, all of the switching was done by the interurban crews. Two Westinghouse semi-automatic 500kw rotary converters were located at the pit site and the power came from the Union Traction's power lines. The additional capacity was used to power the large clamshell earth mover. A heavy-duty cable ran over the ground from the end of the trolley wire to the clamshell.

The pit was a major source of stone and gravel for delivery via both rail lines. Indiana Railroad had commitments to move a considerable amount of the pit's output and, for that reason, continued a portion

Above Western Indiana Gravel Company's decrepit box motor was a former Indianapolis and Southeastern Railroad passenger car. Operational ability was more important than appearance. After it was accidentally burned, salvaged parts were used to build center-cab motor 103. *Jerry D. Pruden photo*

Above Indiana Railroad 775 was sold to Western Indiana Gravel Company for the Dundee operation in April 1934. A similar motor worked the Western Indiana's pit on the southeast side of Anderson. Neither of these cars or the box motor appears to be lettered or numbered. *Jerry D. Pruden photo*

of the Alexandria-Tipton line (west from Orestes to Tipton) after passenger service ended in 1931. The stone and gravel continued to move until March 2, 1932. The connection with the Nickel Plate was continued as an active interchange point. Since the pit had no motive power, Western Indiana needed motive power and acquired a box motor from the abandoned Indianapolis & Southeastern. In December 1933, the former THI&E 179 was purchased, painted, lettered for Western Indiana and numbered 102. The 102 was known to have been at the Indiana Railroad Anderson shop in 1936 but disappeared afterwards. In December 1934, Indiana Railroad's work motor 775 was purchased. The former 775 worked the pit and the box motor did the road hauling to the Nickel Plate. Apparently neither of these cars was re-lettered or numbered by Western Indiana.

The box motor was struck by lightning in 1947, and the upper body work was destroyed by fire. Western Indiana took the remains to its facilities in the former Indiana Railroad shops at Elwood and, using the trucks, motors and controls, constructed a new center-cab work motor with the number 103.

Both the 775 and the new 103 continued to work the pit and interchange tracks until 1953 when the gravel operation ceased. The entire rail and equipment facilities were sold to an area salvage dealer for $5,000.

An Abbreviated Equipment Roster

A companion volume will be issued by Central Electric Railfans' Association to give detailed coverage of the extensive equipment roster of Indiana Railroad System's rail and motor bus equipment.

As an aid to the reader, this abbreviated list provides basic information on the cars and types most frequently mentioned in the text and, for the most part, those cars owned by the company. The list omits many cars that were leased from Indiana Service Corporation, Public Service Company of Indiana and those taken over from the Terre Haute, Indianapolis & Eastern and Northern Indiana Power.

Interurban Passenger Cars

No.	Builder	Built	Trucks	Notes
50-63	AC&F	1931	Commonwealth	Highspeeds, coach-lounge
64-84	Pullman	1931	Commonwealth	Highspeeds, coach-baggage
90-99	Cummings	1930	Cummings	Lightweight cars, ex-NI Ry
301-306	Jewett and Niles	1905-1907	Peckham	Trailers from Public Service Co.
323-326	St. Louis	1924	Commonwealth	Medium-weight cars from ISC
327	St. Louis	1916	Commonwealth	Medium-weight rebuilt car, from ISC
375-377	St. Louis	1926	Baldwin	Railway Post Office cars, from ISC
400, 402-408	Cincinnati	1913	Baldwin and Standard	Steel cars, never one-manned
427-441	St. Louis	1925	Standard	Converted to one-man cars
442-443, 445	Jewett	1913	Baldwin	Converted to one-man cars
446-449	Cincinnati	1923	Baldwin	Converted to one-man cars
450-456	Cincinnati	1920	Baldwin	Converted to one-man cars, from Public Service Co.
457-458	St. Louis	1926	Baldwin	Converted to one-man cars, from ISC
Indiana, Purdue	Jewett	1919	Baldwin	Parlor trail cars

City Cars

No.	Builder	Built	Trucks	Notes
31-45	Brill	1919	Baldwin	Birneys used at Richmond
49-89	St. Louis	1915-1923	St. Louis	Birneys (built or rebuilt by St. Louis) used at Anderson, Marion and Muncie
200-205	Kuhlman	1927	Brill	Double-truck suburban cars
207-212	Cincinnati	1913	Brill	Double-truck city cars
459-534	American	1918-1920	Brill	Birneys used at Terre Haute

Freight and Work Car Groups

700-738	Box Freight Motors	1150-1161	Wreck Cars
750-754	Locomotives	1170-1173	Snow Sweepers
760-773	Line Cars	1176-1178	Snow Plows
777-795	Work Motors	1182-1193	Service Cars

Appendix A
Public Timetables

Timetables given to the public had an information and marketing purpose: to convert readers into riders. Staple-bound booklets about 9 by 8 inches in size, they were folded in half. That way they could be displayed in racks in hotels, depots and other distribution points. The format emulated steam railroad practice rather the cluttered sheets of some interurbans. Thus Indiana Railroad could compete in the transportation market dominated by steam trains serving the same principal towns. The more frequent schedules of the electric line would attract short- and intermediate-distance passengers, but only if the public could readily learn of the service.

Indiana Railroad System's early "folders" required twelve pages. In later years, the folders were smaller, eight pages after route and schedule retrenchments in 1932. A list of system-wide folders known to have been issued during the period of rail service appears on page 202.

In addition, timetables were sometimes issued for specific portions of the system. Perhaps the first was a reissue on August 1, 1930, of the Union Traction folder. It was only a stopgap—"issued for temporary information," it advised—until Indiana Railroad System could release its first consolidated folder the following month.

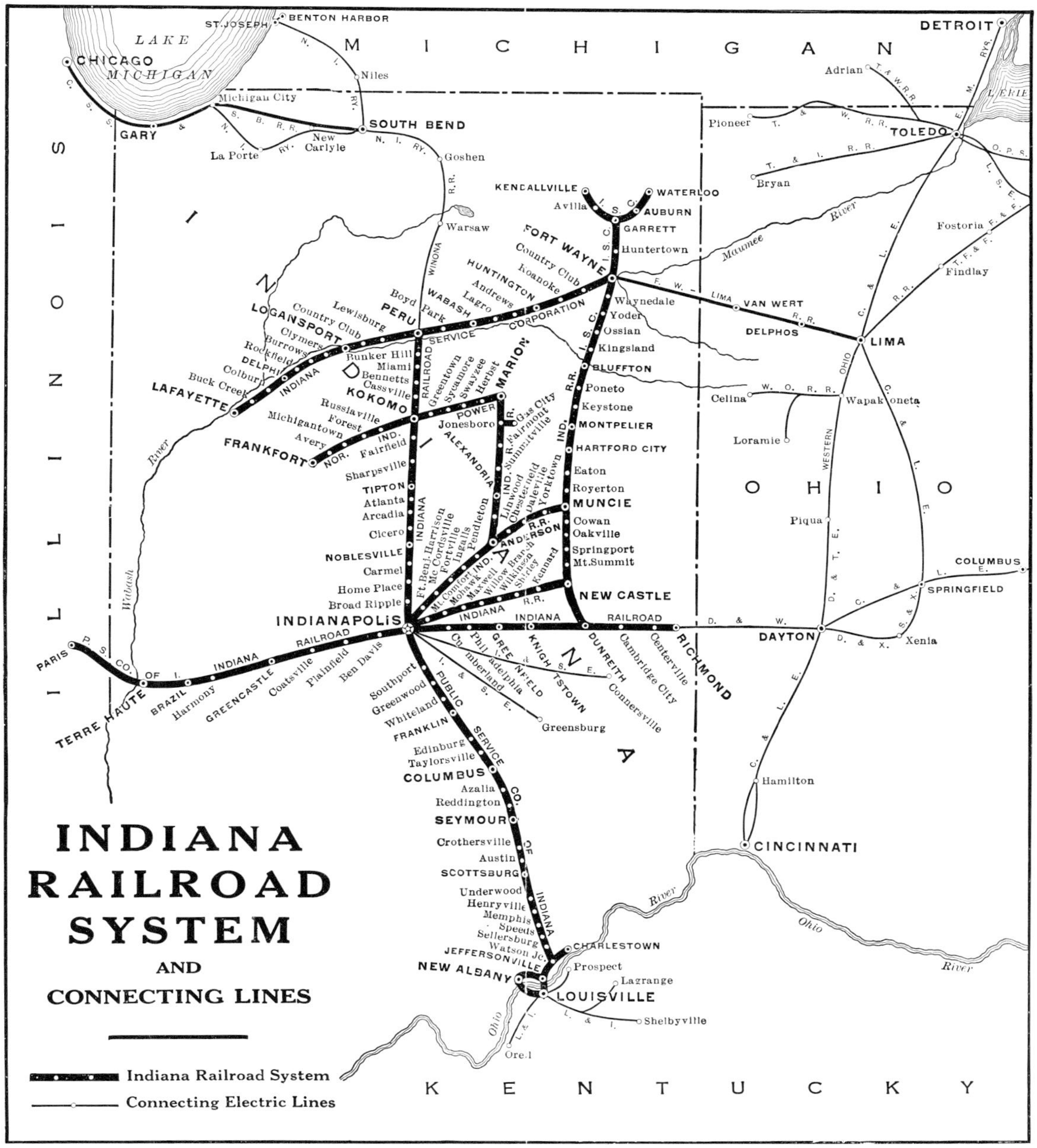

Above and Right Reproduced in reduced size on pages 201-206 is all (except an identical half of the cover) of Indiana Railroad's folder showing the most interurban route mileage ever in one issue. Another edition, also dated September 27, 1931, was produced first, then came this one in an improved arrangement. *George K. Bradley collection*

Right Opening the timetable of September 27, 1931, the traveler learned of impressively fast travel for rural America in that era. Including stops, the overall speed was 39 mph—creditable given the existing track geometry.

SYSTEM-WIDE PUBLIC TIMETABLES ISSUED DURING THE PERIOD OF RAIL OPERATION

Date	Corrected to	Date	Corrected to
9/28/30	—	4/28/35	—
9/28/30	12/ 1/30	9/29/35	—
9/28/30	1/ 5/31	9/29/35	12/ 1/35
9/28/30	3/15/31	9/29/35	1/27/36
4/26/31	—	4/26/36	—
—	5/19/31	8/ 9/36	—
—	7/ 1/31	9/ 6/36	—
*9/27/31	—	9/27/36	—
1/ 5/32	—	9/27/36	*11/ 1/36
1/26/32	—	9/27/36	1/17/37
5/ 1/32	—	9/27/36	3/15/37
5/22/32	—	9/27/36	6/ 1/37
7/10/32	—	9/26/37	—
9/25/32	—	4/ 3/38	—
10/10/32	—	4/ 3/38	4/24/38
10/10/32	12/15/32	9/ 6/38	—
4/30/33	—	9/ 6/38	10/16/38
4/30/33	5/ 6/33	12/ 4/38	†11/23/38
4/30/33	7/ 1/33	4/30/39	—
10/ 1/33	—	9/24/39	—
10/ 1/33	2/ 1/34	10/ 1/39	—
3/12/34	—	11/ 1/39	—
4/29/34	—	1/11/40	—
4/29/34	6/15/34	1/11/40	4/21/40
9/30/34	—	9/29/40	—
9/30/34	11/15/34	9/29/40	11/ 3/40
9/30/34	2/ 1/35		

*At least two distinguishable printings.
†Note anomalous dates.

Below So many motorists laid up their cars in summer 1936 rather than endure a long, inconvenient detour around paving of the National Road (U. S. 40) that Indiana Railroad ran extras from Terre Haute at 4:10, 5:45, 7:25, 9:15 and 3:30 six days a week. They appeared only in a special folder probably produced by a local job printer. *George Krambles collection*

Right The *Hoosierland* trains with observation-lounge cars stopped only at principal towns. Locals would serve any established flagstop. Interurban timetables customarily did not list the country stops—over a hundred of them on this run. Passengers were expected to identify the locals in the timetable and estimate when the train was due.

NOW---TRAVEL FASTER!
On the Finest of all Electric Trains

3 Hours Indianapolis to Louisville
70 Miles an Hour or More --- in Safety and Comfort at Lowest Cost.

3 Hours 10 Min. Indianapolis to Fort Wayne
Luxurious Observation-Lounge Compartment on all Limited Trains---No Extra Charge.

A New Era in High Speed Service

Another major improvement in modern interurban transportation! New schedules, adopted by the Indiana Railroad System on September 27th, permit faster running time between Indianapolis, Louisville, Fort Wayne and all intermediate cities. Thirty minutes saved from Indianapolis to Louisville. Thirty-five to fifty minutes saved from Indianapolis to Fort Wayne.

70 Miles an Hour in Safety

More than $1,450,000 has been spent in giving our patrons one of the world's finest electric interurban systems. The new high-speed coaches are easily capable of gliding along at 70 miles an hour or faster. Their stream-line design, lower center of gravity and powerful electro-magnetic brakes set entirely new standards of speed and safety in travel.

MATCHLESS RIDING COMFORT

The riding ease of these new coaches is unsurpassed in public or private transportation. The *coaches* with air-cushioned individual leather seats, head pillows and arm rests; wide vision windows, and steady lighting intensity—and the *deluxe* cars with tapestry davenports, thick carpets, reading tables and lamps, afford distinctly the safest, fastest and most economical inter-city transportation. The temperature in the cars is automatically maintained at 70 degrees during the colder months by an electrically controlled thermostat.

For information about passenger or freight service write or call your nearest Indiana Railroad System traffic representative, or

W. L. SNODGRASS, General Superintendent Traffic.

Left To make the Louisville run in three hours required extremely fast travel on open stretches as much of the route was slow street running. Each city station stop took a few minutes to exchange passengers and baggage. With no stops, the competing Pennsylvania Railroad carded the *South Wind*, its streamlined coach train, at 2 hours 8 minutes.

Below Passengers could travel between Indianapolis and Spring Valley or intermediate stops on some of the locals which continued to Muncie. But they could do so on Fort Harrison cars featured in a pocket-size folder for "suburban" fares, a few cents less. If Indiana Railroad had a growth market, this was it! In 1931 Americans appreciated the difference between a 23-cent and a 35-cent fare. *George K. Bradley collection*

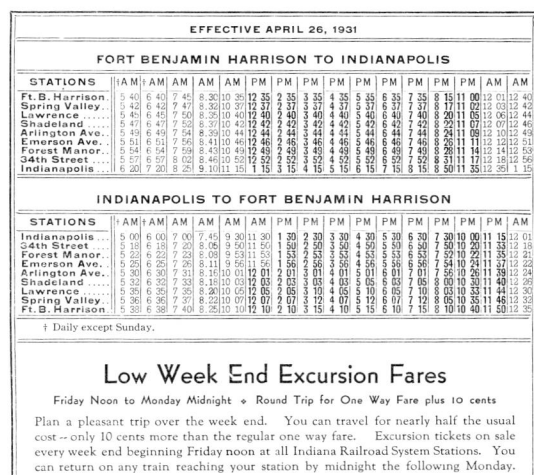

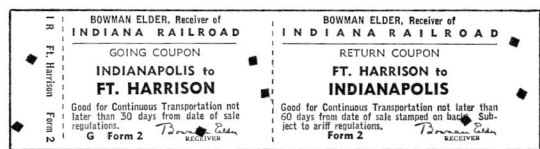

Above Regular round-trip fare after 1933 was 1.5 cents per mile, even less than the "suburban" fare of earlier years. This printer's sample lacks serial numbers and also some needed corrections in the wording. *George K. Bradley collection*

Left The lesser Fort Wayne route (via Peru) received less service than the line through Muncie and had to use five-year-old equipment. But the folder listed it as prominently as the major route on the facing page.

Right In the September 27, 1931 timetable, the "O-L" trains were the *Dixie Flyer* (southbound) and the *Hoosier Flyer* (northbound). Charlestown had just a shuttle to Watson Junction or on some trips to Jeffersonville. Indiana Railroad folders frequently were not explicit about the need to change cars.

Right and Below A long headway between trains operating on the single track rail line was adequate near Indianapolis because of diversion of short-haul business to the company's buses. *George K. Bradley collection*

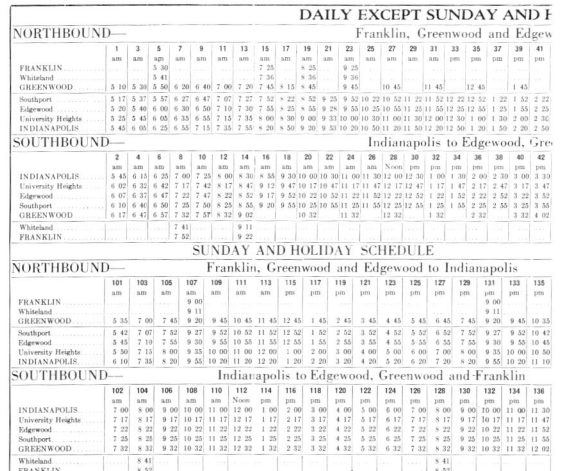

Right The Lafayette line was an impressive run along the Wabash River valley. However, half the distance (the busier half) was previously seen in Table 2.

Left The "main" ex-THI&E line was another route with local, limited and "name" trains, the *Highlander*, translation from the French of Terre Haute's name and winner of a public contest many years earlier. But the 21-mile Terre Haute-Paris line was more typical of interurban railways. Its frequent schedules emphasize the short-haul nature of interurban travel.

Below Flashier advertising techniques brought illustrations and two-color printing. These three cover designs were used successively. Upon conversion of the Terre Haute line in 1940, highspeeds and buses shared the covers. *George K. Bradley collection*

Left Frankfort-Anderson had only recently been combined into one route over the tracks of IR and Northern Indiana Power Company—a route of operating convenience, not a "desire line" of travel.

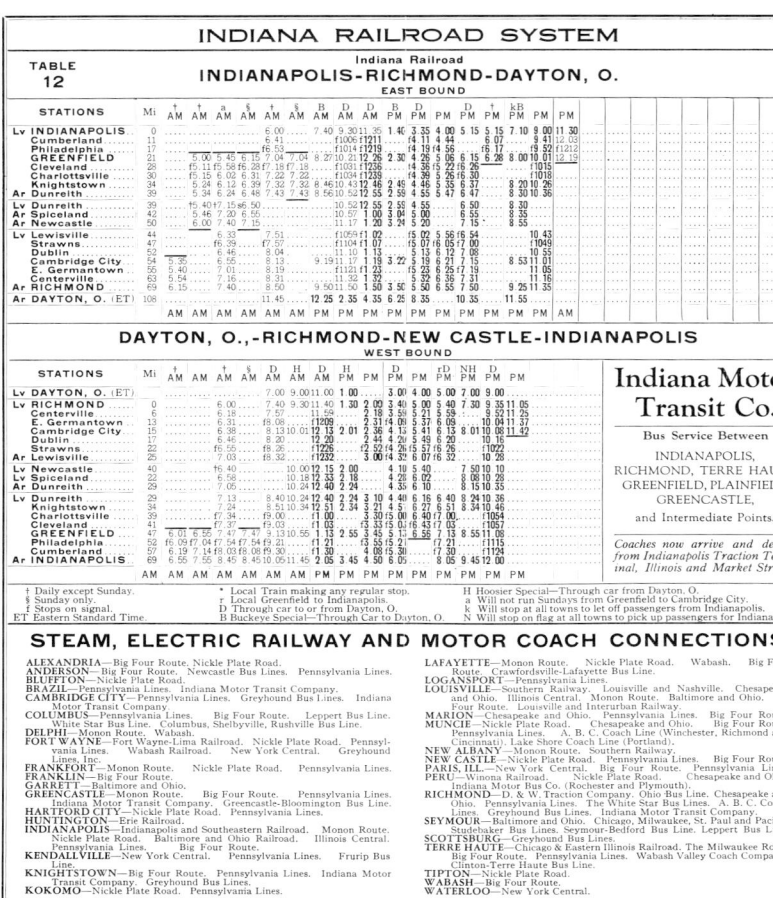

Left Indianapolis-Richmond, the former THI&E Eastern Division, still offered through cars on some trips over the Dayton & Western Traction Company to that Ohio city. The New Castle branch had only a shuttle car from the hamlet of Dunreith. For a while car 72, an old THI&E motor which had been steel-plated, held down this run.

Below The late 1930's saw a trend toward separate timetables for each division. Here is the inside of the "three-quarter size" folder of November 1, 1939 for the Seymour line, later reprinted in a different color. A folder for the Indianapolis-Muncie-Fort Wayne, Fort Harrison and Muncie-New Castle rail services is known with dates of April 28 and September 29, 1940. There is even an Indianapolis-Terre Haute bus timetable dated January 8, 1940, the intended starting time. *George K. Bradley collection*

Below A short-lived route served residents around Greenfield, Maxwell and Pendleton, towns on the former interurban routes to Richmond, New Castle and Anderson. The schedule was precisely tailored to shifts in the war plants. *George K. Bradley collection*

Left A few long-distance motor coach trips to Richmond, Terre Haute and Louisville met a competitive need. The company's small buses provided little capacity: those transportation corridors were served by a greater number of rail schedules protected by the big traction cars or even multi-car trains. This concludes the September 27, 1931 timetable.

Below Relatively frequent city transit service had less need than interurbans for public timetables. Regular riders expected a car at "so many" minutes after the hour. Or they knew an inbound car always came soon after they heard the outbound pass the house. Even so, Marion Railways, for marketing advantage, periodically revised its undated timetable. *George K. Bradley collection*

Below Around New Albany was the other long-surviving rail transit network with origins in the Indiana Railroad System. Frustrated by telephone inquiries, management printed this information on its services. Though its closest headway was 15 minutes, wartime demands on the State-Vincennes line required a double-truck car or "double-headed" birneys on each trip. *J. R. McFarlane collection*

Below Of course interurban bus services continued. This attractive card announced Indiana Railroad's return to southern Indiana. Jeffersonville and Charlestown had been Public Service interurban cities fifteen years before, but the remainder of the territory south of New Castle was new to the company. *George K. Bradley collection*

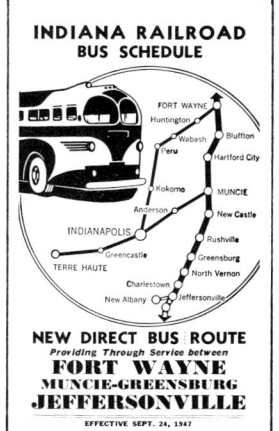
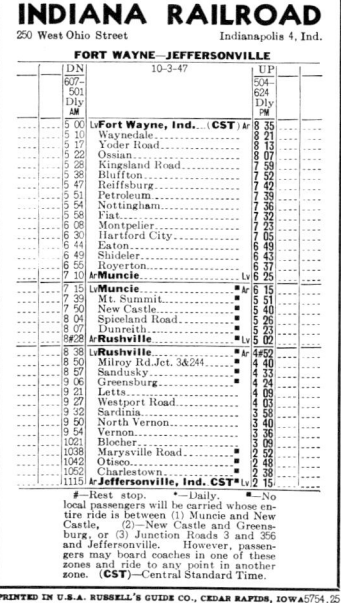

Appendix B
Employee Timetables

Timetables giving trains the right to operate over the railroad are called employee timetables or operating timetables. They specify meeting points. The points listed are, for the most part, sidings rather than passenger stations.

Accompanying the illustrations of selected employee timetables on pages 208-223 are lists of all issued by the Indiana Railroad or Indiana Railroad System. For each division the existing timetable of the previous management (not listed) remained in effect after Indiana Railroad was formed until the next revision.

Unless otherwise noted, all are titled Indiana Railroad.

All are "bedsheet" type tables unless otherwise noted. Most of the single sheet timetables had special instructions on the reverse, often for more divisions than the schedules covered. Provided was operating information such as mandatory reporting points, speed limits and "rings" on the party-line telephones in depots and substations.

The variety of sizes which appeared under the "System" management resulted from a requirement, in some cases, to show the name of the underlying owner or lessor of the property and the printing methods where the metal type for printed forms was kept "standing" for the periodic revisions, thereby reducing typesetting costs. The "common," multi-division backside was also the result of using one set of standing metal type. Some of the divisions used a book format: these are indicated with a (B).

The last issue for each division is known and these are noted with an (L).

As on any railroad, trains had even numbers in one direction and odd numbers in the other direction. Where available, the lowest and highest train numbers in each group are indicated. Train numbers which have been found only in public timetables are indicated with (P). Some intermediate numbers were not used. Some trains did not operate the entire route.

Early in its existence, Indiana Railroad eliminated second class trains and scheduled freights. The interurban passenger trains, and even the Gas City and Fort Harrison suburban runs, continued to be first class trains. The freight trains became extras as regarding their right to the track under dispatching rules, even though many of them were called for the same time each day. Some exceptions, before these practices were developed, are indicated by notes.

Jerry Marlette initiated this listing with a number of interested railfans providing information about various issues. It has taken several years to develop the listing of 112 employee timetables. There are only 11 issues for which a copy has not been located. Mr. Marlette provided a date for each missing issue and he believes these are within a few days of the actual issue date, if not the actual issue date. Since these are in question they are marked with (?).

Left Card tickets measuring 1 3/16 by 2 1/4 inches were sold for one-way rides to popular destinations, this one in 1939. *George K. Bradley collection*

INDIANA SERVICE CORPORATION
INDIANA CENTRAL LINES
Direction of even-numbered trains: Eastbound (Northbound Bluffton-Ft. Wayne)
(An illustration appears on page 220)

Time table no.	Date	Supersedes time table	Fort Wayne-Peru	Peru-Lafayette	Fort Wayne-Bluffton
43(B)	9/28/30	42	1-29	1-30	51-68
44(B)	4/26/31	43	†200-229	202, 251-266	‡2-47
45(B)	8/30/31	44	†200-229	202, 251-266	‡2-39
46(B)	5/ 1/32	45	†200-223	251-264	‡2-33

Peru-Lafayette line was abandoned after this issue. For other lines, next issue was ISC All Divisions time table 47.
†Westbound trains continue southbound from Peru to Indianapolis with the same numbers.
‡Southbound trains continue south and westbound from Bluffton to Indianapolis with the same numbers.

NDIANA POWER COMPANY
RT - KOKOMO - MARION DIVISION
TIME TABLE NO. 11

This Time Table for the government of employees only.
Read Special Instructions and Rules Carefully.

EAST BOUND—FRANKFORT TO MARION—Read Up

Distance from Marion	STATIONS AND SIDINGS	Distance from Frankfort	DAILY		FIRST CLASS						DAILY		
			2	4	6	8	10	12	14	Note B 16	Note A 18		
			Loc	Loc	Loc	Loc	Loc	Loc	Loc	Loc			
			AM	AM	AM	AM	PM	PM	PM	PM	PM		
.00	MARION Y	52.80	7.45	8.50	11.50	2.50	5.50	7.05	......	10.20			
1.10	IRON	51.70	7.84³	8.39	11.39¹¹	2.39	5.39¹¹	6.56¹³	......	10.08¹⁷			
2.58	BELT	50.22	7.30	8.35	11.35	2.35	5.35	6.53	......	10.04			
4.82	ROSEBURG	47.98	7.23	8.28	11.28	2.28	5.28	6.48	......	9.59			
7.45	BABB	45.35	7.21	8.26	11.26	2.26	5.26	6.46	......	9.57			
7.95	HERBST	44.85	7.19	8.24	11.24	2.24	5.24	6.44	......	9.55			
9.88	WYE Y	42.92	7.16	8.21	11.21	2.21	5.21	6.41	......	9.52			
10.03	SWAYZEE	42.77	7.15	8.20	11.20	2.20	5.20	6.40	......	9.51			
11.81	SIMS	40.99	7.11	8.16	11.16	2.16	5.17	6.37	......	9.49			
13.62	MARSH	39.18	7.10	8.15	11.15	2.15	5.15	6.35	......	9.47			
15.03	SYCAMORE	37.77	7.08	8.13	11.13	2.13	5.13	6.32	......	9.44			
17.59	JINKENS	35.21	7.04	8.09³	11.09	2.09	5.09	6.29	......	9.41			
17.84	GREENTOWN Y	34.96	7.03	8.08	11.08	2.08	5.08	6.28	......	9.40			
18.33	PIT	34.47	7.01	8.06	11.06	2.06	5.06	6.26	......	9.38			
22.33	BLAKELY	30.47	6.57	8.02	11.02	2.02	5.02	6.22¹¹	......	9.30			
25.50	JUNCTION	27.30	6.53	7.58	10.58	1.58	4.58	6.17	......	9.28			
27.23	KOKOMO Y	25.57	6.45	7.50	10.50	1.50	4.50	6.10	9.20	9.20¹³	11.00		
28.79	SHOPS Y	24.01		7.40	10.40⁵	1.40	4.40⁹	6.05	9.11¹⁵		10.47		
29.46	BUSBY	23.34		7.38	10.38	1.37	4.38	6.03	9.09		10.44		
31.55	SMITH	21.25		7.34	10.34	1.33	4.34	5.59	9.04		10.40		
33.63	MIDDLETON	19.17		7.30	10.31	1.29⁷	4.31	5.56	9.01		10.37		
36.36	RUSSIAVILLE Y	16.17		7.26	10.26	1.25	4.27	5.52	8.57		10.33		
39.20	NEFF	13.60		7.22	10.22	1.21	4.22	5.47	8.52		10.30		
41.48	FOREST	11.32		7.19	10.19	1.18	4.19	5.44	8.49		10.28		
41.72	NUTTER	11.08		7.18	10.18	1.17	4.18	5.43	8.48		10.27		
45.54	HAYES	7.26		7.13	10.13	1.12	4.13	5.38	8.43		10.23		
45.64	MICHIGANTOWN	7.16		7.12	10.12	1.11	4.12	5.37	8.42		10.22		
48.52	AVERY	4.28		7.07	10.07	1.07	4.07	5.32	8.37		10.17		
52.80	FRANKFORT Y	.00		7.00¹	10.00³	1.00	4.00	5.25⁹	8.30		10.10¹⁵		
				AM	AM	AM	PM	PM	PM	PM	PM	PM		
				Loc	Loc	Loc	Loc	Loc	Loc	Loc	Loc		
				2	4	6	8	10	12	14	16 Note B	18 Note A		

C. C. LENTZ,
Supt. Transportation.

N. K. SMITH,
Trainmaster.

Right Ten-ride commutation tickets consisted of a cardboard strip of ride coupons (this is number 6) folded into a cover good for the tenth trip. "R24" denotes Gray's stop, 5.9 miles south of Noblesville.   *Joseph M. Canfield collection*

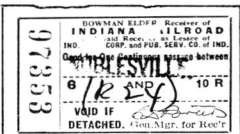

INDIANA SERVICE CORPORATION
ALL DIVISIONS
Direction of even-numbered trains: Northbound (Eastbound Peru-Ft. Wayne)

Time table no.	Date	Supersedes time table	Fort Wayne-Peru†	Fort Wayne-Bluffton‡	Northern Division*
47(B)	9/25/32	46 & Nor. 36	200-217	4-33	501-522
48(B)	4/30/33	47	200-217	4-33, 300-301	501-522
49(B)	10/ 1/33	48	200-220	2-35	501-528
50(B)	4/29/34	49	200-221	4-37, 300-303	501-524

Next issues were:
 Fort Wayne-Peru Division time table 51 (*See page 221 for list*)
 Fort Wayne-Muncie Division time table 158 (*See page 218 for list*)
 Northern Division time table 52.
* Trains operating between Kendallville and Waterloo change at Garrett from odd to even numbers.
† Westbound trains continue southbound from Peru to Indianapolis with the same numbers.
‡ Southbound trains continue south and westbound from Bluffton to Indianapolis with the same numbers.

Left Operating late trips on weekends, bringing celebrants home, was common. After severe service cuts of May 1, 1932 on many branches, the last weekday trips from Marion were unusually early.   *George K. Bradley collection*

FRANKFORT-KOKOMO-MARION DIVISION
(Northern Indiana Power Company)
Direction of even-numbered trains: Eastbound

Time table no.	Date	Supersedes time table	Train numbers
9	4/26/31	8	1-20
10	9/27/31	9	*1-20
11(L)	5/ 1/32	10	*1-18

*Eastbound trains change at Marion to odd numbers and continue to Anderson.

Below On any division the dispatcher's permission to start each trip was transcribed on a clearance slip. This operator prepared for train 28 (see page 61 for his schedule). He used the margin as a reminder to identify cars 57 and 69 on train 23, which the timetable tells him to meet before entering single track at Long. He is also expecting cars 429 and 449 on trains from Fort Harrison.   *George Krambles collection*

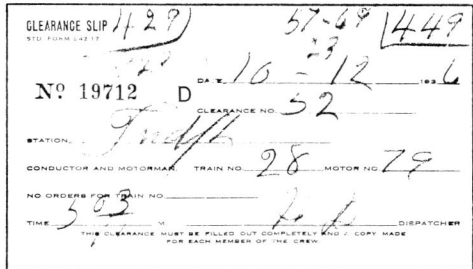

INDIANA SERVICE CORPORATION
NORTHERN DIVISION
Fort Wayne-Garrett-Kendallville-Waterloo
Direction of even-numbered trains: Northbound

Time table no.	Date	Supersedes time table	Train numbers*
33(B)	9/28/30	32	501-558
34(B)	4/26/31	33	501-558
35(B)	9/27/31	34	501-558
36(B)	5/ 1/32	35	501-528

Next issue was ISC All Divisions time table 47.
*Trains operating between Kendallville and Waterloo change at Garrett from odd to even numbers.

NORTHERN DIVISION
(Indiana Service Corporation)
Direction of even-numbered trains: Northbound
(*An illustration appears on pages 116-117*)

Time table no.	Date	Supersedes time table	Train numbers*
52	9/30/34	50	501-522
53	4/28/35(?)		501-524(P)
54	9/29/35	53	501-542
55	4/26/36	54	501-542
56(L)	9/27/36	55	501-540

*Trains operating between Kendallville and Waterloo change at Garrett from odd to even numbers.

Effective Sunday, May 1, 1932.
At 4:01 A. M. Central Standard Time.
Superseding Time Table No. 3.
Destroy all Time Tables of previous date.

INDIANA RAI[LROAD]
ANDERSON AND MARIO[N]
TIME TABLE N[o. 4]

SOUTH BOUND—Read Down

FIRST CLASS

STATIONS AND SIDINGS	FREIGHT STATION NUMBERS		337	Note H 65	335	333	331	63	329	61	327	325	59	323	57	321	319	317	55	315	313	311	53	309	307	51	Note G 305	Note F 303	Note E 301	Distance From Marion	STATIONS AND SIDINGS
			Loc	Loc	Loc	Loc	Loc	Loc	Loc	Loc	Loc	Loc	Loc	Loc	Loc	Loc	Loc	Loc	Loc	Loc	Loc	Loc	Loc	Loc	Loc	Loc	Loc	Loc	Loc		
			PM	PM	PM	PM	PM	PM	PM	PM	PM	PM	PM	PM	PM	PM	PM	PM	PM	PM	PM	PM	PM	AM	AM	AM	AM	AM	AM		
MARION	4534		10.40	10.20	9.40	8.40	7.40	7.10	6.40	5.50	5.40	4.40	4.00	3.40	2.50	2.40	1.40	12.40	11.50	11.40	10.40	9.40	8.50	8.40	7.40	6.50	6.40	5.40	4.40		MARION
HOME	4531		336 10.53	336 10.30	64-334 9.52	332 8.52	62-330 7.18	328 7.00	62-330 6.52	329 6.00	60-326 5.52	324 4.52	322 4.10	322 3.52	58-320 3.00	318 2.52	316 12.52	56-314 12.00	312 11.52	54-310 10.52	308 9.52	308 9.00	52-306 8.52	304 7.52	304 7.00	302 6.52	302 5.52	4.52	3.13	HOME
CITY	4529		338-66 11.00	338 10.35	336 10.00	334 9.00	332 8.00	7.22	330 7.00	328 6.05	326 6.00	324 5.00	4.15	322 4.00	320 3.05	318 3.00	316 2.00	314 1.00	312 12.05	310 12.00	308 11.00	306 10.00	9.05	304 9.00	8.00	302 7.05	7.00	6.00	5.00	5.84	CITY
JONESBORO	4528			10.36				7.24		6.06			4.16			3.05				12.06			9.06		7.06					6.27	JONESBORO
SCHOOL	4527			10.38				7.26		6.08			4.18			3.08				12.08			54 9.08		52 7.08					7.09	SCHOOL
BRICK	4526			10.40				7.31		6.10			4.20			3.10				12.10			9.10		7.10					8.15	BRICK
FAIRMOUNT	4523			10.45				7.36		6.15			4.25			3.15				12.15			9.15		7.15					11.21	FAIRMOUNT
DEAN	4521			10.49				7.39		6.19			4.29			3.19				12.19			9.19		7.19					12.85	DEAN
CLARK	4518			10.51				7.41		6.21			4.31			3.21				12.21			9.21		7.21					15.38	CLARK
SUMMITVILLE	4517			10.53				7.43		6.23			4.33			3.23				12.23			9.23		7.23					16.66	SUMMITVILLE
ALLEN	4516			10.54				7.45		6.25			4.35			3.25				12.25			9.25		7.25					18.06	ALLEN
STAR	4513			66 10.56				7.48		6.27			4.39			3.29				12.29			9.29		7.29					20.37	STAR
MONROE				10.58				7.50		62 6.31			4.42			3.32				12.32			9.32		60 7.32					22.35	MONROE
ALEXANDRIA	4511			11.00				7.52		6.33			4.44			3.33				12.33			9.33		7.33					22.65	ALEXANDRIA
BLOCK	4510			11.01				7.54		6.36			4.46			3.36				12.36			9.36		7.36					23.28	BLOCK
CASTLE	4509			11.02				7.57		6.38			4.48			3.38				12.38			9.38		7.38					24.36	CASTLE
STRONG	4508			11.05				8.00		6.41			4.51			3.41				12.41			9.41		7.41					25.59	STRONG
LINWOOD	4506			11.08				8.03		6.44			4.54			3.44				12.44			9.44		7.44					27.49	LINWOOD
HUNT	4504			11.10				8.07		6.48			4.58			3.48				12.48			9.48		7.48					29.68	HUNT
YARD	4503			11.12				64 8.09		6.50			5.00			60 3.50				58 12.50			56 9.50		54 7.50					30.99	YARD
ANDERSON	4500			11.20				8.15		7.00			5.10			4.00				1.00			10.00		8.00					33.68	ANDERSON

HEAVY FACE TYPE denotes meeting points.
Note E—Train No. 301 is Annulled on Sunday and Decoration Day, July 4th, Labor Day, Thanksgiving, Christmas Day and New Years Day
Note F—Train No. 303 is Annulled on Sunday and Decoration Day, July 4th, Labor Day, Thanksgiving, Christmas Day and New Years Day
Note G—Train No. 305 is Annulled on Sunday and Decoration Day, July 4th, Labor Day, Thanksgiving, Christmas Day and New Years Day
Note H—Train No. 65 Runs Saturday and Sunday and Decoration Day, July 4th, Labor Day, Thanksgiving, Christmas Day and New Years Day

L. M. BROWN, Gen. Supt. Transportation   C. C. LENTZ, Supt. Transportation

Above "City" was the junction of the short Gas City branch, which apparently ran without formal timetable authority. Most of this huge sheet (28 inches wide) was occupied by Gas City trains—all of which used a single one-man suburban car! *George K. Bradley collection*

Below The first, "except Sunday," train was printed nearest the station column; time advanced "backwards" (from right to left) on the "read down" side. *George K. Bradley collection*

INDIANA SERVICE CORPORATION, Marion and Bluffton Division
TIME TABLE No. 27
Superseding Time Table No. 26
Effective Sunday, September 28, 1930
4.01 A. M. Central Standard Time
East Bound—Read Down   West Bound—Read Up

18	16	14	12	10	8	6	4	2	TRAIN No.		1	3	5	7	9	11	13	15	17
P.M.	P.M.	P.M.	P.M.	P.M.	A.M.	A.M.	A.M.	A.M.	Miles	STATIONS	Miles	A.M.	A.M.	A.M.	P.M.	P.M.	P.M.	P.M.	P.M.
9.00	6.50	5.15	3.30	12.50	11.40	8.50	7.00	5.30	0.00	Marion	31.80	6.45	8.25	10.10	12.25	2.10	4.45	6.35	8.10	10.50
9.02	6.52	5.17	3.32	12.52	11.42	8.52	7.02	5.32	0.30	Marion Spur	31.50	6.43	8.24	10.08	12.24	2.08	4.43	6.34	8.08	10.47
9.03	6.53	5.18	3.33	12.53	11.43	8.53	7.03	5.33	0.70	McClure's Siding	31.10	6.42	8.23	10.07	12.23	2.07	4.42	6.33	8.07	10.46
9.07	6.57	5.22	3.37	12.57	11.47	8.57	7.07	5.37	2.94	Feighner Siding	28.90	6.38	8.19	10.03	12.19	2.03	4.38	6.29	8.03	10.42
9.13	7.02	5.27	3.42	1.02	11.52	9.02	7.13	5.42	5.10	Hicks Siding	26.70	6.33	8.14	9.58	12.14	1.58	4.33	6.24	7.58	10.37
9.18	7.06	5.31	3.46	1.06	11.56	9.06	7.18	5.46	6.94	Oil Siding	24.83	6.29	8.09	9.54	12.09	1.54	4.29	6.19	7.54	10.32
9.23	7.11	5.35	3.50	1.11	11.30	9.11	7.23	5.50	9.33	Race Siding	22.47	6.24	8.04	9.49	12.04	1.49	4.24	6.14	7.49	10.27
9.29	7.15	5.38	3.53	1.15	11.33	9.15	7.29	5.53 10.20	Van Buren "Y"	21.60	6.19	7.59	9.44	11.59	1.44	4.19	6.09	7.44	10.25
9.35	7.21	5.45	3.58	1.21	11.38	9.21	7.35	5.58 12.55	Studebaker Siding	19.25	6.13	7.53	9.38	11.53	1.38	4.13	6.03	7.38	10.19
9.38	7.24	5.48	4.00	1.24	11.40	9.24	7.38	6.00 13.55	Barnes Siding	18.25	6.10	7.50	9.35	11.50	1.35	4.10	6.00	7.35	10.17
9.45	**15 7.30**	**13 5.55**	**11 4.05**	**9 1.30**	**7 11.45**	**5 9.30**	**3 7.45**	**1 6.05** 16.57	Warren "Y"	15.23	**2 6.05**	**4 7.45**	**6 9.30**	**8 11.45**	**10 1.30**	**12 4.05**	**14 5.55**	**16 7.30**	10.12
9.49	7.34	5.59	4.09	1.34	11.49	9.34	7.49	6.09 17.44	Fair Siding	14.36	6.01	7.43	9.27	11.41	1.27	4.01	5.52	7.27	10.06
9.55	7.41	6.05	4.15	1.40	11.56	9.41	7.56	6.15 21.12	Buckeye Siding	10.68	5.55	7.37	9.22	11.35	1.22	3.55	5.47	7.22	10.06
17 10.00	7.46	6.10	4.22	1.46 12.10	9.46	8.01	6.22 24.96	Liberty Center	6.84	5.47	7.30	9.15	11.27	1.15	3.47	5.40	7.15	**18 10.00**
10.05	7.51	6.15	4.27	1.51 12.06	9.51	8.06	6.27 27.34	Fisher Siding	4.46	5.42	7.25	9.10	11.22	1.10	3.42	5.35	7.10	9.55
10.09	7.55	6.19	4.31	1.55 12.10	9.55	8.09	6.31 29.90	N. K. P. Transfer	1.90	5.37	7.21	9.06	11.17	1.06	3.37	5.30	7.06	9.51
10.10	7.56	6.20	4.32	1.56 12.10	9.56	8.11	6.32 30.57	Car House	1.23	5.36	7.20	9.05	11.16	1.05	3.36	5.30	7.05	9.50
10.15	8.00	6.25	4.40	2.00 12.15	10.00	8.15	6.40 31.80	Bluffton	0.00	5.30	7.15	9.00	11.10	1.00	3.30	5.25	7.00	9.45
P.M.	P.M.	P.M.	P.M.	P.M. P.M.	A.M.	A.M.	A.M. Miles	STATIONS	Miles	A.M.	A.M.	A.M.	A.M.	P.M.	P.M.	P.M.	P.M.	P.M.
18	16	14	12	10	8	6	4	2	Train No.		1	3	5	7	9	11	13	15	17

Full faced type with small numbers above indicate schedule meeting points.
Trains No. 1 and No. 2 annulled on Sundays, New Years Day, Decoration Day, July Fourth, Labor Day, Thanksgiving Day and Christmas.

HENRY BUCHER, Vice President.   L. M. BROWN, General Supt. Interurban Lines.   H. F. COLEMAN, Trainmaster.

ANDERSON AND MARION DIVISION
Direction of even-numbered trains: Northbound

Time table no.	Date	Supersedes time table	Train numbers Anderson-Marion	Marion-Gas City
1	9/28/30	UT 46	50-73, *290-293	201-238
2	4/26/31	1	50-71	301-338
3	9/27/31	2	†51-69	301-338
4(L)	5/ 1/32	3	†51-66	301-338

*Second-class freight trains.
† Northbound trains change at Marion to odd numbers and continue to Frankfort.

INDIANA SERVICE CORPORATION MARION AND BLUFFTON DIVISION
Direction of even-numbered trains: Eastbound

Time table no.	Date	Supersedes time table	Train numbers
27	9/28/30	26	1-18
28(L)	4/26/31	27	51-66

L ROAD
N DIVISION

NO. 4 NORTH BOUND—Read Up

This Time Table for the government of employees only.
Read Special Instructions and Rules Carefully.

Distance From Anderson	Note A 302 Loc AM	Note B 304 Loc AM	52 Loc AM	Note C 306 Loc AM	308 Loc AM	54 Loc AM	310 Loc AM	312 Loc AM	56 Loc AM	314 Loc AM	316 Loc AM	318 Loc AM	58 Loc AM	320 Loc PM	322 Loc PM	324 Loc PM	60 Loc PM	326 Loc PM	328 Loc PM	62 Loc PM	330 Loc PM	332 Loc PM	64 Loc PM	334 Loc PM	336 Loc PM	338 Loc PM	Note D 66 PM	STATIONS SIDINGS AND CAR CAPACITY OF SIDINGS
33.68	5.35	6.35	7.30	7.35	8.35	9.30	9.35	10.35	11.30	11.35	12.35	1.35	2.30	2.35	3.35	4.35	5.30	5.35	6.35	7.20	7.35	8.35	9.30	9.35	10.35	11.35	11.40	MARION........DT
30.55	5.20	6.21	307 7.16	307 7.21	309-53 8.21	9.17	311 9.21	313 10.21	315-55 11.16	315-55 11.21	317 12.21	319 1.21	321-57 2.16	321-57 2.21	323-59 3.21	325 4.21	327-61 5.16	327-61 5.21	329-63 6.21	7.09	7.18	8.21	9.16	9.21	10.21	11.21	11.29	HOME........DT
27.84	301 5.15	303 6.15	305-51 7.11	305-51 7.15	307 8.15	309 9.11	309 9.15	311 10.15	313 11.11	313 11.15	315-55 12.15	317 1.15	319 2.11	319 2.15	321-57 3.15	323-58 4.15	325 5.11	325 5.15	327-61 6.11	7.04	7.12	8.15	9.11	9.15	10.15	11.15	11.24	CITY........12 CARS
27.41			7.09		9.09		11.09						2.09				5.09			7.02			9.09				11.22	JONESBORO....2 CARS
26.59			51 7.08		53 9.08		11.08						2.08				5.08			7.00			9.08				11.20	SCHOOL......6 CARS
25.53			7.05		9.05		11.05						2.05				5.05			6.58			9.05				11.17	BRICK........5 CARS
22.47			7.00		9.00		11.00						2.00				5.00			6.50			9.00				11.13	FAIRMOUNT...3 CARS
20.83			6.56		8.56		10.56						1.56				4.56			6.46			8.56				11.09	DEAN........5 CARS
18.30			6.53		8.53		10.53						1.53				4.53			6.43			8.53				11.06	CLARK........4 CARS
17.02			6.50		8.50		10.50						1.50				4.50			6.40			8.50				11.03	SUMMITVILLE..7 CARS
15.62			6.48		8.48		10.48						1.48				4.48			6.38			8.48				10.59	ALLEN........5 CARS
13.31			6.45		8.45		10.45						1.45				4.45			6.35			8.45				65 10.56	STAR..........7 CARS
11.33			6.42		8.42		10.42						1.42				59 4.42			61 6.31			8.42				10.53	MONROE.....
11.03			6.40		8.40		10.40						1.40				4.40			6.29			8.40				10.51	ALEXANDRIA...6 CARS
10.40			6.36		8.36		10.36						1.36				4.36			6.26			8.36				10.47	BLOCK........5 CARS
9.32			6.35		8.35		10.35						1.35				4.35			6.25			8.35				10.45	CASTLE........7 CARS
8.09			6.33		8.33		10.33						1.33				4.33			6.23			8.33				10.43	STRONG......7 CARS
6.19			6.30		8.30		10.30						1.30				4.30			6.20			8.30				10.40	LINWOOD....6 CARS
4.00			6.28		8.28		10.28						1.28				4.28			6.18			8.28				10.38	HUNT........6 CARS
2.69			6.26		51 8.26		53 10.26						55 1.26				57 4.26			6.16			63 8.26				10.36	YARD........DT
			6.20		8.20		10.20						1.20				4.20			6.10			8.20				10.30	ANDERSON........DT

Note A—Train No. 302 is Annulled on Sunday and Decoration Day, July 4th, Labor Day, Thanksgiving, Christmas Day and New Years Day
Note B—Train No. 304 is Annulled on Sunday and Decoration Day, July 4th, Labor Day, Thanksgiving, Christmas Day and New Years Day
Note C—Train No. 306 is Annulled on Sunday and Decoration Day, July 4th, Labor Day, Thanksgiving, Christmas Day and New Years Day
Note D—Train No. 66 Runs Saturday and Sunday and Decoration Day, July 4th, Labor Day, Thanksgiving, Christmas Day and New Years Day

N. K. SMITH, Trainmaster.

WATSON AND CHARLESTOWN

NORTH BOUND — FIRST CLASS

Daily 323 A.M.	Daily 321 P.M.	Daily 319 P.M.	Daily 317 P.M.	Daily 315 P.M.	Daily 313 P.M.	Daily 311 P.M.	Daily 309 A.M.	Daily 307 A.M.	Daily 305 A.M.	Daily 303 A.M.	Daily 301 Except Sunday A.M.	Distance from Watson	Station	Distance from Charlestown	Daily 302 Ex. Sun A.M.	Daily 304 A.M.	Daily 306 A.M.	Daily 308 A.M.	Daily 310 A.M.	Daily 312 P.M.	Daily 314 P.M.	Daily 316 P.M.	Daily 318 P.M.	Daily 320 P.M.	Daily 322 P.M.	Daily 324 A.M.
12.33	9.03	7.03	6.22	4.40	1.48	12.51	10.21	9.34	7.48	6.20	5.35	6.86	A. CHARLESTOWN "Y" L		5.37	6.50	8.15	9.40	11.40	1.10	1.55	4.50	6.25	7.40	9.35	12.34
12.15	8.54	6.55	6.13	4.32	1.41	12.44	10.14	9.27	7.41	6.12	5.28	3.40	...CRUM...	3.46	5.45	6.58	8.22	9.48	11.48	1.18	2.03	4.58	6.33	7.48	9.43	12.42
12.07	8.45	6.46	6.04	4.23	1.32	12.35	10.05	9.18	7.32	6.03	5.20		L..WATSON JUNCTION..A	6.86	5.55	7.05	8.30	9.56	11.56	1.26	2.11	5.06	6.40	7.56	9.51	12.49

No. 302 Connects with No. 2
No. 304 Connects with No. 4
No. 305 Connects with No. 103
No. 308 Connects with No. 102
No. 310 and 311 Connects with No. 104 and 35
No. 312 and 313 Connects with No. 109
No. 318 and 319 Connects with No. 49
No. 320 Connects with No. 112
No. 321 Connects with No. 115
No. 322 Connects with No. 114 and 51
No. 323 Connects with No. 93

INDIANAPOLIS-LOUISVILLE
Direction of even-numbered trains: Southbound

Time table no.	Date	Supersedes time table	Train numbers Mainline trains	Charlestown trains
(Interstate Public Service Company)				
17*	9/28/30	16	3-94, 102-115	301-324
(Public Service Company of Indiana)				
18*	4/26/31	17	3-94, 102-115	301-324
19*	9/27/31	18	3-94, 102-115	301-324
20	5/ 1/32	19	1-26	—
21	9/25/32	20	1-21	—
22	4/29/34		1-24(P)	—
23	9/30/34	22	1-30	—
24	4/28/35(?)		1-30(P)	—
25	9/29/35	24	1-35	—
26	4/26/36	25	1-40	—
27	9/27/36	26	1-38	—
28	9/26/37	27	1-36	—

Above This Charlestown timetable was on the back of the mainline sheet of April 26, 1931. Discontinued in 1932, the branch used a light interurban which Interstate had reworked to resemble one of its big limiteds. *George Krambles collection*

INDIANAPOLIS AND SEYMOUR DIVISION
Direction of even-numbered trains: Southbound
(An illustration appears on page 214)

Time table no.	Date	Supersedes time table	Train numbers
(Indiana Railroad)			
29	11/ 1/39	28	101-132
(Public Service Company of Indiana)			
30(L)	1/19/41	29	1-2

*Includes Watson and Charlestown Branch.

Right Sidings clearing only a few cars were adequate for most interurban lines—note the many 3- and 4-car tracks listed here. On the Louisville line a number of *long* sidings were a legacy of the emphasis on freight trains that had been made in the early 1920's by Interstate Public Service. *George K. Bradley collection*

Above A ticket dater mark was the "signature" of the agent. Cities had full-time railroad employees, but commission agencies were common in smaller places. The proprietor of a store or other enterprise served as the interurban's representative. In exchange for a percentage of the revenue, he or she sold tickets, handled dispatch freight and provided a place for passengers to await their trains. This was one of the few railroad jobs allowed to women in the interurban era. *George K. Bradley collection*

PUBLIC SERVIC
TI
FOR T

EFFECTIVE 4.01 A. M., SUNDAY, SEPT. 26, 1937.
Superseding Time Table No. 27, Dated Sept. 27, 1936.

FIRST CLASS—NORTH BOUND TRAINS

STATIONS AND SIDINGS	STATION NUMBERS			Express 35 Daily P.M.	Limited 33 Daily P.M.	Limited 31 Daily P.M.	Express 29 Daily P.M.	Express 27 Daily Note A	Limited 25 Daily P.M.	Express 23 Daily P.M.	Limited 21 Daily P.M.	Express 19 Daily P.M.	Limited 17 Daily P.M.	Express 15 Daily P.M.	Limited 13 Daily P.M.	Express 11 Daily A.M.	Limited 9 Daily A.M.	Express 7 Daily Note A	Limited 5 Daily A.M.	Express 3 Daily A.M.	Express 1 Daily A.M.
INDIANAPOLIS	001			11.30	8.50	7.55		6.50	5.55	4.50	3.50	2.50	1.50	12.50	11.50	10.50	9.50	8.50	7.50	6.45
THE LOOP				11.11(34)	8.30(32)	7.35		6.30(28)	5.35(26)	4.29(24)	3.29(22)	2.29(20)	1.29(18)	12.29(16)	11.29(14)	10.29(12)	9.29(10)	8.29(8)	7.22(6)	6.22
MADISON	1006			11.08	8.28	7.30		6.28	5.30	4.25	3.25	2.25	1.25	12.25	11.25	10.25	9.25	8.25	7.19	6.19
EDGE	1007			11.06	8.26	7.29		6.26	5.29	4.23	3.23	2.23	1.23	12.23	11.23	10.23	9.23	8.23	7.17	6.17
PORT	1008			11.04	8.25	7.27		6.25	5.27	4.21	3.21	2.21	1.21	12.21	11.21	10.21	9.21	8.21	7.15	6.15
OAK	1010			11.02	8.23	7.25		6.23	5.25	4.19	3.19	2.19	1.19	12.19	11.19	10.19	9.19	8.19	7.13	6.13
JOHNSON	1013			10.58	8.19	7.21		6.19	5.21	4.14	3.14	2.14	1.14	12.14	11.14	10.14	9.14	8.14	7.09	6.09
GREEN				10.57	8.18	7.20		6.18	5.20	4.13	3.13	2.13	1.13	12.13	11.13	10.13	9.13	8.13	7.08	6.08
MILLER	1014			10.55	8.15(30)	7.19		6.15(26)	5.18(24)	4.11(22)	3.11(20)	2.11(18)	1.11(16)	12.11(14)	11.11(12)	10.11(10)	9.11(8)	8.11(6)	7.06(4)	6.06
SMITH	1017			10.52	8.12	7.16		6.12	5.15	4.08	3.08	2.08	1.08	12.08	11.08	10.08	9.08	8.08	7.03	6.03
STORY	1021			10.50	8.07	7.12		6.07	5.10	4.03	3.03	2.03	1.03	12.03	11.03	10.03	9.03	8.03	6.56	5.58
FRANKLIN Y	1022			10.47	8.04	7.09		6.04	5.07	4.00	3.00	2.00	1.00	12.00	11.00	10.00	9.00	8.00	6.53	5.55
STOCK	1023			10.43	7.59	7.04(28)		5.59	5.01	3.55	2.55	1.55	12.55	11.55	10.55	9.55	8.55	7.55	6.50	5.50
HAM	1024			10.42	7.57	7.01		5.57	4.56	3.52	2.52	1.52	12.52	11.52	10.52	9.52	8.52	7.52	6.49	5.48
BARROW	1026			10.39	7.54	6.59		5.54	4.53	3.49	2.49	1.49	12.49	11.49	10.49	9.49	8.49	7.49	6.45	5.46
ROSS	1027			10.37	7.52	6.58		5.52	4.50	3.47	2.47	1.47	12.47	11.47	10.47	9.47	8.47	7.47	6.43	5.45
ADAMS	1029			10.36	7.51	6.53		5.51	4.48	3.46	2.46	1.46	12.46	11.46	10.46	9.46	8.46	7.46	6.41	5.43
DURHAM	1030			10.34	7.50	6.51		5.50	4.47	3.45	2.45	1.45	12.45	11.45	10.45	9.45	8.45	7.45	6.39	5.41
IRWIN Y	1031			10.32(32)	7.49	6.48		5.48	4.43	3.43	2.43	1.43	12.43	11.43	10.48	9.43	8.43	7.43	6.37	5.40
EDINBURG	1032			10.29	7.48	6.47		5.47	4.40	3.42	2.42	1.42	12.42	11.42	10.42	9.42	8.42	7.42	6.36	5.39
ELK	1033			10.29(26)	7.44	6.40		5.43(24)	4.35(22)	3.38(20)	2.35(18)	1.38(16)	12.35(14)	11.38(12)	10.35(10)	9.38(8)	8.35(6)	7.38	6.32	5.35
KING	1034			10.25	7.43	6.36		5.42	4.30	3.37	2.30	1.37	12.30	11.37	10.30	9.37	8.30	7.37	6.28	5.31
TAYLOR	1036			10.23	7.41	6.35		5.40	4.26	3.31	2.26	1.34	12.26	11.34	10.26	9.34	8.26	7.34	6.25	5.29
BROOK	1041			10.19	7.37(28)	6.30		5.36	4.22	3.29	2.22	1.29	12.22	11.29	10.22	9.29	8.22	7.29	6.21	5.25
LONG				10.16	7.34	6.28		5.34	4.20	3.27	2.20	1.27	12.20	11.27	10.20	9.27	8.20	7.27	6.18	5.23
COLUMBUS Y	1043			10.13	7.31	6.25		5.31	4.17	3.25	2.17	1.25	12.17	11.25	10.17	9.25	8.17	7.25	6.16	5.20
BROWN	1045			10.07	7.25	P.M.		5.25	P.M.	3.20	P.M.	1.20	P.M.	11.20	A.M.	9.20	8.10	7.19	6.13	A.M.
TROY	1047			10.05	7.23			5.23		3.18		1.18		11.18		9.18	8.08	7.16	6.09	
NEWSOM	1049			10.02	7.21			5.21		3.16		1.16		11.16		9.16	8.06	7.14	6.06	
AZALIA	1052			10.00	7.18			5.18		3.13		1.13		11.13		9.13	8.02	7.11	6.03	
CRUMP	1054			9.58	7.16			5.16		3.11		1.11		11.11		9.11	7.58	7.08	6.01	
GIBBONS	1056			9.56	7.14			5.14		3.09		1.09		11.09		9.09	7.56	7.06	5.59	
RED	1057			9.55	7.12(26)			5.12(22)		3.07(18)		1.07(14)		11.07(10)		9.07(6)	7.54(4)	7.04	5.57	
WALSH	1061			A.M.	9.51	7.08			5.08		3.02		1.02		11.02		9.02	7.49	7.00	5.53
SEYMOUR Y	1062				12.43	9.48	7.04		5.04		2.59		12.59		10.59		8.59	7.45	6.57	5.50
B. & O.					12.39	9.44	6.57		4.57		2.53		12.53		10.53		8.53	7.42	6.52	A.M.
WARD	1063				12.37	9.42	6.54		4.54		2.50		12.50		10.50		8.50	7.39	6.49	
FARM	1065				12.35	9.40	6.52		4.52		2.48		12.48		10.48		8.48	7.36	6.46	
CHEST	1068				12.33	9.37	6.50		4.50		2.46		12.46		10.46		8.46	7.34	6.43	
LANGDON	1072				12.30	9.33(30)	6.46		4.46		2.42		12.42		10.42		8.42	7.28(6)	6.39	
RUDE	1074				12.28	9.29	6.44		4.43		2.40		12.40		10.40		8.40	7.23	6.36	
CROTHERSVILLE	1075				12.27	9.27	6.42		4.42		2.39		12.39		10.39		8.39	7.22	6.35	
AUSTIN	1078				12.23	9.22	6.39		4.37		2.34		12.34		10.34		8.34	7.17	6.30	
LAKE Y	1082				12.19	9.18	6.35		4.33		2.30		12.30		10.30		8.30	7.12	6.26	
SCOTTSBURG	1083				12.17	9.16	6.33	5.40(22)	4.31		2.28		12.28		10.28		8.28	7.10	6.25	
VIENNA	1085				12.13	9.11	6.28	5.33	4.26		2.23		12.23		10.23		8.23	A.M.	6.18	
HOUGHLAND	1087				12.11	9.09	6.26	5.31	4.23		2.21		12.21		10.21		8.21		6.16	
WOOD	1089				12.09	9.07	6.25	5.29	4.22		2.20		12.20		10.20					
HENRY	1093				12.05(36)	9.03	6.20	5.24	4.18		2.15		12.15		10.15		8.15		6.11(2)	
MEMP	1097				12.01	8.59	6.16	5.19	4.13		2.11		12.11		10.11		8.11		6.06	
HILL	1100				11.58	8.56	6.12(22)	5.14(18)	4.09(14)		2.09(10)		12.09(8)		10.09(4)		8.09		6.03	
SPEEDS	1102				11.56	8.54	6.09	5.12	4.06		2.06		12.06		10.06		8.06		6.01	
SELLERSBURG	1103				11.53	8.51	6.04	5.08	4.02		2.02		12.02		10.02		8.02		5.57	
BELKNAP	1104				11.50	8.48	6.01	5.02	3.59		1.59		11.59		9.59		7.59		5.54	
BRIDGE	1105				11.49	8.47	6.00	5.00	3.58		1.58		11.58		9.58		7.58		5.53	
WATSON	1107				11.46	8.44	5.56	4.57	3.54		1.54		11.54		9.54		7.54		5.49	
PINES	1110				11.42	8.41	5.52	4.52	3.51		1.51		11.51		9.51		7.51		5.46	
R.VER	1112				11.41	8.40	5.51	4.51	3.50		1.50		11.50		9.50		7.50		5.45	
JEFF Y	1114				11.35(30)	8.35(26)	5.45	4.45(18)	3.45		1.45		11.45		9.45		7.45		5.40	
LOUISVILLE Y	1117				11.20	8.20	5.30	4.30	3.30		1.30		11.30		9.30(2)		7.30		5.25	
				P.M. Express 35 Daily	P.M. Limited 33 Daily	P.M. Limited 31 Daily	Express 29 Daily	P.M. Express 27 Note A	P.M. Limited 25 Daily	Express 23 Daily	P.M. Limited 21 Daily	Express 19 Daily	A.M. Limited 17 Daily	Express 15 Daily	A.M. Limited 13 Daily	Express 11 Daily	A.M. Limited 9 Daily	A.M. Express 7 Note A	A.M. Limited 5 Daily	Express 3 Daily	Express 1 Daily

NOTE A—Trains 6, 7 and 27 will run daily except Sundays, Decoration Day, July 4th, Labor Day, Thanksgiving, Christmas and New Years.
NOTE B—Train 36 will run on Sundays and Holidays only.
Trains will meet on double track between Indianapolis Terminal and The Loop.
Trains will meet on double track between Jeffersonville and Louisville.

E COMPANY OF INDIANA

ME TABLE NO. 28

HE GOVERNMENT OF EMPLOYEES ONLY

The safety of passengers and trains is of the first importance, and all operations of working, repair or construction [illegible] be subservient thereto.

Every person in the service of the Company is expected to be courteous and obliging toward the public and his associates.

FIRST CLASS—SOUTH BOUND TRAINS

Distance from Louisville	Stations and Sidings	Distance from Indianapolis	Express 2 Daily	Limited 4 Daily A. M.	Express 6 Note A A. M.	Limited 8 Daily A. M.	Limited 10 Daily A. M.	Express 12 Daily A. M.	Limited 14 Daily A. M.	Express 16 Daily P. M.	Limited 18 Daily P. M.	Express 20 Daily P. M.	Limited 22 Daily P. M.	Express 24 Daily P. M.	Limited 26 Daily P. M.	Express 28 Daily P. M.	Limited 30 Daily P. M.	Express 32 Daily P. M.	Express 34 Daily P. M.	Express 36 Note B	Stations and Sidings and Car Capacity of Sidings
117.16	A... INDIANAPOLIS...L			5.25	6.25	7.30	9.30	10.30	11.30	12.30	1.30	2.30	3.30	4.30	5.30	6.15	7.30	9.30	11.45		INDIANAPOLIS
112.84	(4.32) THE LOOP	4.32		5.43	[1] 6.43	[3] 7.49	[7] 9.49	[9] 10.49	[11] 11.49	[13] 12.49	[15] 1 49	[17] 2.49	[19] 3.49	[21] 4.52	[23] 5.52	[25] 6.35	[29] 7.50	[31] 9 50	[33] 12 04		THE LOOP
111.36	(1.48) MADISON	5.80		5.46	6.46	7.52	9.52	10.52	11.52	12.52	1.52	2.52	3.52	4.55	5.55	6.38	7.53	9.53	12.07		MADISON 6 CARS
110.43	(0.93) EDGE	6.73		5.47	6.47	7.53	9.53	10.53	11.53	12.53	1.53	2.53	3.53	4.57	5.57	6 39	7.54	9.54	12.08		EDGE 15 CARS
109.27	(1.16) PORT	7.89		5.49	6.49	7.55	9.55	10.55	11.55	12.55	1.55	2.55	3.55	5.00	5.59	6.41	7.56	9.56	12.10		PORT 4 CARS
107.37	(1.90) OAK	9.79		5 51	6.51	7.57	9.57	10 57	11 57	12 57	1.57	2.57	3 57	5.02	6.01	6.43	7 58	9 58	12 12		OAK 20 CARS
105.06	(2.31) JOHNSON	12.10		5.56	6.56	8.02	10.02	11.02	12.02	1.02	2.02	3.02	4.02	5.06	6.05	6.48	8.03	10.03	12.17		JOHNSON
104.56	(0.50) GREEN	12.60		5.57	6.57	8.03	10.03	11.03	12.03	1.03	2.03	3.03	4.03	5 07	6.06	6.49	8.04	10.04	12.18		GREEN 4 CARS
102.69	(1.87) MILLER	14.47		5.59	6.59	8.05	10.05	11.05	12.05	1.05	2.05	3.05	4.05	5.10	6.08	6.51	8.06	10.06	12.20		MILLER 9 CARS
99.97	(2.72) SMITH	17.19		[1] 6.03	[3] 7.03	[5] 8.08	[9] 10 08	[11] 11.08	[13] 12.08	[15] 1.08	[17] 2.08	[19] 3.08	[21] 4.08	[23] 5.15	[25] 6.12	6 54	[31] 8 12	10.08	12.22		SMITH 5 CARS
96.33	(3.64) STORY	20.83		6 07	7.07	8.12	10.12	11.12	12.12	1.12	2 12	3 12	4.12	5.19	6.16	6 58	8.16	10 12	12 26		STORY 16 CARS
95.54	(0.79) FRANKLIN "Y"	21.62		6.11	7.12	8.16	10.16	11.16	12.16	1.16	2.16	3.16	4.16	5.22	6.20	7 01	8.20	10.16	12.29		FRANKLIN Y 4 CARS
94.88	(0.66) STOCK	22.28		6.14	7.15	8.19	10.19	11.19	12.19	1.19	2.19	3.19	4.19	5.26	6.25	[29] 7.04	8.24	10.19	12 32		STOCK 3 CARS
93.61	(1.27) HAM	23.55		6.16	7.17	8.21	10.21	11.21	12.21	1.21	2.21	3.21	4.21	5.27	6.26	7.05	8.25	10.21	12.34		HAM 3 CARS
91 15	(2.46) BARROW	26.01		6.18	7.20	8.23	10.23	11.23	12.23	1.23	2.23	3.23	4.23	5.29	6.28	7.07	8.27	10.23	12 36		BARROW 7 CARS
89.86	(1.29) ROSS	27.30		6.20	7.22	8.25	10.25	11.25	12.25	1.25	2.25	3.25	4.25	5.30	6.30	7 08	8.28	10.25	12 38		ROSS 4 CARS
88.46	(1.40) ADAMS	28.70		6.21	7.23	8.26	10.26	11.26	12 26	1 26	2.26	3 26	4.26	5 31	6.31	7.09	8 29	10.26	12 39		ADAMS 13 CARS
86.88	(1.58) DURHAM	30.28		6.23	7.25	8.28	10.28	11.28	12.28	1.28	2.28	3.28	4.28	5.33	6.33	7.11	8.31	10 29	12.41		DURHAM 6 CARS
85.38	(1.50) IRWIN "Y"	31.78		6.25	7.27	8 30	10.30	11.30	12.30	1.30	2.30	3.30	4 30	5.35	6.35	7.12	8.33	[33] 10.32	12 43		IRWIN Y 13 CARS
85.19	(0.19) EDINBURG	31.97		6.27	7.30	8.32	10.32	11.32	12.32	1.32	2.32	3.32	4.32	5.37	6.37	7.14	8.35	10.34	12.45		EDINBURG 2 CARS
84.38	(0.81) ELK	32.78		[3] 6.32	7.34	[7] 8.35	[11] 10.35	11.35	[15] 12.35	1.35	[19] 2.35	3.35	[23] 4.35	5.40	[29] 6.40	7.18	8.38	10.37	12.48		ELK 3 CARS
82.98	(1.40) KING	34.18		6.33	[5] 7.37	8.36	10.36	[13] 11.37	12.36	[17] 1.37	2.36	[21] 3.37	4.37	[25] 5.42	6.41	7.19	8.39	10 38	12 49		KING 4 CARS
80.69	(2.29) TAYLOR	36.47		6 36	7.39	8 38	10 38	11.42	12 38	1 42	2 38	3 42	4.40	5 47	6 43	7 25	8 40	10 40	12 51		TAYLOR 12 CARS
76.53	(4.16) BROOK	40.63		6.40	7.43	8.42	10.42	11.46	12.42	1.46	2.42	3.46	4.45	5.51	6.47	7 30	8.44	10.44	12.55		BROOK 9 CARS
74.36	(2.17) LONG	42.80		6.44	7.46	8.45	10.45	11.50	12.45	1.50	2.45	3.50	4 48	5.54	6.50	[31] 7.34	8.47	10.47	12.58		LONG 13 CARS
73.85	(0.51) COLUMBUS "Y"	43.31		6.48	7.50	8.50	10.50	11.55	12.50	1.55	2.50	3.55	4 53	6 00	6 55	7.40	8 50	10.50	1.05		COLUMBUS Y 13 CARS
72.48	(1.37) BROWN	44 68		6 51	7.52	8.52	10.52	A.M.	12 52	P.M.	2.52	P.M.	4 56	P.M.	6.57	P.M.	8.52	10.51	A.M.		BROWN 15 CARS
69.88	(2.60) TROY	47 28		6 53	7.51	8 54	10.54		12.54		2 54		4 58		6.59		8.54	10 55			TROY 8 CARS
67.83	(2.05) NEWSOM	49.33		6.55	7.57	8.57	10.57		12.57		2.57		5.01		7.02		8.56	10.58			NEWSOM 6 CARS
64.79	(3.04) AZALIA	52.37		6.57	[7] 8.02	9.00	11.00		1.00		3.00		5 04		7.05		8.59	11.01			AZALIA 4 CARS
63.38	(1.41) CRUMP	53.78		6.59	8.04	9.03	11.03		1.03		3.03		5.07		7 08		9.00	11.02			CRUMP 18 CARS
61.43	(1.95) GIBBONS	55.73		7.01	8.07	9.04	11.04		1.04		3.04		5.08		7.09		9.02	11.04			GIBBONS 5 CARS
60.14	(1.29) RED	57.02		[5] 7.04	8 10	[9] 9 07	[13] 11 07		[17] 1.07		[21] 3 07		[25] 5 12		[31] 7.12		9.04	11.06			RED 7 CARS
55.79	(4.35) WALSH	61.37	A.M.	7.09	8.14	9.11	11.11		1.11		3.11		5.16		7.16		9.07	11.10		P.M.	WALSH—Stub 7 9 CARS
54.70	(1.09) SEYMOUR "Y"	62 46	5.25	7.15	8.22	9.17	11.17		1.17		3.17		5.22		7.22		9 13	11.15		11.22	SEYMOUR Y 3 CARS
54.47	(0.23) B. & O.	62 69	5.27	7 17	8 24	9.19	11.19		1 19		3.19		5.24		7.24		9 15	P.M.		11 21	B. & O. 2 CARS
53.96	(0.51) WARD	63.20	5.29	7.19	8.26	9.21	11.21		1.21		3.21		5.26		7.26		9 17			11.26	WARD 18 CARS
51.73	(2.23) FARM	65.43	5.31	7.21	8.28	9.23	11.23		1.23		3.23		5.28		7.28		9 19			11.28	FARM 13 CARS
49.31	(2.42) CHEST	67.85	5.33	7 24	8.31	9.26	11.26		1.26		3 26		5.31		7.31		9.21			11.31	CHEST 4 CARS
45.45	(3.86) LANGDON	71.71	5.38	[7] 7.28	8.35	9.30	11.30		1.30		3.30		5.35		7.35		9 24			11.35	LANGDON 3 CARS
42.98	(2.47) RUDE	74.18	5.40	7.30	[9] 8.40	9.33	11.33		1.33		3.33		5.38		7.37		[33] 9 29			11.38	RUDE 11 CARS
42.54	(0.44) CROTHERSVILLE	74.62	5.42	7.32	8 43	9.34	11 34		1.34		3 34		5.39		7 39		9 32			11.39	CROTHERSVILLE 7 CARS
38.87	(3.67) AUSTIN	78.29	5.47	7.38	8 47	9.38	11.38		1.38		3.38		5.43		7.43		9.36			11.43	AUSTIN 32 CARS
34.97	(3.90) LAKE "Y"	82.19	5.52	7.42	8.51	9.42	11.42		1.42		3.42		5.47		7.47		9.42			11.47	LAKE Y 26 CARS
34.24	(0.73) SCOTTSBURG	82.92	5.55	7.46	8.54	9.46	11.46		1.46		3.46		[27] 5.51		7.51		9 46			11.51	SCOTTSBURG 7 CARS
31.75	(2.49) VIENNA	85.41	5.58	7 50	8.58	9.50	11 50		1.50		3.50		5 55		7.55		9.50			11.55	VIENNA 3 CARS
29.90	(1.85) HOUGLAND	87.26	6.01	7.53	9.01	9.53	11.53		1 53		3.53		5.58		7 58		9 53			11.58	HOUGHLAND 3 CARS
28.08	(1.82) WOOD	89 08	6.03	7.55	9.03	9.55	11.55		1.55		3 55		6 00		8 00		9.55			12.00	WOOD 3 CARS
24.08	(4.00) HENRY	93.08	[5] 6.11	8.00	9.08	10.00	12.00		2 00		4.00		6.05		8.05		10.00			[35] 12.05	HENRY 7 CARS
19.80	(4.28) MEMP	97.36	6.18	8 05	9.12	10.05	12.05		2.05		4.05		6.09		8.10		10.05			12.10	MEMP 11 CARS
17.20	(2.60) HILL	99.96	6.22	[9] 8.09	9.16	[13] 10.09	[17] 12.09		[21] 2.09		[25] 4.09		[31] 6.12		8.12		10 07			12.14	HILL 5 CARS
15.31	(1.89) SPEEDS	101.85	6.24	8.12	9.18	10.12	12.12		2.12		4 12		6.14		8.14		10 09			12.15	SPEEDS 12 CARS
13.82	(1.49) SELLERSBURG	103.34	6.30	8.15	9.21	10.15	12.15		2.15		4.15		6.19		8.19		10.11			12.18	SELLERSBURG
12.76	(1.06) BELKNAP	104 40	6.34	8.18	9.24	10.18	12 18		2 18		4 18		6 22		8.22		10 14			12 21	BELKNAP 42 CARS
11.93	(0.83) BRIDGE	105.23	6.35	8.19	9.25	10.19	12 19		2.19		4.19		6.23		8.23		10.15			12 22	BRIDGE 20 CARS
9.73	(2.20) WATSON	107.43	6.40	8.23	9.28	10.23	12 23		2.23		4.23		6.26		8.26		10.18			12.25	WATSON
6.71	(3.02) PINES	110.45	6.45	8.26	9.32	10.26	12.26		2.26		4.26		6.29		8.29		10.21			12.28	PINES 6 CARS
5.45	(1.26) RIVER	111.71	6.47	8.28	9 34	10.28	12.28		2.28		4 28		6.30		8.30		10.22			12.29	RIVER 13 CARS
3.32	(2.13) JEFF "Y"	113.84	6.55	8.33	9.39	10.33	12.33		2.33		4.33		6.35		8 34		10.28			12.35	JEFF Y
	(3.32) L...LOUISVILLE "Y"..A.	117.16	[9] 7.10	8.50	[13] 9.55	10.50	12.50		2.50		[27] 4.50		6 50		[33] 8.50		[35] 10 45			12.50	LOUISVILLE Y
			A.M. Express 2 Daily	A.M. Limited 4 Daily	A.M. Express 6 Note A	A.M. Limited 8 Daily	P.M. Limited 10 Daily	Express 12 Daily	P.M. Limited 14 Daily	Express 16 Daily	P.M. Limited 18 Daily	Express 20 Daily	P.M. Limited 22 Daily	Express 24 Daily	P.M. Limited 26 Daily	Express 28 Daily	P.M. Limited 30 Daily	Express 32 Daily	Express 34 Daily	A.M. Express 36 Note B	

L. M. BROWN, Gen. Supt. Transportation. **G. L. HARMON, Train Master.**

```
PUBLIC SERVICE COMPANY OF INDIANA
           TIME TABLE NO. 30
   EFFECTIVE 4:01 A. M. SUNDAY, JANUARY 19, 1941
SUPERSEDING INDIANA RAILROAD TIME TABLE NO. 26 DATED NOVEMBER 1, 1940
       INDIANAPOLIS AND SEYMOUR DIVISION
```

North Bound Train #1 Daily A.M.	Miles	Stations and Sidings	Miles	South Bound Train #2 Daily P.M.
10:10	62.18	A....INDIANAPOLIS....L	.00	3:30
9:45	57.82	THE LOOP	4.36	3:54
9:41	56.34	MADISON	5.84	3:56
9:39	55.40	EDGE	6.78	4:00
9:36	54.24	PORT	7.94	4:03
9:33	52.34	OAK	9.84	4:06
9:28	50.13	JOHNSON	12.05	4:11
9:27	49.59	GREEN	12.59	4:12
9:25	47.72	MILLER	14.46	4:15
9:20	45.05	SHIFF	17.13	4:19
9:15	41.44	STORY	20.74	4:24
9:12	40.65	FRANKLIN "T"	21.53	4:28
9:07	39.99	STOCK	22.19	4:32
9:05	38.69	HAM	23.49	4:35
9:02	36.23	BARROW	25.95	4:37
8:56	33.53	ADAMS	28.65	4:41
8:54	31.95	DURHAM	30.23	4:43
8:51	30.45	IRWIN "T"	31.73	4:45
8:49	30.26	EDINBURG	31.92	4:46
8:48	29.45	ELK	32.73	4:49
8:46	28.05	KING	34.13	4:51
8:43	25.76	TAYLOR	36.42	4:55
8:35	21.61	BROOK	40.57	5:00
8:33	19.44	LONG	42.74	5:05
8:30	18.98	COLUMBUS "T"	43.20	5:08
8:25	17.82	BROWN	44.36	5:12
8:22	15.21	TROY	46.97	5:16
8:19	13.16	NEWSOM	49.02	5:19
8:14	10.12	AZALIA	52.06	5:23
8:12	8.72	CRIMP	53.46	5:25
8:09	6.77	GIBBONS	55.41	5:28
8:07	5.39	RED	56.79	5:31
8:04	1.05	WALSH	61.13	5:35
8:00	.00	KEYMOUR "T"	62.18	5:40
A.M.				P.M.
#1 Daily				#2 Daily

L. M. BROWN
DIVISION SUPERINTENDENT

Above In 1941 the final service changed from "railroad time" to daylight time. *George Krambles collection*

Below Train orders could modify the timetable. The last train to Terre Haute on the last night (see timetable opposite) was late at Belt. The dispatcher changed a meet from Bunton to Rynerson, keeping oncoming train 126 "on time." In addition, 123 must meet extras 439 and 436, no longer needed overnight at Terre Haute or Duffs (near Greencastle). Without an order, the extras would face a long wait for late train 123. *George K. Bradley collection*

TRAIN ORDER
STD. FORM 542-1S
H N° 8593
HANG ON HOOK HERE

INDIANA RAILROAD SYSTEM
"BE SURE YOU ARE RIGHT, THEN GO AHEAD"

TO CONDUCTOR AND MOTORMAN: 1-19   19 41
TRAIN NO. 123   CAR NO. 428   AT   Belt

Train 123 Car 428 and Train Ex E Car 439 Will Meet At _____
Train 123 Car 428 and Train 126 Car 429 Will Meet At Rynerson
Train 123 Car 428 and Train Ex Car 436 Will Meet At Duffs

MOTORMAN | CONDUCTOR | TRAIN NO. | ORDER NO. | DISPATCHER | COMPLETE
| | | 123 | 49 | | 9:47 P.M.

Above Duplex receipts accounted for cash fares paid when the Ohmer fare register was out of order or on two-man cars. Those printed in the 1930's bore the Indiana Railroad name. In 1941 with only the daily Seymour round trip remaining, Public Service Company still used this form. By then the term "conductor" was an anachronism. *Joseph M. Canfield collection*

PUBLIC SERVICE COMPANY OF INDIANA
Conductor's Cash Fare Slip
PASSENGER WILL NOTICE THAT THE MARGINAL PROJECTIONS ABOVE SHOW THE FULL AMOUNT PAID TO .... Conductor
NO REFUND Three projections are absolutely necessary on each receipt.
V.-Pres. & Gen'l Mgr.
Form C. F. 53312

Below In interpreting interline tickets, note that coupons were detached from the bottom up. Each connecting carrier (even the intracity transfer) turned in its "lift" to IR to claim its share of the fare. Wabash Valley Coach reached south to Evansville. *George K. Bradley collection*

Issued by Bowman Elder, Receiver of Indiana Railroad.
Form Interline 3 T. H.
AGENT'S STUB NOT GOOD FOR PASSAGE
RATE $_____
RATE $_____
ONE WAY FARE $_____
From INDIANAPOLIS, Ind.
To _____
Via I. R. R. To TERRE HAUTE, Ind.
Via TERRE HAUTE TRANSFER CO.
Via WABASH VALLEY COACH CO.
Good for continuous transportation commencing not later than 30 days after date of sale stamped on back. Subject to tariff regulations.
PUGH, CIN'TI, O.

ISSUED BY BOWMAN ELDER, RECEIVER OF INDIANA RAILROAD.
Form Interline 3 T. H.
NOT GOOD IF DETACHED.
Via WABASH VALLEY COACH CO.
From TERRE HAUTE, Ind.
To _____

ISSUED BY BOWMAN ELDER, RECEIVER OF INDIANA RAILROAD.
Form Interline 3 T. H.
NOT GOOD IF DETACHED.
Via TERRE HAUTE TRANSFER CO.
From INDIANA RAILROAD Station
To Wabash Valley Coach Co. Bus Station

ISSUED BY BOWMAN ELDER, RECEIVER OF INDIANA RAILROAD.
Form Interline 3 T. H.
NOT GOOD IF DETACHED.
From INDIANAPOLIS, Ind.
To TERRE HAUTE, Ind.

Effective Sunday, September 26, 1937.
At 4:01 A. M. Central Standard Time.
Superseding Time Table No. 312.
Destroy all Time Tables of previous date

STATIONS AND SIDINGS	STATION NUMBERS
INDIANAPOLIS	001
BELT RAILWAY	2002
DARNELLS	2004
GUN CLUB	2005
BEN DAVIS	2007
BRIDGEPORT	2009
VESTALS	2012
PLAINFIELD	2014
BOYS' SCHOOL	2015
DILLEY	2018
VAN JUNCTION	2019
RYNERSON	2020
CLAYTON	2021
PECKSBURG	2024
AMO	2026
COATESVILLE	2029
BRYAN	2032
FILLMORE	2033
BUNTON	2035
TUCKER	2038
GREENCASTLE	2040
DUFFS	
SHOPS	2041
LIMEDALE	2042
TORRS	2044
JOHNS	2046
GIRTON	2050
APPEL	2052
JUNCTION	2054
MORGANS	
BRAZIL	2057
MILLERS	2059
GRAVEL PIT	2060
MIAMI	2063
W. SEELYVILLE	2064
STOCK FARM	2067
FRUITRIDGE AVE.	
TERRE HAUTE	2072

HEAVY FACE TYPE denotes meeting points.
L. M. BROWN, Gen. Supt. Tr.

Right Revenue passes for an unlimited number of rides were offered by many city transit systems of the 1930's, but on interurbans they were less common. *George K. Bradley collection*

INDIANA RAILROAD
WEEKLY PASS

Not Redeemable. Baggage will not be checked on this ticket. Good for transportation on regular trains during week beginning first train Sunday, December 6th and arriving at destination on or before 12:00 Midnight Saturday December 12, 1931, between

_____ and _____
or intermediate stations
FOR THE PERSONAL USE OF
Mr.
Miss
Mrs. _____
Personal signature of purchaser _____
Selling agent's stamp on back.
Form W. P.   *Henry Bracken* V.P. & Gen. Mgr.

INDIANAPOLIS AND TERRE HAUTE DIVISION
Direction of even-numbered trains: Eastbound

Time table no.	Date	Supersedes time table	Train numbers
301	9/27/31	THI&E 32	101-128
302	5/ 1/32	301	101-122
303	9/25/32	302	101-124
304	4/30/33	303	101-124
305	9/24/33(?)		101-126(P)
306	4/29/34(?)		101-126(P)
307	9/30/34	306	101-128
308	4/28/35(?)		101-128(P)
309	9/29/35	308	101-128
310	12/ 1/35	309	101-128
311	4/26/36(?)		103-128(P)
312	9/27/36(?)		103-138(P)
313(L)	9/26/37	312	101-128

Below The footnote about the *Highlander* refers to agency stations (towns), not country flagstops. Named runs were usually "county seat trains," but these had in effect been downgraded to ordinary limiteds. *George K. Bradley collection*

BOWMAN ELDER, RECEIVER OF
INDIANA RAILROAD
INDIANAPOLIS AND TERRE HAUTE DIVISION
TIME TABLE NO. 313

This Time Table for the government of employees only.
Read Special Instructions and Rules Carefully.

WEST BOUND—Read Down   EAST BOUND—Read Up

FIRST CLASS — DAILY												DISTANCE FROM INDIANAPOLIS	STATIONS AND SIDINGS	DISTANCE FROM TERRE HAUTE	DAILY — FIRST CLASS											STATIONS AND SIDINGS AND CAR CAPACITY OF SIDINGS
125 Loc	123 Lim	121 Hld	119 Lim	Note B 117 Loc	115 Lim	113 Hld	111 Lim	109 Lim	107 Lim	105 Loc	Note B Note C 103	101 Loc				102 Loc	Note A 104 Lim	Note B 106 Hld	108 Lim	110 Lim	112 Lim	114 Lim	116 Lim	118 Lim	120 Loc	122 Lim	124 Hld	126 Loc	128	
PM	PM	PM	PM	PM	PM	PM	PM	AM	AM	AM	AM	AM				AM	AM	AM	AM	AM	AM	PM	PM	PM	PM	PM	PM	PM	AM	
11.45	9.30	7.35	5.45	5.15	4.25	3.30	1.25	11.30	9.30	7.30				INDIANAPOLIS	71.88	7.10		7.50	8.50	9.50	10.50	12.50	2.45	4.45	6.55		8.55	11.25		INDIANAPOLIS
11.54	9.40	7.45	5.54	5.25	4.35	3.39	1.35	11.40	9.40	7.40		2.00	2.00	BELT RAILWAY	69.88	6.57		7.35	8.39	9.37	10.33	12.39	2.32	4.33	6.43		8.42	11.14		BELT RAILWAY
11.57	9.43	7.48	5.56	5.28	4.38	3.42	1.38	11.43	9.43	7.43		4.00		DARNELLS	67.88	6.54		7.32	8.36	9.34	10.36	12.36	2.29	4.30	6.40		8.40	11.11		DARNELLS 15 CARS
11.59	9.45	7.50	5.58	5.30	4.40	3.44	1.40	11.45	9.45	7.45		5.47		GUN CLUB	66.47	6.52		7.30	8.34	9.32	10.34	12.34	2.27	4.28	6.38		8.38	11.09		GUN CLUB 6 CARS
12.00	9.47	7.52	6.00	5.31	4.42	3.45	1.42	11.46	9.46	7.46		6.52		BEN DAVIS	65.36	6.51		7.28	8.32	9.31	10.32	12.32	2.25	4.27	6.37		8.37	11.08		BEN DAVIS 8 CARS
12.03	9.51	7.55	6.03	5.34	4.46	3.48	1.46	11.49	9.49	7.49		9.31		BRIDGEPORT	62.57	6.48		7.24	8.27	9.28	10.27	12.27	2.21	4.23	6.33		8.33	11.04		BRIDGEPORT 5 CARS
12.06	9.54	7.59	6.07	5.37	4.49	3.52	1.49	11.52	9.52	7.52		12.18		VESTALS	59.70	6.44		7.21	8.24	9.25	10.24	12.24	2.18	4.20	6.29		8.30	11.01		VESTALS 12 CARS
12.11	9.56	8.03	6.11	5.41	4.53	3.56	1.53	11.58	9.58	7.58		14.01		PLAINFIELD	57.87	6.40		7.18	8.21	9.23	10.21	12.21	2.15	4.18	6.25		8.27	10.58		PLAINFIELD 1.83 CARS
12.13	9.57	8.04	6.12	5.42	4.54	3.57	1.54	11.59	9.59	7.59		14.44		BOYS' SCHOOL	57.44	6.38		7.17	8.20	9.22	10.20	12.20	2.14	4.17	6.24		8.26	10.57		BOYS' SCHOOL 0.63
12.19	10.01	8.10	6.18	5.48	5.00	4.03	2.00	12.05	10.05	8.05		17.86		DILLEY	54.02	6.32		7.11	8.14	9.17	10.14	12.14	2.09	4.12	6.18		8.20	10.52		DILLEY 5 CARS
12.20	10.02	8.11	6.21	5.49	5.01	4.04	2.01	12.06	10.06	8.06		18.38		VAN JUNCTION	53.50	6.31		7.10	8.13	9.16	10.13	12.13	2.08	4.11	6.17		8.19	10.51		VAN JUNCTION 8 CARS
12.23	10.05	8.15	6.25	5.53	5.05	4.08	2.05	12.10	10.10	8.10		20.47		RYNERSON	51.41	6.28		7.07	8.10	9.13	10.10	12.10	2.05	4.08	6.13		8.15	10.48		RYNERSON
12.24	10.06	8.16	6.26	5.54	5.06	4.09	2.06	12.12	10.12	8.12		20.67		CLAYTON	51.21	6.27		7.06	8.08	9.12	10.08	12.08	2.03	4.06	6.12		8.14	10.47		CLAYTON 2 CARS
12.26	10.09	8.20	6.30	5.59	5.09	4.12	2.09	12.16	10.16	8.16		23.31		PECKSBURG	48.57	6.22		7.02	8.03	9.08	10.03	12.03	1.57	4.00	6.08		8.09	10.43		PECKSBURG 12 CARS
12.28	10.11	8.22	6.33	6.04	5.11	4.14	2.11	12.18	10.18	8.18		25.50		AMO	46.29	6.20		7.00	8.01	9.05	10.00	12.00	1.55	3.57	6.04		8.07	10.41		AMO 5 CARS
12.30	10.15	8.26	6.37	6.08	5.15	4.18	2.15	12.22	10.22	8.22		28.66		COATESVILLE	43.22	6.15		6.55	7.56	9.01	9.56	11.56	1.51	3.53	5.58		8.02	10.37		COATESVILLE 7 CARS
12.33	10.22	8.30	6.41	6.12	5.19	4.24	2.19	12.26	10.26	8.26		31.03		BRYAN	39.95	6.12		6.51	7.52	8.57	9.52	11.52	1.47	3.49	5.54		7.57	10.33		BRYAN 6 CARS
12.35	10.24	8.32	6.43	6.14	5.21	4.24	2.21	12.28	10.28	8.28		33.23		FILLMORE	38.65	6.10		6.49	7.50	8.55	9.50	11.50	1.45	3.47	5.52		7.55	10.31		FILLMORE 1 CAR
12.39	10.28	8.35	6.46	6.17	5.24	4.27	2.24	12.31	10.31	8.31		35.71		BUNTON	36.93	6.07		6.47	7.48	8.53	9.48	11.48	1.43	3.44	5.49		7.53	10.28		BUNTON 12 CARS
12.43	10.30	8.39	6.50	6.21	5.28	4.31	2.28	12.35	10.35	8.35		37.70		TUCKER	34.18	6.04		6.44	7.45	8.50	9.45	11.45	1.40	3.40	5.45		7.50	10.25		TUCKER 12 CARS
12.50	10.40	8.44	6.55	6.25	5.35	4.38	2.35	12.40	10.40	8.40	6.35	5.35		GREENCASTLE	32.25	6.00	6.35	6.40	7.40	8.45	9.40	11.40	1.35	3.35	5.40	6.25	7.45	10.20	12.27	GREENCASTLE 1.39
	10.41	8.45	6.56		5.38	4.39	2.36	12.41	10.41	8.43	6.36	5.36		DUFFS	31.95		6.33		7.37	8.43	9.37	11.37	1.32	3.32	5.38	6.23	7.41	10.17	12.25	DUFFS 0.27
	10.42	8.46	6.57		5.39	4.40	2.37	12.42	10.42	8.45	6.37	5.37		SHOPS	31.20		6.32		7.36	8.41	9.36	11.36	1.29	3.31	5.33	6.22	7.40	10.16	12.24	SHOPS 0.75
	10.43	8.47	6.58		5.40	4.42	2.39	12.44	10.46	8.46	6.39	5.39		LIMEDALE	30.08		6.30		7.34	8.39	9.34	11.34	1.26	3.29	5.31	6.21	7.38	10.14	12.23	LIMEDALE 12 CARS
	10.46	8.51	7.02		5.43	4.46	2.43	12.48	10.48	8.48	6.43	5.43		TORRS	27.74		6.27		7.30	8.35	9.30	11.30	1.21	3.25	5.27	6.17	7.34	10.11	12.19	TORRS 8 CARS
	10.48	8.54	7.05		5.46	4.49	2.46	12.51	10.51	8.53	6.47	5.45		JOHNS	25.49		6.22		7.27	8.31	9.27	11.27	1.18	3.22	5.24	6.13	7.31	10.08	12.16	JOHNS 5 CARS
	10.52	8.58	7.09		5.50	4.53	2.50	12.55	10.55	8.57	6.51	5.49		GIRTON	21.84		6.18		7.23	8.28	9.23	11.23	1.14	3.18	5.20	6.09	7.27	10.05	12.12	GIRTON 4 CARS
	10.55	9.01	7.12		5.53	4.56	2.53	12.58	10.58	9.00	6.55	5.53		APPEL	19.20		6.15		7.19	8.25	9.20	11.20	1.11	3.15	5.17	6.06	7.24	10.02	12.09	APPEL 12 CARS
	10.58	9.04	7.14		5.56	4.59	2.56	1.02	11.02	9.03	6.58	5.56		JUNCTION	17.51		6.12		7.16	8.22	9.17	11.17	1.09	3.12	5.15	6.03	7.21	10.00	12.06	JUNCTION 4 CARS
	11.01	9.07	7.18		6.00	5.03	3.00	1.06	11.05	9.07	7.02	6.00		MORGANS	16.17		6.09		7.12	8.19	9.14	11.14	1.06	3.09	5.12	6.00	7.18	9.57	12.03	MORGANS
	11.05	9.11	7.23		6.05	5.08	3.05	1.10	11.10	9.10	7.05	6.05		BRAZIL	15.33		6.05	7.00	7.08	8.14	9.10	11.10	1.01	3.05	5.08	5.54	7.12	9.53	11.59	BRAZIL
	11.11	9.17	7.30		6.12	5.14	3.11	1.16	11.16	9.15	7.13	6.09		MILLERS	12.58		5.59		7.02	8.08	9.03	11.03	12.56	2.57	4.58	5.47	7.04	9.47	11.53	MILLERS 4 CARS
	11.13	9.18	7.32		6.14	5.16	3.13	1.18	11.18	9.16	7.15	6.10		GRAVEL PIT	10.33		5.57		7.00	8.06	9.01	11.01	12.51	2.55	4.57	5.44	7.02	9.46	11.51	GRAVEL PIT 4 CARS
	11.16	9.21	7.35		6.18	5.19	3.16	1.21	11.20	9.17	7.17	6.13		MIAMI	9.27		5.54		6.56	8.03	8.58	10.58	12.48	2.52	4.53	5.40	6.59	9.43	11.48	MIAMI
	11.18	9.24	7.39		6.22	5.22	3.19	1.24	11.22	9.20	7.20	6.19		W. SEELYVILLE	7.47		5.52		6.53	8.00	8.56	10.56	12.46	2.49	4.50	5.38	6.56	9.41	11.45	W. SEELYVILLE 4 CARS
	11.21	9.27	7.43		6.26	5.25	3.22	1.27	11.25	9.25	7.24	6.22		STOCK FARM	5.13		5.49		6.48	7.57	8.53	10.53	12.43	2.45	4.45	5.35	6.53	9.38	11.43	STOCK FARM 11 CARS
	11.25	9.32	7.47		6.31	5.30	3.27	1.32	11.29	9.29	7.28	6.26		FRUITRIDGE AVE	2.55		5.45		6.44	7.52	8.48	10.48	12.39	2.40	4.40	5.30	6.48	9.33	11.38	FRUITRIDGE AVE
	11.35	9.40	7.55		6.40	5.40	3.35	1.40	11.40	9.40	7.40	6.35		TERRE HAUTE			5.35		6.35	7.43	8.40	10.40	12.30	2.30	4.30	5.20	6.40	9.25	11.30	TERRE HAUTE
AM	PM	PM	PM	PM	PM	PM	PM	PM	AM	AM	AM	AM				AM	AM	AM	AM	AM	AM	PM	PM	PM	PM	PM	PM	PM	PM	
Loc	Lim	Hld	Lim	Loc	Lim	Hld	Lim	Lim	Lim	Loc	Note B Note C	Loc				Loc	Lim	Hld	Lim	Lim	Lim	Lim	Lim	Lim	Loc	Lim	Hld	Loc		
125	123	121	119	Note B 117	115	113	111	109	107	105	103	101				102	Note A 104	Note B 106	108	110	112	114	116	118	120	122	124	126	128	

Note A—Train 104 will run on Mondays and day after holidays only.
Note B—Trains 103, 106, 117, and 122 will not run on Sundays, Decoration Day, July 4th, Labor Day, Thanksgiving, Christmas and New Year's.
Note C—Train 103 will go to Court House.

Highlander stops at all stations on signal.

G. L. HARMON, Trainmaster

Right Muncie-New Castle timetables really were printed on end like this. On all routes the men folded their sheets to show their own train's column.
George K. Bradley collection

MUNCIE, NEW CASTLE AND INDIANAPOLIS DIVISION
Direction of even-numbered trains:
North and eastbound

Time table no.	Date	Supersedes time table	Train numbers‡
101	8/ 1/30(?)		
102	4/26/31	101	*701-722

INDIANAPOLIS-NEW CASTLE-RICHMOND DIVISION
MUNCIE-NEW CASTLE BRANCH
Direction of even-numbered trains:
North and eastbound

103	1/ 5/32	102 & THI&E 38	701-724, 401-420
104	5/ 1/32	103	701-720, 401-416
105	9/25/32	104	701-724, 401-414
106	4/30/33	105	701-724, 401-412
107	10/ 1/33	106	701-718, 401-416
108	3/11/34	107 & suppl. 1	701-722, 401-416
109	4/29/34	108	701-724, 401-416
110	4/28/35	109	701-725, 401-416
111	9/29/35	110	701-724, 401-418, 301, 304

INDIANAPOLIS-RICHMOND-DAYTON DIVISION
MUNCIE-NEW CASTLE BRANCH
Direction of even-numbered trains:
North and eastbound

112	8/ 9/36†	111 & D&W 8	601-632, 401-418, 301, 304
113	9/ 6/36	112	601-632, 401-418, 301, 304
114	9/27/36	113	601-632, 401-418, 301, 304
115(L)	1/17/37	114	601-636, 401-418, 301, 304

Indianapolis-Richmond-Dayton line was abandoned after the issue. Muncie-New Castle Branch continues on Fort Wayne-Muncie Division time table 163 *(See page 218 for list).*

* Includes first-class freight trains 711 and 716.
† Beginning August 2, Richmond-Dayton was run by IR, but dispatching was not yet unified at Muncie.
‡ Trains numbered in 300's and 400's operated on the Muncie-New Castle branch; the others on the main portion of the division.

Above Newspapers were carried on passenger trains in small lots—as low as one pound. The motormen threw off individual papers or small bundles without even pausing at rural crossings.
George K. Bradley collection

BOWMAN ELDER, RECEIVER OF

INDIANA RAILROAD

INDIANAPOLIS - RICHMOND - DAYTON DIVISION

This Time Table for the government of employees only. Read Special Instructions and Rules Carefully.

ST BOUND—Read Down

TIME TABLE NO. 113

NORTH AND EAST BOUND—Read Up

ASS TRAINS

621	Note D 619	Note C 617	615	613	611	609	607	Note B 605	603	Note A 601	Distance from Dayton	STATIONS AND SIDINGS
Loc	Loc	Loc	Loc	Loc	Loc	Loc	Loc	Loc	Loc	Loc		
P M	P M	P M	P M	P M	A M	A M	A M	A M	A M	A M		
5.15	4.45	(618) 4.15	3.00	1.00	11.00	9.00	(604-606) 7.00	(602-604) 6.00	(602) 5.00	....	0.0	DAYTON
(620) 5.38	(620) 5.10	4.38	(618) 3.23	(616) 1.23	(614) 11.23	(612) 9.23	(610) 7.23	(606) 6.23	(604) 5.19	....	3.8	KEMP
5.40	5.13	4.41	3.25	1.25	11.25	9.25	7.25	6.25	5.21	....	4.5	CROWN
5.43	5.16	4.44	3.28	1.28	11.28	9.28	7.28	6.28	5.23	....	5.9	HUNTER
5.46	5.19	4.48	3.31	1.31	11.31	9.31	7.31	6.31	5.26	....	7.6	SNYDER
5.49	5.22	(620) 4.52	3.33	1.33	11.33	9.33	7.33	6.33	5.29	....	9.1	HECKS
5.53	5.26	4.57	3.37	1.37	11.37	9.37	7.37	6.36	5.32	....	10.7	NEW LEBANON
5.54	5.27	4.58	3.38	1.38	11.38	9.38	7.38	6.37	5.33	....	11.1	M. & S.
5.57	5.30	5.01	3.41	1.41	11.41	9.41	7.41	6.40	5.35	....	12.5	JOHNSVILLE
6.00	5.33	5.04	3.44	1.44	11.44	9.44	7.44	(610) 6.43	5.38	....	14.8	MILLER
6.03	5.36	5.07	3.47	1.47	11.47	9.47	7.47	6.47	5.40	....	16.2	BISHOP
6.08	5.40	5.11	3.51	1.51	11.51	9.51	7.52	6.52	5.43	....	18.2	W. ALEXANDRIA
6.10	5.43	5.14	3.54	1.54	11.54	9.54	7.55	6.55	(606) 5.46	....	18.8	VOGUE
6.14	5.47	5.18	3.57	1.57	11.57	9.57	7.58	6.58	5.49	....	20.7	KITSON
6.16	5.49	5.20	4.00	2.00	12.00	10.00	8.02	7.01	5.52	....	22.2	RENSMAN
(622) 6.23	(622-624) 5.54	5.25	4.05	2.05	12.05	10.05	(612) 8.11	7.08	5.57	....	23.9	EATON
6.26	....	5.28	4.08	2.08	12.08	10.08	8.14	7.11	6.01	....	25.4	PENN
6.28	....	5.30	4.11	2.11	12.11	10.11	8.16	7.13	6.04	....	26.7	HARTS
6.30	....	5.32	(620) 4.14	(618) 2.14	(616) 12.14	(614) 10.14	8.18	7.16	6.05	....	28.1	STRADER
6.32	....	5.34	4.19	2.19	12.19	10.19	8.20	7.19	(610) 6.10	....	29.6	HOPE
6.35	....	5.37	4.22	2.22	12.22	10.22	8.22	7.22	6.13	....	31.4	WATTS
6.38	....	5.40	4.26	2.26	12.26	10.26	8.26	7.26	6.17	....	34.2	NEW WESTVILLE
6.42	....	5.44	4.30	2.30	12.30	10.30	8.30	7.30	6.22	....	37.1	W. DRIVING PARK
6.44	....	5.46	4.32	2.32	12.32	10.32	8.32	7.32	6.24	....	37.6	AUSTIN
(624) 6.54	....	(622) 5.56	4.42	2.42	12.42	10.42	8.42	(608-612) 7.42	(608) 6.30	....	39.5	RICHMOND
6.58	....	6.00	4.46	2.46	12.46	10.46	8.46	7.46	6.37	....	40.6	OHIO
7.02	....	6.04	4.50	2.50	12.50	10.50	8.50	7.50	6.41	....	43.0	JONES
7.06	....	6.08	4.54	2.54	12.54	10.54	8.55	7.55	6.45	....	45.3	CENTERVILLE
7.10	....	6.12	4.58	2.58	12.58	10.58	8.59	7.59	6.48	....	47.5	JACKSON PARK
7.13	....	(624) 6.19	5.01	3.01	1.01	11.01	9.03	8.03	6.51	....	49.7	HISER
7.18	....	6.24	5.06	3.06	1.06	11.06	9.07	8.07	6.55	....	52.4	E. GERMANTOWN
7.23	....	(626) 6.29	(622) 5.11	(620) 3.11	(618) 1.11	(616) 11.11	(614) 9.13	8.12	(612) 7.00	5.15	54.6	CAMBRIDGE CITY
(626) 7.27	....	....	5.15	3.15	1.15	11.15	9.17	8.16	7.05	5.18	55.3	AUBURN
7.31	....	....	5.19	3.19	1.19	11.19	9.21	8.19	7.07	5.21	56.6	DUBLIN
7.34	....	....	5.22	3.22	1.22	11.22	9.24	8.22	7.10	5.24	59.0	KENSINGER
7.37	....	....	5.25	3.25	1.25	11.25	9.27	8.24	7.13	5.26	60.6	E. STRAWN
7.38	....	....	5.26	3.26	1.26	11.26	9.28	8.25	7.14	5.27	61.0	STRAWN
7.40	....	....	5.28	3.28	1.28	11.28	9.30	8.27	7.17	5.29	62.3	OGLE
7.42	....	....	5.30	3.30	1.30	11.30	9.32	8.30	7.20	5.32	63.7	E. LEWISVILLE
7.43	....	....	5.31	3.31	1.31	11.31	9.33	8.31	7.21	5.33	64.4	LEWISVILLE
7.44	....	....	5.32	3.32	1.32	11.32	9.34	8.33	7.22	5.34	65.3	FLAT ROCK
7.49	....	....	5.37	3.37	1.37	11.37	9.39	8.38	7.27	5.40	68.5	DUNREITH
(628) 7.54	....	....	(624) 5.41	3.41	1.41	11.41	9.43	(614) 8.42	7.29	5.44	70.6	DRAPER
7.55	....	....	5.42	3.42	1.42	11.42	9.44	8.43	7.30	5.45	71.1	SPICELAND
7.57	....	....	5.44	3.44	1.44	11.44	9.46	8.45	7.33	5.48	72.3	CATES
8.01	....	....	5.48	3.48	1.48	11.48	9.50	8.50	7.37	5.52	74.6	CARPENTER
8.06	....	....	5.53	3.53	1.53	11.53	9.55	8.54	7.41	5.56	78.2	CHAMBERS
8.10	....	....	6.00	4.00	2.00	12.00	10.00	9.00	7.45	(612) 6.02	79.4	NEW CASTLE
8.15	....	....	6.06	4.06	2.06	12.06	10.06	9.07	7.53	6.07	80.3	BLUE
8.18	....	....	6.11	(622) 4.11	(620) 2.11	(618) 12.11	(616) 10.11	9.10	7.57	6.10	83.2	LOWE
8.21	....	....	6.14	4.14	2.14	12.14	10.14	9.13	8.01	6.13	85.2	PITTS
8.26	....	....	6.18	4.18	2.18	12.18	10.18	9.17	(614) 8.07	6.16	88.3	KEN
8.30	....	....	(626) 6.22	4.22	2.22	12.22	10.22	9.21	8.12	6.20	91.0	SHIRLEY
8.35	....	....	6.27	4.27	2.27	12.27	10.27	9.26	8.18	6.26	94.6	WILK
8.39	....	....	6.31	4.31	2.31	12.31	10.31	9.30	8.23	6.30	97.3	POLK
(630) 8.44	....	....	6.36	4.36	2.36	12.36	10.36	9.35	8.29	6.35	101.9	MAX
8.49	....	....	6.41	(624) 4.41	2.41	12.41	10.41	(616) 9.40	8.34	6.40	105.8	DUNN
8.54	....	....	(628) 6.46	4.46	2.46	12.46	10.46	9.46	8.40	6.45	109.8	COMFORT
8.59	....	....	6.51	4.51	2.51	12.51	10.51	9.51	8.46	6.51	114.2	HALL
9.04	....	....	6.56	4.56	2.56	12.56	10.56	9.56	8.51	6.57	117.3	SHANK
9.07	....	....	7.00	5.00	3.00	1.00	11.00	10.00	8.56	7.02	120.2	WOOD
9.09	....	....	7.02	(626) 5.02	(622) 3.02	(620) 1.02	(618) 11.02	10.02	8.59	(614) 7.06	121.4	BROOK
9.30	....	....	(630) 7.25	(628) 5.25	(624) 3.25	1.25	11.25	(618) 10.25	9.20	7.30	124.3	INDIANAPOLIS
P M	P M	P M	P M	P M	P M	P M	A M	A M	A M	A M		
Loc	Loc	Loc	Loc	Loc	Loc	Loc	Loc	Loc	Loc	Loc		
621	Note D 619	Note C 617	615	613	611	609	607	Note B 605	603	Note A 601		

FIRST CLASS TRAINS

STATIONS AND SIDINGS	Distance from Indianapolis	Note E 602	604	Note F 606	Note G 608	610	Note I 612	614	616	618	620	622	Note H 624	626	Note J 628	630	632	STATIONS, SIDINGS AND CAR CAPACITY OF SIDINGS
		Loc	Loc	Loc	Loc	Loc	Loc	Loc	Loc	Loc	Loc	Loc	Loc	Loc	Loc	Loc	Loc	
		A M	A M	A M	A M	A M	A M	A M	P M	P M	P M	P M	P M	P M	P M	A M	A M	
DAYTON	124.3	(603-605) 5.05	(605-607) 5.45	(607) 6.40	....	7.30	9.15	11.25	1.25	(617) 3.25	5.25	(623) 7.25	....	(627) 9.45	....	12.10	....	DAYTON
KEMP	120.5	4.38	(603) 5.19	(605) 6.19	....	(607) 7.06	(609) 8.51	(611) 11.03	(613) 1.03	(615) 3.03	(619-621) 5.03	7.03	....	9.25	....	11.45	....	KEMP
CROWN	119.8	4.34	5.17	6.16	....	7.03	8.49	11.00	1.00	3.00	5.00	7.00	....	9.22	....	11.43	....	CROWN 7 CARS
HUNTER	118.4	4.31	5.14	6.13	....	7.00	8.46	10.57	12.57	2.57	4.57	6.57	....	9.19	....	11.41	....	HUNTER 5 CARS
SNYDER	116.7	4.28	5.11	6.09	....	6.56	8.43	10.54	12.54	2.54	4.54	6.54	....	9.16	....	11.39	....	SNYDER 6 CARS
HECKS	115.2	4.25	5.09	6.07	....	6.54	8.41	10.52	12.52	2.52	(617) 4.52	6.52	....	9.14	....	11.37	....	HECKS 1 CAR
NEW LEBANON	113.6	4.22	5.06	6.04	....	6.51	8.38	10.49	12.49	2.49	4.49	6.49	....	9.11	....	11.34	....	NEW LEBANON
M. & S.	113.2	4.21	5.05	6.03	....	6.50	8.37	10.48	12.48	2.48	4.48	6.48	....	9.10	....	11.33	....	M. & S. 1 CAR
JOHNSVILLE	111.8	4.18	5.02	6.00	....	6.47	8.34	10.45	12.45	2.45	4.45	6.45	....	9.07	....	11.30	....	JOHNSVILLE
MILLER	109.5	4.15	4.58	5.56	....	(605) 6.43	8.30	10.41	12.41	2.41	4.41	6.41	....	9.03	....	11.27	....	MILLER 1 CAR
BISHOP	108.2	4.13	4.56	5.54	....	6.40	8.28	10.39	12.39	2.39	4.39	6.39	....	9.01	....	11.25	....	BISHOP 5 CARS
W. ALEXANDRIA	106.1	4.10	4.52	5.50	....	6.36	8.24	10.35	12.35	2.35	4.35	6.35	(623) 7.35	8.57	....	11.21	....	W.ALEX'NDRIA 3 CARS
VOGUE	105.5	....	4.48	(603) 5.46	....	6.32	8.20	10.32	12.32	2.32	4.32	6.32	7.32	(623) 8.53	....	(627) 11.18	....	VOGUE 1 CAR
KITSON	103.6	....	4.46	5.41	....	6.29	8.18	10.29	12.29	2.29	4.29	6.29	7.29	8.47	....	11.15	....	KITSON 7 CARS
RENSMAN	102.2	....	4.44	5.39	....	6.27	8.16	10.27	12.27	2.27	4.27	6.27	7.27	8.45	....	11.13	....	RENSMAN 2 CARS
EATON	100.5	....	4.40	5.35	....	6.23	(607) 8.11	10.23	12.23	2.23	4.23	(619-621) 6.23	(619) 7.23	8.41	....	11.09	....	EATON 3 CARS
PENN	98.9	....	....	....	....	6.18	8.07	10.19	12.19	2.19	4.19	6.19	7.19	8.37	....	11.05	....	PENN 8 CARS
HARTS	97.6	....	....	....	....	6.16	8.05	10.17	12.17	2.17	4.17	6.17	7.17	8.35	....	11.03	....	HARTS 6 CARS
STRADER	96.2	....	....	....	....	6.13	8.03	(609) 10.14	(611) 12.14	(613) 2.14	(615) 4.14	6.14	7.14	8.32	....	11.01	....	STRADER 8 CARS
HOPE	94.7	....	....	....	....	(603) 6.10	8.00	10.10	12.10	2.10	4.10	6.10	7.10	8.29	....	10.59	....	HOPE 6 CARS
WATTS	92.9	....	....	....	....	6.04	7.57	10.07	12.07	2.07	4.07	6.07	7.07	8.26	....	10.56	....	WATTS 8 CARS
NEW WESTVILLE	90.1	....	....	....	....	5.58	7.53	10.02	12.02	2.02	4.02	6.02	7.02	8.21	....	10.51	....	N.WESTVILLE 4 CARS
W. DRIVING PARK	87.2	....	....	....	....	5.53	7.48	9.57	11.57	1.57	3.57	5.57	6.57	8.16	....	10.46	....	W. DRIV'G PK. 7 CARS
AUSTIN	86.7	....	....	....	....	5.51	7.46	9.55	11.55	1.55	3.55	5.55	6.55	8.14	....	10.44	....	AUSTIN 3 CARS
RICHMOND	84.8	....	....	....	(603-605) 6.25	5.45	(605) 7.33	9.42	11.42	1.42	3.42	(617) 5.42	(621) 6.42	8.02	(623) 9.00	10.35	....	RICHMOND
OHIO	83.7	....	....	....	6.15	....	7.27	9.38	11.36	1.36	3.36	5.36	6.36	7.56	8.50	(625) 10.29	....	OHIO D. T.
JONES	81.3	....	....	....	6.10	....	7.22	9.33	11.31	1.31	3.31	5.31	6.31	7.51	8.45	10.24	....	JONES 16 CARS
CENTERVILLE	79.0	....	....	....	6.05	....	7.17	9.28	11.25	1.25	3.25	5.25	6.25	7.46	8.40	10.19	....	CENTERVILLE 6 CARS
JACKSON PARK	76.8	....	....	....	6.02	....	7.14	9.25	11.22	1.22	3.22	5.22	6.22	7.43	8.37	10.16	....	JACKSON P'K 7 CARS
HISER	74.6	....	....	....	5.58	....	7.10	9.22	11.19	1.19	3.19	5.19	(617) 6.19	7.40	8.33	10.13	....	HISER 6 CARS
E. GERMANTOWN	71.9	....	....	....	5.54	....	7.06	9.18	11.15	1.15	3.15	5.15	6.16	7.37	8.29	10.09	....	E. GERMAN'N 11 CARS
CAMBRIDGE CITY	69.7	....	....	....	5.50	....	(603) 7.00	(607) 9.13	(609) 11.11	(611) 1.11	(613) 3.11	(615) 5.11	6.11	(617) 7.32	8.25	(623) 10.06	....	CAMBRIDGE CITY
AUBURN	69.0	....	....	....	....	....	6.56	9.10	11.06	1.06	3.06	5.06	6.06	(621) 7.27	8.20	10.00	....	AUBURN 5 CARS
DUBLIN	67.7	....	....	....	....	....	6.53	9.07	11.03	1.03	3.03	5.03	6.03	7.23	8.16	9.57	....	DUBLIN 4 CARS
KENSINGER	65.3	....	....	....	....	....	6.49	9.04	10.59	12.59	2.59	4.59	5.59	7.19	8.12	9.53	....	KENSINGER 4 CARS
E. STRAWN	63.7	....	....	....	....	....	6.47	9.01	10.57	12.57	2.57	4.57	5.57	7.17	8.10	9.51	....	E. STRAWN 11 CARS
STRAWN	63.3	....	....	....	....	....	6.46	9.00	10.56	12.56	2.56	4.56	5.56	7.16	8.09	9.50	....	STRAWN
OGLE	62.0	....	....	....	....	....	6.44	8.58	10.54	12.54	2.54	4.54	5.54	7.14	8.07	9.48	....	OGLE 5 CARS
E. LEWISVILLE	60.6	....	....	....	....	....	6.42	8.55	10.52	12.52	2.52	4.52	5.52	7.12	8.05	9.46	....	E.LEWISVILLE 16 CARS
LEWISVILLE	59.9	....	....	....	....	....	6.41	8.54	10.51	12.51	2.51	4.51	5.51	7.11	8.04	9.45	....	LEWISVILLE
FLAT ROCK	59.0	....	....	....	....	....	6.40	8.52	10.50	12.50	2.50	4.50	5.50	7.10	8.03	9.44	....	FLATROCK 5 CARS
DUNREITH	55.8	....	....	....	....	....	6.35	8.47	10.45	12.45	2.45	4.45	5.45	7.05	7.58	9.39	....	DUNREITH 16 CARS
DRAPER	53.7	....	....	....	....	....	6.31	(605) 8.42	10.41	12.41	2.41	4.41	(615) 5.41	7.01	(621) 7.54	9.35	....	DRAPER 3 CARS
SPICELAND	53.2	....	....	....	....	....	6.30	8.41	10.40	12.40	2.40	4.40	5.40	7.00	7.53	9.34	....	SPICELAND
CATES	52.0	....	....	....	....	....	6.28	8.39	10.37	12.37	2.37	4.37	5.37	6.57	7.50	9.31	....	CATES 1 CAR
CARPENTER	49.7	....	....	....	....	....	6.24	8.35	10.34	12.34	2.34	4.34	5.34	6.54	7.47	9.28	....	CARPENTER 2 CARS
CHAMBERS	46.2	....	....	....	....	....	6.19	8.30	10.29	12.29	2.29	4.29	5.29	6.49	7.42	9.24	....	CHAMBERS 12 CARS
NEW CASTLE	44.9	....	....	....	....	....	(601) 6.15	8.26	10.25	12.25	2.25	4.25	5.25	6.45	7.38	9.20	12.50	NEW CASTLE 3 CARS
BLUE	44.0	....	....	....	....	....	....	8.18	10.15	12.15	2.15	4.15	5.17	6.38	7.29	9.13	12.45	BLUE 25 CARS
LOWE	41.1	....	....	....	....	....	....	8.15	(607) 10.11	(609) 12.11	(611) 2.11	(613) 4.11	5.12	6.34	7.25	9.10	12.42	LOWE 5 CARS
PITTS	39.1	....	....	....	....	....	....	8.12	10.08	12.08	2.08	4.08	5.08	6.30	7.21	9.07	12.39	PITTS 4 CARS
KEN	36.0	....	....	....	....	....	....	(603) 8.07	10.03	12.03	2.03	4.03	5.04	6.26	7.16	9.02	12.36	KEN 8 CARS
SHIRLEY	33.3	....	....	....	....	....	....	8.02	9.59	11.59	1.59	3.59	5.01	(615) 6.22	7.12	8.58	12.32	SHIRLEY 7 CARS
WILK	29.7	....	....	....	....	....	....	7.55	9.53	11.53	1.53	3.53	4.54	6.14	7.07	8.53	12.27	WILK 5 CARS
POLK	27.0	....	....	....	....	....	....	7.51	9.49	11.49	1.49	3.49	4.50	6.08	7.03	8.49	12.23	POLK 5 CARS
MAX	22.4	....	....	....	....	....	....	7.45	9.44	11.44	1.44	3.44	4.46	6.02	6.58	(621) 8.44	12.18	MAX 5 CARS
DUNN	18.5	....	....	....	....	....	....	7.40	(605) 9.40	11.39	1.39	3.39	(613) 4.41	5.56	6.52	8.39	12.13	DUNN 3 CARS
COMFORT	14.5	....	....	....	....	....	....	7.35	9.34	11.34	1.34	3.34	4.34	5.50	(615) 6.46	8.34	12.08	COMFORT 4 CARS
HALL	10.1	....	....	....	....	....	....	7.29	9.29	11.29	1.29	3.29	4.29	5.45	6.40	8.29	12.04	HALL 4 CARS
SHANK	7.0	....	....	....	....	....	....	7.24	9.24	11.24	1.24	3.24	4.24	5.40	6.35	8.24	11.59	SHANK 4 CARS
WOOD	4.1	....	....	....	....	....	....	7.19	9.19	11.19	1.19	3.19	4.19	5.35	6.30	8.19	11.54	WOOD 10 CARS
BROOK	2.9	....	....	....	....	....	....	(601) 7.17	(603) 9.17	(607) 11.17	(609) 1.17	(611) 3.17	4.17	(613) 5.32	6.27	8.17	(623) 11.52	BROOK D. T
INDIANAPOLIS	0	....	....	....	....	....	....	7.00	9.00	(605) 11.00	1.00	3.00	(611) 4.00	5.15	(613) 6.10	(615) 8.00	11.30	INDIANAPOLIS D. T.
		A M	A M	A M	A M	A M	A M	A M	A M	A M	P M	P M	P M	P M	P M	P M	P M	
		Loc	Loc	Loc	Loc	Loc	Loc	Loc	Loc	Loc	Loc	Loc	Loc	Loc	Loc	Loc	Loc	
		Note E 602	604	Note F 606	Note G 608	610	Note I 612	614	616	618	620	622	Note H 624	626	Note J 628	630	632	

Note A—Train 601 annulled Cambridge City to Newcastle Sundays and Holidays.
Note B—Train 605 annulled Sundays and Holidays.
Note C—Train 617 annulled Sundays and Holidays.
Note D—Train 619 annulled Sundays and Holidays.
Note E—Train 602 annulled Sundays and Holidays.
Note F—Train 606 annulled Sundays and Holidays.
Note G—Train 608 annulled Sundays and Holidays.
Note H—Train 624 annulled Sundays and Holidays.
Note I —Train 612 annulled New Castle to Cambridge City Sundays and Holidays.
Note J —Train 628 will run from Cambridge City to Richmond on Saturday only.
Note K—Train 625 will run on Saturday only.

C. C. Lentz, Trainmaster, Indianapolis.

Effective Sunday, April 24, 1938.
at 4:01 A. M. Central Standard Time
Superseding Time Table No. 163.
Destroy all Time Tables of previous date.

SOUTH BOUND—Read Down

FIRST CLASS

STATIONS AND SIDINGS	STATION NUMBERS	307 Loc PM	37 Loc PM	35 Loc PM	33 Loc PM	31 Loc PM	Note A 29 Lim PM	Note A 305 Lim PM	27 Loc PM	25 Lim PM	23 Loc PM	21 Lim PM	19 Lim PM	17 Loc AM	15 Lim AM	13 Loc AM	Note A 11 Loc AM
FT. WAYNE	7123	11.00	9.10	6.05		5.10	4.15	4.00		1.45		12.00		10.00	8.00	7.00
BDY. & TAYLOR (Y)		11.05	9.15	6.10		5.15	4.20	4.05		1.50		12.05		10.05	8.05	7.05
BROAD		11.10	9.19	6.14		5.18	4.25	4.08		1.55		12.10		10.08	8.08	7.08
FARM	7120	11.11	9.20	6.15		5.19	4.26	4.09		1.56		12.11		10.09	8.09	7.09
POINT	7119	11.13	9.22	6.16		5.21	4.28	4.11		2.00		12.12		10.11	8.10	7.10
MASON	7118	11.15	9.24	6.18		5.23	4.31	4.12		2.01		12.14		10.13	8.13	7.13
FERGUSON	7116	11.18	9.27	6.20		5.26	4.33	4.15		2.04		12.17		10.15	8.15	7.16
LAND	7114	11.19	9.28	6.21		5.28	4.34	4.16		2.06		12.18		10.16	8.16	7.17
YODER	7113			Note C												
SPRANG	7112	11.22	9.31	6.25		5.33	4.38	4.19		2.09		12.21		10.19	8.20	7.21
OSSIAN	7109	11.25	9.34	6.28		5.38	4.41	4.22		2.12		12.24		10.22	8.23	7.24
ERIE	7107	11.26	9.36	6.29		5.40	4.42	4.23		2.13		12.25		10.24	8.25	7.25
KINGSLAND	7106															
MACK	7105	11.30	9.40	6.33		5.44	4.45	4.27		2.17		12.29		10.28	8.29	7.30
PAXON	7102	11.33	9.43	6.36		5.48	4.48	4.30		2.20		12.33		10.32	8.32	7.33
VILLA	7100	11.35	9.46	6.38		5.50	4.50	4.32		2.22		12.35		10.34	8.35	7.36
BLUFFTON (Y)	7099	11.40	9.51	6.43		5.55	4.55	4.37		2.25		12.38		10.37	8.38	7.40
ROTARY	4098		9.54	6.46			4.40			2.28		12.41		10.40	8.40	7.45
NOT	4094		9.57	6.50			4.44			2.32		12.45		10.44	8.44	7.50
BELL	4091		10.00	6.53			4.47			2.36		12.48		10.47	8.47	7.53
KEY	4087		10.03	6.57			4.51			2.39		12.52		10.51	8.51	7.57
OIL	4086		10.06	7.00			4.54			2.42		12.55		10.54	8.54	8.00
PELIER (Y)	4085		10.08	7.03			4.57			2.44		12.56		10.55	8.56	8.01
RACE	4084		10.10	7.05			4.59			2.46		12.58		10.57	8.58	8.03
MAN	4082		10.13	7.08			5.02			2.49		1.01		11.00	9.01	8.05
BURNS	4079		10.15	7.11			5.04			2.51		1.04		11.03	9.04	8.08
CLEVE	4078		10.18	7.15			5.06			2.54		1.07		11.06	9.07	8.10
BLAKE (Y)	4077		10.19	7.16			5.07			2.55		1.08		11.07	9.08	8.11
FORD	4075		10.22	7.20			5.11			3.00		1.13		11.10	9.12	8.15
HURST	4073		10.27	7.24			5.16	3.05			1.18		11.15	9.17	8.20
ERVIN	4070		10.29	7.27			5.19	3.08			1.21		11.18	9.19	8.23
EATON STA.	4067															
POWER	4066		10.34	7.32			5.24	3.13			1.26		11.23	9.24	8.28
LEARD	4065		10.35	7.33			5.25	3.14			1.27		11.24	9.25	8.29
ROY	4062		10.39	7.37			5.28	3.18			1.30		11.27	9.29	8.33
TRENT	4060		10.41	7.41			5.31	3.22			1.34		11.31	9.32	8.36
KUHNER	4059		10.44	7.43			5.32	3.24			1.35		11.32	9.33	8.37
HIGH	4058		10.46	7.44			5.35	3.25			1.37		11.34	9.35	8.38
MUNCIE	4057		10.55	7.52			5.43	3.35			1.45		11.43	9.45	8.47

HEAVY FACE TYPE denotes meeting point.

NOTE A—Daily
NOTE B—Daily
NOTE C—Train 3

L. M. BROWN, Gen. Supt. Transportation.

Above At 5:16 PM at Hurst, a southbound train met both the RPO and a local, and the local overtook the mail train. Nervous with another train right behind, the conductor on the RPO car was brisk with people getting off at country stops near Eaton. *George K. Bradley collection*

MUNCIE AND BLUFFTON DIVISION
Direction of even-numbered trains: Northbound

Time table no.	Date	Supersedes time table	Train numbers
151	9/28/30	UT 47	*509-525
152	4/26/31	151	†5-45, *17, *28
153	9/27/31	152	†3-37
154	5/1/32	153	†4-33
155	9/25/32	154	†4-33
156	10/1/33	155	†4-35
157	4/29/34	156	†4-37

* First-class freight trains.
† Southbound trains continue westbound from Muncie to Indianapolis with the same numbers. Northbound trains continue beyond Bluffton to Fort Wayne with the same numbers.

FORT WAYNE-MUNCIE DIVISION
Direction of even-numbered trains: Northbound

Time table no.	Date	Supersedes time table	Train numbers — Main part of route	Muncie-New Castle
158	9/30/34	157 & ISC 50	†2-37	—
159	4/28/35	158	†2-37, 300-303	—
160	9/29/35	159	†2-37, 301-305	—
161	4/26/36	160	†2-37, 301-307	—
162	9/27/36	161	†2-37, 301-307	—
163‡	9/26/37	162	†2-37, 301-307	301, 304, 401-420
164‡	4/24/38	163	†2-37, 301-307	301, 304, 403-420
165‡(L)	9/24/39	164	†2-37, 301-307	301, 304, 403-420

† Southbound trains continue westbound from Muncie to Indianapolis with the same numbers.
‡ Includes Muncie-New Castle Branch.

INDIANA RAILROAD
BOWMAN ELDER, RECEIVER OF
FORT WAYNE – MUNCIE DIVISION
TIME TABLE NO. 164

This Time Table for the government of employees only. Read Special Instructions and Rules Carefully.

NORTH BOUND—Read Up

[Timetable with station listings from Ft. Wayne to Muncie showing train schedules for trains 9, 301, 7, 5, 1-3, 302, 2, 4, 6, 8, 10, 12, 14, 16, 18, 20, 304, 22, 24, 26, 28, 30, 32, 34, 36 with distances and siding capacities]

C. C. LENTZ, Trainmaster.

MUNCIE-ANDERSON-INDIANAPOLIS DIVISION
Direction of even-numbered trains: Eastbound
(An illustration appears on pages 60-61)

Time table no.	Date	Supersedes time table	Indianapolis-Muncie	Indianapolis-Ft. Harrison
201	9/28/30	UT 45		
202	4/26/31	201	*1-45	901-932
203	9/27/31	202	*1-38	901-932
204	4/24/32(?)	203	*1-34(P)	
205	9/25/32	204	*3-34	901-930
206	10/1/33	205	*1-36	901-932
207	4/29/34	206	*1-37	901-932
208	9/29/35	207	*1-37	902-931, 300, 303
209(L)	9/26/37	208	*1-37	902-933, 300, 303

*Eastbound trains continue northbound from Muncie to Fort Wayne with the same numbers.

Right Children's half rates, excursions and other less-used fares were sold as paper tickets filled in by the agents. It would be impossible to maintain a full range of preprinted forms at every agency. *George K. Bradley collection*

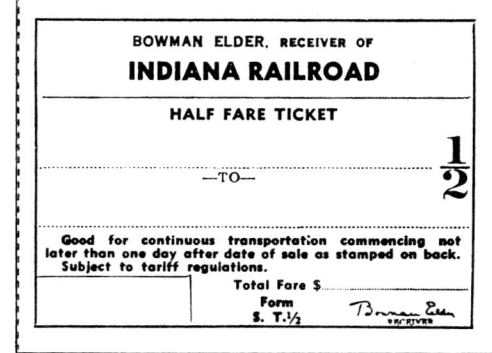

219

BE SURE YOU ARE RIGHT—THEN GO AHEAD

PERU—LAFAYETTE
WEST BOUND TRAINS

Distance in Miles from Fort Wayne	STATION AND SIDING NAMES	FIRST CLASS						
		Daily Express 251 A.M.	Daily Express 253 A.M.	Daily Express 255 A.M.	Daily Express 257 P.M.	Daily Express 259 P.M.	Daily Express 261 P.M.	Daily Express 263 P.M.
	FORT WAYNE	8.10						
58.7	PERU	6.30	9.20	11.30	1.30	3.20	5.30	7.40
59.4	GRANT	6.34	9.24	11.34	1.34	3.24	5.34	7.44
60.7	GAS	6.38	9.28	11.38	1.38	3.28	5.38	7.49
61.6	OGLE	6.40	9.30	11.40	1.40	3.30	5.40	7.51
64.2	SHURK	6.43	9.33	11.43	1.43	3.33	5.42	7.54
66.7	LEWISBURG	6.46	9.36	11.46	1.46	3.36	5.45	7.57
70.1	JONES	6.50	9.40	11.50	1.50	3.40	5.49	8.01
70.7	KEEFER	6.51	9.41	11.51	1.51	3.41	5.50	8.02
72.0	BAKER	6.53	9.43	11.53	1.53	3.43	5.52	8.03
73.3	I.R.R. JCT.	6.55	9.45	11.55	1.55	3.45	5.53	8.04
74.3	DORNER	6.57	9.47	11.57	1.57	3.47	5.55	8.06
75.7	LOGANSPORT	7.05	9.55	12.05	2.05	3.55	6.02	8.12
76.5	LINK	7.09	9.59	12.09	2.09	3.59	6.06	8.16
79.3	PORTER	7.14	10.04	12.14	2.14	4.04	6.10	8.20
81.4	CLYMERS	7.17	10.08	12.17	2.17	4.08	6.13	8.24 (264)
83.3	GRAYS	7.20	10.11	12.20	2.20	4.11	6.16	8.28
85.1	BURROWS	7.23	10.15	12.23	2.23	4.15	6.20 (262)	8.31
87.9	MARTINS	7.26	10.18 (254)	12.26 (256)	2.26 (258)	4.18 (260)	6.23	8.34
89.5	ROCKFIELD	7.29	10.22	12.30	2.30	4.22	6.26	8.38
91.6	LOYS	7.32 (252)	10.26	12.33	2.33	4.26	6.29	8.41
93.5	MEARS	7.35	10.29	12.36	2.36	4.29	6.31	8.44
95.2	CAMDEN	7.39	10.32	12.39	2.39	4.32	6.33	8.47
96.2	DELPHI (Y)	7.43	10.35	12.43	2.43	4.35	6.37	8.51
98.0	SPRING	7.46	10.39	12.46	2.46	4.39	6.41	8.54
100.1	VONN	7.49	10.41	12.49	2.49	4.41	6.44	8.57
101.1	COLBURN							
102.1	ELM	7.53	10.45	12.53	2.53	4.45	6.48	9.01
104.7	BUCK CREEK	7.56	10.48	12.56	2.56	4.48	6.51	9.05
106.4	PENCE	7.59	10.51	12.59	2.59	4.51	6.54	9.08
108.7	HILEMAN	8.02	10.54	1.02	3.02	4.54	6.57	9.11
110.5	VALE	8.05	10.57	1.05	3.05	4.57	7.00	9.15
111.5	MONON	8.08	11.00	1.08	3.08	5.00	7.03	9.18
113.3	LAFAYETTE	8.20	11.10	1.20	3.20	5.10	7.15	9.30
	Schedule No. 44 In Effect April 26, 1931	Express 251 A.M.	Express 253 A.M.	Express 255 A.M.	Express 257 P.M.	Express 259 P.M.	Express 261 P.M.	Express 263 P.M.

BE SURE YOU ARE RIGHT—THEN GO AHEAD

LAFAYETTE—PERU
EAST BOUND TRAINS

Distance in Miles from Lafayette	STATION AND SIDING NAMES	FIRST CLASS						
		Daily Express 202 A.M.	Daily Express 252 A.M.	Daily Express 254 A.M.	Daily Express 256 P.M.	Daily Express 258 P.M.	Daily Express 260 P.M.	Daily Express 262 P.M.
54.6	PERU	6.20	8.40	11.20	1.20	3.20	5.20	7.10
53.9	GRANT	6.14	8.34	11.14	1.14	3.14	5.14	7.04
52.7	GAS	6.11	8.30	11.10	1.10	3.10	5.10	7.00
51.7	OGLE	6.10	8.28	11.08	1.08	3.08	5.08	6.58
49.1	SHURK	6.07	8.25	11.05	1.05	3.05	5.05	6.55
46.7	LEWISBURG	6.04	8.22	11.02	1.02	3.02	5.02	6.52
43.3	JONES	5.59	8.18	10.58	12.58	2.58	4.58	6.48
42.6	KEEFER	5.58	8.17	10.57	12.57	2.57	4.57	6.47
41.5	BAKER	5.56	8.15	10.55	12.55	2.55	4.55	6.45
40.0	I.R.R. JCT.	5.54	8.13	10.53	12.53	2.53	4.53	6.43
39.1	DORNER	5.52	8.11	10.51	12.51	2.51	4.51	6.41
37.8	LOGANSPORT	5.45	8.05	10.45	12.45	2.45	4.45	6.36
36.8	LINK		8.00	10.40	12.41	2.41	4.41	6.32
34.1	PORTER		7.57	10.37	12.38	2.38	4.38	6.29
32.0	CLYMERS		7.54	10.34	12.35	2.35	4.35	6.26
30.0	GRAYS		7.51	10.31	12.32	2.32	4.32	6.23 (261)
28.2	BURROWS		7.48	10.28	12.29	2.29	4.29	6.20
25.5	MARTINS		7.45 (255)	10.25 (253)	12.26	2.26 (257)	4.26 (259)	6.15
23.8	ROCKFIELD		7.42	10.22	12.22	2.22	4.22	6.12
21.7	LOYS		7.38	10.18	12.18	2.18	4.18	6.09
19.8	MEARS		7.35 (251)	10.15	12.15	2.15	4.15	6.05
18.1	CAMDEN		7.31	10.12	12.12	2.12	4.12	6.02
17.1	DELPHI (Y)		7.28	10.10	12.10	2.10	4.10	5.58
15.3	SPRING		7.25	10.06	12.06	2.06	4.06	5.55
13.2	VONN		7.22	10.02	12.02	2.02	4.02	5.52
12.2	COLBURN							
11.2	ELM		7.18	9.58	11.58	1.58	3.58	5.48
8.6	BUCK CREEK		7.15	9.55	11.55	1.55	3.55	5.45
7.0	PENCE		7.12	9.52	11.52	1.52	3.52	5.42
4.7	HILEMAN		7.08	9.48	11.48	1.48	3.48	5.38
2.8	VALE		7.04	9.44	11.44	1.44	3.44	5.34
2.0	MONON		7.01	9.41	11.41	1.41	3.41	5.31
0.0	LAFAYETTE		6.50	9.30	11.30	1.30	3.30	5.20
	Schedule No. 44 In Effect April 26, 1931	Express 202 A.M.	Express 252 A.M.	Express 254 A.M.	Express 256 P.M.	Express 258 P.M.	Express 260 P.M.	Express 262 P.M.

INDIANA SERVICE CORPORATION

Time Table
No. 44

Superseding Time Table No. 43

For the Government of Employes Only

Effective 4:01 a.m., April 26, 1931
(Central Standard Time)

HENRY BUCHER   H. F. COLEMAN
Vice President   Trainmaster

BE SURE YOU ARE RIGHT—THEN GO AHEAD

PERU—LAFAYETTE
WEST BOUND TRAINS

Distance in Miles from Fort Wayne	STATION AND SIDING NAMES	FIRST CLASS
		Daily Express 265 P.M.
	FORT WAYNE	
58.7	PERU	9.30
59.4	GRANT	9.34
60.7	GAS	9.38
61.6	OGLE	9.40
64.2	SHURK	9.43
66.7	LEWISBURG	9.46
70.1	JONES	9.50
70.7	KEEFER	9.51
72.0	BAKER	9.53
73.3	I.R.R. JCT.	9.55
74.3	DORNER	9.57
75.7	LOGANSPORT	10.05
76.5	LINK	10.09
79.3	PORTER	10.14
81.4	CLYMERS	10.17
83.3	GRAYS	10.20
85.1	BURROWS	10.23
87.9	MARTINS	10.26
89.5	ROCKFIELD	10.29
91.6	LOYS	10.32
93.5	MEARS	10.35
95.2	CAMDEN	10.38
96.2	DELPHI (Y)	10.42
98.0	SPRING	10.45
100.1	VONN	10.48
101.1	COLBURN	
102.1	ELM	10.51
104.7	BUCK CREEK	10.54
106.4	PENCE	10.56
108.7	HILEMAN	10.59
110.5	VALE	11.02 Note (E)
111.5	MONON	11.00 (266)
113.3	LAFAYETTE	11.15
	Schedule No. 44 In Effect April 26, 1931	Express 265 P.M.

BE SURE YOU ARE RIGHT—THEN GO AHEAD

LAFAYETTE—PERU
EAST BOUND TRAINS

Distance in Miles from Lafayette	STATION AND SIDING NAMES	FIRST CLASS	
		Daily Express 264 P.M.	Daily Express 266 A.M.
	FORT WAYNE		
54.6	PERU	9.10	
53.9	GRANT	9.04	
52.7	GAS	9.00	
51.7	OGLE	8.58	
49.1	SHURK	8.55	
46.7	LEWISBURG	8.52	
43.3	JONES	8.48	
42.6	KEEFER	8.47	
41.5	BAKER	8.45	
40.0	I.R.R. JCT.	8.43	
39.1	DORNER	8.41	
37.8	LOGANSPORT	8.35	12.10
36.8	LINK	8.30	12.07
34.1	PORTER	8.27 (263)	12.04
32.0	CLYMERS	8.24	12.01
30.0	GRAYS	8.21	11.59
28.2	BURROWS	8.18	11.56
25.5	MARTINS	8.15	11.53
23.8	ROCKFIELD	8.12	11.50
21.7	LOYS	8.09	11.47
19.8	MEARS	8.06	11.44
18.1	CAMDEN	8.03	11.41
17.1	DELPHI (Y)	8.01	11.37
15.3	SPRING	7.58	11.34
13.2	VONN	7.55	11.31
12.2	COLBURN		
11.2	ELM	7.51	11.28
8.6	BUCK CREEK	7.48	11.25
7.0	PENCE	7.43	11.22
4.7	HILEMAN	7.40	11.19
2.8	VALE	7.37	11.15 Note (E)
2.0	MONON	7.35	11.12 (265)
0.0	LAFAYETTE	7.25	11.00
	Schedule No. 44 In Effect April 26, 1931	Express 264 P.M.	Express 266 P.M.

Above The cover of the ISC timetable book and the pages for the early-abandoned west end. Trains in opposite directions appeared on facing pages, a common practice on many steam and electric railroads—convenient in single-track operation, where crews had to keep track of oncoming trains.

George K. Bradley collection

Effective Sunday, April 3, 1938.
At 4:01 A. M., Central Standard Time.
Superseding Time Table No. 55.
Destroy all Time Tables of previous Date.

FORT WAYNE TO PERU—READ DOWN

STATIONS AND SIDINGS	Freight Station Numbers					223
						Loc
						P. M.
FORT WAYNE	6000					216 10.00
TAYLOR & BROADWAY	6001					10.06
TAYLOR	6002					10.09
FREEMAN	6003					
ARDMORE	6004					10.11
PAUL'S	6005					10.14
ELLISON'S	6008					10.17
AMBERS	6010					10.21
WEBER	6013					10.24
ROANOKE	6016					10.28
MAHON	6018					10.32
ZINT	6020					10.35
ROCK	6023					10.38
McKEES	6024					10.39
WHEEL	6025					10.40
HUNTINGTON	6026					10.45
PARK	6028					
POLAR	6030					
ANDREWS	6032					
COSS	6034					
FOX	6036					
LAGRO	6039					
STOUP	6041					
RANKIN	6043					
WABASH	6045					
WOLF	6047					
KINGS	6049					
BOYD	6051					
BUTT'S	6053					
HOOVER	6055					
SMITH	6058					
PERU	6059					
						P. M.
						Loc
						223

HEAVY FACE TYPE denotes meeting points.

L. M. BROWN, Gen. Supt. Transportation

FORT WAYNE-LIMA RAILROAD COMPANY
Not operated in Indiana Railroad System but under the same supervision
Direction of even-numbered trains: Eastbound

Time table no.	Date	Supersedes time table	Train numbers
49(B)	9/28/30	48	101-130
50(B)	4/26/31	49	101-128
51(B)(L)	9/27/31	50	101-130

FORT WAYNE-PERU DIVISION
(Indiana Service Corporation)
Direction of even-numbered trains: Eastbound

Time table no.	Date	Supersedes time table	Train numbers†
51	9/30/34	50	200-226
52	9/29/35	51	200-223, 350
53	4/26/36(?)		200-223, 350(P)
54	9/27/36	53	200-223, 350
55	9/26/37	54	200-223, 350
56(L)	4/3/38	55	200-223

†Westbound trains continue southbound from Peru to Indianapolis with the same numbers.

Below Another common practice on the longer routes. First train in each direction started mid-line rather than come from the end of the division so early that it would have been nearly empty for the first hour. Tying up the last evening trains at Huntington balanced equipment and, again, avoided a very late underused trip. Cars spent the night at numerous towns around the system, even at outlying sidings. *George K. Bradley collection*

Right Officials of the line and connections, or long-time employees, were granted wallet-sized card passes according them free transportation.

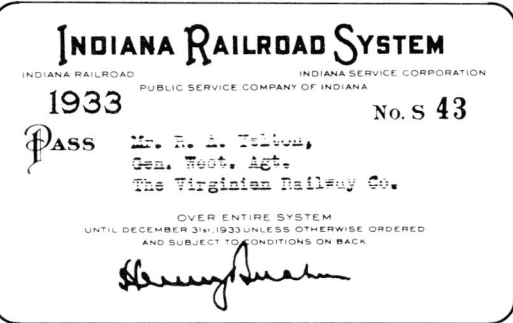

Right Newer employees could request a pass for a specific round trip—occasionally. *Both: George K. Bradley collection*

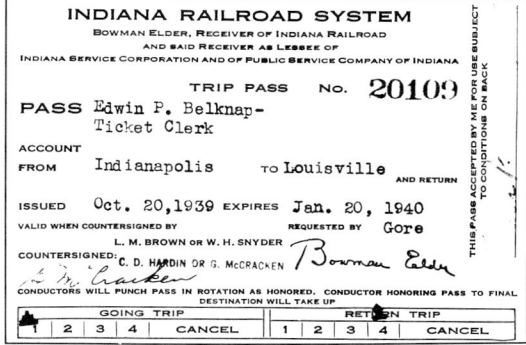

INDIANA SERVICE CORPORATION
FORT WAYNE - PERU DIVISION
TIME TABLE No. 56

This Time Table for the government of employees only.
Read Special Instructions and Rules carefully.

WEST BOUND / PERU TO FORT WAYNE—READ UP—EAST BOUND

[Detailed timetable with train numbers 221, 219, 217, 215, 213, 211, 209, 207, 205, 203, 201 westbound and 200, 202, 204, 206, 208, 210, 212, 214, 216, 218, 220, 222 eastbound, showing stations: Fort Wayne, Taylor & Broadway, Taylor, Freeman, Ardmore, Paul's, Ellison's, Ambers, Weber, Roanoke, Mahon, Zint, Rock, McKees, Wheel (Y), Huntington, Park, Polar, Andrews, Coss, Fox, Lagro, Stoup, Rankin, Wabash, Wolf, Kings, Boyd, Butt's, Hoover, Smith, Peru with mileages and car capacities of sidings.]

Note A—Trains 214 and 217 annulled on Sundays and Holidays.

C. C. Lentz, Trainmaster.

Effective Sunday, April 3, 1938,
At 4:01 A. M. Central Standard Time
Superseding Time Table No. 60.
Destroy all Time Tables of previous date.

BOWMAN ELDER, RECEIVER OF

INDIANA RAILROAD
INDIANAPOLIS-KOKOMO-PERU DIVISION
TIME TABLE NO. 61

This Time Table for the government of
Read Special Instructions and Rules Ca

PERU TO INDIANAPOLIS—READ DOWN—SOUTH BOUND

INDIANAPOLIS TO PERU—READ UP—NORTH BOUND

STATIONS AND SIDINGS	Freight Station Numbers			221 Loc PM	219 Loc PM	217 Loc PM	215 Loc PM	213 Loc PM	211 Loc PM	209 Loc PM	207 Loc AM	Note A 205 Loc AM	203 Loc AM	Note C 201 Loc AM	Distance from Peru	STATIONS AND SIDINGS	Distance from Indianapolis	Note B 202 Loc AM	Note A 204 Loc AM	206 Loc AM	208 Loc PM	210 Loc PM	212 Loc PM	214 Loc PM	216 Loc PM	Note A 218 Loc PM	220 Loc PM	222 Loc AM	
PERU	5076			220 10.15	212 7.40		210 4.35	208 2.40	12.40	207 9.40			6.10		.00	PERU	75.48	207 8.15		10.35	211 1.40	213 3.40	219 6.05		8.05		221 10.15		
RIVER	5075			10.16	7.41		4.36	2.41	12.41	9.41			6.11		.48	RIVER	75.00	8.12		10.34	1.36	3.36	6.05		8.00		10.10		
CREEK	5073			10.19	7.44		4.40	2.45	12.45	9.44			6.14		2.93	CREEK	72.55	8.09		10.31	1.32	3.33	5.58		7.57		10.07		
BETS	5070			10.22	7.47		4.43	2.48	12.48	9.48			6.17		5.62	BETS	69.86	8.05		10.27	1.28	3.30	5.55		7.54		10.04		
BUNKER HILL	5068														7.30	BUNKER HILL	68.18												
BUNKER	5067			10.26	216 7.50		4.46	2.52	12.52	9.51			6.20		7.55	BUNKER	67.93	8.01		10.24	1.25	3.26	5.51		219 7.50		10.01		
HAGG	5066			10.28	7.54		4.48	2.54	12.54	9.53			6.22		8.99	HAGG	66.49	7.58		10.22	1.23	3.24	5.49		7.48		10.00		
MIAMI	5065														10.40	MIAMI	64.99												
SHOE	5064			10.31	7.57		4.51	2.58	12.58	9.57			6.26		11.61	SHOE	63.93	7.54		10.18	1.19	3.20	5.45		7.44		9.56		
BENNETT'S	5063														12.57	BENNETT'S	62.91												
CASTOR	5062			10.35	8.01		4.54	3.01	1.01	10.00			6.29		13.21	CASTOR	62.27	7.51		10.15	1.16	3.17	5.42		7.41		9.53		
CASSVILLE															14.31	CASSVILLE	61.17												
LEN	5060			10.38	8.04		4.57	3.05	1.05	10.03			6.32		15.29	LEN	60.19	7.48		10.13	1.13	3.13	5.38		7.37		9.50		
POT	5058			10.41	8.07		5.00	210 3.09	208 1.09	206 10.08			6.35		17.56	POT	57.92	7.45		207 10.08	209 1.09	211 3.09	5.35		7.34		9.47		
KOKOMO	5056			10.48	8.15		5.13	3.18	1.18	204 10.15	202-204 9.15		6.43		19.51	KOKOMO	55.97	7.35	205-207 9.03	10.01	1.01	3.02	5.28		7.25		9.40		
MARKL'D AVE	5055			10.51	8.19		5.16	3.21	1.20	10.18	9.18		6.45		20.39	MARKL'D AVE	55.09	7.28	9.00	9.57	12.57	2.57	5.23		7.22		9.36		
LIMIT	5054			10.54	8.23		212 5.20	3.24	1.22	10.21	9.21		6.48		21.25	LIMIT	54.23	7.26	8.57	9.54	12.54	2.54	213 5.20		7.19		9.33		
DYER	5052			10.57	8.26		5.23	3.27	1.25	10.25	9.25		6.51		23.82	DYER	51.66	7.24	8.54	9.51	12.51	2.51	5.14		7.16		9.29		
FAIRFIELD	5051														24.56	FAIRFIELD	50.92												
WILSON	5049			11.01	8.29		5.26	3.31	1.29	10.29	9.29		6.55		26.14	WILSON	49.34	7.20	8.50	9.47	12.47	2.47	5.10		7.12		9.25		
SHARP-SPUR				11.02	8.30		5.27	3.33	1.31	10.31	9.31		6.57		27.28	SHARP-SPUR	48.20	7.18	8.49	9.46	12.45	2.46	5.09		7.11		9.24		
SHARPSVILLE	5048														27.54	SHARPSVILLE	47.94												
HARP	5046			11.06	8.34		5.31	3.37	1.35	10.34	9.34	7.00			29.11	HARP	46.37	7.15	8.46	9.42	12.41	2.42	5.04		7.07		9.21		
JACKSON															31.27	JACKSON	44.21												
JACK	5044			11.09	8.37		5.35	3.40	1.39	10.37	206 9.38	7.03			31.57	JACK	43.91	7.11	8.42	205 9.38	12.38	2.39	5.00		7.03		9.18		
CRAIL	5042			11.12	8.40		5.38	3.43	1.42	10.40	9.42	202 7.07			33.71	CRAIL	41.77	203 7.07	8.39	9.35	12.35	2.36	4.57		7.00		9.15		
TIPTON	5041			11.17	218 8.46		216-218 7.50	5.45	3.48	1.48	10.45	9.47	7.12	5.45	34.92	TIPTON	40.56	7.02	8.34	9.30	12.30	2.31	4.50		6.54	215-2.9 7.45	9.10	12.25	
INNIS	5040			11.19	8.48		7.52	5.47	3.50	1.50	10.47	9.49	7.14	5.47	35.78	INNIS	39.70	6.57	8.31	9.27	12.26	2.27	4.46		6.51	7.41	9.07	12.21	
COX	5038			11.22	8.51		7.55	5.49	3.53	1.53	10.50	9.52	7.17	5.50	37.73	COX	37.75	6.54	8.28	9.24	12.23	2.24	4.43		6.49	7.39	9.04	12.18	
ATLANTA	5036			11.25	8.54		7.58	5.52	3.56	1.56	10.53	9.55	7.20	5.53	39.57	ATLANTA	35.91	6.51	8.25	9.21	12.20	2.21	4.40		6.46	7.36	9.01	12.15	
STAR	5034			11.28	220 8.58		8.01	5.55	3.59	1.59	10.56	9.58	7.23	5.56	41.39	STAR	34.09	6.48	8.22	9.18	12.17	2.18	4.37		6.43	7.33	219 8.58	12.12	
ARCADIA	5033														42.61	ARCADIA	32.87												
MIDWAY	5032			11.33	9.03		8.06	6.00	4.04	2.04	11.01	10.03	7.28	6.01	43.97	MIDWAY	31.51	6.43	8.17	9.13	12.12	2.14	4.32		6.38	7.29	8.53	12.07	
CICERO	5030														45.65	CICERO	29.83												
NEAL	5029			11.37	9.08		8.11	6.05	4.09	210 2.09	11.06	10.08	7.33	6.06	46.48	NEAL	29.00	6.38	8.12	9.08	12.07	209 2.09	4.27		6.34	7.25	8.49	12.03	
BRAY	5027			11.40	9.11		8.14	6.08	4.13	2.13	11.09	10.11	7.36	6.10	48.58	BRAY	26.90	6.35	8.09	9.05	12.04	2.05	4.24		6.31	7.22	8.46	12.00	
SUBVILLE	5025			11.44	9.15		8.18	6.12	4.16	2.16	11.13	10.15	7.39	6.14	51.31	SUBVILLE	24.17	6.31	8.05	9.02	12.00	2.02	4.20		6.27	7.18	8.43	11.56	
NOBLESVILLE	5024			11.45	9.16		8.19	6.14	212 4.18	2.18	11.15	10.16	7.40	6.17	51.58	NOBLESVILLE	23.90	6.30	8.04	9.01	11.59	2.01	211 4.18		6.26	7.17	8.42	11.55	
BRICK	5023			222 11.50	9.22		8.25	216 6.20	4.24	2.24	11.21	10.22	7.46	202 6.23	52.82	BRICK	22.66	201 6.23	7.58	8.55	11.53	1.53	4.11		213 6.20	7.11	8.37	221 11.50	
MOORE	5021			11.54	9.24		8.27	6.22	4.26	2.26	11.23	10.24	7.48	6.25	53.81	MOORE	21.47	6.19	7.56	8.53	11.50	1.51	4.09		6.15	7.09	8.35	11.48	
HAZEL	5018			11.58	9.28		220 8.31	6.26	4.30	2.30	11.27	10.28	7.52	6.29	56.42	HAZEL	18.06	6.16	219 7.52	8.48	11.47	1.48	4.05		6.11	7.05	215 8.31	11.44	
CARMEL	5016														60.21	CARMEL	15.27												
HAWK	5015			12.03	9.33		8.36	6.31	4.35	2.35	11.32	10.33	7.58	6.34	60.40	HAWK	15.08	6.12	7.46	8.43	11.42	1.43	3.59		6.05	7.00	8.26	11.39	
GROVE	5013			12.08	9.38		8.41	6.36	4.40	2.40	208 11.37	10.37	8.02	6.40	62.80	GROVE	12.73	6.07	7.41	8.38	207 11.37	1.38	3.54		6.00	6.55	8.21	11.34	
AKERS	5010			12.12	9.42		8.46	6.40	4.44	2.44	11.42	10.42	8.07	6.45	65.18	AKERS	9.93	6.04	7.37	8.34	11.34	1.34	3.49		5.55	6.50	8.17	11.31	
RIPPLE	5007			12.16	222 9.45		8.50	218-220 6.46	216-218 4.48	212 4.18	210 11.47	208 10.47	206 8.12	204-206 6.50	67.78	RIPPLE	7.70	6.00	201 7.32	201-203 8.30	205 11.28	207 1.30	209 3.15		211 5.50	211-213 6.45	213 8.13	219 11.28	
INDIANAPOLIS	001			12.45	10.15		9.20	7.20	5.20	3.20	12.20	11.20	8.50	7.25	75.48	INDIANAPOLIS	.0	5.35	7.00	8.00	11.00	1.00	3.15		5.10	6.15	7.45	11.00	
				AM	PM		PM	PM	PM	PM	PM	AM	AM	AM				AM	AM	AM	AM	PM	PM	PM	PM	PM	PM	PM	
				Loc	Loc		Loc	Loc	Loc	Loc	Loc	Loc	Loc	Loc				Loc	Loc	Loc	Loc	Loc	Loc	Loc	Loc	Loc	Loc	Loc	
				221	219	217	215	213	211	209	207	Note A 205	203	Note C 201				Note B 202	Note A 204	206	208	210	212	214	216	Note A 218	220	222	

HEAVY FACE TYPE denotes meeting points.

Note A—Trains 204, 205, 215 and 218 annulled on Sundays and Holidays.
Note B—Train 202 annulled from Indianapolis to Tipton on Sunday.
Note C—Train 201 annulled from Tipton to Indianspolis on Sundays.

L. M. Brown, Gen. Supt. Transportation

C. C. Lent

Above Timetables omitted schedule times at town stations where trains did not clear the main track. Trains 202 and 213 carried the RPO six days a week, including holidays. Having a two-man crew, they took the siding for meets at Limit and Crail. *George K. Bradley collection*

INDIANAPOLIS-KOKOMO-PERU DIVISION
Direction of even-numbered trains: Northbound (Eastbound on Tipton-Alexandria Branch)

Time table no.	Date	Supersedes time table	Train numbers Indianapolis-Peru	Tipton-Alexandria
51†	9/28/30	UT 48	300-331, *380-385	400-425, *487-488
52†	4/26/31	51	‡201-230	400-419
53	5/ 1/32	52	‡201-226	—
54	9/25/32	53	‡201-218	—
55	10/ 1/33	54	‡201-224	—
56	4/29/34	55	‡201-222	—
57	9/20/34	56	‡201-224	—
58	9/29/35	57	‡201-222	—

Time table no.	Date	Supersedes time table	Train numbers Indianapolis-Peru	Tipton-Alexandria
59	9/27/36	58	‡201-222	—
60	9/26/37	59	‡201-222	—
61(L)	4/ 3/38	60	‡201-222	—

*Second-class freight trains.
†Includes Tipton-Alexandria Branch.
‡Northbound trains continue eastbound from Peru to Fort Wayne with the same numbers.

Bibliography

Preliminary work on the Indiana Railroad history began over ten years ago. A serious careful study begun in 1981 continues to the present. The author used, wherever possible, primary sources including a sizable wealth of company papers, statistical records, advertisements, timetables, etc. as well as contemporary publications. Individuals with first-hand knowledge were contacted in person and by letter, and information which they contributed was made part of the file. A number of secondary sources, including *National Railway Bulletin*, *Traction & Models* and *Trolley Talk* were reviewed and any reasonable leads furnished by related articles were pursued by contacting the authors or checking additional primary sources.

Books and Pamphlets

R. M. Bates, *Interurban Railways of Allen County Indiana* (Fort Wayne: Public Library, 1958).

R. G. Benedict, *The Interurban from Marion to Bluffton* (Chicago, 1980).

G. K. Bradley, *Fort Wayne and Wabash Valley Trolleys* (Chicago: Bulletin 122 of the Central Electric Railfans' Association, 1983).

G. K. Bradley, *Fort Wayne's Trolleys* (Chicago: Owen Davies, 1963).

Electric Railways of Indiana, Part 1 (Chicago: Bulletin 101 of the Central Electric Railfans' Association, 1958).

Electric Railways of Indiana, Part 2 (Chicago: Bulletin 102 of the Central Electric Railfans' Association, 1959).

Electric Railways of Indiana, Part 3 (Chicago: Bulletin 104 of the Central Electric Railfans' Association, 1960).

G. W. Hilton and J. F. Due, *The Electric Interurban Railways in America* (Stanford: Stanford University Press, 1960).

Indiana Railroad System (Chicago: Bulletin 17 of the Central Electric Railfans' Association, 1940).

Indiana Railroad System (Chicago: Bulletin 91 of the Central Electric Railfans' Association, 1950, rev. 1975).

Indiana Railroad System Railway Post Office Cars (Chicago: Bulletin 21 of the Central Electric Railfans' Association, 1941).

Indiana Service Corporation (Fort Wayne: ISC, 1926).

J. Keenan, *Cincinnati & Lake Erie Railroad, Ohio's Great Interurban System* (San Marino: Golden West Books, 1974).

E. E. King, *Railway Signaling* (New York: McGraw Hill, 1921).

F. McDonald, *Insull* (Chicago: University of Chicago Press, 1962).

J. Marlette, *Electric Railroads of Indiana* (Indianapolis: Hoosier Heritage Press, 1980).

D. H. Mitchell, *Northern Indiana Public Service Company* (Princeton: Newcomen Society in North America, 1960).

Moody's Manual of Investments—Public Utilities (New York: Moody's Investment Service, Inc., 1920-1943).

J. E. Schramm. W. H. Henning and R. R. Andrews, *When Eastern Michigan Rode the Rails, Book 1* (Glendale: Special 94 of Interurban Press, 1984, rev. 1989).

Terre Haute, Indianapolis and Eastern Traction Co. (Chicago: Bulletin 30 of the Central Electric Railfans' Association, 1941).

Union Traction Company of Indiana (Chicago: Bulletin 62 of the Central Electric Railfans' Association, 1945).

Union Traction Company of Indiana Roster (Chicago: Bulletin 63 of the Central Electric Railfans' Association, 1945).

Utilities Investigation: 70th Congress, Senate Document 92 (70-1), Serial Set 8858.6-77 (Washington: United States Government Printing Office, 1930-1935). Volumes used:

8858-8 *Investigation of Utility Companies, pt. 22, American Gas and Electric Co., Electric Bond and Share Co.*

8858-17 *Investigation of Utility Companies, pt. 33 and 34, The North American Company and Subsidiaries.*

8858-21 *Investigation of Utility Companies, pt. 38, Middle West Utilities Co. and Subsidiaries.*

8858-34 *Investigation of Utility Companies, pt. 51, Insull Companies, United Gas Improvement Co.*

8858-37 *Investigation of Utility Companies, pt. 54, United Gas Improvement Co. and Subsidiaries.*

8858-42 *Investigation of Utility Companies, pt. 59, Middle West Utilities Co., Adirondack Power and Light Corp., Peoples Gas and Electric Co. of Oswego, Municipal Gas Co. of Albany, Cohoes Power and Light Corp.*

8888-43 *Investigation of Utility Companies, pt. 60, Midland United Co., Midland Utilities Co., Northern New York Utilities, Inc.*

8858-57 *Investigation of Utility Companies, pt. 72A, Economic, Financial, and Corporate Phases of Holding and Operating Companies of Electric and Gas Utilities.*

8858-63 *Investigation of Utility Companies, pt. 77, American Natural Gas Corp., Southern Natural Gas Corp., Commonwealth and Southern Corp. Group, Allied Engineers, Inc., Cities Service Co. Schedule E.*

Company and Private Papers

Harold L. Stuart (Halsey, Stuart & Co.) Report (in Insull Papers).

Indiana Railroad, Corporate Minute Books—1942-1949.

Insull Papers, Chicago: Loyola University of Chicago, University Archives, E. M. Cudahy Memorial Library.

Wesson Company, Chicago, IL (Financial reports prepared by Arthur Andersen & Co. in 1943 and 1944).

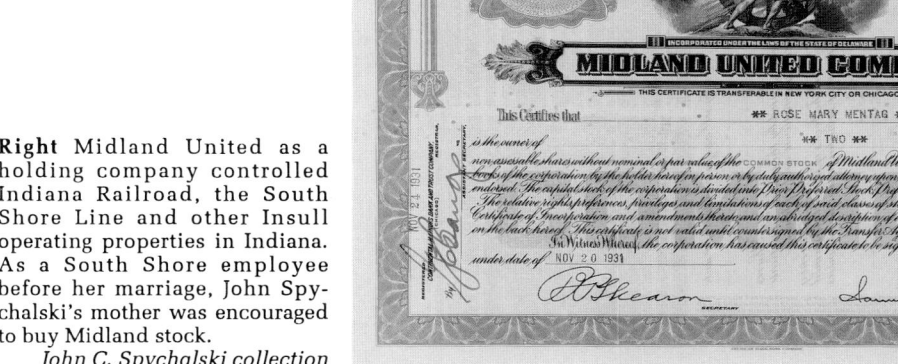

Right Midland United as a holding company controlled Indiana Railroad, the South Shore Line and other Insull operating properties in Indiana. As a South Shore employee before her marriage, John Spychalski's mother was encouraged to buy Midland stock.
John C. Spychalski collection

Miscellaneous Papers

A variety of Indiana Railroad materials are held by:
Allen County-Fort Wayne Public Library, Fort Wayne, IN (Indiana Service Company corporate records).
Indiana Transportation Museum, Noblesville, IN.
Public Service Company of Indiana, Plainfield, IN (Real estate, financial data, predecessor companies information, subsidiary company data, I&SE RR corporate data and electric power information).
Southeastern Trailways, Inc., Indianapolis, IN (Motor bus records).
Other sources of company and miscellaneous related data are the private collections of:

George K. Bradley,   George Krambles,
Norman Carlson,   David W. Peat,
James F. Cook,   Robert M. Stacy.

Court Records

Consolidated Colliers Company vs. Terre Haute, Indianapolis and Eastern Traction Company, Cause No. A-54658 and Consolidated Cause No. A-59833 dated April 21, 1930. Marion County (IN) Superior Court, Room 5 at Indianapolis, IN.
General Electric Company vs. Indiana Railroad, Cause 72820 et al., June 27, 1933 through June 23, 1942. Marion County (IN) Superior Court, Room 5, Indianapolis, IN. (Includes a record of 692 receivership actions following the appointment of a receiver for Indiana Railroad on June 28, 1933.)
Terre Haute, Indianapolis and Eastern Traction Company; Deeds, Elmer W. Stout, as receiver, to Indiana Railroad—Dated July 28, 1931. (Individual deeds recorded in the following Indiana counties: Boone, Clay, Hancock, Hendricks, Henry, Marion, Morgan, Montgomery, Putnam and Wayne.)
Union Traction Company of Indiana; Deed, Arthur W. Brady, as receiver, to Indiana Railroad—Dated July 17, 1930. (A real estate and physical property deed which covers all the property and equipment (except rolling stock) of the Union Traction Company of Indiana including those lines abandoned prior to the purchase and not normally considered as property of the Indiana Railroad as an operating railway company.)
Westinghouse Electric Company vs. Union Traction Company of Indiana, Consolidated Cause No. 7202, Final Decree, June 6, 1930. Madison County (IN) Circuit Court at Anderson, IN.

Newspapers

Anderson *Daily Bulletin*
Anderson *Herald*
Brazil *Daily Times*
Columbus *The Evening Republican*
Fort Wayne *Journal-Gazette*
Fort Wayne *News-Sentinel*
Greencastle *Herald*
Indianapolis *News*
Indianapolis *Star*
Jeffersonville *The Evening News*
Kokomo *Tribune*
Muncie *Evening Press*
Muncie *Morning Star*
New Albany *Tribune*
Richmond *Palladium*
Terre Haute *Tribune-Star*
Wabash *Plain Dealer*

Periodicals

Aera (New York: American Electric Railway Association, 1912-1932).
Bus Transportation (New York: McGraw-Hill).
Indiana Service Corporation, *Annual Reports,* 1930-1942.
Indianapolis Railways, Inc., *Annual Reports,* 1932-1942.
Indianapolis Street Railway Company, *Annual Reports,* 1928-1931.
Mass Transportation and its predecessors: *Interurban Railway Journal* (1905), later *Electric Traction Weekly* (1906), then *Electric Traction* (1912), next *Electric Traction & Bus Journal* (1932), name changed to *Mass Transportation* (1935). (Chicago: Kenfield-Davis)
Midland United Company, *Annual Reports,* 1931-1932.
Motor Coach Transportation and its predecessors: *Better Buses: The Bus Men's Journal* (1923-1925), later *Better Buses and Motor Coach Transportation* (April-June 1926) and next *Motor Coach Transportation* (July-Dec. 1926). (Pittsburgh: McCracken-Robinson Co.)
Proceedings of the American Electric Railway Engineering Association, 1911-1914, Report of the Committee on Block Signals (New York: American Electric Railway Association, 1911-1914).
Public Service Commission of Indiana, *Annual Reports,* 1931-1942.
Public Service Company of Indiana, *Annual Reports,* 1932, 1941-1942.
Railway Signal and its predecessors: *The Signal Engineer* (1912), later *Railway Signal Engineer* (1917), next *Railway Signal* (1925) and discontinued in 1931. Last published by McGraw-Hill, New York.
Transit Journal and its predecessors: Founded in 1884 as the *Street Railway Journal* and became the *Electric Railway Journal* upon its merger with the *Electric Railway Review* in June 1908. The *Electric Railway Review* had been founded in 1891 as the *Street Railway Review* and operated under its original name until July 1906. The *Electric Railway Journal* became the *Transit Journal* in 1932 and was discontinued in 1942. (New York: McGraw-Hill)

Company Publications

The following were published for passengers and/or employees:
Hoosier Traveler (1931).
Indiana Service News (1927-1930).
Power News (1930-1931), which became *Public Service News* (1931-1932).
Selling System Service (1939-1940).
Union Traction Booster (1927).
Union Traction News (1928-1930).

Below Long shadows signify the approaching end of a winter day in 1941. Car 71, crossing from the unpaved center of Martindale Avenue to the roadside of Sutherland Avenue, foreshadows the impending departure of frequent interurban service from the capital city. The symbolic view ends this book's observation of Indiana Railroad, the "magic" interurban.   *M. D. McCarter collection*